Developments in Amer

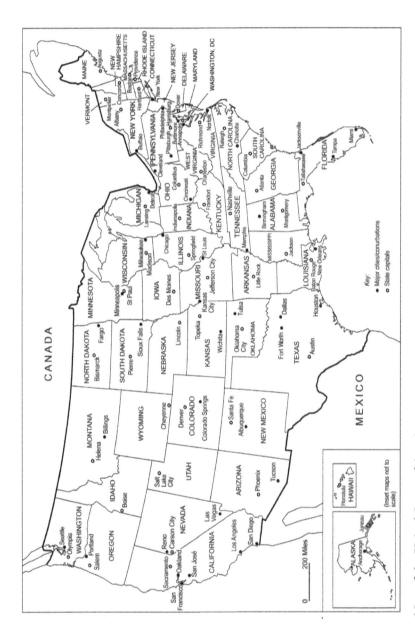

Map of the United States of America

Gillian Peele · Bruce E. Cain · Jon Herbert ·
Andrew Wroe
Editors

Developments
in American Politics 9

Editors
Gillian Peele
Lady Margaret Hall
University of Oxford
Oxford, UK

Bruce E. Cain
Department of Political Science
Stanford University
Stanford, CA, USA

Jon Herbert
School of Social, Political and Global
Studies
Keele University
Staffordshire, UK

Andrew Wroe
School of Politics and International
Relations
University of Kent
Canterbury, Kent, UK

ISBN 978-3-030-89739-0   ISBN 978-3-030-89740-6   (eBook)
https://doi.org/10.1007/978-3-030-89740-6

Cover credit: Marian Weyo

This Palgrave Macmillan imprint is published by the registered company Springer Nature
Switzerland AG
The registered company address is: Gewerbestrasse 11, 6330 Cham, Switzerland

PREFACE

This is the ninth volume of *Developments in American Politics*. It comes at a time of huge challenge for the American political system. The transition from the presidency of Donald Trump to that of Joe Biden was bitterly contested by Trump himself and supporters who thought the election had been fraudulent. Unprecedented efforts to prevent by force a peaceful handover of power, although unsuccessful, shocked observers and caused many to speculate about how close the United States had come to experiencing a coup. Certainly the events following the 2020 elections raised a series of questions both about how far its constitutional arrangements and political institutions retained legitimacy and support in all sections of the population. Those events also revealed the deeply polarized character of American society as it entered a new presidential term. Our individual chapters focus on the workings of the key institutions of American government and on the dynamics of contemporary American political life to place them against the background of a society which had visibly become deeply divided.

We have been able to recruit a distinguished team of authors from both sides of the Atlantic. There have been some major changes to our editorial team. Christopher Bailey and B. Guy Peters who were involved in the volumes from their start—Professor Bailey from the first edition in 1992 and Professor Peters from the second volume in 1995—have retired from the editorship. We are enormously grateful to them both for all their intellectual contribution and friendship over those years. We have strengthened our existing editorial team by the recruitment of Andrew Wroe from the University of Kent. The Covid-19 pandemic and the extensive period of university closure and lockdown has meant that the editorial work on the book was conducted in circumstances which we could not have foreseen when the last volume was produced. However editorial contact via regular virtual meetings has greatly facilitated the process. Remembering the comment in our first preface that the editors were grateful for help from that essential 'tool of modern scholarship', the fax machine, is a startling reminder of the pace of technological change over the course of our volumes.

This volume is structured rather differently from its predecessor. The publishers make individual chapters available as well as the book as a whole and so we now place the references and further reading related to each chapter at the end of that chapter rather than at the end of the book. American spelling is used throughout. We would like to thank Madison Allums our publisher at Palgrave and to Zobariya Jidda and the production team at Springer Nature for all their expert help and careful copy-editing and type-setting.

We also thank those who have given research advice and assistance to the authors of individual chapters: Laura Mattioli (Chapter 4) and Josh Pe (Chapter 14).

Finally we would like to thank our colleagues at the Universities of Oxford, Stanford, Keele and Kent for their support and stimulating company.

Oxford, UK	Gillian Peele
Stanford, USA	Bruce E. Cain
Staffordshire, UK	Jon Herbert
Canterbury, UK	Andrew Wroe

CONTENTS

List of Contributors

Mark D. Brewer Department of Political Science, University of Maine, Orono, ME, USA

Bruce E. Cain Department of Political Science, Stanford University, Stanford, CA, USA

James M. Curry Department of Political Science, University of Utah, Salt Lake City, UT, USA

Philip John Davies Faculty of Business and Law, De Montfort University, Leicester, UK

Ursula Hackett Department of Politics and International Relations, Royal Holloway, University of London, London, UK

Jon Herbert School of Social, Political and Global Studies, Keele University, Staffordshire, UK

Althea Legal-Miller School of Humanities and Educational Studies, Canterbury Christ Church University, Canterbury, UK

Emma Long School of Art, Media and American Studies, University of East Anglia, Norwich, UK

Trevor McCrisken Department of Politics and International Studies, University of Warwick, Coventry, UK

Jonathan Oberlander Department of Health Policy and Management, University of North Carolina, Chapel Hill, NC, USA

Gillian Peele Lady Margaret Hall, University of Oxford, Oxford, UK

Bert A. Rockman Department of Political Science, Purdue University, West Lafayette, IN, USA

Gregory L. Rosston Stanford Institute for Economic Policy Research, Stanford University, Stanford, CA, USA

Virginia Sapiro Department of Political Science, Boston University, Boston, MA, USA;
Department of Political Science, University of Wisconsin-Madison, Madison, WI, USA

Robert J. Spitzer Political Science Department, The State University of New York (SUNY), Cortland, NY, USA

Margaret Weir Department of Political Science, Brown University, Providence, RI, USA

Andrew Wroe School of Politics and International Relations, University of Kent, Canterbury, UK

Hye Young You Wilf Family Department of Politics, New York University, New York, NY, USA

ABBREVIATIONS AND ACRONYMS

ABA	American Bar Association
ACA	Affordable Care Act
ACE	Affordable Clean Energy
ACLU	American Civil Liberties Union
AEI	American Enterprise Institute
AFDC	Aid to Families with Dependent Children
ALEC	American Legislative Exchange Council
AMA	American Medical Association
ANES	American National Election Study
APAs	Asylum Protection Agreements
APSA	American Political Science Association
ARP	American Rescue Plan
ARRA	American Recovery and Reinvestment Act 2009
BCRA	Bipartisan Campaign Reform Act 2002
BIPOC	Black Indigenous and People of Color
BLM	Black Lives Matter
CAA	Clean Air Act
CAFE	Corporate Average Fuel Economy
CARA	Comprehensive Addiction and Recovery Act 2016
CARES	Coronavirus Aid Relief and Economic Security Act
CBN	Christian Broadcasting Network
CBO	Congressional Budget Office
CBP	Customs and Border Protection
CDC	Center for Disease Control and Prevention
CFPB	Consumer Financial Protection Bureau
CIS	Citizenship and Immigration Services
CPP	Clean Power Plan
CPTPP	Comprehensive and Progressive Agreement for Trans-Pacific Partnership
CRA	Congressional Review Act 2016
CRD	Civil Rights Division (of the Department of Justice)
CSIS	Center for Strategic and International Studies
CTC	Child Tax Credit

DACA	Deferred Action for Childhood Arrivals
DAPA	Deferred Action for Parents of Americans
DHHS	Department of Health and Human Services
DNC	Democratic National Committee
DOD	Department of Defense
DOJ	Department of Justice
DOL	Department of Labor
DOMA	Defense of Marriage Act 1996
DOT	Department of Transportation
DREAM	Development, Relief and Education for Alien Minors
EEA	Early Eligibility Age
EITC	Earned Income Tax Credit
EO	Executive Order
EOP	Executive Office of the President
EPA	Environmental Protection Agency
FBI	Federal Bureau of Investigation
FEC	Federal Election Commission
FECA	Federal Election Campaign Act
FEMA	Federal Emergency Management Agency
FOI	Freedom of Information
GAO	General Accounting Office
GDP	Gross Domestic Product
GOP	Grand Old Party
HAVA	Help Americans Vote Act
HEROES	Health and Economic Recovery Omnibus Emergency Solutions Act 2020
HUD	Housing and Urban Development
IBO	New York Independent Budget Office
ICE	Immigration and Customs Enforcement
INF	Intermediate-Range Nuclear Forces
IRGC	Islamic Revolutionary Guard Corps
IRS	Internal Revenue Service
JCPOA	Joint Comprehensive Plan of Action
JPA	Justice in Policing Act
LDA	Lobbying Disclosure Act
LGBTQ+	Lesbian Gay Bisexual Trans Queer and Others
MAGA	Make America Great Again
MPPs	Migrant Protection Protocols
NAACP	National Association for the Advancement of Colored People
NAFTA	North America Free Trade Area/Agreement
NAR	National Association of Realtors
NEP	National Election Pool
NFIB	National Federation of Independent Business
NOAA	National Oceanic and Atmospheric Administration
NRA	National Rifle Association
NSS	National Security Strategy
NYPD	New York Police Department
OANN	One America News Network
OECD	Organisation for Economic Cooperation and Development
OIRA	Office of Information and Regulatory Affairs

OMB	Office of Management and Budget
PAC	Political Action Committee
PPE	Personal Protective Equipment
RINO	Republican in Name Only
SALT	State and Local Tax
SCC	Social Cost of Burning Carbon
SEC	U.S. Securities and Exchange Commission
SNAP	Supplemental Nutrition Assistance Program
START	Strategic Arms Reduction Treaty
TANF	Temporary Assistance to Needy Families
TCJA	Tax Cuts and Jobs Act
TPP	Trans-Pacific Partnership
TPS	Temporary Protected Status
USMCA	United States-Mexico-Canada Agreement
VRA	Voting Rights Act
WTO	World Trade Organization

LIST OF FIGURES

CHAPTER 1

Introduction: From Trump to Biden

Gillian Peele, Bruce E. Cain, Jon Herbert, and Andrew Wroe

The inauguration of Joe Biden as the 46th President of the United States in January 2021 stood out from previous such ceremonies in a number of ways. Instead of the usual crowds observing the spectacle, the audience for the proceedings was sparse as a result of distancing restrictions imposed in the wake of the deadly Covid-19 pandemic which was sweeping the United States. The atmosphere in Washington DC itself was tense and much of the central downtown area was cut off and guarded in a massive security operation by military forces following an invasion of the Capitol two weeks earlier by protesters claiming, against all the evidence, that Biden's election was fraudulent and that his predecessor Donald Trump had really won. Trump's role

G. Peele (✉)
Lady Margaret Hall, University of Oxford, Oxford, UK
e-mail: gillian.peele@lmh.ox.ac.uk

B. E. Cain
Department of Political Science, Stanford University, Stanford, CA, USA
e-mail: bcain@stanford.edu

J. Herbert
School of Social, Political and Global Studies, Keele University, Staffordshire, UK
e-mail: j.n.herbert@keele.ac.uk

A. Wroe
School of Politics and International Relations, University of Kent, Canterbury, UK
e-mail: a.j.wroe@kent.ac.uk

G. Peele et al. (eds.), *Developments in American Politics 9*, https://doi.org/10.1007/978-3-030-89740-6_1

1

in these demonstrations was at best reckless and at worst he was complicit in, even encouraging of, an insurrection against the democratic system. His continued refusal to accept his election defeat meant that not merely was he absent from Biden's inauguration, although three previous presidents followed normal custom and attended the ceremony; Trump also refused to extend the normal courtesies of an outgoing to an incoming president in relation to Biden's move into the White House.

Biden's inaugural speech inevitably acknowledged the extraordinary circumstances that surrounded the opening of his presidency, especially the impact of Covid-19 on the lives and prosperity of Americans which, as he put it, was a 'once in a century virus'. Biden also highlighted the threat which had been posed to the US constitutional system by the violent extremism which he said had 'shaken the very foundations' of the 'hallowed ground of the Capitol.' Biden pledged himself to pursue an ambitious political agenda—to defeat the pandemic and remedy its effects, to take action to preserve the planet from climate change, to answer the cry for racial justice and to address the profound problems of political extremism, white supremacy and domestic terrorism which had become such troubling features of American political life. The newly elected president made unity the key goal of his tenure, and pledged to overcome what he called the 'uncivil wars' that put red against blue, rural against urban, and conservative against liberal in US society. Whether Biden can overcome the polarizing divisions which have come to mark the United States is an open question, however. As the chapters of this book will discuss, those divisions run deep and ameliorating them poses a daunting challenge. Moreover, although Biden had secured a decisive win both in the popular vote and in the electoral college, the legitimacy of his presidency continued to be contested by elements of the Republican elite and the Republican rank and file. Democratic control of Congress is based on narrow majorities, making the passage of legislation no easy matter and rendering the administration vulnerable both to Republican obstruction and to Democratic factionalism. The remorseless timetable of American democracy means also that, whatever the Democrats' eventual triumph at the polls in 2020, the 2022 midterm elections already loomed in official Washington's calculations and threatened to change the political arithmetic as they had for President Clinton in 1994 and for President Obama in 2010. Indeed, even as Biden completed his first one hundred days, observers were speculating on whether the midterms would prove disastrous for the Democrats.

THE ROAD TO THE 2020 ELECTIONS AND AMERICAN GOVERNANCE

Elections shape how American presidents govern. Donald Trump had won the Electoral College vote but lost the popular vote to Hillary Clinton in 2016. The Electoral College margin of 306–232 which secured him the presidency was larger than that of John F. Kennedy in 1960, of Richard Nixon in 1968, of Jimmy Carter in 1976 and of George W. Bush in both 2000 and 2004. Yet Trump's 2016 victory hinged on a vote margin of fewer than 80,000 votes in three previously blue (that is, Democratic) midwestern states.

President Trump then governed for four years in a manner that was designed to win reelection by appealing, as he had in his 2016 campaign, to the resentments of white voters who felt victimized by the free trade, immigration, and automation policies which benefitted the educated urban elites on both US coasts. Rather than trying to broaden his coalition, his strategy was to sharpen and exploit the divisions within the American electorate. The divisiveness of his campaign was underlined a day after his inauguration in 2017, when women staged the largest single-day march in American history in protest at the contemptuous attitude to women he had displayed and at his election. It was clear from the start of Trump's term that he would have little chance of winning a majority of women's votes in 2020.

In office, Trump gave symbolic and substantive support to different sections of his base. Very shortly after his inauguration, he reinstated the 'Mexico City policy' which banned foreign aid to international groups that counseled on or performed abortions. By the end of July 2017, he had withdrawn from a free trade agreement, the Trans-Pacific Partnership (TPP), instituted a travel ban on seven African and middle eastern countries, suspended the US refugee admissions policy for 120 days, nominated a conservative, Neil Gorsuch, to the Supreme Court and begun a roll back on environmental protections. In short, instead of attempting to broaden his coalition to attract some of those who did not support him in 2016, he doubled down on policies that pleased his base. The Electoral College strategy that got him into office became his governing strategy as well.

Despite the ostensible chaos of his governing style (including the constant staff turnovers, the feuds with the press and the Twitter controversies) Trump's basic reelection strategy rarely wavered. The tax cuts and regulatory relief would appease the traditional conservative wing of the Republican Party and the Supreme Court appointments pleased the conservative religious element. The protectionist trade policies, restrictions on immigrants and refugees, some construction of a wall on the Mexican border, demonization of urban areas, and support for far-right extremist groups all delivered on promises to the Trump base. Heading into the 2018 midterm elections, the Mueller investigation into Russian interference in the 2016 elections and the Trump campaign's involvement in it as well as the confirmation battle of Supreme Court nominee Brett Kavanaugh, who was accused of sexual assault, hardened what was already a wide partisan gulf.

The 2018 midterm elections proved to be largely a disaster for Republicans in the House but not in the Senate, a foreshadowing of the mixed results in 2020. Republicans in 2018 lost control of the House with the Democrats picking up 41 seats but Republicans retained control of the Senate by winning two extra seats. Two years later in 2020 the Democrats won the presidency and picked up three seats in the Senate and retained control of the House,

albeit with ten fewer seats. The outcome gave President Biden nominal control
of Congress when he took office in 2021 but only because Vice President
Kamala Harris could exercise the casting vote in the 50–50 Senate. And while
President Trump had lost both the popular and the Electoral College vote, he
did win more votes in 2020 than in 2016, and the margin of victory in several
critical states was close enough to warrant a recount. The voters had rejected
Trump in 2020 but not decisively; nor had they really reaffirmed their support
for the Democrats. Other ballot results below the federal level further muddied
the meaning of the 2020 election. Republicans increased their trifecta control
in the states (where one party controls both houses of the state legislature and
the governorship), giving them a 23–15 margin over the Democrats in terms
of controlling each state. The 2020 elections thus seemed to give no clear
mandate to either party.

What lessons should we draw from these results? Trump's divisive policies
hardened an already highly polarized electorate along racial, gender, education, and rural–urban lines. Democrats did well with racial minority, female,
urban/suburban, and better educated voters while Trump drew support from
white, older, male, rural/exurban, and less well-educated voters. There was
never much chance of the conversion of either base to the other side. The
name of the game was destined to be mobilization for both parties. The
strongest mobilizing force was fear of the other party and its values. Republicans feared that Democrats would bring socialism and allow urban disorder;
Democrats feared that four more years of Trump would be a disaster for
climate change, race relations and the composition of the federal court system,
especially the Supreme Court.

The even division of the electorate between Republicans and Democrats
meant that the outcome of the 2020 election hinged on the swing of independent voters in a handful of so-called 'purple' (competitive) states. While
the Democrats in 2020 were firmly united against Trump, the progressive
wing of the party, represented by Bernie Sanders and Elizabeth Warren, had
grown in strength. The early 2020 Democratic primaries, contests over who
would become the party nominee, showed greater support for the progressive candidates than for the moderate ones. However, black voters rallied to
Joe Biden in the South Carolina primary and created the momentum which
ultimately took him to the nomination. Underlying the Democratic Party's
stance after South Carolina's primary was the overwhelming interest in putting
forward the candidate who would be hardest for Trump to defeat: a decent
person from the moderate wing of the Party and one who had experience in
government, most recently as President Obama's Vice President.

But strategy aside, elections are also shaped by economic conditions and
unexpected events. Prior to March 2020 when many businesses had to close
down due to Covid-19, President Trump was counting on strong economic
conditions to help him win reelection. But the Covid-19 pandemic hurt him
in at least two ways. First, it severely damaged his economic record as unemployment soared and economic growth slowed. Second, it exposed Trump's

inability to govern competently. Anxious to be always in charge, his off-the-cuff remarks at televised press conferences revealed an appalling lack of medical and scientific knowledge. Moreover, his defiance of medical expertise regarding social distancing and mask-wearing undermined his support among the small number of undecided voters in the handful of competitive states. A study by Brady and Parker (2021) reveals that in Georgia, Michigan, and Pennsylvania, 81 percent of those who switched their 2016 vote for Trump to a 2020 vote for Biden said that Covid-19 was a major factor in their decision. By comparison, less than half of them thought that recent Black Lives Matter protests were a major factor. Trump's strategy of playing primarily to his base did not seem to stop him garnering slightly higher than usual levels of support from some Hispanic groups in Florida and Texas, but his erratic management in government in relation to the pandemic in the end cost him the election in the competitive states.

Biden's First One Hundred Days

Despite the lack of cooperation from the head of the outgoing administration, Biden's transition planning nevertheless went ahead as best it could. It was clear from the preparations for governing which Biden and his transition team made that his administration would place emphasis on expertise in government, in marked contrast to Trump's suspicion of what he and his supporters regarded as a hostile 'deep state'. The cabinet names and policy teams indeed reflected Biden's own extensive governmental experience. There was also an emphasis on diversity with key posts going to women and to members of minority groups.

Biden faced a series of massive policy problems and a deeply divided society. The Republican Party, although itself absorbed in a battle about its future and the future role of Trump, was in no mood to be cooperative or conciliatory. Bipartisan compromise in Congress seemed as far away as ever. The Democratic Party, while for the most part supportive of its president, had its own tensions. The progressive wing associated with Bernie Sanders and younger figureheads such as Alexandria Ocasio-Cortez wanted to shift policy in a leftwards direction. And there were individuals like Senator Joe Manchin of West Virginia who has consistently taken a more conservative line on policy than the party leadership.

The first initiatives which Biden took involved using executive orders to reset policies initiated by Trump. There were a raft of policies designed to enhance the United States's response to Covid-19 including creating a new position to coordinate strategy against the pandemic, expanding the vaccination drive, and encouraging more mask-wearing. The United States also signaled its intention to reengage with the World Health Organisation (WHO). The permit for the XL Keystone pipeline was revoked and the United States rejoined the Paris climate agreement. Restrictions on abortion funding were withdrawn and the president signaled his intention to combat discrimination on the basis of sexual preference and gender identity, which included repealing Trump's ban on transgender persons serving in the military. Construction of the border wall was halted and a program offering protection from deportation to young illegal immigrants was restored. Biden took early advantage of his power to nominate judges to federal judicial positions, although his announcement of a commission to study the appointments process for the Supreme Court seemed calculated to give ammunition to the right without any likelihood of promoting substantial change (Wheeler 2021).

The real character of Biden's agenda however seemed to be revealed by three major initiatives which together represent a major extension of government spending and a retreat from the philosophy of limited government which had come to dominate American politics in the period from Reagan onwards. The first was a massive Covid Relief Bill which aimed to direct $1.9 trillion of public spending toward helping individuals and families economically damaged by the pandemic. This legislation was passed in March 2021 and was overwhelmingly popular, not surprisingly perhaps as it made payments to large numbers of Americans. The second and third legislative packages outlined in his State of the Union message in April 2021 confirmed a desire on Biden's part to be a radical president, to reset the public philosophy, transform the architecture of American social provision and modernize the infrastructure of the country. The speech outlined a $1.8 trillion package for families and a $2.3 trillion package for infrastructure. Biden's blueprint for strengthening government provision for families was predictably quickly attacked by Republican Senators Mitch McConnell and Tim Scott as threatening a takeover of American society while Senator Josh Hawley, a Senator on the far right of the GOP, attacked it as 'lefty social engineering.' While it is likely that Republicans will continue their attacks both on the cultural impact of Biden's vision as well as on the costs and the implications of such spending for higher taxes, it is possible that some of these priorities may be enacted. Biden appears to be pursuing the mantle of a twenty-first century Franklin Delano Roosevelt and to be taking the Party in the direction of a new New Deal. There are of course obstacles to realizing this ambition not least in Congress, and many of the other priorities which he has outlined may well be stymied. But Biden knows that, if there is to be action on the scale he wants, he must act quickly and certainly before the 2022 midterms threaten his ability to set the agenda.

THE CHAPTERS

The individual chapters focus on different aspects of US institutions and politics as the country enters this new phase. Bruce Cain analyses the reasons why the rules and machinery of the US electoral system have become the subject of such partisan contestation and he explores the racial dimension of the debates about restricting or extending voting eligibility. The chapter shows how Republican states tried to limit the impact of demographic change which they saw as threatening their interests. They did this by adopting a variety of tactics calculated to make it more difficult for presumed likely Democratic voters to exercise their vote while Democrats in turn tried to encourage electoral participation by making the process easier especially by the use of postal voting. The legitimacy of the 2020 elections was inevitably made even more contentious because the Covid pandemic made many voters reluctant to vote in person. Partisan control of America's election machinery undermines the legitimacy of election outcomes. Yet while the parties see an interest in maintaining their ability to shape the rules the prospects of reform are gloomy.

The next two chapters look at social movements which grew rapidly over the course of the Trump presidency and transformed the American political agenda. Althea Legal-Miller looks at the growth of the Black Lives Matter (BLM) movement and its impact on the debate about policing and law enforcement in the United States. She explains how the traditions and practice of policing in America are rooted in the experience of slavery and white supremacy and how these origins continue to shape the way in which black Americans experience the many incidents of police brutality. The early stages of the Black Lives Matter movement prompted a series of reforms under Barack Obama. These initiatives were largely reversed by the Trump administration which increasingly saw the protection of the police as key to its defense of law and order against the allegedly anarchistic goals of the BLM protesters and proposals which would limit police powers and defund the police as currently organized. Although on assuming office President Biden issued a series of executive orders designed to tackle racial injustice in the United States, efforts to pass comprehensive police reform in the shape of the Justice in Policing Act (JPA) seem likely to fail as a result of Republican opposition in the Senate. As is clear from the author's analysis, while the death of George Floyd and the transformation of the BLM movement into a movement of global significance marked a new point in the US awareness of its racial injustices, the ability of the political system to address those injustices is anything but straightforward.

Virginia Sapiro looks at the changing politics of the women's movement. She places her analysis in the context of a series of profound changes in the understanding of sex and gender identity and a growing tolerance of sexualities which diverge from the heterosexual norm. As she argues, although that growing tolerance has been fuelled by generational shifts, there are still very marked differences between the two major parties on issues to do with sexuality—including same-sex marriages and transgender issues. Such issues have stoked the contemporary culture wars and reflect also the continuing influence of religion in American life. As the author emphasizes there has also been a massive growth in women's consciousness and mobilization against sexual harassment, especially through the Me Too movement. And there has been a significant expansion of women's presence in political life both in congressional representation and other elective offices and in government. The selection of Kamala Harris as President Biden's running mate brought a woman to the vice-presidency for the first time ever.

Mark Brewer looks at the role of political parties in American democracy, particularly the changing nature of the parties' electoral coalitions. He notes that while parties were regarded with suspicion by many of the Founding Fathers and that today many observers blame them for the vitriolic tone of American public life, parties are an essential element of a democracy. Yet as he details American parties have changed to reflect the wider developments in society, sometimes dramatically and sometimes incrementally. Two periods in their evolution over the last hundred years are of particular importance to understanding the character of the parties today. The New Deal period of the 1930s saw Franklin Delano Roosevelt put together an enlarged Democratic coalition which dominated American party competition until the late 1960s. The period of the Reagan ascendancy (1981–89) saw an expansion of Republican support to take in cultural as well as fiscal conservatives and to sharpen its appeal to white southerners, white men, surburbanites, and religious conservatives especially evangelicals but also traditionalist Roman Catholics. Increasingly also from the 1980s the parties became intensely polarized, a process which the Trump presidency exacerbated. Few observers believe that the rise in what is called 'affective polarization' is a healthy feature of a democracy but the trend is one which is likely to be difficult to reverse, especially in the short term. The Republican coalition as it operates in the present period may also be under strain for two reasons: the demographics of its components are changing in a way which reduces their strength and the experience of the Trump defeat in 2020 has left the Party divided about what its future strategy should be. As Brewer is clearly aware, attempting to predict the future shape of the parties is a task beset by a range of unknowns, but analyzing how parties have changed in the past is a crucial first step toward understanding their current and likely future role in shaping American politics.

Hye Young You then examines the controversial role of interest groups and money in American politics. As she notes, competition between interest groups is an essential part of American democracy but it presents troubling problems, especially the inequality of the different voices in the American political arena and the likelihood that listening to interest groups may cause politicians to misrepresent the views of the general public. This misrepresentation occurs for example when general support for tighter gun regulation is consistently underestimated as a result of aggressive lobbying by pro-gun activist groups. The role of money in US politics also has a profound impact on the quality of American democracy. Here the dynamics have changed significantly since the efforts to control the role of money in election campaigns after the Watergate scandal in the 1970s. This effort was undermined by a series of decisions by a conservative leaning Supreme Court that struck down a number of limitations on campaign spending in the name of protecting the constitutional right to spend money in an election campaign, which in the Court's view was a form of free speech. The author discusses how the decision in *Citizens United* has led to a massive growth in independent expenditures by SuperPACs (a type of organization that makes independent expenditures in elections) which takes place alongside the formal expenditures by party organizations and candidates. This growth can shape the political agenda in a way which is often negative and largely unaccountable. On the donation side, she explains how there has been a rise in the influence of individual donors as opposed to PACs (Political Action Committees) and that this changing balance may have the effect of favoring more extreme candidates and issue positions. The chapter also explores the motivations for lobbying which is ubiquitous at all levels of the system. Overall, she argues, the way interest groups and money operate in the American system serves not so much to produce an efficient balance of interests, as Madison suggested, but rather to entrench inequalities of access and systematic distortions of representation.

Philip Davies analyses Donald Trump's use of the media. He shows that Trump displayed a high degree of media skill before he came to the presidency and was an object of fascination for the media on account of his celebrity, wealth, and lifestyle. Once in office, however, relations with the mainstream media became strained and Trump came to rely increasingly on sympathetic media channels and social media to promote his version of political reality. Not merely did Trump attack any media source which challenged him but Democrats and Republicans came to live in two quite separate media worlds. The Trump administration's determination to deny the seriousness of the Covid-19 pandemic led to public confusion and brought Trump into disrepute as he promoted nonsensical remedies for the virus. The peddling of lies, euphemistically labeled as 'truthful hyperbole' or 'alternative facts' became a hallmark of Trump's handling of the media and his presidency as a whole. It culminated in Trump's refusal to accept that he had lost the 2020 election and his assertion that it had been stolen, an outlandish claim which nonetheless gained credibility with many of his supporters. Although Trump's campaign to overturn the election result ultimately failed and he was debarred at least temporarily from Twitter and Facebook, his ruthless strategy of exploiting the new media landscape and his disdain for truth not only showed how a politician could shape the political terrain to his advantage but also provided a dangerous model for future emulation.

In the first of a series of five chapters looking at the institutions of the US political system Jon Herbert examines the changed character of the presidency. The rise of partisanship in the system has done much to change presidential opportunities for leadership. The author shows how the presidency has evolved from an institution where a president negotiated and bargained with other actors and agencies by seeking compromise in the center ground of the political system to one where the presidency operates more often as a highly partisan instrument. Trump's presidency seemed, at first blush, likely to break this pattern as an outsider challenging all things establishment came to office. Yet, despite a highly personalized style of communication and presidential management, Trump and the Republicans engineered an accommodation that gave the party significant gains and protected Trump in office despite the flaws of his governing style.

James Curry's discussion of the legislature analyses the dynamics of the contemporary Congress, the evolution of its policy-making processes and its discharge of the representative function. He argues that, although much has changed in the way Congress goes about its business—especially the extent to which party leadership directs the legislative process—there is much that is stable in its operations. Although the tendency of observers is to focus on the legislative measures which deeply divide the parties, much legislation is still on the basis of cross-party support and is informed by the intricate system of committees which shape policy outcomes reflecting specialist knowledge and expertise. Of course, there have been changes in the role of committees as a result of the strengthening of centralized party direction and there has been a growth in unorthodox legislative mechanisms which allow the tortuous process of committee deliberation to be by-passed to some extent. But Curry's argument is that the element of continuity should not be underestimated. So too with representation. Today's Congress is more diverse than it was a generation ago and is thus in many respects more representative of American society, although it should be noted that much of that diversity (on race, on religion, on gender, and on sexual preference) is contained in the Democratic Party rather than in the Republican ranks. It is also more representative of issue divisions within the United States as party sorting has clarified the ideological and policy differences between the parties. Changes in technology have allowed members of Congress to communicate directly with their constituents via social media rather than having to rely on mass media to reach their electorates. Yet, as Curry emphasizes, the notion of the geographical representation of a single area or state is still key to the way Congress interacts with the public; and building a personal vote remains an important factor in how congressional members order their priorities.

Emma Long's essay on the Supreme Court shows how Trump's approach to the federal court system and especially the Supreme Court has had a profound impact on the role of courts in the American political system. His ability to fill a large number of vacancies, including appointing to three Supreme Court vacancies, by defying normal conventions will shape the composition of the courts for many years to come. Equally, she argues, Trump's treatment of the courts has altered the culture in which the legal system operates; Trump treated judicial appointments as part of the spoils of electoral victory and attempted to exert control over and secure cooperation from the courts in legal disputes involving the administration. When a judge or court did not deliver the 'win' Trump expected he would often denounce the judge personally. The consequence of such an approach is that the public will increasingly see legal processes in partisan political terms and that in turn will undermine the legitimacy of the judiciary and of constitutional interpretation. Of course, there has always been an element of political calculation in the processes surrounding court nominations and legal processes in the United States. Trump's approach has made those calculations more blatant and obvious, blurring the distinctions between liberal and conservative jurisprudential positions and Democratic and Republican ones. Long offers a careful overview of some recent cases which the Supreme Court has decided, showing the changing agenda of cases before the Court, the impact of the new appointees on outcomes, and the political significance of the decisions. She notes the appointment by President Biden of a commission to study the role of the Court and, although she recognizes the dangers associated with any charge of 'court-packing', she also sees the commission's deliberations as offering a possible way back from today's hyper-partisanship.

Bert Rockman's chapter analyses the changing approach to the federal executive and the bureaucracy in the Trump years. He traces the historic expansion in the size and role of the federal government and shows how the Republican Party became increasingly suspicious of the bureaucracy. All presidents want a responsive governmental machine and take steps to try to control it effectively. For Trump the bureaucracy was seen as the 'deep state', a hostile force seeking to undermine him. As a result, Trump emphasized personal loyalty rather than expertise and there was a high turnover of personnel at all levels of his administration as officials who challenged the president's policies or displeased him in some way were removed or sidelined. Trump was also disdainful of the institutions and administrative procedures which are an essential part of decision-making. Thus initiatives such as the attempt to ban Muslim migrants to the United States and the effort to exclude non-citizens from the 2020 US census count were struck down by the courts and had to be revised or abandoned. Rockman shows that Trump's general approach to government resulted in a loss of policy competence and damaging loss of morale in the bureaucracy, qualities which the Biden government will have to work hard to rebuild.

Ursula Hackett examines the workings of federalism and the subnational system of government in the United States. Although federalism is sometimes seen as a formal constitutional artefact, she argues that its fifty states and 90,000 local government units make a dynamic ecosystem in which a variety of actors seek to influence policy by exploiting constitutional and extra-constitutional resources. It is a system characterized by collaboration and competition: collaboration generated by the desire to share information and expertise especially through organizations such as the National Governors Association (NGA) and competition generated by the pursuit of investment and resources including federal funding. The autonomy that states enjoy allows a high degree of policy innovation over such matters as access to abortion and the decriminalization of cannabis as well as taxing and spending decisions. That autonomy is not unlimited. In addition to the constraints imposed by the courts, the federal government may seek to control state initiatives, especially if state and federal governments are controlled by different parties. Thus the federal government under Trump has sought to use federal grant allocations to challenge so-called sanctuary cities (where information about illegal immigrants is withheld from federal authorities) and to distribute the medical supplies needed in the pandemic to politically sympathetic states. The author shows how the states can have a major impact on social policy and indeed on the quality of democracy itself through actions on health care and through changes to voting rights. State and local government will thus have a profound impact on the everyday lives of citizens, and gridlock in Washington, DC may be expected to put increased pressure on the states to fill the gaps left by federal inaction.

In the first of a series of chapters which examine key issues on the American political agenda Andy Wroe explores the issue of immigration. He argues that immigration is inextricably linked to the question of the United States' individual and collective identity and to the narratives which the country tells about itself. There are of course profoundly different versions of those narratives—the rosy picture of the United States as a nation of immigrants and the less rosy narrative which emphasizes the xenophobic and racist antagonism experienced by successive waves of newcomers. That antagonism has taken a new form over the last sixty years as the demographics of the United States are changing radically. Although as of 2020 just over 60 percent of the population is white, it is projected that proportion will decline to around 48 percent by 2055 while the rapidly increasing Hispanic and Asian populations will grow to around 24 percent and 14 percent of the population respectively. Taken together with the 13 percent of the population which is black, these projections mean that the white segment of the population will be a minority by 2055. As Wroe demonstrates, the immigration issue was central to Trump's agenda and his exploitation of anti-immigrant fears fuelled his 2016 and 2020 campaigns. However, as Wroe also points out, despite the nativist rhetoric and appeal to cultural nationalism, Trump's ability to translate his agenda into policy achievements was much more limited, constrained by both the effects of a political system which tends to impede radical initiatives and by his own leadership failings.

In the next chapter Greg Rosston looks at the handling of economic policy under Trump and assesses the likely trajectory of President Biden's approach to the economy. Three themes stand out about Trump's economic record. First, it was an approach to the economy which deviated in significant ways from Republican orthodoxy, reflecting as it did Trump's determination to move away from free trade toward greater protection for American businesses. It also was relatively unconcerned about cutting spending and placed a heavy emphasis on cutting taxes. Secondly, it displayed a short-term emphasis and was geared toward initiatives that could generate growth in the near future and yield immediate political popularity while neglecting longer term costs whether to the environment or indeed to consumers. This approach reflected Trump's campaign promises to make a difference and his perception that growth and improved employment figures would fuel a sense of economic resurgence and hence enhance his reelection prospects. The third theme of the chapter is how the impact of the Covid-19 pandemic had a devastating effect on the economy sending unemployment rates soaring and causing a paralysis of much of the retail sector. With that devastation Trump's prospects of reelection were greatly reduced.

Jonathan Oberlander then looks at the highly polarized politics of health care policy. He explains why the United States had for so long failed to provide a comprehensive system of health care for the population, pointing to such factors as the anti-government environment in the United States, its fragmented political institutions, and the fact that health care reform seemed to threaten major interests in the policy sector. However with Obama's Affordable Care Act (ACA) of 2010 (dubbed by its opponents as 'Obamacare') a major step forward was taken. The intense controversy surrounding the legislation did not, as initially anticipated, recede after its passage. Bitter opposition continued. Republican gains in 2010 at the midterms further inflamed the debate and many Republican states refused to implement the ACA's key provisions. Trump came to the presidency in 2017 pledged to repeal the ACA. Yet, although there was a major threat to the legislation, in practice it survived. The Republicans were divided over repeal and what might replace it. Moreover, the new system had become more established and its benefits began to be appreciated by the public. The author shows how, despite the new legislation, the experience of the Covid-19 pandemic exposed continuing gaps in the health care system and its inequities in relation to the poor, the unemployed, and those with preexisting medical conditions. The Biden administration has now to assess how far it can take reform forward, knowing that any major further initiative will likely generate renewed controversy and opposition.

Robert Spitzer explores the issue of guns and gun control in the United States. He shows that there is much misunderstanding and mythology surrounding the history of America's relationship with guns and that the regulation of firearms has a long pedigree in the United States. Indeed it was not until *DC v Heller* in 2008 that the Supreme Court decided that the Second Amendment protected an individual's right to keep a firearm for the purposes of self-defense in the home, although the Court also recognized that right was not unlimited and could be regulated. Spitzer also shows how, despite its clout as a pressure group, the National Rifle Association (NRA) has experienced a period of internal turmoil in recent years culminating in having to file for Chapter 11 bankruptcy. It was also outspent in the 2020 elections by the forces advocating stricter gun regulation which have gained support in the aftermath of a series of deadly gun massacres. Nevertheless, although gun reform legislation is likely to command support in the House of Representatives, the prospect of substantial reform is remote while the Senate retains its power to block change. Moreover, the conservative tilt of the Supreme Court is also likely to act as a further barrier to any meaningful tightening of the laws.

Margaret Weir then analyses America's patchy system of social policy which has long displayed a number of gaps and inadequacies by comparison with the systems in place in most other advanced democracies. Weir shows how the system's work-oriented policies provide little for those who most need support—those at the bottom end of the labor market and the unemployed.

The long-standing inadequacies of the system especially in relation to unemployment support, housing, and health care were cruelly exposed by the onset of Covid-19. As Weir notes, the pandemic initiated a new stage in the debate about social policy, the inadequacies of the existing system, and its racial bias. Although some emergency measures were introduced to put a floor under the system, there remains profound disagreement between the parties as to the direction of any future reform. Republicans are reluctant to commit to high levels of spending especially when directed to programs aimed at the poorest groups and not linked to work. Democrats are looking to expand the scope of social protection in a more permanent and comprehensive manner to make the United States more in line with the welfare systems of other advanced democracies and address the poverty which persists despite US wealth.

Trevor McCrisken's examination of foreign and security policy concludes the series of issue-based chapters. He argues that the advent of the Biden presidency finds the United States at a turning point in relation to foreign and security policy as it tries to extract itself from a series of military commitments made in the aftermath of the 9/11 attacks. McCrisken highlights the different policy approaches of alternating Republican and Democratic administrations. He shows how Trump, by comparison with his predecessor Obama, opted for a more unilateralist set of objectives encapsulated in the idea of peace through strength. However, Trump's combative and unorthodox style, his lack of finesse and attention to detail, as well as the frequent changes of key personnel made it difficult to sustain this as a successful strategy. The author shows how Russia and China have emerged as obvious threats to US national interests but he suggests that the international arena also now presents a set of complex issues, not least climate change and pandemics, which require the United States to adapt its foreign and security policy thinking and to move on from its traditional mindset. While it is by no means clear that the US foreign policy-makers can make this adaptation, there is some cause for optimism in Biden's approach and his emphasis on expertise and openness in foreign policy-making and a willingness to engage with multinational organizations once more.

Gillian Peele concludes the book by assessing Trump's legacy. She looks at the different aspects of his impact on the US political system: the legacy of his highly unconventional style, the legacy of his deliberate exacerbation of identity politics, his policy legacy and his legacy for the Republican Party. Each of these legacies she argues has had disruptive effects on the wider political, social, and constitutional system. While their longer term impact may not be known for some time (and much may depend on Trump's decision about his own political future), his period in the presidency has been one from which the United States will move on with difficulty.

REFERENCES

Brady, D., and B. Parker. 2021. This is how Biden Eked Out his 2020 Victory. *Washington Post*, February 12.

Wheeler, R. 2021. *Biden's First One Hundred Days and the Judiciary: Prompt Action and a Supreme Court Vacancy*. Washington, DC: The Brookings Institution, April 27.

CHAPTER 2

The Elections of 2020

Bruce E. Cain

Sometimes, unanticipated events or circumstances beyond the candidate's control such as global economic downturns, national security crises, or extreme natural disasters play a pivotal role in elections. They constitute the 'known unknowns' in vote prediction models, uncontrollable contextual factors that have shaken up voting outcomes in the past. The prospect of a major pandemic disrupting the conduct of a national election had seemed very remote in recent decades. Although the Spanish Flu reduced turnout in the 1918 midterm election by ten percent (Marisam 2010), the faded memory of that event over time and the assumption that contemporary medicine could better handle novel infectious diseases had put this possibility out of mind. By the time American officials realized that conducting a Presidential election during a public health crisis would be a serious challenge, the matter had already become strongly politicized along party lines.

President Trump's strategy of talking down Covid-19's danger ensured that a larger share of his voters as opposed to Biden's would turn out in person to vote in November. And since Biden's supporters tended to take the pandemic threat more seriously, efforts to make it easier for voters to cast an absentee ballot would on balance favor their turnout. When Republican efforts to block these accommodations and later to have the courts throw them out ultimately failed, President Trump ramped up his assertions that the election was stolen

B. E. Cain (✉)
Department of Political Science, Stanford University, Stanford, CA, USA
e-mail: bcain@stanford.edu

© The Author(s), under exclusive license to Springer Nature
Switzerland AG 2022
G. Peele et al. (eds.), *Developments in American Politics 9*,
https://doi.org/10.1007/978-3-030-89740-6_2

from him, adding new inflammatory material to a long-simmering partisan and racialized disagreement over political participation. Determining who could vote and how had increasingly become a partisan tactic with the consequence of progressively eroding bipartisan consensus over electoral administration at all levels of American government (Hasen 2012). This corrosive trend made Donald Trump's unsubstantiated claims more credible to many Republicans and fed the far right's political paranoia that culminated in the January 6 assault on the Capitol and a new round of voting restrictions in 2021. In the sections that follow, I will first discuss how the Covid-19 pandemic disrupted the strategies and conduct of the 2020 Presidential election. Then I will trace the roots of this contemporary dispute to America's racialized history of electoral participation and conclude with some reflections about how the ballot wars have affected America's perceptions of democratic legitimacy and its ability to govern.

THE CONTEXT OF THE 2020 ELECTION

Despite the continuous turmoil of his presidency, Donald Trump entered the 2020 campaign with strong reelection prospects. Throughout his term in office, Trump's job approval numbers never dropped below 37 percent and usually hovered just above 40 percent no matter what he said or did. When on March 13, President Trump declared a national emergency to deal with the pandemic, he only trailed Joe Biden by 4 points in the intended vote. His polling numbers were even better in the swing states that would ultimately determine the Electoral College outcome. And because he enjoyed widespread support in the Republican base, there was no serious opponent in the Republican primary who might have forced him to deplete his campaign coffers or left him with a residual split in the Republican ranks to mend. The Democratic field, by contrast, was 28 strong. When former Vice-President Joe Biden finally emerged victorious from the scrum, he was far behind Donald Trump in money and staff organization, forcing him to make some policy platform compromises that pulled him to the left in order to prevent potential defections from voters on the progressive wing and leaving Biden open to the charge that his policies in office would be more extreme than his campaign rhetoric suggested.

While Trump never led Biden in national polling during the entire campaign, his popularity in the critical swing states was such that he could realistically aspire to be the first presidential candidate to be elected twice without winning the popular vote. A major reason for this was the unevenness of the underlying playing field. For various geopolitical reasons including the inefficient over-concentration of Democrats in large coastal states and the Republican advantage in smaller states, the Electoral College calculations in recent years have tilted discernibly in a Republican direction. The polling-focused website fivethirtyeight.com predicted that Donald Trump could win the Electoral College even if he lost the national popular vote by as much as three to four percent. By this calculation, Biden would have had to win the popular vote by 5–7 points to be confident of an Electoral College victory. In the end, Joe Biden's final margin in the popular vote was under five points (i.e., 51.3 percent to 46.9 percent), enough to secure a 306–232 Electoral College victory, but only after weeks of close re-examination of the outcome in several swing states such as Arizona, Georgia, and Pennsylvania.

The Republican playing field advantages also extended down ballot due to such factors as the small state bias in US Senate elections, the Republican skew in federal and state district boundaries from line-drawing after the 2010 census, and numerous restrictive voting rules enacted by Republican state legislatures for the ostensible purpose of preventing extensive voter fraud. Democrats feared that the election would be stolen from them by efforts to suppress the vote. Republicans feared that the election would be stolen from them by efforts to expand the vote. As a consequence, the 2020 election was as much about partisan disagreements over the voting process as it was about competing visions over policy and ideology.

The Historical Pathway to Voting Disputes

As in 2000, the 2020 presidential contest exposed the American electoral system's vulnerability to partisanship, political gaming, and judicial contestation. In 2000, the Democratic candidate, Al Gore, lost the Electoral College 271–266 even though he carried the popular vote by 48.4 percent to 47.9 percent. The ensuing recounts and legal battles revealed flaws in ballot design, a faulty but widely used punch card voting system and gaping holes and ambiguities in federal and state election law. Republicans referred to the Florida hand recount process as 'slow motion grand larceny,' but they were not referring at the time to voter fraud (such as ineligible people voting or the same person voting multiple times). Rather, the current Republican preoccupation with voter fraud evolved in the decades after the 2000 election.

Donald Trump did not originate either the contemporary Republican preoccupation with election security or the racialized debate over expanding or restricting voter eligibility. The latter had deep historical roots extending back in time to when voting restrictions were imposed on African-Americans by Democrats in the Southern Confederate states during the Jim Crow era. After the Civil War, the passage of the 13th, 14th, and 15th amendments ended slavery and supposedly guaranteed the voting rights of the black population. However, fearing the political impact of black enfranchisement, the southern states adopted measures such as literacy tests and poll taxes that sometimes had the pretextual claim of being legitimate 'qualifications' for voting, but had the intent and effect of severely suppressing black voter participation in the American South. The contemporary political practice of using electoral administration to suppress minority voting is a modern variation of post-Civil War tactics that were widely employed in the predominantly Democratic South from the latter part of the nineteenth century until the civil rights era of the mid-twentieth century (Kousser 2000).

After decades of often futile litigation against these vote suppression efforts, Congress eventually passed the Voting Rights Act (VRA) in 1965, which removed supervision of voting rights litigation from Southern judges and gave it over to the DC Circuit Court and the US Justice Department. It also banned the use of poll taxes and literacy tests, and gave the civil rights legal community better tools to combat some of the subtler methods of disfranchising black voters such as allowing cities to selectively annex lands in a manner that bypassed black neighborhoods or drawing district boundaries that diluted the impact of the black vote by 'cracking' or 'packing' their communities.

Over time, the case law under Sections 2 and 5 of the VRA developed clearer guidelines for determining when changes in voting rules might have a discriminatory effect and the grounds under which either the courts or the Justice Department could intervene to remedy the racial vote dilution problem. While the VRA was extremely successful in increasing black voting rates, its passage set in motion a significant partisan realignment. White conservative Democrats in the South gradually separated themselves during the Reagan era from the party that imposed civil rights legislation upon them and moved into the Republican ranks while liberal whites, Latinos, and African-Americans consolidated into the Democratic coalition. The cumulative effect of racial, ideological, and partisan sorting (i.e., the realignment of a voter into socially and economically consistent party coalitions) created more homogeneous and polarized parties that were much more consistently liberal or conservative across social, racial, and economic issues (Cain and Zhang 2016).

This is the political context that Donald Trump emerged from in 2016 and operated in during the four years of his administration. With a few notable exceptions, Trump's racial, economic, and social themes fit quite comfortably with those favored by the Republican Party base. His court appointments pleased the religious right even if his personal life hardly resembled that of a devout Christian. His efforts to lessen the burdens of regulation and to implement tax cuts were sufficient to retain the support of the party's fiscal conservatives even though his trade policies and tariffs deviated from long-standing Republican party orthodoxy. Even in racial matters, Trump's policies, though more extreme than previous Republican presidential candidates, were largely consistent with the recent sentiments in the base.

Similarly, Trump's views about stolen elections fit comfortably with the growing fear within the Republican ranks that if demographic trends continued, their party would eventually be relegated to minority status. Throughout the 1980s and 1990s, Republican elected officials had either supported or at least not actively opposed the Voting Rights Act. One reason may have been that the VRA spurred the creation of new black and Latino seats that came at the expense of white Democratic incumbents. But Section 5 gave the federal government supervision over the election administration decisions of many southern jurisdictions due to their fraught racial histories, and increasingly became a source of tension between the political parties. In addition, Section 5 had been employed by the civil rights community in recent decades to prevent Republican legislatures in areas that were covered (i.e., designated for special scrutiny due to a history of discriminatory behavior) from redistricting black and Latino voters into ultra-safe districts for partisan advantage or adding new administrative burdens (e.g., proof of citizenship, photo identification) that might discourage disadvantaged minority group participation. The election of Barack Obama caused many across the political spectrum to assume naively that the US was finally post-racial, and therefore, that vulnerable minority groups did not need the VRA protection. When the conservative majority on the Supreme Court in effect nullified Section 5 of the VRA in *Shelby County v Holder* (2013), on the grounds that the preclearance formula used to identify areas of the country that deserved closer judicial scrutiny due to past racism was woefully outdated, the civil rights community lost a valuable tool for preventing the passage of voting restrictions that would adversely affect minority communities.

By the time Donald Trump formally entered the political arena, there was a pre-existing partisan divide over election rules, particularly as it applied to nonwhites. Democrats favored preserving and enhancing minority voting rights protection and making the electorate more inclusive, including restoring voting rights to felons upon completion of their incarceration. Democrats also favored making registration and voting less burdensome, advocating such methods as same-day registration, less stringent purging of the voter rolls, voting on the weekends, early voting, easier paths to correcting ballot errors, and third-party voting assistance to low voting communities.

Republicans, on the other hand, citing their concerns about voter fraud, favored more stringent protections such as stricter voter identification laws, proof of citizenship when voting and less expansive voter outreach. From their perspective, immigration was bringing in more potential Democratic voters and the rules that made it easier to vote were accelerating the effects of demographic trends that would eventually marginalize them. The Republican autopsy following Romney's loss to Barack Obama in 2012 recommended that the party attract more women and nonwhite voters. Donald Trump, however, showed them a path in 2016 that did not require that kind of politically fraught adjustment. The Republican Party could instead limit the influx of immigrants who might eventually vote Democratic and ramp up its existing efforts to install more restrictive voting procedures. President Trump had already fastened on the issue of illegal voting to explain why he did not win the popular vote in 2016 and even established a commission to look into the evidence for his allegations. In the end, as with many previous voter fraud investigations, the evidence proved to be largely anecdotal and the commission dissolved without resolving the issue one way or the other.

Questions about the legitimacy of American elections over the course of history have emanated from both ends of the political spectrum. Al Gore's 2000 election loss was a wake-up call to Democrats that the Electoral College could produce results that were not consistent with the popular vote. When Trump voters in 2020 questioned whether the voting machines were rigged to discount their votes, they were mimicking the Gore voters who suspected that a voting machine owned by a Republican supporter was miscounting their votes, the legacy of which is that now many states require a paper trail for electronic voting machine ballots (Smyth 2003). The failure of subsequent efforts either to get rid of the Electoral College or to persuade states to sign a compact that would pledge their Electoral College votes to the popular vote winner enhanced the fear on the left that they would be unfairly disadvantaged in future elections by this relic institution from an earlier, less 'small d' democratic era. Those fears were amplified in 2016 with Trump's Electoral College victory. But there was little Democrats could do about it. Red states were not going to surrender their advantage.

The concerns on both ends of the spectrum feed off one another. The more aggressively Democrats have taken steps to ease registration and voting, the more they heightened Republicans' paranoia and their determination to counter with voting restrictions. This syndrome leads to a reinforcing cycle of declining faith in the legitimacy of American elections. The point here is not to defend efforts at vote suppression or to say that goals of expanding or restricting the franchise and voter participation are morally equivalent, but simply to understand the mindset that Republicans have adopted in the face of rapid demographic change and potential political marginalization.

How political actors in the US think about the electoral process is inevitably tied to how it affects their prospects of winning or losing. In some ideal world, the rules of the electoral game would enjoy bipartisan consensus based on a shared sense of fairness behind a 'veil of ignorance' as to how it affects their political advantage. But with a closely divided American electorate, massive revenues and major policies at stake, and a raft of campaign professionals dedicated to advising the candidates how to win, such high-mindedness is easily pushed aside as naive. For the players and many activists, the rules of the political battle are fair game for manipulation in order to achieve a partisan advantage. Donald Trump in his inimitable manner took this mindset to the next level.

PARTISANSHIP AND EMERGENCY MEASURES

The well-handled crisis can sometimes work to the incumbent office-holder's advantage: voters have retrospectively rewarded presidents for successful military operations or economic recoveries in the past. But the way President Trump handled the Covid-19 crisis ensured that the country would divide not unite over his actions. On the plus side of the political credit ledger, the Trump administration did organize a massive campaign for vaccine development called 'Operation Warp Speed,' and, while his motives were suspect, he was probably correct to try to limit travel from China to prevent the spread from overseas. But the ban he implemented allowed Americans who were in

China to return to the US and ignored the threat from Western Europe. His discomfort with letting medical advisors take the lead (especially Director of the National Institute of Allergy and Infectious Diseases, Dr. Fauci), refusal to promote and personally adhere to the guidance on masking and social distancing, advocacy for hydroxychloroquine despite medical evidence, and speculations about bleach as a cure unnerved many voters. The president had hoped to campaign on a strong economy, but the pandemic brought many economic sectors such as tourism, entertainment, and restaurants to a stand-still and swelled the ranks of the unemployed. It also diverted attention away from the Black Lives Matter unrest that he had hoped would win some conser-vative Democrats and Independents to his side. Instead, Covid-19 deaths and overwhelmed hospitals dominated the news.

Moreover, Covid-19 opened up a contentious debate about how to conduct an election during a public health emergency, which in turn tapped into the steadily evolving partisan divide over whether to ease voting requirements and expand the electorate versus make them stricter and more exclusive. Trailing in the polls and aware that his 2016 Electoral College victory was determined by the narrow margin of 76,000 votes in the three blue states (Wisconsin, Michigan, and Pennsylvania) that he flipped to red, Trump's 2020 campaign needed to squeeze every vote he could get in the swing states. The Republi-cans had lost control of the House of Representatives in 2018 thanks in large part to the defection of educated suburban voters. While his loyal base gave him a hard floor of support, his unpopularity with college-educated voters meant that he had a hard ceiling as well. There was not a lot of wavering voters after 4 years of the Trump presidency. The challenge was to mobilize the base through rallies and repeating 'Make America Great Again' themes.

The turnout problems loomed larger for the Democrats than the Republi-cans at the outset of the 2020 campaign. While presidential elections normally generate a higher turnout, especially among young and nonwhite voters, turnout in 2020 would be complicated by the partisan divide over masking, social distancing, and divisions over the seriousness of the Covid-19 threat. It became clearer as the pandemic unfolded that Democrats would be more reluctant to go to the polling places and stand in line to vote because they took the health threat more seriously. Republicans were primed by their president to discount the danger of in-person activities and hence could be counted on to be less worried about voting in person. Trump hard-core supporters were even willing to attend political rallies closely bunched in crowded venues and unmasked. The president had placed a political appointee in charge of the US Postal Service who implemented cost-cutting measures that were likely to lead to delivery delays that could result in mailed absentee ballots arriving too late, or worse, getting lost in route. The battles of previous participation wars had found new expression in disagreements over whether the pandemic emer-gency warranted accommodations to absentee and early voting that would allow voters to avoid exposure to Covid-19 in the polling day lines.

Before delving into how specific ballot access controversies ballooned into claims that the election was stolen, it is helpful to bear in mind several distinctive aspects of the American electoral administration. To begin with, it is shaped by America's strong institutional emphasis on checks and balances and electoral accountability: the former explains why voting rules are so complex and variable, and the latter why Americans think it is acceptable to let partisan officials oversee the conduct of elections as opposed to neutral, nonpartisan bureaucrats.

Written in the late eighteenth century, the US Constitution was designed to prevent or at least limit an excessive concentration of power in any branch or level of government through checks and balances. It means in effect that laws and administrative actions cannot be exercised without multiple layers of political consent. This fracturing of power has a horizontal (across the branches of government) and a vertical dimension (across the national, state, and local levels). Polarization has increased party discipline, especially in the Republican ranks. When one party controls all the branches of government, partisan polarization helps the party with 'trifecta control' to maintain enough party discipline to overcome many of the usual obstacles to legislation. But when control of the branches is divided and the parties are polarized, taking bold legislative action becomes more difficult.

This is relevant because President Trump would likely have been able to override many of the state emergency provisions with respect to elections for federal offices if the Republicans had retained control of the House of Representatives in the 2018 mid-terms. The authority to do so resides in Article 1, Section 4, Clause 1 of the US Constitution:

> The Times, Places and Manner of holding Elections for Senators and Representatives, shall be prescribed in each State by the Legislature thereof; but the Congress may at any time by Law make or alter such Regulations, except as to the Places of chusing Senators.

In other words, states have the authority to determine their election rules for federal elections unless Congress itself decides otherwise. President Trump with unified Republican control in 2020 would likely have considered using this power to limit mail-in and early voting accommodations. The Democrats with trifecta control in 2021, for instance, introduced a sweeping electoral reform bill (H.R.1) that aimed to impose reforms on the states that would make it easier to vote and harder to restrict participation in the future elections. As former Republican Senate leader Mitch McConnell lamented: 'The same party that wants to change Senate rules when they lose a vote, pack the Supreme Court when they lose a case and throw out the electoral college every time they lose the White House now wants to forcibly rewrite 50 states' election laws from Washington.' Few would doubt that McConnell would have done the same in 2020 if he had had the requisite support from the House.

Failing radical Congressional action of this sort, the vertical fracture of authority across the states created a highly varied and complex electoral administration landscape. Giving individual states the autonomy to make rules about congressional elections generated a wide variation in the processes governing absentee ballots and early voting. This was complicated by a second distinctive feature of US electoral administration: the partisanship of election administrators. The chief election officer in 47 of the 50 states is the Secretary of State. Out of the 47, there were 20 who ran as Democrats, 25 as Republicans, 1 as an independent, and 1 as nonpartisan. Half of all US local officials are either appointed by or elected as partisans. Fortunately, partisan officials do not always favor their own party. A number of Republican election officials in critical swing states—Arizona, Michigan, Georgia, and Pennsylvania—heroically refuted Trump's claims of widespread voter fraud and defended the integrity of their voting systems. But many did not, underlining the danger of allowing partisan officials to conduct elections and adjudicate voting disputes. The partisanship of elected officials also came up in the 2000 presidential election dispute in Florida, but the strong inertia behind keeping processes that have been in place for decades combined with the American proclivity to prioritize accountability to the voters over neutral expertise combined to prevent any significant progress toward remediating the partisan bias problem.

One last feature to bear in mind is the breadth of discretion that state governors have during extreme weather and public health emergencies. A system with so much built-in policy inertia of necessity needs to have strong emergency powers to deal with unanticipated civil emergencies (e.g., riots) or natural disasters. Droughts, flooding events, and hurricanes routinely enable governors to authorize expenditures and take actions that would normally require legislative consent. But in this case, one party or the other could be differentially advantaged by adhering to or easing rules about when and how one could vote in the 2020 election. Moreover, whatever a state did, it would inevitably result in litigation as the language of the Constitution is ambiguous as to who in the state could make changes in election laws. Article 1, for instance, states that the election laws are 'prescribed in each State by the legislature thereof,' which leaves open a partisan disagreement over whether the term 'legislature' means only the state legislatures or a legislative process broadly defined that includes the governor or other entities that delegated legislative power (Morley and Tolson 2021). This led to legal challenges when Republican legislatures were overridden by Democratic governors and state courts.

Bearing these features in mind, another reason that many Republicans came to believe that the 2020 election was stolen from them—in addition to President Trump's unproven insistence that Democrats benefited from extensive voter fraud—may have been the sheer number and extent of the changes made in 2020 to permit more absentee and early voting. To clarify terms, absentee voting in the US referred originally to votes cast prior to an election on a ballot that was mailed to eligible voters because they would be out of the state for some valid reason and could not reasonably be expected to vote in person. Mail-in absentee voting refers to those who send in by post, which was a concern for many Democrats because the postal service was experiencing delays due to Republican cuts in its budget. All-mail balloting refers to a handful of states that mail out and accept ballots mailed back to them by all eligible voters. And early voting refers to opportunities to vote in person or to drop off a ballot at voting stations before the election.

Prior to the 2020 election, there had been a several decade upward trend in so-called convenience voting: that is, people who availed themselves of the convenience of filling out their ballot at home and either dropping it off at a polling place or mailing it in. Americans have lengthy ballots requiring many choices among elected federal, state, and local candidates. In addition, many states and local governments also decide many policies and bond questions by direct democracy. Voters who have not diligently gone through the voting materials to decide in advance how to mark the ballot could be in a polling booth for 15 minutes or more as they make their decisions. This in turn can contribute to waiting in long lines at the polling place.

The prospect of Covid-19 spreading while people waited in lines or interacted with election officials was a serious concern. The option of filling out a ballot at home and then returning it by mail or in a dropbox was an attractive option for those who took the pandemic seriously. Post-election studies revealed that 58 percent of people who stated that they were worried about family members catching Covid-19 reported that they voted by mail versus 27 percent among those not so worried. Democrats were more likely than Republicans to be worried about catching Covid (62 percent to 41 percent) and more likely to report voting by mail (35 percent to 25 percent) despite the fact that Republican voters were on average older and more likely to suffer serious consequences or death from a Covid-19 infection (Persily and Stewart 2021). In sum, making voting accommodations for public health reasons had different tactical consequences for the two parties. Election rules in the highly partisan, closely divided, and highly professionalized campaign setting in 2020 were ripe for politicization.

According to data collected by the Brennan Center, 29 states and the District of Columbia enacted 79 bills expanding ballot access in 2020, including 4 states that mailed a ballot to every voter and a dozen that mailed out absentee applications, both for the first time. In addition, eight states expanded voting by mail by eliminating excuse requirements or making Covid-19 a valid excuse. Still, others newly allowed voters to correct mistakes in their ballot such as forgetting to sign the envelope, extended the deadlines for ballot receipts, provided pre-paid postage, and allowed pre-processing of mailed-in ballots. The latter might not seem important, but delays in processing mailed-in ballots can lead to substantial delays in the final count, leading to heightened suspicions when the leads between candidates change days after the election. States also relaxed the rules on who could be a poll worker and raised their compensation in light of the dangers of Covid-19 infection and the preponderance of people over 60 who traditionally served as poll workers on election day. In addition to the $400 million allocated by Congress under the CARES Act to upgrade election security and safety, private individuals donated even more to upgrade voting processes, including $400 million from the founder of Facebook, Mark Zuckerberg. All of this helped to produce a record turnout of 158 million voters, up 7 percentage points from 2016. But all this activity also fed the Republican belief that the election was stolen from them. The analysis by Persily and Stewart revealed a 58 percent gap between Democrats and Republicans in belief in the fairness of the election, and that 'simply living in a state Trump barely won is worth approximately 40 points in confidence in whether state votes were counted properly among Republicans, compared to living in a state Trump barely lost' (Persily and Stewart 2021). Republican discontent, they found, was highest in states where Trump lost by three points or less (i.e., swing states) and where the use of mail balloting was the highest (i.e., blue states like California, Washington, and Oregon).

POST-ELECTION CONTROVERSY

Trump tweeted incessantly about the election being rigged in November and December after he lost. His lawyers filed 62 lawsuits at the state and federal level, losing 61 of them either for lack of standing or failure to provide any credible evidence of systematic voter fraud by the Democrats. A majority of these lawsuits centered on the six swing states that Biden won and that Trump had counted on winning (i.e., Arizona, Georgia, Michigan, Nevada, Pennsylvania, and Wisconsin). The judicial decisions against Trump's allegations were supported by judges appointed by Democratic and Republican leaders, including some he nominated, such as Amy Coney Barrett. His judicial setbacks included two US Supreme Court decisions that refused to take on the question of whether the November election outcome should be overturned. One of these cases, *Kelly et al. v. Pennsylvania*, claimed that the Republican-controlled legislature violated the Pennsylvania constitution when it expanded absentee voting. The Court dismissed it with one brief sentence. In sum, the American judiciary proved to be far less partisan and more loyal to precedent than the state legislatures, a reminder of the value of checks and balances.

Trump also pushed for recounts in some of the contested states, which provided further evidence that Trump's allegations regarding election fraud were specious. Two recounts in Georgia only found enough uncounted votes to reduce Biden's victory margin by 2417 votes to 11,779. The recount in Wisconsin only garnered 2343 votes, leaving Biden with a lead of 20,682. To be clear, President Trump was entitled to recounts in states where the margin of victory was below a threshold level and to challenge the results in court on procedural grounds as well. But when he refused to accept the outcome of these decisions and recounts, he went further than any losing incumbent president before him by calling an election official in Georgia to persuade him to overturn the state-certified vote and convening a rally about the stolen election that precipitated the January 6 invasion of the Capitol. Trump's last desperate ploy to retain the presidency was to try to persuade his Vice President to misuse his largely ceremonial role of opening and announcing the certified results of the Electoral College votes from each state to declare Trump the winner.

The battle over voter participation did not end with Joe Biden's Inauguration. As mentioned earlier, Democrats in the House of Representatives immediately introduced a bill H.R.1 that included a sweeping set of reforms aimed at fixing a wide range of election problems such as redistricting, election administration, campaign finance and voting rights. Democrats in just two months also introduced bills in 37 state legislatures that attempted to enhance mail voting, early voting, voter registration, and minority voting rights. For their part, Republicans in 33 states in the same period introduced over 165 bills that would limit mail voting, impose stricter voter identification requirements, constrain voter registration opportunities, and enable aggressive voter registration purges. This included Georgia, the site of not only Trump's defeat but also of two Republican US Senate seats lost, in large part, due to heavy organizing and high turnout in the African-American community. One of those bills aimed at eliminating Sunday early voting and negating a popular get-out-the-vote event in the black community called 'souls to the polls.' The sheer number of voting bills by both Republican 'restrictionists' and Democratic 'expansionists' far exceeded what had been introduced at comparable time periods previously—further evidence that the 2020 election supercharged the politicization of the ongoing participation battle between Democrats and Republicans.

THE IMPLICATIONS OF ELECTION WARS

Despite the bitterness of the presidential campaign and the disturbing events of January 6, there were some reassuring signs for American democracy in the 2020 election. The Electoral College bias did not prevent Joe Biden from defeating Donald Trump. Biden received 51.3 percent of the popular vote and 56 percent of the Electoral College votes. The margins in some of the swing states were quite narrow as they were in 2016, but that mirrors the situation in the country as a whole as reflected in the down-ballot outcomes. Neither party got a clear mandate out of the election. The Republicans picked up 11 seats in the House but lost 2 in the Senate. There were only two state legislative chambers that flipped in 2020, both gains by Republicans in New Hampshire. The split after the 2020 elections was 27R-23D for the governors. In all, the Republicans had trifecta control of state governments in 21 states and the Democrats in 15 states. The rest had divided governments. In short, neither US party was strongly preferred in 2020, and there is little indication that the power balance will change in the immediate future.

America's checks and balances largely held up. The courts and many election officials put their oaths of office before their political attachments. But it is disturbing that so many Republicans supported the unproven allegations of voter fraud, and that 140 House Members and 6 Senators voted against the certification of the Electoral College results. The peaceful transition of power that is central to the operation of any democracy requires that those who lose an election accept the results after they have exhausted all the available options for appeal and review. Moreover, it is also worrying that the conjoining of race, ideology and party identity have amplified the perceived stakes of every procedural battle, even when victory only confers small tactical advantages to the winners. Ironically, the avid pursuit of tactical advantage goes forward despite any clear academic evidence that making it harder and/or easier to vote is really an effective strategy (Grimmer et al. 2018). The findings of many political science studies fail to identify consistent effects on turnout in states that adopt these measures. The reason in part may be that the Democrats have successfully adjusted their grassroots activities to mobilize around these restrictions and that efforts to make voting easier do not matter if people are unexcited by their options.

All of that said, the intense voting wars of recent elections are not a good development for many reasons. First, the blatant conflation of partisan advantage and election rule design undermines confidence in the legitimacy of the political system. This in turn fuels opposition to anything the incoming government tries to achieve and enhances the growing partisan polarization and alienation from government. It becomes unnecessarily difficult to solve problems like holding an election during a pandemic emergency in a bipartisan way.

The political parties used to share a bipartisan consensus that campaign finance disclosure was important, but that has disappeared. Americans used to believe that voting was a civic duty that should be promoted widely, but that too has broken down. Partisanship has paralyzed both the Federal Election Commission and neutered the Election Assistance Commission that was formed after the 2000 election to improve voting in the US.

Election reforms often entail pluses and minuses. 'No excuse' absentee ballots are more convenient, but they more frequently than in-person voting result in uncounted ballots due to such oversights as voters failing to sign the outside of the envelope that contains the ballot or mailing the ballots in too late. Without poll workers to supervise and the secret ballot to protect the voter, an abusive spouse can control a partner's ballot, or give it to a third party to fill out. It is one thing to use mail-in voting during a public health emergency, but another to institute it permanently versus relying more on early and weekend in-person voting. It would be better if the debate focused on weighing the pros and cons of reform supported by evidence, not based on who gets the upper hand politically. But that does not seem possible at this point in the US.

The ballot wars are also not good for policy-making. The battle for tactical advantage has no natural stopping point. If the process merely serves the interests of those in power, then every rule is evaluated in that light. When power shifts, political actors conveniently shift their points of view about the rules that govern the political process generally, not just about voting. This for instance describes the Senate filibuster debate. When a party is in power, the super-majority rule needed to invoke cloture of a filibuster seems like an infuriating obstructive tool. When that party is out of power, it favors retaining the filibuster as leverage to induce compromise or prevent laws they oppose. As the expression goes in politics, where you stand depends upon where you sit. The mentality of shaping the electoral process for political advantage bleeds over into policy-making and back again.

The danger in this is not just policy instability, but undercutting confidence in the political system as a whole. In a closely divided society, power will inevitably shift from one party to the other. Once in power, the majority party can shape the electoral and legislative rules for electoral advantage, but when power shifts in the other direction, the new party can reverse the processes and policies of the previous party. The US Constitution is protected from short-term political manipulation by the super-majority rules required to change it, but congressional procedures and election rules are not spelled out in any detail and are subject to shifting majority rule.

As the American political system has become more professionalized and the stakes of government policies rise, short-run tactical advantages loom larger and long-term consequences recede. 'Grab it while you can' becomes the mantra. But when power shifts back and forth, the ensuing disruptions and reversals of regulatory policy or program support can adversely affect many different sectors of the economy and the population. Major problems like decarbonizing the economy and rebuilding an aging infrastructure cannot be solved in fits and starts. America's political parties are stuck in a non-cooperative rut at a time when the long term needs the utmost attention. Whether it is possible to break out of this pattern is the challenge moving forward.

REFERENCES

Cain, Bruce E., and Emily R. Zhang. 2016. Blurred Lines: Conjoined Polarization and Voting Rights. *Ohio St. LJ* 77: 867.

Grimmer, Justin, Eitan Hersh, Marc Meredith, Jonathan Mummolo, and Clayton Nall. 2018. Obstacles to Estimating Voter ID Laws' Effect on Turnout. *Journal of Politics* 80: 1045–1051.

Hasen, Richard L. 2012. *The Voting Wars: From Florida 2000 to the Next Election Meltdown.* New Haven, CT: Yale University Press.

Kousser, J. Morgan. 2000. *Colorblind Injustice: Minority Voting Rights and the Undoing of the Second Reconstruction.* Chapel Hill, NC: University of North Carolina Press.

Marisam, Jason. 2010. Judging the 1918 Election. *Election Law Journal* 9: 141–152.

Morley, Michael, and Franita Tolson. 2021. Elections Clause. Available at: https://constitutioncenter.org/interactive-constitution/interpretation/article-i/clause s/750.
Persily, Nathaniel, and Charles Stewart. 2021. The Miracle and Tragedy of the 2020 U.S Election. *Journal of Democracy* 32: 159–178.
Smyth, Julie Carr. 2003. Voting Machine Controversy. *Cleveland Plain Dealer*.

FURTHER READING

There is vast literature on the history of Jim Crow laws and subsequent battles over minority voting rights. The most authoritative study of efforts to use the civil rights amendments to the US Constitution and the 1965 Voting Rights Act to undo literacy tests, poll taxes and other efforts aimed at suppressing black voting in the South can be found in *Quiet Revolution in the South: The Impact of the Voting Rights Act, 1965–1990* edited by Chandler Davison and Bernard Grofman (1994, Princeton: Princeton University Press). Efforts to push back against this civil rights expansion are chronicled in J. Morgan Kousser's book *Minority Voting Rights and the Undoing of the Second Reconstruction* (2000, Chapel Hill: University of North Carolina Press), and Richard Hasen's study *The Voting Wars: From Florida 2000 to the Next Election Meltdown* (2012, New Haven: Yale University Press). For those interested in how Donald Trump become President, the leading political science account is John Sides, Michael Tesler, and Lynn Vavreck's book, *Identity Crisis: The 2016 Presidential Campaign and the Battle for the Meaning of America* (2019, Princeton: Princeton University Press). For a comprehensive overview of the various battles over election rules in the 2020 election see Nathaniel Persily and Charles Stewart. 'The Miracle and Tragedy of the 2020 U.S. Election.' in the *Journal of Democracy* (32: 159–178). While Jason Marisam's article, 'Judging the 1918 election.' in the *Election Law Journal* (9: 141–152) was written before the 2020 pandemic stuck, it provides a prescient account of how pandemics could disrupt electoral business.

CHAPTER 3

Race, Policing, and Black Lives Matter

Althea Legal-Miller

In March 2020, George Floyd, an African American man, lost his job as a security guard after Minnesota issued a statewide order to close all bars and restaurants in the early stages of the coronavirus pandemic. The following month he tested positive for Covid-19. At once, Floyd faced two social risk factors with significant racial disparities—unemployment and a coronavirus infection. A month later, he did not survive a third social risk factor with racial disparities—a lethal encounter with the police. On May 25, 2020, Floyd was murdered by Minneapolis Police Department officers after he was taken into custody on suspicion of using a counterfeit $20 bill at a local convenience store. As Officer Tou Thao engaged in 'crowd control,' Officers J. Alexander Kueng and Thomas Lane used their body weight to pin Floyd face down on the ground, while Officer Derek Chauvin knelt on his neck. For almost five minutes, Floyd begged for his life, stating 27 times 'I can't breathe.' Bystanders pleaded with the four officers to provide life-saving care, but they were ignored and threatened to 'back off.' In total, nine minutes and 29 seconds passed before Chauvin removed his knee from Floyd's neck at the insistence of paramedics who needed to carry Floyd's lifeless body into an ambulance. He was pronounced dead at the hospital, with the county medical examiner subsequently ruling the death a homicide.

A. Legal-Miller (✉)
School of Humanities and Educational Studies, Canterbury Christ Church University, Canterbury, UK
e-mail: althea.legal-miller@canterbury.ac.uk

G. Peele et al. (eds.), *Developments in American Politics 9*,
https://doi.org/10.1007/978-3-030-89740-6_3

The protracted extrajudicial execution of Floyd, captured for eight minutes and 46 seconds on the infamous smartphone recording that went viral, exposed the deadly convergence of policing and anti-Black racism, and sparked Black Lives Matter (BLM) protests across the United States and around the world. This chapter traces the rise of BLM demands for police accountability, which originated under the Obama presidency. The actions of the Obama and Trump Administrations amid critiques of racial bias in policing are explored, followed by an evaluation of the significance of the 2020 BLM protests in terms of federal, state, and local level outcomes. The chapter concludes with an assessment of President Biden's early efforts to address racial justice and police reform. The chapter begins, however, by providing a snapshot of race and policing in the United States. By so doing, the chapter hopes to show how police violence and the debate over the future of policing has deep political implications for the nature of American society more generally.

THE SIGNIFICANCE OF RACE IN POLICING

Academic scholars have argued that racial bias has deep roots in American policing. The origin of modern policing in the American South is rooted in the 'Slave Patrol.' Organized slave patrols, operating at times with impunity, had the primary functions of catching and returning enslaved escapees, terrorizing enslaved communities as a means of deterring slave rebellions, and using force to ensure adherence to 'slave codes' (Brown 2019). Slave codes were legal restrictions on enslaved people designed to regulate all aspects of their life: from religion to marriage, from cohabitation to imprisonment, from crimes to corporal punishment. With the vast majority of African Americans living in the South, 'policing' and its attendant functions of control and surveillance became the frontline of defense against threats to the institution of slavery and the maintenance of white supremacy. Following the Civil War and the constitutional abolition of slavery in 1865, slave patrols evolved in modern Southern police departments to limit the movement of free Black people, to ensure accessibility to cheap or unfree labor, and later to enforce the legal disenfranchisement of African Americans through 'Jim Crow' segregation laws. The development of policing is significant to understanding the contemporary relationship between the police and Black communities, because traditions and practices rooted in white supremacy were blended into modern policing. To be clear, changes in societal norms and laws and the implementation of professional standards have improved many aspects of American policing. However, for hundreds of years, Black Americans experienced differential and discriminatory treatment at the hands of patrols and the police.

And this experience is not confined to the past. Significant portions of the American public are inclined to believe that police actions are influenced by race. According to a 2019 Pew Research Center survey, 84 percent of Black and 63 percent of white Americans reported that Black people are treated less fairly than whites in dealing with the police and by the criminal justice system in general (Pew Research Center 2019).

When it comes to street-level policing, Black Americans disproportionately experience stops, searches, surveillance, arrests, and force that cannot be easily explained away by legal factors. There is compelling evidence that historical racial bias against Black Americans, and the enduring profitability of their incarcerated bodies (from plantations workers to prison workers, for example), have influenced and continue to influence the arrest decision-making of police officers. Studies reveal that race is a statistically significant factor in arrest outcomes, even when controlling for various legal and extralegal factors including, but not limited to, the offense or conduct of the arrestee, deference to the police, or the presence or preference of the victim (Brown 2019). In meta-analysis of approximately forty studies spanning data collected between 1966 and 2004, researchers found that the chances of arrest for people of color were 30 percent higher than that of white suspects (Kochel et al. 2011). Naturally, an arrest is only one of many discretionary choices police officers make, and Black Americans are susceptible to disparate racial impacts in stop and search, procedural justice, assistance to victims, and use of force. According to the Bureau of Justice Statistics (2015), Black Americans were more likely to be stopped by police, both in traffic and street stops, than white or Hispanic Americans. The same study also reveals that for Black Americans, those encounters are more likely to happen multiple times in a year, more likely to be initiated by police, and more likely to involve the use of force.

While the majority of public encounters with the police begin and end safely in the United States, Bureau of Justice data indicates that in comparison to white Americans, Black and Hispanic Americans are twice as likely to be subjected to the threat or use of physical force. In Minneapolis, Minnesota, where Floyd was killed and Black people make up just 19.4 percent of the population, police data revealed that between January 1, 2008, and June 8, 2020, there were 18,659 cases of use of force by police officers, of which 62 percent involved a Black person (Amnesty International 2020). The disproportionate use of lethal force by the police against Black Americans should be seen in the context of a wider pattern of racial profiling, stops and searches, and use of force by law enforcement personnel.

Notably, statistics on racial disparities in fatal police encounters are limited because mandatory or comprehensive records on these incidents have yet to be established by federal and local governments. But deadly force data-collection projects, such as those launched by *The Guardian* and *The Washington Post*, have found that Black men are 2.5 times more likely than white men to be killed by police during their lifetime. Media launched data-collection projects also suggest that about 1000 civilians are killed in officer-involved shootings each year in the United States, but that Black Americans killed by the police are twice as likely as white Americans to be unarmed (Campbell et al. 2017). In response to public pressure, the Federal Bureau of Investigation (FBI) established the first national database on the fatal use of force by police officers in 2019, although its data is compiled from only 40 percent of US law enforcement officers and relies on voluntary submissions.

Despite data limitations, researchers have linked racial disparities in the police's use of deadly force to structural racism. For example, Aldina Mesic et al. (2018) found that during 2013–2015 unarmed Black people were shot at a rate 4.5 times higher than unarmed white people in states with 'higher markers of structural racism'—a calculation formed by elevated rates of Black residential segregation, incarceration, unemployment, poverty, and lower educational attainment. The correlation in racial disparities and deadly police force goes some way to contextualizing historian Keeanga-Yamahtta Taylor's (2020) argument that 'police brutality has been the single most important political rallying cry across Black communities for decades, because it is the most visceral evidence of the second-class citizenship of poor and working-class African-Americans.'

Although the National Advisory Commission on Civil Disorders, appointed by President Lyndon B. Johnson, reported in 1968 that Black Americans held a 'widespread belief … in the existence of police brutality,' more recently smartphones and social media have provided unprecedented capacities to monitor the police and expose, circulate, and mobilize around discriminatory policing and use of deadly force. Indeed, the United States has been forced to reckon with the realities of racial disparities in fatal police encounters, and the discourse it has sparked is at the center of the BLM movement.

FROM OBAMA TO TRUMP IN THE ERA OF BLACK LIVES MATTER

A new movement for racial justice began during the presidency of Barack Obama when George Zimmerman was acquitted of the murder of a Black teenager Trayvon Martin in 2013. Addressing the despondency of Black communities to the exoneration of Zimmerman, community organizer Alicia Garza created the hashtag #blacklivesmatter to challenge the historical dehumanization of Black life. Alongside fellow activists Patrisse Cullors and Opal Tometi, Garza transformed the hashtag into an online community to help combat anti-Black racism in a vast array of guises, ranging from ending state violence to full employment. The #blacklivesmatter moment was transformed into a movement by the 2014 fatal shooting of Black teenager Michael Brown by a white police officer in Ferguson, Missouri. Brown's killing, the callous handling of the case by municipal authorities, and the militarized posturing of police officers against peaceful protesters, triggered an uprising in Ferguson that police sought to quell with tanks, tear gas, and rubber bullets. The Ferguson rebellion was the focal point of Black discontent, but BLM protests erupted across the United States in response to Brown's shooting and a series of other high-profile fatal police encounters, all in 2014, which saw Eric

Garner choked to death, John Crawford III and Ezell Ford shot to death, and Dante Parker tasered multiple times before dying in police custody.

In the aftermath of Ferguson and BLM protests, the Obama Administration set up a task force to review police practices and use of force. Outrage over images of militarized police in Ferguson amplified criticism of the Department of Defense's (DOD) 1033 program, which facilitates the transfer of controlled surplus military-grade equipment to state, local, and tribal law enforcement. The Obama Administration responded by limiting the program and prohibiting the transfer of specific military-grade equipment such as camouflage, 0.50-caliber ammunition, armored vehicles, and grenade launchers. Additionally, Obama's Department of Justice (DOJ) launched 25 'pattern or practice' investigations into police departments—a legal mechanism used to identify persistent patterns or practices of misconduct within a given police department. These investigations uncovered a pattern of unlawful racial bias against Black Americans, as illuminated by systematic civil rights violations, use of excessive force, and 'for-profit policing'—arrests motivated by the reliance of municipalities on the police and courts for local budget revenue generated from fines, fees, citations, and tickets (Taylor 2016). From those investigations, the DOJ entered into consent decrees with 14 departments, mandating them to adopt and implement procedural justice practices and training. At the state level, thirty-four states and the District of Columbia adopted seventy-nine laws by 2016 addressing racial profiling, use of force, de-escalation training, and body-worn cameras. While some observers claimed that state and federal policy responses to BLM were narrowly reformist in nature, one of the most valuable contributions of the early movement, as Taylor (2016) writes, was 'its ability to articulate the dehumanizing aspects of anti-Black racism in the United States' (p. 182).

The issue of excessive police force was at the top of the national agenda when Donald Trump formally announced his run for president in June 2015. Yet Trump, who positioned himself as the 'law and order' candidate, promised to prioritize police safety and morale. The election of President Trump brought a complete shift in police oversight priorities, and one day after the Senate confirmed Jeff Sessions as Attorney General in February 2017, Trump used his executive authority to direct the DOJ to explore new legislation that would make attacks on police officers a federal crime. The move mimicked several state initiatives, including Louisiana's, which became the first state to pass a 'Blue Lives Matter' law extending hate crime protections to law enforcement. Critics argued that 'Blue Lives Matter' legislation was a manifest backlash to BLM advocacy, and that hate crime laws—traditionally reserved for characteristics like race, gender, religion, national origin, disability, and sexual orientation—should not be extended to occupations. President Trump also used an executive order, 'Restoring State, Tribal, and Local Law Enforcement's Access to Life-Saving Equipment and Resources,' to reverse Obama's ban on the transfer of military equipment to police departments.

Under Trump's first Attorney General Jeff Sessions, the focus of an Obama-era community policing body, known as the Collaborative Reform Initiative, was redirected away from identifying best practices toward offering support with gang violence and protests. Another Obama-era program, the National Initiative for Building Community Trust and Justice, which sought to address implicit police bias, was abandoned altogether. During the Trump presidency, only one narrow DOJ 'pattern or practice' investigation was launched, and not a single consent decree was entered into with a police department. Indeed Sessions, a vocal opponent of such decrees, called them 'dangerous,' believing that they undermined respect for the police. Shortly before Trump fired him in 2018, Sessions signed a memorandum limiting the DOJ's ability to use these court-enforceable agreements to monitor and adjust the actions of local law enforcement agencies. Jeff Sessions' replacement, Attorney General William Barr, continued the tradition of diverging from the reformist law enforcement agenda of the Obama Administration. Notably, this included Barr's 2019 intervention to reject the recommendation from the DOJ's Civil Rights Division to file charges against the New York City police officer who choked Eric Garner to death, and his 2020 refusal to open a federal 'pattern or practice' investigation into the Minneapolis Police Department in the aftermath of Floyd's murder. For observers, the push for police reform was made more difficult under a Trump federal government that not only retreated from a leadership role, but actively pursued an adversarial stance to addressing systemic racism and bias in law enforcement.

THE REEMERGENCE OF BLACK LIVES MATTER PROTESTS

In May 2020, Floyd died from a cardiopulmonary arrest caused through 'neck compression' and 'restraint' while in the custody of Minneapolis Police Department officers. The extraordinary occurrence of witnessing Floyd's murder-by-asphyxiation marked the beginning of a series of BLM protests across the United States. As many as 26 million Americans participated in the largest racial justice movement in US history. As political scientist Deva Woodly notes, this was considerably higher than participation in the US civil rights protests of the 1960s, which involved 'hundreds of thousands of people, but not millions' (Buchanan et al. 2020). The momentum of street demonstrations and other direct actions were partially sustained for the entire summer of 2020 in response to Floyd's 'modern-day lynching' and other contemporaneous police killings of Black people. They included Elijah McClain, who died after being put in a chokehold by Aurora, Colorado, police and injected with ketamine by a paramedic on August 24, 2019; Manuel Ellis, who died of hypoxia due to physical restraint by Tacoma, Washington, police on March 3, 2020; Breonna Taylor, fatally shot by plainclothes Louisville, Kentucky, police during a nighttime raid at her home on March 13, 2020; Tony McDade, a transgender man, fatally shot by Tallahassee, Florida, police on May 27, 2020; Rayshard Brooks, fatally shot by Atlanta, Georgia, police on June 12, 2020;

Dijon Kizzee, fatally shot by Los Angeles County, California, police on August 21, 2020; and Jonathan Dwayne Price, tasered and fatally shot by Wolfe City, Texas, police on October 3, 2020.

The nationwide rallying cry of 'Black Lives Matter' resulted in over 8500 demonstrations by the close of 2020 and produced historic changes in perceptions of racial justice and the BLM movement (*Economist* Staff 2020). A Monmouth University study that tracked five years of American public opinion on the severity of racial justice issues revealed that while 51 percent considered racism and discrimination a 'big problem' in 2015, it surged to 76 percent in the wake of Floyd's death and the 2020 BLM protests (Russonello 2020). According to a Pew study, 67 percent of Americans said they supported the BLM movement. While the strength of that support was highest among Black Americans (86 percent), majorities of white (60 percent), Hispanic (77 percent), and Asian (75 percent) Americans expressed at least some support (Pew Research Center 2020).

Opinion polls taken amid the 2020 protests also revealed the public's appetite for police reform. A Kaiser Family Foundation survey found that majorities of the public supported two key reforms aimed at reducing the use of excessive force by police—prohibiting the use of chokeholds (a maneuver used by police to kill Floyd and Garner) and banning 'no-knock' warrants (Breonna Taylor was killed by police officers who entered her home under this authorization). The same poll found broad and bipartisan support for other police reform proposals, including requiring verbal warnings before discharging a weapon, mandating officers to intervene and prevent the use of excessive force by fellow officers, providing public access to police disciplinary records, and allowing individuals subjected to excessive force to sue police officers (Kaiser Family Foundation 2020). In the years following the police killing of Brown, BLM advocates have achieved significant but incremental changes to policing, including training on discriminatory profiling, and according to the Bureau of Justice Statistics, the adoption of body cameras by 60 percent of local police departments. However, scholars observe that while many police departments have adopted new training and policies, the rate of fatal shootings and attendant racial disparities have remained steady (Fagan and Campbell 2020).

FEDERAL AND STATE RESPONSES: REFORM

Sustained BLM protests in all 50 states and the District of Columbia provoked swift responses at the federal level. By mid-June 2020, the Democrats and Republicans both introduced police reform bills to Congress. The Democrats' bill, the George Floyd Justice in Policing Act of 2020 (JPA), co-sponsored by Congressional Black Caucus Chairwoman Karen Bass, passed in the House by a 236-181 vote—gaining support from three Republicans. However, Republican then-Senate Majority Leader Mitch McConnell refused to bring the bill to the Senate floor for debate. The Republicans' police reform bill, 'Just and

Unifying Solutions to Invigorate Communities Everywhere [JUSTICE] Act,'
introduced by Senator Tim Scott, the sole African American Republican in
the Senate, was rejected by the Democrats in a 55-45 vote—where 60 votes
were required to overcome the filibuster and advance. The Democrats' opposition to the bill was welcomed by civil liberties groups, who argued that the
'JUSTICE Act' failed to establish legal changes that would directly address
systemic police misconduct and misuse of force. Indeed, unlike the Democrats'
JPA, the Republican bill included no proposals to end qualified immunity
for law enforcement (a legal interpretation that provides police officers with
broad immunity from being sued in civil court if they violate the constitutional
rights of an individual); fund independent counsels to prosecute police misconduct; strengthen 'pattern and practice' investigations; or ban racial profiling,
chokeholds as a use of deadly force, and no-knock warrants for narcotics
operations.

Concurrent to congressional action to address policing practices and law
enforcement accountability, President Trump signed an executive order on
'Safe Policing for Safe Communities' on June 16, which included the establishment of a public national police misconduct registry and incentives for law
enforcement collaborations that would require experts in mental health, addiction, and homelessness to respond with police to nonviolent calls. The order
did not, however, ban chokeholds as a use of deadly force, or seek to end
qualified immunity. Nevertheless, Trump's use of executive action was interpreted by some pundits as a long-awaited acknowledgment that police reform
was indeed a national imperative. However, just two weeks after issuing the
order, Trump denounced Black Lives Matter as a 'symbol of hate,' and allies
repeatedly echoed his opposition to the protests through attempts to discredit
the overwhelmingly peaceful movement by focusing on isolated incidents of
violence.

For some political analysts, Trump's demagoguery in response to the 2020
protests and his promise to veto the JPA bill, assisted him in securing 2020
reelection endorsements from several prominent police unions. In 2020, the
'tough on crime' messaging that had underpinned Trump's 2016 campaign
was recalibrated to encompass BLM, and viscerally demonstrated in his
support for the use of chemical irritants and kinetic impact projectiles against
protesters, and his threat to invoke the Insurrection Act of 1807—a federal
law that empowers the president to send military forces to states to quell civil
unrest. Human rights and civil liberties groups were highly critical of Trump's
provocations, as well as Attorney General William Barr's deployment of some
3000 heavily armed riot police in military-style uniforms without insignias to
guard specific buildings and areas in Washington, DC. (This level of organization or show of force would be absent just months later when the United
States Capitol was breached and vandalized by white rioters on January 6,
2021.) Further, Trump's decision to send armed federal officers and several
paramilitary-style units to street demonstrations in Portland, Oregon, drew

the ire of critics who challenged the legal authority of federal agents in camouflage military fatigues with generic 'POLICE' patches and unmarked vehicles to police demonstrations and arbitrarily detain people (Amnesty International 2020). The Trump Administration's offensive against the 2020 BLM movement would extend to executive orders that established a 'patriotic education' commission to prohibit a 'divisive' founding story that centered on slavery, and a ban on 'anti-American' racial bias training for federal agencies, the military, government contractors and recipients of federal grants, including universities and nonprofits. These decisions may go some way to explaining why a 2020 Pew survey found that six-in-ten Americans thought the president was delivering 'the wrong message' in response to the BLM protests and that half-believed Trump had generally made race relations worse in America (Pew Research Center 2020).

The highly decentralized nature of policing in the United States (with some eighteen thousand state and local independent police departments) presented BLM activists with exceptional opportunities to drive reviews of existing laws and demand new police reforms at local and state levels. With legislative interest in policing and police accountability at an unprecedented high, states that were either finished or close to ending the regular legislative calendar at the time of Floyd's death held special sessions or moved quickly to pass police reform bills prior to the summer recess. While police groups supported some measures and opposed others, one month into the Floyd protests, 18 states, Washington, DC, and Puerto Rico had introduced 166 bills and/or executive orders covering issues of police oversight, data collection, training, policing alternatives, and use of force. From the day of Floyd's murder on May 25, through to the end of 2020, a total of 36 states and Washington, DC had introduced more than 700 bills addressing police accountability, of which nearly 100 were enacted (National Conference of State Legislators 2021a). However, moves to eliminate qualified immunity were largely excluded from the legislation. A notable exception was Colorado, which passed one of the most comprehensive 2020 police accountability bills and became the first state to legislate against qualified immunity by placing statutory limits on its use as a defense in law enforcement cases at the state level. Connecticut also passed legislation to eliminate governmental immunity as a defense, albeit without explicitly addressing qualified immunity (National Conference of State Legislators 2021b).

Local Responses: Reimagination

Many criminal justice experts noted the unusual 'lightning pace to pass significant policing reform proposals that in some cases [had] languished for years' (Suderman 2020). Movement activists seized the extraordinary moment to push beyond conventional reform proposals and moved a spectrum of calls to 'defund,' 'dismantle,' and 'abolish' the police from the margins to the center of a national conversation on the future of American policing. While these demands differ significantly, they share roots in the prison abolitionist movement, which seeks to replace the 'prison-industrial complex' with alternative community-based interventions that engage the approaches of 'transformative justice' and 'restorative justice' (Davis 2003; Gilmore 2007). Many community groups advocating defunding were not proposing the complete dismantlement of police departments or abolition of police forces. Rather, proponents urged US cities and states to cut law enforcement budgets amid a dramatic rise in spending on policing, and divert those funds to vital social services and programs. The call from activists to defund the police did not signal the abandonment of reform as one essential strategy. But the conversation about divestment from policing and the simultaneous reinvestment in social welfare did raise crucial questions about the possibility of alternative solutions to 'protecting and serving' communities that would not require the presence of armed first responders—an observation supported by studies revealing that the majority of calls to the police are less crime-related and more a response to social service needs (Jacobs et al. 2021).

Over the 2020 election season, President Trump, and presidential candidate Joe Biden, both vehemently rejected calls to defund the police. However, some city councils appeared receptive, with Portland, Boston, Los Angeles, San Francisco, and New York City all making public commitments to explore reducing police department budgets in response to activists' demands. Yet for community organizers, none of the proposed or approved cuts, including the 2021 budget cut of $420 million to the New York Police Department (NYPD), have reached a level to 'effect a cultural shift' that would fundamentally change policing (Okeowo 2020). Indeed, according to an assessment from New York's Independent Budget Office (IBO), the budget cut to the NYPD will in large part be achieved by capping overtime spending, not redirecting police funding to social services, and critical aspects of the public sector (Pozarycki 2020).

In June 2020, BLM protests led to a significant commitment to defund the Minneapolis Police Department—the city where Floyd was murdered. With a majority, the Minneapolis City Council announced its intention to dismantle the city's police department through its budgetary and policy powers. In the face of President Trump labeling the decision 'crazy,' together with opposition from Minneapolis Mayor Jacob Frey, law enforcement officials and the police union, Minneapolis Council President Lisa Bender explained:

> Our efforts at incremental reform have failed, period. Our commitment is to do what's necessary to keep every single member of our community safe and to tell the truth: that the Minneapolis police are not doing that. Our commitment is to end policing as we know it and to recreate systems of public safety that actually keep us safe. (Levin 2020)

However, in November 2020, the Minneapolis Charter Commission—an unelected board of volunteers that trends older, whiter and wealthier than the city as a whole—voted unanimously to reject the city council's charter amendment to replace the traditional police department with a new public safety model. Critics of the amendment argued that it left questions about the future of public safety unanswered, with Charter Commissioner Gregory Abbott cautioning that changes in law enforcement should not be motivated by 'policy disputes of the moment.' Yet, community leaders cited a long history of excessive force complaints and the high-profile Minneapolis police killings of Jamar Clark, Philando Castile, and Thurman Blevins in 2015, 2016, and 2018, respectively. Since 2015, Minneapolis police have used force against Black people at a rate at least seven times that of white people. And, while Minneapolis residents have mixed views on decreasing the size of the police force, a 2020 poll conducted by local media outlets reported that 73 percent of Minneapolitans thought that the city should redirect some police funding to social services like violence prevention, drug treatment, and mental health programs; a position that broadly supports the city council's intention to create alternatives to armed police (Hazzar 2020). The decision to 'defund' the Minneapolis Police Department will likely be decided when residents are afforded the opportunity to vote for the city council's amendment in a 2021 ballot initiative.

Looking Forward: The Biden Presidency and Black Lives

The scale and global influence of the 2020 Black Lives Matter protests have renewed a reassessment of the role and investment in US law enforcement and its function in upholding white supremacy. An inescapable reality is that police in the United States kill people at a rate that far outpaces other comparable wealthy democratic countries (Taylor 2016). And over the course of the 2020 election year, BLM argued that recalibrating the scale, scope, and social function of the police was an essential step toward redressing police violence (Akbar 2020). In a speech responding to the police killing of Floyd, presidential candidate Joe Biden remarked: 'The very soul of America is at stake. We must commit as a nation to pursue justice with every ounce of our being.' Months later in his January 20, 2021 inauguration speech, President Biden pledged to defeat 'white supremacy,' and as part of his day one actions issued an executive order on 'Advancing Racial Equity and Support for Underserved Communities.' In part, the order revoked Trump's ban on federal government engagement in antiracist training programs and disbanded his so-called 'patriotic education' commission—a project Biden denounced as 'offensive' and 'counter-factual.' The order also reinstated Diversity and Inclusion training in the federal government, established an Equitable Data Working Group, and directed federal agencies to review and report on federal equity and diversity efforts within 200 days.

In a move to fulfill a key campaign promise made during the height of the 2020 BLM protests, President Biden used his executive authority on January

26, 2021, to address racial discrimination in federal housing policies; end the DOJ's use of private prisons; commit to tribal sovereignty and consultation; and combat xenophobia against Asian American and Pacific Islanders. In remarks by Biden at the signing of these four executive actions on racial equity, he stated:

> What many Americans didn't see, or had simply refused to see, couldn't be ignored any longer. Those 8 minutes and 46 seconds that took George Floyd's life opened the eyes of millions of Americans and millions of people around — all over the world. It was the knee on the neck of justice, and it wouldn't be forgotten. It stirred the conscience of tens of millions of Americans, and, in my view, it marked a turning point in this country's attitude toward racial justice.

Whether the United States has reached a 'turning point' is yet to be seen. Nevertheless, while executive orders and other similar presidential documents are not legislation (they do have the force of law as formal federal regulations but require no approval from Congress), and a future sitting president can overturn an existing executive directive, their value should not be dismissed. As the first foray of an incoming administration, executive actions can quickly eliminate the policies of a previous administration that do not align with a new agenda and reestablish a baseline upon which policy initiatives and legislation can be pursued. For the Biden Administration, its racial justice baseline includes a commitment to 'embedding equity across federal policymaking and rooting out systemic racism and other barriers to opportunity from federal programs and institutions.'

Despite this progressive reference point for the new administration, social justice groups are concerned that amid calls to defund the police, Biden unveiled a 2020 presidential campaign proposal to allocate $300 million in federal grants 'to reinvigorate community policing.' On the face of it, community policing—envisioned by policymakers as having more police on foot patrol building trust and partnerships with people in the neighborhood—may appear benign and responsive to community concerns. But on deeper examination, Biden's promise appeared to ignore critiques that community policing does not empower communities in meaningful ways or curtail police violence. Moreover, critical race scholars and racial justice advocates argue that community policing expands police power, does not conclusively reduce racial disparities in arrests, and exacerbates the burden of over-policing in Black and brown communities (Akbar 2020; Taylor 2016; Vitale 2017). Indeed, these experts have argued that cutting the size of police departments by curbing funding would be far more effective at reducing police violence than any costly effort to improve the police. However, for now, the Biden Administration remains fixated on investing in the police to repair and relegitimize their social function, rather than exploring a practical agenda toward reimagining public safety.

President Biden has announced that his early agenda will include reinstating Obama-era limits on the transfer of military equipment to local and state law enforcement via the DOD's 1033 program. As a starting point to more transformative change, activists acknowledge that the Biden Administration should reinstitute particular policies seeded in the Obama Administration, but have called on Biden to place a full moratorium on the 1033 program and signal his support for Congress to end the police militarization program altogether (Amnesty International 2021). Although proponents of the program, including President Trump, have cited research to support claims that militarized policing reduces crime, two 2021 peer-reviewed studies have audited newly released data to reveal that the transfer of surplus military equipment through the 1033 program has not served to reduce crime or increase officer safety (Gunderson et al. 2021; Lowande 2021). In addition, activists have demanded that the Biden Administration suspend all federal grant funding for Operation Relentless Pursuit and Operation Legend—two Trump-era DOJ programs that 'surge' federal law enforcement resources and officers into selected US cities. Federal spending, as civil rights advocates argue, 'should nurture the seeds of new community-based public safety systems,' not bolster police militarization and expansion, which are means by which the state enhances its control over Black and other people of color (Stagoff-Belfort 2021).

The passing of the reintroduced George Floyd Justice in Policing Act in the Democratic-controlled House of Representatives on March 3, 2021, was widely hailed as a victory for progressive social policy. President Biden expressed his support for the legislation, declaring that he looked 'forward to working with the Congress to enact a landmark policing reform law.' Yet, months after the height of the 2020 BLM protests, the bipartisan momentum to pass police reforms has dissipated, and Republican opposition in the House and Senate has become increasingly hostile. This will make securing the three-fifths support the JPA bill needs to overcome the Senate filibuster exceedingly difficult.

One of the provisions in the JPA bill, long sought by civil rights advocates, lowers the intent standard in cases of police use of lethal force. Presently, it is especially arduous to hold police officers accountable for lethal excessive force as a jury must agree that the acts in question were done 'willfully.' In a bid to remove a legal standard that often works to shield police officers from liability, the bill seeks to lower the intent standard to 'knowingly or with reckless disregard.' During the Senate confirmation process for President Biden's Attorney General Merrick B. Garland, advocates cautiously welcomed his willingness to discuss the possibility of lowering the willfulness standard with the DOJ's Civil Rights Division. A DOJ investigation into Derek Chauvin, the white police officer who was convicted of second-degree murder, third-degree murder, and second-degree manslaughter in Floyd's death, will also be an early racial justice test for the Biden Administration.

As ubiquitous representatives of the state, police have an immense effect on how citizens perceive and experience government (Vitale 2017). Biden has been resolute in stating his commitment to 'hold police officers accountable for abuses of power and tackle systemic misconduct – and systemic racism – in police departments' (Sonmez and Itkowitz 2021). But he faces fierce opposition from federal and state level Republican legislators who are mounting a racialized backlash against police reform. Indicative of this partisan conflict is the passage of a bill by the Republican-majority state Senate in Kentucky (the state where Breonna Taylor was killed and the site of high-profile BLM protests) that would criminalize insulting a police officer. Specifically, the bill not only enhances penalties for crimes related to civil unrest and prohibits early release on such offenses, but it makes it a misdemeanor to taunt or challenge an officer with words or gestures 'that would have a direct tendency to provoke a violent response from the perspective of a reasonable and prudent person.' A conviction would be punishable by up to 90 days in jail and fines of up to $250. Critics, including the American Civil Liberties Union of Kentucky, have condemned the move as an obvious attempt to criminalized protesters and 'stifle' free speech and dissent (Iati 2021).

In May 2020, the world came to know of George Floyd, and the United States was forced to confront the dehumanizing impacts of a law enforcement system etched in racism. Although the executive orders and official presidential statements issued by Biden have signaled an intent to change American policing, executive actions and reprising Obama-era policies will not achieve the Biden Administration's transformative goals for law enforcement. Fortunately, public support for police reform remains strong, which will aid the push to seek a range of reforms and defunding initiatives that refocus the need for true reinvestment in US social welfare.

REFERENCES

Akbar, A. 2020. An Abolitionist Horizon for (Police) Reform. *California Law Review* 108: 1781–1846.

Amnesty International. 2020. USA: The World Is Watching Mass Violations by U.S. Police of Black Lives Matter Protesters' Rights.

———. 2021. Domestic Human Rights Policies Biden-Harris Administration Must Address in Early 2021, February 18. Available at: https://www.amnestyusa.org/wp-content/uploads/2021/02/Amnesty-International-Judiciary-proirities-Biden-Admin-.pdf.

Brown, R. 2019. Policing in American History. *Du Bois Review: Social Science Research on Race* 16: 189–195.

Buchanan, L., Q. Bui, and J. Patel. 2020. Black Lives Matter May Be the Largest Movement in U.S. History. *The New York Times*, July 3.

Bureau of Justice. 2015. Contacts Between Police and the Public. Available at: www.bjs.gov/content/pub/pdf/cpp15.pdf.

Campbell, B., E. Byers, and G. Alpert. 2017. A Bird's Eye View of Civilians Killed by Police in 2015. *Criminology & Public Policy* 16: 309–340.

Davis, A.Y. 2003. *Are Prisons Obsolete?* New York: Seven Stories Press.

Economist Staff. 2020. Six Months After Mass Protests Began, What Is the Future of BLM? *The Economist*, December 10.

Fagan, J., and A. Campbell. 2020. Race and Reasonableness in Police Killings. *Boston University Law Review* 100: 951–1015.

Gilmore, R.W. 2007. *Golden Gulag: Prisons, Surplus, Crisis, and Opposition in Globalizing.* Berkeley, CA: University of California Press.

Gunderson, A., E. Cohen, K.J. Schiff, T.S. Clark, A.N. Glynn, and M.L. Owens. 2021. Counterevidence of Crime-Reduction Effects from Federal Grants of Military Equipment to Local Police. *Nature Human Behaviour* 5: 194–204.

Hazzar, A. 2020. Minneapolis Charter Commission's Slow-Rolling of Public Safety Amendment Follows Pattern. *Southwest Journal*, August 19.

Iati, M. 2021. Kentucky Senate Votes to Criminalize Insulting Police in Way That Could Cause "Violent Response". *The Washington Post*, March 12.

Jacobs, L.A., M.E. Kim, D.L. Whitfield, R.E. Gartner, M. Panichelli, S.K. Kattari, M.M. Downey, S.S. McQueen, and S.E. Mountz. 2021. Defund the Police: Moving Towards an Anti-Carceral Social Work. *Journal of Progressive Human Services* 32: 37–62.

Kaiser Family Foundation. 2020. KFF Health Tracking Poll—June 2020, June 26. Available at: https://www.kff.org/racial-equity-and-health-policy/report/kff-health-tracking-poll-june-2020/.

Kochel, T., D. Wilson, and S. Mastrofski. 2011. Effect of Suspect Race on Officers' Arrest Decisions. *Criminology* 49: 473–512.

Levin, S. 2020. Minneapolis Lawmakers Vow to Disband Police Department in Historic Move. *The Guardian*, June 8.

Lowande, K. 2021. Police Demilitarization and Violent Crime. *Nature Human Behaviour* 5: 1–7.

Mesic, A., L. Franklin, A. Cansever, F. Potter, A. Sharma, A. Knopov, and M. Siegel. 2018. The Relationship Between Structural Racism and Black-White Disparities in Fatal Police Shootings at the State Level. *Journal of the National Medical Association* 110: 106–116.

National Conference of State Legislators. 2021a. Law Enforcement Statutory Database, January 26. Available at: https://www.ncsl.org/research/civil-and-criminal-justice/law-enforcement-statutory-database.aspx.

———. 2021b. Qualified Immunity, January 12. Available at: https://www.ncsl.org/research/civil-and-criminal-justice/qualified-immunity.aspx.

Okeowo, A. 2020. How to Defund the Police. *The New Yorker*, June 26.

Pew Research Center. 2019. Race in America 2019.

———. 2020. Amid Protests, Majorities Across Racial and Ethnic Groups Express Support for the Black Lives Matter Movement.

Pozarycki, R. 2020. Not Even Close: NYC Shifting Far Less Than a Billion from NYPD in Budget, Report Finds. *AMNY*, August 18.

Russonello, G. 2020. Why Most Americans Support the Protests. *The New York Times*, June 5.

Sonmez, F, and C. Itkowitz. 2021. 'House Passes Expansive Policing Overhaul Bill Named in Honor of George Floyd.' *The Washington Post*, March 3.

Stagoff-Belfort, A. 2021. Biden Plans to "Reinvigorate" a Community Policing Office That Has a Dark History. *Slate*, February 24.

Suderman, A. 2020. States Race to Pass Policing Reforms After Floyd's Death. *The Washington Post*, August 8.

Taylor, K. 2016. *From #BLACKLIVESMATTER to Black Liberation*. Chicago, IL: Haymarket Books.

———. 2020. We Should Still Defund the Police. *The New Yorker*, August 14.

Vitale, A.S. 2017. *The End of Policing*. Brooklyn: Verso.

FURTHER READING

The breadth and impact of Black Lives Matter has been extraordinary. Between 2012 and 2020, millions of people in the United States have marched, rallied, held vigils, and engaged in direct actions to protest and draw attention to state and vigilante violence against Black people. For key accounts that outline the scope and genealogy of the Black Lives Matter movement, see Keeanga-Yamahtta Taylor (2016) *From #BLACKLIVESMATTER to Black Liberation* (Chicago, IL: Haymarket Books), Christopher J. Lebron (2017) *The Making of Black Lives Matter: A Brief History of an Idea* (New York, NY: Oxford University Press), and Barbara Ransby (2018) *Making All Black Lives Matter: Reimagining Freedom in the Twenty-First Century* (Oakland, California: University of California Press). Smartphone recordings of fatal police encounters have provided much of the brutal raw material that has powered the Black Lives Matter movement. For more on the intersection of smartphones, social media, and social justice, see Allissa V. Richardson (2020) *Bearing Witness While Black: African Americans, Smartphones, and the New Protest #Journalism* (New York, NY: Oxford University Press, 2020). The Black Lives Matter website (blacklivesmatter.com) is an excellent resource for up-to-date information on BLM campaigns and demands.

In the United States, modern policing partially grew out of southern slave patrols. For more on the racialized origins and evolution of American policing, see Sally E. Hadden (2001) *Slave Patrols: Law and Violence in Virginia and the Carolinas* (Cambridge, Massachusetts: Harvard University Press). For historical and theoretical perspectives on anti-Black and racially biased policing, see Michelle Alexander (2010) *The New Jim Crow: Mass Incarceration in the Age of Colorblindness* (New York: The New Press), Khalil G. Muhammad (2010) *The Condemnation of Blackness: Race, Crime, and the Making of Modern Urban America* (Cambridge, Massachusetts: Harvard University Press), and Stephen K. Rice and Michael D. White (eds.) (2010) *Race, Ethnicity, and Policing: New and Essential Readings* (New York: New York University Press). On state-sanctioned police violence, see Noel A. Cazenave (2018) *Killing African Americans: Police and Vigilante Violence as a Racial Control Mechanism* (New York, NY: Routledge). On police abolition and creating new public safety alternatives, see Alex S. Vitale (2017) *The End of Policing* (Brooklyn: Verso).

CHAPTER 4

Gender Politics in the Trump Era

Virginia Sapiro

August 26, 2020 was the centennial of the ratification of the 19th Amendment to the US Constitution which reads, 'The right of citizens of the United States to vote shall not be denied or abridged by the United States or by any State on account of sex.' Clearly, much changed in that century, but the 2020 celebrations were almost universally marked by the recognition that the change toward equality and inclusion was disappointing and tenuous. President Donald Trump managed to invigorate the women's movement by embodying a perceived threat to progress through his words and actions. From the point of view of feminist activists, the United States had faced a fork in the road in 2016 with a choice between Trump and electing the first woman President and went the wrong way. As the 2020 election approached, they feared the United States would go further down the wrong road.

Through most of the period since the ratification of the 19th Amendment, most people have seemed very certain about what sex and, later, gender meant. For most people, *sex* and *gender* are probably synonyms. However, for scholars and scientists since the 1970s, and eventually a portion of the public, *sex* refers to a biological phenomenon while *gender* refers to the cultural, social, and symbolic meanings human communities attribute to sex (Rubin 1975).

V. Sapiro (✉)
Department of Political Science, Boston University, Boston, MA, USA
e-mail: vsapiro@bu.edu

Department of Political Science, University of Wisconsin-Madison, Madison, WI, USA

© The Author(s), under exclusive license to Springer Nature Switzerland AG 2022
G. Peele et al. (eds.), *Developments in American Politics 9*,
https://doi.org/10.1007/978-3-030-89740-6_4

As the Trump era dawned, the consensus among scholars and scientists who studied sex and gender questioned even that convention. Research in biology shattered the older, more simple understandings of the biological basis of our gendered lives (Roughgarden 2013). Likewise, concepts of and attitudes toward sexuality were changing in some dramatic ways.

Sex, gender, and sexuality are fundamental to our understandings of self and society, so it is not surprising that they became implicated in the increasingly polarized politics of the era and important subjects of political debate. This chapter begins with an exploration of how conventional notions of gender have been destabilized, looking in succession at sexuality, gender identity (especially transgender issues), and intersectionality. It then considers gender, power, and engagement, emphasizing social movements aimed at redressing power inequalities, followed by an examination of women in political leadership. It concludes with a discussion of political polarization, women, and politics.

Gender Isn't What It Used to be: Sexuality

As Nathaniel Hawthorne's classic novel, *The Scarlet Letter*, tells us, American society from the beginning has taken issues of sexuality, especially deviation from conventional sexuality, very seriously. Of course, sexual behavior—and sometimes sexual thoughts—have been core to religion and morality and important subjects of law and policy for as long as we have historical memory. American society is not unusual in having held a dominant norm of 'compulsory heterosexuality' (Rich 1980), the belief that heterosexuality is the only acceptable form of sexuality, a mark of 'real' men and women, and actions that do not conform to that should be suppressed (Canaday 2009).

There have long been social movements and organizations aimed at ending laws and policies that discriminate against homosexuality—certainly since before the 1969 'Stonewall Riots,' which are often identified as the launch of the gay rights movement (Frank 2014). A conservative backlash against that movement shaped new discriminatory laws and policies. In 1973 Maryland became the first of many governmental units explicitly to *ban* same-sex marriage. The 1996 federal Defense of Marriage Act (DOMA), passed by a Republican Congress but signed into law by Democratic President Bill Clinton, 'defended' marriage by defining marriage as a union between one man and one woman.

An increasingly large and professional gay rights movement was nevertheless remarkably effective in a relatively brief time (Frank 2018). The first two decades of the twenty-first century witnessed a remarkable change in public attitudes toward homosexual rights, especially after 2010. The generational change clearly fueled the shift, but growing tolerance emerged across generations (Pew Research Center 2013). Most social groups showed an increasing liberalization of attitudes toward sexuality during this period, although some groups moved faster than others. There was, however, a great divide across parties and religious groups which remains, with Republicans, white evangelical Protestants, and Black Protestants taking the conservative side, and Democrats and more liberal denominations taking the liberal side (Baldassarri and Park 2020).

Although the term *culture wars* emerged in the early 1990s, the phenomenon of liberal and conservative leaders and their followers engaging in a struggle over the meaning of what constituted 'American values' with respect to private life, social identity, and cultural institutions such as education, the arts, and religion, goes back longer (Hunter 1991; Hartman 2016). The two sides even differed over language, with liberals advocating what they defined as inclusive and respectful communication, which conservatives lambasted as 'political correctness.' Years later, by the end of the Trump era, conservatives had taken to attacking 'cancel culture,' which they defined as the denigration or silencing of conservative views. The growing political and partisan polarization was fueled by and in turn shaped conflicts over identity, culture, and a sense of what is appropriately American (Klein 2020).

Political leadership mattered in this polarization process. Political science research has long shown that partisan and social group leadership is crucial in guiding the views of mass partisans (Zaller 1992). This appears true even with respect to apparently fundamental and personal values as those related to sexuality and gender. As Patrick J. Egan (2020) has shown, partisan polarization around identity and values leads to at least some re-sorting of identities at the mass level. That is, rather than viewing identities and values as necessarily deeper than and preceding partisanship, the sharp conflicts over these issues at the leadership level appear to move some partisans at the mass level to shift their identities and ideology. This effect became apparent as evangelical Christians, strong supporters of the Republican Party, seemed to become more tolerant of immoral sexual attitudes and behavior because of the sexual attitudes and behavior of President Trump.

Two Supreme Court cases represent both the change and backlash that occurred in the United States, one decided during the Obama Administration, one during the Trump Administration. In *Obergefell v Hodges* (2015) the Court decided in a 5–4 decision that, because the Due Process Clause of the 14th Amendment guarantees the right to marry as a protected fundamental right, the Equal Protection Clause means that same-sex couples must be protected in the same way as different-sex couples. In contrast, *Masterpiece Cakeshop, Ltd v. Colorado Civil Rights Commission* (2017) concluded in a 7–2 decision that, although individuals have a right to marry a person of their own sex, the cake shop owner in question had a right to refuse to bake a wedding cake for a same-sex wedding because same-sex marriage offended his religious beliefs. The Court's majority believed the Colorado Civil Rights Commission displayed hostility to religion in its determination that the cake must be baked as a matter of equal marriage rights. The wedding cake issue was a cause célèbre dividing liberals and conservatives.

The composition of generations of elected government officials reveals shifts in cultural norms toward sexuality among the American public. Aspiring politicians used to have to conform to the heterosexual norm to be successful, but that informal requirement weakened considerably, at least among Democrats. The 'firsts' are relatively recent, and include Tammy Baldwin (D-WI), who became the first openly gay person elected to Congress as a non-incumbent in 1998, and achieved a similar landmark when she won her Senate seat in 2012. Jared Polis (D-CO) became the first openly gay person elected to become governor of a US state in 2018. The barriers to office holding posed by alternative sexualities were further lowered among Democratic politics during the Trump era. At the beginning of the 116th Congress (2019–2021) about ten Democratic members were openly gay, and, unlike the case for most gay members in earlier days, they were not 'outed' by other people, but announced themselves. In 2020 one of the major contenders for the Democratic presidential nomination, Pete Buttigieg, was married to a man. He later became the first openly gay Cabinet member in 2021 when he was confirmed as Secretary of Transportation. The Republican closet doors still appear to be closed, however.

Changes in the relationship of *sexuality* to politics and policy are important in and of themselves, but they are also part of the destabilization of traditionally stable binary understandings of *gender*. Sexuality is an important element of how people perceive and define gender because the 'performance' of gender—how we present ourselves and act in order to signal our gender 'appropriately'—has conventionally depended on and been interpreted as the degree to which we act in ways that accord with dominant heterosexual norms and expectations (Chang and Wildman 2017). 'Real' men and women act in conventional heterosexual ways. Thus shifts in understanding of sexuality are linked to shifts in understanding of *gender*.

Gender Isn't What It Used to be: Gender Fluidity and Change

The gender politics boat has been further rocked by the growing salience of transgender issues in public policy. Not long ago discussion of transgender people was rare—no doubt most of the public was largely unaware of them other than perhaps a couple of well-recognized public figures such as Caitlyn Jenner and the tennis star and ophthalmologist Renee Richards. The Obama Administration incorporated transgender rights into mainstream American politics by expanding its conception of equality politics. Congress stayed away from the issue, however, so transgender policy has largely been a subject of executive and judicial politics (Mezey 2019).

President Trump spent four years systematically undoing the policies and impact of Obama wherever possible across a diverse range of policy areas. At least until around 2000, Trump was modestly supportive of gay rights, including civil unions (Samuels and Johnson 2017), and he also evinced some support for abortion rights (Bump 2019). From his presidential candidacy through his presidency Donald Trump changed his stance on these issues and became a hard-liner in pursuit of a right-wing base. His administration's attacks on the rights of transgender students and members of the military and questions over who may use which bathroom inserted these issues ever more volubly into increasingly polarized political debates.

Consider these partisan differences: In late 2017, 80 percent of Republicans thought that gender is determined by sex at birth, compared with 34 percent of Democrats. And, while 60 percent of Democrats thought that society had not gone far enough in 'accepting people who are transgender,' only 12 percent of Republicans did (Brown 2017).

Just as Trump sought to overturn Obama's policies, so President Biden's first executive actions were reversals of some of President Trump's actions which had reinforced discrimination against transgender people. Republicans were simultaneously working on legislation to restrict the ability of transgender people to have access to medical care and to participate in school athletics (Wax-Thibodeaux and Schmidt 2021). Republicans sometimes took the lead in claiming that allowing transgender girls and women to participate in women's sports would set back the cause of women's athletics because women born as female would never again be competitive. This issue has become a global one.

These partisan disagreements about transgender policy signal shifts in policy debates, but they also reflect underlying changes in the relationship between gender and politics. Scholars such as Margot Canaday (2009) and Heath Fogg Davis (2017) underscore how uncritically we tend to accept the assumption that gender categorization is essential for understanding one's relationship to the state, politics, and policy. Yes, gender is a core component of most people's identity; but, as Davis asks, why are we required to name our sex so often? Why do governmental forms almost always ask about our gender? When and why is this information actually relevant? These questions become more pressing when a growing number of people assert that their original sex assignment was wrong or define their gender identity as fluid, or simply identify as male or female. They also unsettle conventional scholarship on gender, politics, policy, and the state, which has traditionally only looked for differences and made comparisons across men and women.

GENDER ISN'T WHAT IT USED TO BE: INTERSECTIONALITY

Concepts of gender have recently become further unsettled as the concept of *intersectionality* has become increasingly influential in our understanding of social categories and identities. Scholars and other people use this concept in different ways—sometimes, unfortunately, more as a buzzword than an analytical tool—but *intersectionality* derives from a remarkably simple observation with implications that challenge conventional analysis of the significance of gender for politics, policy, and the state.

The observation is that there is no common gendered essence of being a woman or a man that is immune to variations by age, class, race, or other critical categories of social location and identity. Being a woman (or man) is not the same for babies, children, young adults, older adults. Cultural expectations and the treatment of women as women or men as men vary across class, race, nationality, and other categories of social location and identity. How do women or men dress or speak or act or interact as gendered persons? That depends. This socially contingent aspect of gender is the core of what scholars mean by intersectionality, and it follows that we cannot truly understand gender without integrating into our analysis these cross-cutting aspects of our social lives.

This recognition of the importance of intersectionality makes studying gender and politics harder than it used to be. Seeking to understand gender in politics without recognizing, for example, the impact of race on its relationship with gender leaves our analysis superficial and misleading. But it is simply not possible to incorporate a full recognition of intersectionalities in any given gender analysis—for example by considering all the ways that gender politics depends on race, age, class, ethnicity, religion, nationality and so forth. Any attempt to do so would leave the concept of gender shattered on the floor in a multitude of cross-cutting considerations.

The gender and race politics of the Trump era brought questions of intersectionality, especially between gender and race, to the fore. For example, after decades of focus on the *gender gap*—the tendency for women to identify and vote more Democratic than men, and for men to identify and vote more Republican than women—the 2016 National Election Pool (NEP) exit poll used by CNN, ABC, the *New York Times* and many other news outlets showed that the majority of white women (52 percent) and white men (62 percent) voted for Donald Trump while only 25 percent of Latina woman and four percent of Black women did so (Kenski 2018). Although later work with verified votes found 47 percent of white women voted for Trump (still more than the 45 percent who voted for Clinton), it is nonetheless clear that without a discussion of race we cannot understand the significance or impact of any gender gap. In fact, a marginal majority of white women have usually voted Republican in presidential elections (Zhang and Fox 2020), and in 2020 Trump increased his majority among white women to 55 percent, according to the NEP's (unvalidated) exit poll.

In both 2016 and 2020, people of color—especially African American women—provided the margin that gave the Democratic presidential candidate the majority of the popular vote, if not the keys to the White House in 2016. But there was a gender gap among African Americans also despite their overwhelming support for Democrats. In 2016, 81 percent of Black men but fully 98 percent of Black women voted for Hillary Clinton.

The size of gender differences both within and across racial groups varies across elections because contextual factors shape gender's effect on voting behavior. In the two January 2021 Senate runoff elections in Georgia, which flipped a normally Republican state Democratic and gave the Democrats control of the Senate, there were only modest gender differences in the vote. The relatively large African American population was largely responsible for the Democratic victory.

Many people attributed this critical partisan shift to the leadership of Stacey Abrams, an African American woman who had narrowly lost the race for Georgia governor two years previously and turned her attention to political organizing efforts that increased voter registration and turnout among African Americans. African American women are gaining prominence as political strategists, and they tend to emphasize the intersection of their race and gender in their analysis of politics. The 2020 elections witnessed another widely observed and apparently effective point of organization among African American women: the coordinated nation-wide activism of members and alumnae of black sororities, social and philanthropic organizations on college campuses, especially in support of their fellow 'soror,' Kamala Harris, the successful Democratic vice-presidential candidate (Ross 2019).

The prominence of black women in the Democratic base brings us back to the question of why, given conventional understandings of the gender gap, did a majority (or plurality) of white women vote for the antifeminist, perhaps misogynistic, candidate and party? Unfortunately, many people—including pundits and journalists—have often misunderstood the gender gap and the gender basis of voting. The gender gap does not mean—and never did mean— that most women vote for Democrats and most men vote for Republicans. It refers to the fact that since the time when many men who would traditionally have been part of the Democratic Party began pulling away from that party in the 1970s, there has been a tendency, albeit a variable tendency, for men to vote more Republican than women, and women to vote more Democratic than men (Kaufmann and Petrocik 1999; Ondercin 2017). This is true among white voters, it is true among black voters, it is sometimes true among Latinx voters. But it does not mean that a majority of women vote for one party and a majority of men vote for the other.

The vast majority of people vote on the basis of their party identification—a type of identity that tends to be established very early in life and remains relatively stable over the long haul. Although women are more likely to identify as Democrats than are men, and men are more likely than women to identify as Republicans, at least until recently white people tended to identify at least marginally more with Republicans than with Democrats. Since the Roosevelt era, African Americans have tended to identify massively more as Democrats than Republicans. So two things are true: there has been a clear gender gap among both white and Black people, but because people tend to vote their partisanship, in this polarized era white women vote more Republican than Democratic, but not nearly to the degree that white men do. And African American women vote overwhelmingly Democratic, even more than African American men.

The intersectionality of gender analysis was also prominent during the 19th Amendment's centennial celebrations. As crucial as that constitutional amendment was, it did not 'give women the right to vote,' contrary to what is often claimed. First, many states, especially in the Midwest and the West, had already banned gender discrimination in voting by the time of ratification in 1920. But more important for our intersectional analysis, the 19th Amendment gave the right to vote only to women whose rights had previously been denied on the basis of sex and only on the basis of sex. That was a lot of women, including African American women in some parts of the country. But throughout much of the country, especially in the South, African American women, like African American men, were barred from voting on account of race. Removing the sex restriction did nothing for them. This is a good example of why intersectional analysis is necessary.

Gender, Power, and Political Engagement

The first two decades of the twenty-first century have been marked by a series of large-scale protests and social movements revolving around gender questions and involving women prominently in numbers and leadership. The most obvious are the #MeToo Movement and the January 2017 Women's March, which was followed by annual women's marches through to 2020. But other protest events and social movements also placed women center stage and stimulated women's political engagement. Some major examples of these events and movements were the Parkland School Shooting activists, the March for Our Lives, and Black Lives Matter. Even the growing and militant right-wing movements that formed part of President Trump's base included a notable number of women.

The name of the #MeToo Movement was borrowed from the work of Tarana Burke, an African American woman who founded a nonprofit organization, Just Be Inc., in 2003 to support survivors of domestic violence, sexual harassment, and abuse. A broader worldwide social movement was launched and gained momentum beginning in 2017, after two years of multiplying headline news stories of sexual harassment and abuse by prominent and powerful men in many walks of life. Most, but not all of the victims of these famous abusers were women and girls. This movement highlighted a pattern of powerful men taking advantage of their institutional power over women, especially at the early stages of women's careers when they were most vulnerable. Both the frequency of these revelations and the fact that so many of the abusers were powerful, prominent, and widely admired people fueled the energy of the movement. Especially enraging for many women was the 'Access Hollywood' tape in which then-candidate Donald Trump proudly reported his ability to take advantage of and even assault women. ('You can do anything. ... Grab 'em by the pussy. You can do anything.') Trump and his supporters dismissed his comments as mere 'locker room talk,' implying that such behavior was normal and acceptable for men rather than a disqualification for high office.

In October 2017, actress Alyssa Milano encouraged women to share their stories of sexual harassment and abuse on Twitter using #MeToo to help show its ubiquity and to help women understand they are not alone. Thousands responded within hours, and the momentum grew and became international, moving into multiple languages as it crossed the world. The #MeToo phenomenon fueled the launch of a social movement that further revealed the ubiquity of sexual harassment of women and the fact that gender-based power and domination are embedded in institutional power structures such as workplaces and other social institutions. The movement also revealed the large degree to which sexual harassment is shaped by gender-based power relations but also conditioned by other bases of dominance such as race and class (Sapiro 2018).

The #MeToo movement had repercussions for the 2018 Supreme Court confirmation hearings of Brett Kavanaugh, who was accused by Christine Blasey Ford of sexual assault decades before when they were students. The Senate hearings and public reaction to them were reminiscent of the 1991 confirmation hearings of another Supreme Court nominee, Clarence Thomas, when Anita Hill had accused Thomas, her former boss, of sexual harassment. Both cases provoked outcries from feminist groups, an apparent expansion of the number of women reinterpreting their own experiences in light of these stories, and significant increases in the number of Democratic women running for office in the elections of 1992 and 2018.

The 2017 Women's March in Washington, DC, the day after Trump's inauguration, was originally designed to show resistance to the new president's agenda and his visible disrespect for women. It mushroomed into a nationwide, even international, display of political involvement. Between three and five million people took part around the world, with a substantial portion of the marchers wearing the symbolic pink 'pussy hat,' recalling Trump's words in the Access Hollywood tapes. The marches were fueled by a coalition across many women's organizations representing different intersectional populations, as well as political allies such as the National Association for the Advancement of Colored People (NAACP), the American Indian Movement, and Greenpeace. The host of speakers, many of whom were celebrities, emphasized a broad definition of women's issues ranging across health care, education, justice, the environment, and a variety of anti-violence concerns. Smaller marches followed in 2018, 2019, and 2020, but probably more importantly the organization, networks, energy, and anger generated at the time fueled mobilization by women's groups across a range of issues including healthcare, gun control, and #MeToo.

Two other organized episodes of political protest and resistance intersected with the women's marches and anti-harassment movements. The first was the March for Our Lives. In early 2018 a man entered Marjory Stoneman Douglas High School in Parkland, Florida, carrying a semi-automatic rifle. His rampage resulted in the death of seventeen people, including fourteen students, and injuries to many others. Such gun-related attacks had already become all too frequent in the United States, and they have always resulted in a brief upswing of activism among gun control advocates. Women and women's organizations have long been prominent in the gun control movement, but the mass murder at Stoneman Douglas resulted in a new type of political action group: one led largely by a group of surviving students, and ultimately a larger group of young people, among whom many young women were prominent actors. The anti-gun movement has brought a new surge of activism to young people. Following a long international tradition, women also organized against the violence, identifying themselves specifically as mothers, in this case under the name of Moms Demand Action.

Finally, Black Lives Matter, a loose coalition of many organizations and groups across the country focusing on racial justice, has also featured women's activism in addressing issues of political power. Although African Americans have long been the victims of unequally applied standards of justice, in the years since 2013 the news seemed increasingly accented with the killing by police of unarmed African Americans, children, women, and men, often when they were simply carrying out day-to-day activities, or even sleeping in their beds. The breakpoint came with the acquittal of the police officer who had killed a twelve-year-old, Tamir Rice, who was playing by himself in a park with a toy gun.

There were protests and political action around the country, but a new era in African American political history emerged when three women, Patrisse Cullors, Alicia Garza, and Opal Tometi, founded the Black Lives Matter Network, intended as an online platform to facilitate organization and action with regard to racial justice. This evolved into the Movement for Black Lives, a non-centralized coalition of different organizations and groups seeking race justice, including those emphasizing action by women or women's issues relating to racial justice concerns. With each new incident of white violence against Black Americans, the movement grew, and more progressive organizations of many sorts, including feminist organizations affiliated with the coalition. Political action related to Black Lives Matter came to a head in mid-2020 when a disturbing video emerged of a Minneapolis police officer killing an African American man, George Floyd, by kneeling on his neck for nearly nine minutes. Demonstrations and protests under the banner of Black Lives Matter took place across the country, and violence erupted in many locations.

Although the core focus of Black Lives Matter is racial justice, the movement has framed its view around an intersectional understanding of race, especially in relation to gender and sexuality. In a section of the Black Lives Matter website headed 'herstory,' for example, they recognize the importance of women in the founding and organization of the movement and also write:

> Black liberation movements in this country have created room, space, and leadership mostly for Black heterosexual, cisgender men – leaving women, queer and transgender people, and others either out of the movement or in the background to move the work with little or no recognition. As a network, we have

always recognized the need to center the leadership of women and queer and trans people. To maximize our movement muscle, and to be intentional about not replicating harmful practices that excluded so many in past movements for liberation, we made a commitment to lacing those at the margins closer to the center. (Black Lives Matter 2021)

Perhaps not since the nineteenth-century abolition movement has there been such an intensive coalition of gender- and race-focused activists working together in the United States in what they define as a mutual struggle for citizenship rights and empowerment (Sapiro 2020). And, although women have long been prominent in American racial justice movements, the visibility of women and women's issues in Black Lives Matter has been striking.

This escalation of social movement and protest activity does not mean that women and African Americans are abandoning conventional political activities of campaigning and voting. On the contrary, movement leaders have emphasized that all political tactics and strategies matter, especially voting, campaigning, and running for office. Many women candidates cite these movements as part of their inspiration and motivation for running for office.

WOMEN IN POLITICAL LEADERSHIP

The United States continues to lag behind many other democracies in the representation of women in elected governmental positions. In early 2021 the Inter-Parliamentary Union ranked the United States tied for 67th in the world in the percentage of the lower legislative chamber who are women. But even 67th represents an improvement. After the 2020 elections, women held 27 percent of House seats and 24 percent of Senate seats, the highest in history, though still well below the percentage of women in the population. At the same time, women held 32 percent of the statehouse or assembly seats and 28 percent of state senate seats. Turning to elected executive offices, women constituted 23 percent of mayors in cities with a population of over 30,000, 27 percent of mayors in the hundred largest American cities, and 18 percent of governors (Center for American Women and Politics 2021a). In 2020 the United States elected its first female Vice President, although has yet to elect a woman as President.

The United States is a country of vast racial and ethnic diversity, but until recently relatively few of the women who held public elective offices (or relatively few public elective office-holders at all) were people of color. Following the 2020 elections, ten women of color served as mayors of the hundred largest cities in the United States, including six African American women, two Latinas, and two Asian Pacific Islanders, all but one Democrat. Women of color constituted 26 percent of all women state legislators, and nineteen held legislative leadership offices. All but twenty of the 552 women legislators of color were Democrats, as were all of those in leadership positions. Women of color constituted 19 percent of the women serving in statewide elective executive offices, although only one served as governor. A little more than one-third (36 percent) of women serving in Congress were women of color. Of the 51 congressional women of color, all but five were Democrats (Center for American Women and Politics 2021b). Kamala Harris was not only the first woman elected Vice President of the United States, but she was also the first African American and the first Asian American to hold that position.

The history of changes in women's representation in Congress suggests the impact of events that mobilized women in particular, as well as the partisan differences in the recruitment of women to office. Figure 4.1 shows the change in the number of Democratic and Republican women who ran for House of Representatives seats and who won from 1990 to 2020. It demonstrates that the increase in women in Congress is largely a Democratic phenomenon, a fact that also explains why the number of women winning congressional seats fell in 2010 when the Democrats lost control of the House.

The increase in the number of women candidates in the 2000s can partly be attributed to the proliferation of organizations designed to encourage and train women to run for office, including Emerge America (2002), Running Start (2007), VoteRunLead (2014), and Run for Something (2017) as well as others focusing specifically on recruiting candidates of color. The majority of all of these organizations specialized in Democratic recruitment or in the recruitment of candidates likely to be Democrats.

The 2018 midterm elections, the first following the election of Donald Trump and the gathering strength of the #MeToo movement, as well as the reaction to the Supreme Court confirmation hearings of Brett Kavanaugh, provided a burst of electoral energy among Democratic women resulting in the

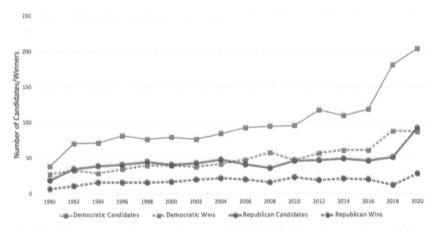

Fig. 4.1 Women Running For Congress, 1990–2020 (Data Source: https://cawp. rutgers.edu/sites/default/files/resources/canwincong_histsum.pdf. Note: Minnesota DFL is treated as Democratic)

second, larger 'Year of the Woman.' The new class of Democratic Congress-members made their presence felt by dressing in suffrage white for their group photo and the 2019 State of the Union Address.

Appointment to the executive office, sometimes requiring legislative approval, is a conspicuous path to power at all levels of American government. Donald Trump appointed three women to his Cabinet. His immediate predecessor, Barack Obama, appointed four women during his first term, then appointed four more in his second term. Women constituted 24 percent of Trump's judicial appointments across all levels, very close to the proportion appointed by the previous Republican president, George W. Bush (at 22 percent), but considerably lower than his immediate predecessor, Barack Obama at 42 percent (Gramlich 2021).

In his early days in office President Biden's profile of appointments reflected to a fair degree his party's stated commitment to social diversity. His Cabinet included five women, including the first American Indian, Deb Haaland, to head the Department of Interior, which includes the Bureau of Indian Affairs. Of his nine other Cabinet-level appointments (executive appointments that hold Cabinet rank but are not in the Cabinet), six were women.

Gender Politics in a Polarized Era

American politics has become increasingly polarized in recent decades. People use this term in many ways, but the political science literature on American politics usually uses polarization to mean that political party identification has become more important to people and increasingly structures a host of political attitudes and policy preferences. Moreover, party identification is increasingly like other social identities, placing us on different teams. It reaches beyond policy preferences to other aspects of social identity and even morality. Attitudes that once did not much sort by party—for example, abortion attitudes—now are closely associated with partisanship. Unlike in the early 1970s, supporters of the pro-choice position align closely with the Democratic Party while pro-life voters are overwhelmingly Republican (Klein 2020).

Gender politics became a critical part of the increasing polarization of the era of transition from Obama to Trump to Biden. This centrality of gender in contemporary politics was not just a matter of ideas about women's equality or inclusion, or even attitudes toward alternative sexualities, as it had been earlier. It has suffused politics in the many different ways described here. It has also spurred women to action in politics, from organizational activity, through protest, to running for office.

Masculinity, not for the first time, has also become an explicit subject of contention. The Republican Party has painted itself as more masculine, supposedly meaning strong-minded, strong-bodied, and capable, while painting the more liberal Democratic Party as effeminate (Winter 2010). Artwork popular with Trump's base often depicted him with a strong jaw and rippling muscles (very unlike his actual body) and the usual array of guns, motorcycles, or historical tableaux. His epithets for political opponents, echoed by his followers, also included gendered terminology; among the more polite was his label 'pussy' for those he deemed not a strong enough Trump supporter, even including his own Vice President in the waning days of their administration. Some of the right-wing, white ethno-nationalist groups involved in the attempted insurrection at the US Capitol on January 6, 2021, are also voluble about their defense of masculinity. They are 'Proud Boys,' indeed.

Although there has been a lot of research on gender differences in public opinion and voting over the years, studies have also detailed the shifting centrality of gender ideology in voting behavior across this period. Brian Schaffner and his colleagues have analyzed the impact of *hostile sexism* on voting during the Trump era. Hostile sexism is measured by a scale of the degree to which people display prejudice and hostility against women, such as agreeing that 'women are too easily offended' or 'most women fail to appreciate fully all that men do for them' (Schaffner et al. 2017).

Schaffner and his co-authors found that hostile sexism (and also a denial of racism) was a significant predictor of voting for Trump in 2016, but a weaker predictor of voting for Republican House candidates in the same election. Their analysis showed that including hostile sexism and denial of racism decreased the well-known effect of educational differences on vote choices in the 2016 election. Hostile sexism and denial of racism were even stronger predictors of 2018 midterm congressional voting, to the detriment of Republicans. Those high on hostile sexism were about equally likely to support Republicans in 2016 and 2018, but those low on hostile sexism moved away from Republican and toward Democratic candidates in 2018 (Schaffner 2020). Follow-up analysis showed that hostile sexism was less related to the presidential vote in 2020 than in 2016 (Zhang and Fox 2020), which can be attributed to a combination of factors, including that both presidential candidates were men, the Coronavirus epidemic, and the sliding economy.

The day after Donald Trump took office, several million women (and a goodly number of men) marched around the world to express their resistance to his political views, and especially his views of women. As he was about to leave office a very different demonstration took place: a large phalanx of demonstrators invaded the US Capitol intent on 'stopping the steal'—that is, they wanted to keep the US Congress from certifying the result of the election that Joe Biden won. Many were armed. They desecrated the building, injured many officers, and many demonstrators hoped to take more lives. Among the right-wing insurrectionists were many women. Among the new right-wing generation of Representatives were women such as Marjorie Taylor Greene (R-Georgia) and Lauren Boebert (R-CO) who, in terms of the issue stands are fierce opponents of feminist movement positions and in terms of gender norms, act nothing like 'traditional women.'

As the Biden Administration took office, two things about gender politics seemed certain. One is that conventional wisdom about gender and gender politics would continue to be undermined and destabilized. The second is that gender politics will remain an important element in polarized politics for some time to come.

References

An Examination of the 2016 Electorate, Based on Validated Voters. Pew Research Center. Available at: https://www.pewresearch.org/politics/2018/08/09/an-exa mination-of-the-2016-electorate-based-on-validated-voters/. Accessed 9 Aug 2018.

Baldassarri, Delia, and Barum Park. 2020. Was There a Culture War? Partisan Polarization and Secular Trends in U.S. Public Opinion. *The Journal of Politics* 82 (3): 809–827.

Black Lives Matter. 2021. Herstory. *Black Lives Matter*. https://blacklivesmatter.com/herstory. Accessed 4 Feb 2021.

Brown, Anna. 2017. Republicans, Democrats have Starkly Different Views on Transgender Issues. Pew Research Center. Available at: https://www.pewresearch.org/fact-tank/2017/11/08/transgender-issues-divide-republicans-and-democr ats/. Accessed 26 Jan 2021.

Bump, Philip. 2019. How Trump Became an Abortion Hard-Liner. *The Washington Post* (May 15). Accessed 23 Mar 2021.

Canaday, Margot. 2009. *The Straight State: Sexuality and Citizenship in Twentieth-Century America*. Princeton: Princeton University Press.

Center for American Women and Politics. 2021a. Current Numbers. Available at: https://cawp.rutgers.edu/current-numbers.

———. 2021b. Women of Color in Elective Office 2021. Available at: https://cawp.rutgers.edu/women-color-elective-office-2021.

Chang, Adam R., and Stephanie M. Wildman. 2017. Gender In/Sight: Examining Culture and Constructions of Gender. *Georgetown Journal of Gender and Law* 43: 43–79.

Davis, Heath Fogg. 2017. *Beyond Trans: Does Gender Matter?* New York: New York University Press.

Egan, Patrick J. 2020. Identity as Dependent Variable: How Americans Shift Their Identities to Align with Their Politics. *American Journal of Political Science* 64 (3): 699–716.

Frank, Nathaniel. 2018. *Awakening: How Gays and Lesbians Brought Marriage Equality to America*. Cambridge, MA: Harvard University Press.

Frank, Walter. 2014. *Law and the Gay Rights Story: The Long Search for Equal Justice in a Divided Democracy*. New Brunswick, NJ: Rutgers University Press.

Georgia Senate Runoff Exit Polls. 2021. NBC News. Available at: https://www.nbcnews.com/politics/2020-elections/georgia-senate-runoff-results. Accessed 8 Feb 2021.

Gramlich, John. 2021. How Trump Compares with Other Recent Presidents in Appointing Federal Judges. Pew Research Center. Available at: https://www.pewresearch.org/fact-tank/2021/01/13/how-trump-compares-with-other-recent-pre sidents-in-appointing-federal-judges/. Accessed 8 Feb 2021.

Hartman, Andrew. 2016. *A War for the Soul of America: A History of the Culture Wars*. Chicago: University of Chicago Press.

Hunter, James Davison. 1991. *Culture Wars: The Struggle to Define America*. New York: Basic Books.

Kaufmann, Karen M., and John R. Petrocik. 1999. The Changing Politics of American Men: Understanding the Sources of the Gender Gap. *American Journal of Political Science* 43 (3): 864–887.

Kenski, Kate. 2018. Gender and the Vote in the 2016 Presidential Election. In *An Unprecedented Election: Media, Communication, and the Electorate in the 2016 Campaign*, eds. Benjamin R. Warner, Dianne G. Bystrom, Mitchell S. McKinney, and Mary C. Banwart, pp.354–68. Santa Barbara, CA: ABC-CLIO, LLC.

Klein, Ezra. 2020. *Why We're Polarized*. New York: Simon & Schuster.

Mezey, Susan Gluck. 2019. *Transgender Rights: From Obama to Trump*. New York: Routledge.

Monthly Ranking of Women in National Parliaments. *IPU Parline*. Available at: https://data.ipu.org/women-ranking?month=1&year=2021.

National Exit Polls: How Different Groups Voted. 2020. *New York Times*.

Ondercin, Heather L. 2017. Who is Responsible for the Gender Gap? The Dynamics of Men's and Women's Democratic Macropartisanship, 1950–2012. *Political Research Quarterly* 70 (4): 749–761.

Pew Research Center. 2018. For Most Trump Voters, 'very warm' Feelings for Him Endured.

———. 2019. Majority of Public Favors Same-Sex Marriage, But Divisions Persist. Available at: https://www.pewresearch.org/politics/2019/05/14/majority-of-pub lic-favors-same-sex-marriage-but-divisions-persist/.

Rich, Adrienne. 1980. Compulsory Heterosexuality and Lesbian Existence. *Signs* 5: 631–661.

Ross, Lawrence C., Jr. 2019. *The Divine Nine: The History of African American Fraternities and Sororities*. New York: Kensington Publishing Co.

Roughgarden, Joan. 2013. *Evolution's Rainbow: Diversity, Gender, and Sexuality in Nature and People*. Berkeley: University of California Press.

Rubin, Gayle. 1975. The Traffic in Women: Notes on the 'political economy' of Sex. In *Toward an Anthropology of Women*, ed. Rayna Rapp Reiter, pp.157–210. New York: Monthly Review Press.

Samuels, Robert, and Jenna Johnson 2017. 'It's not my thing': A History of Trump's Shifting Relationship with the LGBT Community. *The Washington Post* (July 26).

Sapiro, Virginia. 2018. Sexual Harassment: Performances of Gender, Sexuality, and Power. *Perspectives on Politics* 16 (4): 1053–1066.

———. 2020. The Power and Fragility of Social Movement Coalitions: The Woman Suffrage Movement to 1870. *Boston University Law Review* 100: 1557–1611.

Schaffner, Brian, F. Matthew MacWilliams, and Tatishe Nteta. 2017. Hostile Sexism, Racism Denial, and the Historic Education Gap in Support for Trump. In *The 2016 Presidential Election: The Causes and Consequences of a Political Earthquake*, eds. Amnon Cavari, Richard J. Powell, and Kenneth R. Mayer, pp. 99–116. Lanham, MD: Lexington Books.

Schaffner, Brian. 2020. The Heightened Importance of Racism and Sexism in the 2018 U.S. Midterm Elections. *British Journal of Political Science* 1–9. https://doi.org/10.1017/S0007123420000319

Wax-Thibodeaux, Emily, and Samantha Schmidt. 2021. Transgender Girls are at the Center of America's Culture Wars, Yet Again. *Washington Post.*

Winter, Nicholas J.G. 2010. Masculine Republicans and Feminine Democrats: Gender and Americans' Explicit and Implicit Images of the Political Parties. *Political Behavior* 32 (4): 587–618.

Zaller, John. 1992. *The Nature and Origins of Mass Opinion.* New York: Cambridge University Press.

Zhang, Christine, and Brooke Fox 2020. How a Coalition of Women Won it for Joe Biden. *Financial Times* (November 23).

Further Reading

For further exploration about questions of sex, gender, and sexuality, especially their relationship to human biology, see Joan Roughgarden (2013) *Evolution's Rainbow: Diversity, Gender, and Sexuality in Nature and People* (Berkeley: University of California Press). An excellent exploration of the ways that views on sexuality have been embedded in American law and policy is Margot Canaday (2009) *The Straight State: Sexuality and Citizenship in Twentieth-Century America* (Princeton, NJ: Princeton University Press). On social movement activism, see Nathanial Frank (2018) *Awakening: How Gays and Lesbians Brought Marriage Equality to America* (Cambridge, MA: Harvard University Press). For a very useful introduction to how gender designation shape American politics and policy, viewed through the lens of transgender issues, see Heath Fogg David (2017) *Beyond Trans: Does Gender Matter?* (New York: New York University Press).

Further discussion of intersectionality can be found in Patricia Hill Collins and Sirma Bilge (2016), *Intersectionality* (Cambridge: Polity Press).

CHAPTER 5

Political Parties

Mark D. Brewer

The nature and role of political parties in contemporary American politics are the subjects of a great deal of attention. Indeed, this is an area where seemingly everyone—scholars, public officials and political activists, and average citizens—has opinions which they are more than willing to share with anyone who will listen. Many of the opinions offered are negative. One regularly hears commentary bemoaning the high levels of vitriol and incivility currently present in American civic life, with much of the blame laid at the feet of political parties. The same is true regarding government's supposed inability to get much of anything done—political gridlock is caused by the increasingly intractable natures of the Democratic and Republican parties, and their resulting refusal to compromise. Partisan polarization has grown to toxic levels, rendering the public sphere unpalatable, unworkable, and in some instances downright dangerous.

What is the current place of political parties in American politics and governance? This chapter will address this question, explaining not only where parties are but how they got there.

M. D. Brewer (✉)
Department of Political Science, University of Maine, Orono, ME, USA
e-mail: mark.brewer@maine.edu

© The Author(s), under exclusive license to Springer Nature Switzerland AG 2022
G. Peele et al. (eds.), *Developments in American Politics 9*,
https://doi.org/10.1007/978-3-030-89740-6_5

THE PLACE OF PARTIES IN THE AMERICAN POLITICAL SYSTEM

Political parties are not mentioned directly anywhere in the Constitution of the United States, nor are they even hinted at or alluded to. Those who crafted the structure of American governance never intended that governance to be partisan. Indeed, many of the most influential American founders saw political parties as highly negative forces in public life and something to be avoided if at all possible, and tightly controlled and limited if avoidance proved impossible. Two of the most notable of these perspectives come from James Madison, while certainly not the sole architect of the Constitution arguably at least its lead designer, and George Washington, the first president of the United States and almost certainly the most highly esteemed American of his time. It is worth presenting their thoughts here. Beginning with Madison, we can turn to two of his most famous *Federalist* essays, Nos. 10 and 51. In attempting to convince the people of New York State (and by extension other states as well) to support the newly presented Constitution, Madison begins No. 10 by reminding his readers of the threat that individuals brought together by shared interest present to governing arrangements rooted in popular sovereignty:

> Among the numerous advantages promised by a well-constructed Union, none deserves to be more accurately developed that its tendency to break and control faction. The friend of popular government never finds himself so much alarmed for their character and fate as when he contemplates their propensity for this dangerous vice.

Later in No. 10, Madison defines exactly what he means by 'faction':

> By faction I understand a number of citizens, whether amounting to a majority or minority of the whole, who are united and actuated by some common impulse of passion, or of interest, adverse to the rights of other citizens, or to the permanent and aggregate interests of the community.

Madison spends the remainder of No. 10 explaining to his readers why the governing arrangement presented in the Constitution represents the best chance of controlling the 'mischiefs of faction.' Madison returns to this theme in No. 51, explaining how under the Constitution's federal arrangement 'the rights of individuals, or of the minority, will be in little danger from interested combinations of the majority'.

Madison was writing prior to the adoption of the Constitution. Washington, in his Farewell Address of 1796, was writing with over seven years of governance under the Constitution to inform his thoughts. As he prepared to leave the presidency and public life more generally, Washington felt the need to warn his fellow Americans against what he saw as the two biggest threats to the American experiment: foreign entanglements and political parties. It is the latter, of course, that is of interest here. Where Madison spoke at least somewhat ambiguously about faction, Washington was clear that his target was political parties. Washington's enmity toward parties was unmistakable. In his mind, 'the baneful effects of the spirit of party' represent the 'greatest rankness,' 'worst enemy,' 'spirit of revenge,' 'frightful despotism,' and 'ruins of public liberty' in a representative democracy. There is no ambiguity or room for interpretation here.

Madison and Washington were not outliers in their views on parties among the Founding Era elites. While some recent research has challenged the formerly standard view that anti-party spirit was nearly universal during the Founding Era and its immediate aftermath (Huston 2015; Peart 2015), this research largely agrees with the longstanding view that the political elites of the Founding Era were opposed to parties, and that even those who eventually came to dabble in partisan politics did so reluctantly at best (Formisano 1983; Hofstadter 1968). Either way, it did not take long for political parties to entrench themselves in the American system despite the misgivings of the Founders. The Jacksonian Era of the 1820s–1830s saw entities that looked quite a bit like modern American parties come into being. With Martin Van Buren leading the way, Jackson's Democratic Party made the first large scale efforts at partisan mobilization of the masses, and significantly extended the reach and influence of partisanship throughout government more broadly. The opposition Whig Party followed suit in short order. By the time we reach the middle of the nineteenth century, political parties were the dominant institutional actors in American political life. During this period, partisanship permeated all elements of American politics and governance (McGerr 1986; Silbey 1991).

While anti-party reformers such as the Progressives of the late nineteenth and early twentieth centuries attempted to weaken parties and realized some success in these efforts, political parties remained front and center in American politics throughout the twentieth century. In the eyes of many scholars, this was a good thing. In their view, political parties were absolutely essential to democracy in general and American democratic governance in particular. E.E. Schattschneider (2004 [1942]), perhaps the preeminent parties' scholar of his generation, famously said that '[p]olitical parties created democracy and …modern democracy is unthinkable save in terms of the parties…The parties are not therefore merely appendages of modern government; they are in the center of it and play a determinative and creative role in it' (1). Writing a little over fifty years later, prominent parties scholar John Aldrich (1995) opened his now classic work on parties by referencing Schattschneider and agreeing that 'democracy is *unworkable* save in terms of parties' (3). The reason for this view is summarized nicely by equally renowned parties' scholar Clinton Rossiter (1960) in his own classic text on parties. Rossiter fully recognized that everything parties did was in the pursuit and service of their own self-interest. The leaders and supporters of a particular political party wanted to achieve things in opposition to and perhaps even at the expense of other political interests in society and would often go to great lengths to do so. In other words, he agreed with Madison and Washington on this matter.

But where Rossiter disagreed with these authorities was his belief that in the course of nakedly pursuing their own interests, political parties provided things of the utmost importance to the proper functioning of American politics and government: 'We tolerate and even celebrate their [parties'] existence because they do things for us in the public realm that would otherwise be done poorly or not at all' (38). Schattschneider, Aldrich, Rossiter, and many other parties' scholars (including this one) see parties as critical to American representative democracy because of the central role they play in educating, organizing, mobilizing, and offering meaningful choice to voters. Parties also serve as useful heuristic devices, allowing even minimally informed citizens a very strong chance at selecting a candidate that matches their interests on election day. Finally, parties can be very helpful in building connections within the highly fragmented American political arrangement.

THE SHADOWS OF FDR AND REAGAN: PARTISAN CONFLICTS AND CLEAVAGES IN THE TWENTIETH CENTURY

The primary focus of this chapter is the state of American political parties as we enter the third decade of the twenty-first century. But today's Republican and Democratic Parties have long roots. The Democrats trace their origins back to Thomas Jefferson and the very early nineteenth century while the Republicans came into being in the 1850s and like to begin their story with the presidency of Abraham Lincoln. Looking beyond just chronology, the nature of American parties demands that we look at least somewhat to the past in order to understand the present and to a certain degree even speculate on the future. The fluid nature of American society demands that parties change. Occasionally parties change quickly and on a relatively large scale. More often, partisan change occurs slowly in small increments, in a series of fits and starts. Either way, the end result is the same: the parties evolve over time. But even the biggest changes do not result in the complete overhaul of the parties. As the parties are reinvented and reconfigured—sometimes by their own efforts and sometimes by outside forces—they retain at least some elements of their previous incarnation(s). Party leaders, to the degree that they are able, try to think and act strategically in the hopes of obtaining and maintaining political power going forward.

Today's Republican and Democratic parties both contain elements that one can trace back to their earliest days of existence (Gerring 1998). But in order to understand today's parties, their coalitions and factions, their conflicts and divisions, we need to focus in particular on two political eras of the twentieth century and their respective primary leaders and spokesmen: the New Deal era and Franklin Delano Roosevelt of the 1930s and early 1940s and the era of Republican ascension of the 1980s and early 1990s led and overseen by Ronald Reagan. Large parts of the contemporary identities of both of America's major political parties were initiated or solidified in these eras. While

FDR has been dead now for almost 80 years and Reagan approaching 20, their shadows continue to loom large over contemporary American partisanship.

When FDR first won the presidency in 1932 the Democrats had long been the minority party at the national level. Only one Democrat—Woodrow Wilson—had held the presidency since 1896, and he needed a third party challenge by former Republican President Theodore Roosevelt to secure his first win in 1912 (Wilson was reelected in a more traditional two party contest in 1916). Democratic control of Congress was rare in this period as well, limited to a portion of the Wilson administration and the House only in the 72nd Congress (1931–1933). In many ways the Democratic Party of this period was a regional party, dominating the southern states of the former Confederacy but having little success elsewhere. The party was beginning to have success in some of the big cities of the Northeast and Midwest in the 1920s, but this did not translate to elections for federal office. FDR changed this with his victory in the 1932 presidential election and locked in the famous New Deal coalition with his landslide reelection in 1936. Roosevelt and his Democratic Party were able to keep their overwhelming support in the South while adding strong support among the less affluent, city dwellers, organized labor, Catholics, Jews, white ethnics, and Blacks outside the South (there is of course significant overlap among these groups) (Brewer and Stonecash 2009). Such high levels of Democratic success meant that the Republican coalition shrunk during this time, but the GOP was able to hang on to a significant amount of its previous base in the form of still relatively strong support among more affluent Americans and white Protestants outside of the South. Republican support among these groups increased further as the 1930s wore on, at the same time as the party began attracting increased support from rural voters, again outside the South (Axelrod 1972). While today's Democratic and Republican parties have obviously shed some parts of their New Deal era coalitions (while of course adding others), other components of their New Deal bases remain crucial elements of each party's coalition today. As will be discussed in more detail in the next section, today's Democrats still rely heavily on strong support from the less affluent, urbanites, and African-Americans (now joined by other people of color) to win elections, while the GOP continues to count the wealthy and rural Americans as key parts of the party's base.

While some remnants of the New Deal party system still mark the partisanship of today, the continued influence of the Reagan years on the coalitions of both parties is even more readily apparent. And of course the Reagan years did not appear out of nowhere. Reagan's presidential victory in 1980 owes significant debts to the efforts of Strom Thurmond and the Dixiecrats of the late 1940s, George Wallace's presidential campaigns of the 1960s, Richard Nixon's pursuit and apparently successful attraction of his so-called Silent Majority in the late 1960s and early 1970s and perhaps most significantly to Barry Goldwater's 1964 presidential campaign (Perlstein 2001). Not only did Goldwater preview many of the same themes and positions that Reagan successfully used in his 1980 campaign, but a fair number of the conservative activists that first became involved in the GOP due to their support of Goldwater ended up staying active in the party and were critical in Reagan's attaining the 1980 Republican presidential nomination and then winning in the general election. Indeed, Reagan's conversion from New Deal Democrat to conservative Republican was brought about in some part due to his liking of Goldwater and his support for the Arizona Senator in 1964. But Reagan's presidential victories in 1980 and 1984 mark a clear change in the Republican coalition, in much the same way that FDR's wins in 1932 and 1936 did for the Democrats. And just as FDR's victories had coalitional implications for the GOP as well, Reagan's wins also had an impact on the Democratic coalition.

So which groups did Reagan bring into the Republican fold? First and foremost, Reagan's campaign was built on dramatically increasing Republican support among conservatives across the board, whether those conservatives were of the fiscal variety (a group among which the GOP already had a strong foothold) or of the increasingly vocal and politically up-for-grabs cultural variety (Busch 2005; Edsall 2006; Layman 2001). The quest for these conservative voters led Reagan and the Republican Party to a heightened focus on white Southerners, white men, suburbanites, and religious conservatives, primarily white evangelical Protestants but traditionalist Roman Catholics as well. For the fiscal conservatives, Reagan emphasized cutting taxes and shrinking the size of the federal government. For social conservatives, Reagan clearly stated his opposition to abortion, supported the GOP's decision to drop endorsement of the Equal Rights Amendment from its party platform, and actively courted evangelical groups such as the Moral Majority. Reagan dusted off the 'tough on crime' rhetoric, with its often coded racial appeals, first used by Nixon, and signaled his strong support of gun rights. Reagan's muscular foreign policy also had the promise of a conservative appeal (Busch 2005; Edsall 2006).

We know that Reagan won the presidency in both 1980 and 1984, so we can assume that his appeals were at least somewhat successful. Exit polling from these two elections bears out this assumption. Reagan won easily among self-identified conservatives, white southerners, white men, and suburbanites in 1980, and then increased his support among all four of these groups in 1984. While the exit poll data from these two elections do not allow us to look directly at religious conservatives, they do indicate that Reagan received majorities from white Protestants, white Catholics, and born-again or evangelical Christians in 1980 and followed up with even bigger majorities in 1984. Together, voters in these groups represented a significant portion of the electorate in the 1980s. While the exit polls do not allow us to assess how Reagan performed among the more affluent and rural voters—groups that were already key elements of the Republican coalition, data from the American National Election Studies (ANES) do. The results here tell us that Reagan was indeed able to hold the support of these groups. Reagan received over 60 percent of the vote from those in the upper third of the income distribution and rural Americans in 1980 and further increased his support in 1984. When Reagan left office in January 1989, his Republican Party was very much rooted in these groups. The GOP of the Reagan era was built on strong support from conservatives, white men, white Southerners, the more affluent, rural and suburban dwellers, and religious conservatives, especially white evangelicals.

How did the Democrats fare in this period of Republican success? Given that the party lost all three of the presidential elections in the 1980s, one can safely assume that their coalition shrunk from its New Deal era configuration. But where were their losses concentrated? In some instances, answering this is as easy as looking at where Republicans gained. While there are no exit polling data from 1932 to 1936, we know from nascent public opinion polling data and various aggregate vote analyses that New Deal era Democrats did very well among white Southerners, white evangelical Protestants, and white Catholics. Their support among these groups fell dramatically in 1980 and 1984, precipitously among the first two groups. The ANES data also tell us that Democratic support declined among two other core groups in 1980 and 1984. Less than 50 percent of those in the lower third of the family income distribution and city dwellers voted Democratic for president in 1980 and 1984. The ANES data show that Democratic support slipped significantly among union households as well. Perhaps the one area of clear Democratic gain in the Reagan era was among voters of color. The exit polls show that Democrats received 85 percent support among African-Americans and 56 percent of Latinos in 1980, followed by 90 percent and 62 percent respectively in 1984. Both of these groups were also larger portions of the electorate in the 1980s than they were in the 1930s. But the Democratic Party coalition of the 1980s had shrunk dramatically from that of the 1930s. The party lost a good deal of support among white voters, particularly among men, southerners, and evangelical Protestants. It took a hit among urban voters, voters in union households, and the less affluent as well, although these declines were not as dramatic. Support was up among voters of color, but not enough to offset the losses among these other groups.

THE RISE OF POLARIZATION

While the coalitional developments of the New Deal and Reagan eras are clearly important for understanding the American political parties of today, the rise of political polarization rooted in partisanship is even more critical. There has always been a certain degree of partisan polarization present in American politics. But the current levels are unlike anything ever seen before. This hyperpartisan environment has serious implications.

Increasing party polarization in the United States first began to attract scholarly attention in the late 1990s. The earliest research noted the growth in partisan polarization primarily in Congress, although soon increasing polarization was detected outside of Capitol Hill as well. As more work was done on polarization, scholars engaged in debates as to whether party polarization was limited to political elites (Fiorina et al. 2011) or extended to partisans at the mass level (Abramowitz 2010, 2013; Brewer and Stonecash 2007). While scholars were actively debating the existence of polarization, Americans were experiencing its effects on the ground. Americans increasingly saw significant differences between the parties and levels of partisan voting were increasing. So too were levels of partisan animosity.

Today it is taken as a given that contemporary American politics is marked by high levels of partisan polarization at both the elite and mass levels (Abramowitz 2018; Brewer and Stonecash 2015; Campbell 2018; Mason 2018; Pew 2014; Sides et al. 2018). Evidence indicates that polarization manifested more strongly among party elites first, but that this polarization soon spread to partisans at the mass level as well. Not only did party polarization spread from the elites to the masses, it also spread across multiple policy areas. Voters increasingly sorted themselves into the 'correct' partisan camps based on their ideological and partisan preferences (Levendusky 2009). These increased policy differences between Democrats and Republicans led to a rise in partisan animosity (Orr and Huber 2020). Perhaps an even bigger driver of the growing partisan animosity was the increasing presence of so-called 'affective polarization,' where members of one party strongly dislike members of the other party while continuing to like members of their own party, much the way sports fans view fellow supporters of their own teams and supporters of their most hated rivals (Mason 2018). Abramowitz and Webster (2016) label this development the rise of negative partisanship. The rise of partisan media almost certainly contributed to all of these dynamics (Levendusky 2013). The strongest and most active partisans exhibit the highest degrees of polarization, further exacerbating the situation. These partisans are the most likely to exhibit partisan anger and express support for uncivil actions. They are also most likely to see members of the opposing party as less than human, although this growing 'dehumanization' of members of the opposite party extends to a certain degree among all strengths of partisanship among both Democrats and Republicans (Martherus et al. 2021). Trends like these clearly indicate that the growth of partisan polarization in the United States has now reached the point of cause for legitimate concern. Robust partisan differences rooted in principle and strenuous but civil debates over policy proposals are generally positive for representative democracy. But high and still rising levels of partisan anger, increasing support for violence and other uncivil political acts, and a growing likelihood to see supporters of the opposing political party as subhuman are almost certainly indicators of a polity under significant stress.

THE PARTIES NOW AND WHAT THE FUTURE MIGHT BRING

High levels of partisan polarization existed *before* Donald Trump became president in 2017. We are now beginning to understand just how much partisan polarization grew during Trump's four years as president. Research indicates that all presidents during the current era of polarized parties have contributed to the growth of polarization (Wood and Jordan 2018), but Trump of course behaved unlike any president before him, at least in the modern era. Presumably the Trump presidency—where the commander-in-chief routinely called Democrats 'unAmerican' and 'treasonous' actors who were 'trying to destroy the country'—exacerbated an already troubling situation. A recent Pew Research Center study illustrating some of the ways in which Trump fanned the flames of polarization bears this out. During his time in office Trump had an average approval rating of 86 percent among Republicans. Among Democrats this figure was 6 percent. And it was not just Trump's performance that divided Republicans and Democrats. In the words of Michael Dimock and John Gramlich (2021), the authors of this Pew Study:

> Republicans and Democrats weren't just divided over Trump's handling of the job. They also interpreted many aspects of his character and personality in fundamentally opposite ways. In a 2019 survey, at least three-quarters of Republicans said the president's words sometimes or often made them feel hopeful, entertained, informed, happy, and proud. Even larger shares of Democrats said his words sometimes or often made them feel concerned, exhausted, angry, insulted, and confused. The strong reactions that Trump provoked appeared in highly personal contexts, too. In a 2019 survey, 71% of Democrats who were single and looking for a relationship said they would definitely or probably not consider being in a committed relationship with someone who had voted for Trump in 2016. That far exceeded the 47% of single and looking Republicans who said they would not consider being in a serious relationship with a Hillary Clinton voter.

Differences between Republicans and Democrats on issues also increased during Trump's tenure in office, including on many of the most important issues in American public life. Partisan differences on issues such as the Covid-19 pandemic, climate change, racial justice, economic inequality, law enforcement, and the proper nature of America's foreign policy, to name just a few, all reached record highs during the Trump presidency (Pew 2020a, b). Recent research also points to a reignition of the culture wars in American politics, as partisan division over new issues such as religious liberties and transgender rights increased, in much the same way that partisan divides over abortion and homosexual rights marked the 1980s and 1990s (Castle 2019; Hunter 1991). While it is certainly true that partisan conflict is on the rise in many of the world's developed democracies, the partisan divisions in the United States are well beyond the levels seen in other nations (Pew 2020b).

So how might have Trump more specifically and the dramatic rise in partisan polarization more broadly affected the two parties' electoral coalitions? We left off here after the 1984 presidential election, a time just before party polarization began to rise. Exit poll data from the 2016 and 2020 presidential elections show us clearly that the differences between the parties' coalitions have grown substantially. Looking first at groups that were key elements of the GOP during the 1980s, Trump was able to increase Republican support among conservatives from Reagan-era levels and keep levels of support among white men steady. Indeed, Trump won whites overall by a large margin in both 2016 and 2020. Trump also maintained strong levels of support among evangelical Protestants and rural voters. Trump did dip slightly among more affluent voters in 2016 before rebounding in 2020. The one area where Trump underperformed Reagan among the party's base was suburban voters, a decline that proved costly. Trump really did not do much to bring new voters into the party, with the exception of voters with a high school diploma or less. As Johnston et al. (2017) note, for all the talk about Trump changing the Republican Party, there is not much evidence that he did so in terms of the party's electoral coalition. Groups that were Republican under Reagan stayed that way under Trump, except for suburban voters who shifted to more of a swing group status.

Moving to the Democratic coalition presents us with more of a story of change. Again looking first at those groups that were central to the party's coalition in the 1980s, Hillary Clinton and Joe Biden both did very well among African-American voters, Latino voters, and urban dwellers. They also led somewhat of a Democratic rebound among the less affluent and union voters, with the latter group going relatively strong for Biden. But the interesting developments for the Democrats were in the new groups they were able to bring in. If the GOP had consolidated support among conservatives by the 1980s, Democrats have now done likewise among liberals, with Clinton and Biden both winning this group overwhelmingly. Both candidates also did very well among voters with a post-graduate degree, voters with no religion (or 'seculars'), and LGBTQ+ voters. Finally, Clinton and Biden both won women and younger voters, although not by overwhelming margins. This coalition, much more diverse than that of the Republicans, was enough for the Democrats to win the popular presidential vote in both of these elections and the electoral college vote in 2020. Here it is easier to see the possible impact Trump had on the partisan coalitions (Table 5.1).

So what might the future hold for partisanship in the United States? In many ways the political waters are muddy. The future of Donald Trump in American politics remains very much up in the air, although his continued importance to partisan conflict remains clear. While most former presidents tend to fade from public view, gradually at first and then more quickly as increased time passes, it is unclear if this will be the case with Trump. In the early days of his post-(first term?) presidency, Trump is still very active, very much in control of the Republican Party, and is promising to make the 2022 GOP nominating season a referendum on all things Trump. Congress is very closely divided, meaning President Biden may only have two years in order to achieve much in terms of policy. Congressional redistricting is also about to get underway, although it is not yet clear what rules this will take place under. There is also talk of social media regulation, which could dramatically alter the political communication environment in the United States.

Table 5.1 Republican and Democratic presidential vote percentages among various groups, 1980–2020

Group	1980	1984	1988	1992	1996	2000	2004	2008	2012	2016	2020
Republicans											
Conservatives	73	82	80	64	71	81	84	78	82	81	84
White Southerners	61	71	67	49	56	66	70	68	*66*	*69*	–
White Men	59	67	63	40	49	60	62	57	*57*	62	61
White Catholics	51	57	56	37	41	52	56	52	*52*	*56*	**56**
Evangelical Protestants	56	69	74	56	–	–	65	57	60	80	76
Rural Dwellers	*57*	*61*	*56*	*37*	*39*	*51*	57	53	–	61	57
Suburbanites	*58*	*65*	*58*	*36*	*42*	*50*	52	48	–	49	48
Upper Income Third	*56*	*69*	*61*	*39*	*46*	*50*	*57*	*58*	*50*	*45*	54
HS Diploma or Less	*48*	*54*	*47*	*30*	*31*	*43*	*47*	*40*	*45*	*48*	50
Democrats											
Liberals	60	70	81	68	78	80	85	89	86	84	89
Women	45	44	49	45	54	54	51	56	55	54	56
African-Americans	85	90	86	83	84	90	88	95	93	89	87
Latinos	56	62	69	61	72	62	53	67	71	66	66
Seculars	*31*	*52*	*59*	*56*	*57*	*53*	*51*	*61*	*70*	67	65
Urbanites	*56*	*59*	*62*	*63*	*62*	*70*	54	63	–	60	60
Lower Income Third	*52*	*56*	*57*	*60*	*68*	*58*	*57*	*67*	*63*	*54*	55
Post-Graduate Degree	*37*	*50*	*54*	*55*	*49*	*47*	*59*	*51*	*59*	*68*	62
Union Household	*50*	*56*	*58*	*54*	*67*	*58*	*63*	*59*	*57*	*57*	57
Young Voters (18–29)	44	40	47	43	53	48	54	66	60	55	62
LGBTQ+	–	–	–	–	–	–	77	70	76	77	64

Sources All data in regular type are taken from exit poll data as reported by the New York Times. Data in italics are taken from the American National Election Studies Cumulative Datafile, 1948–2016. Data in bold are taken from the 2020 Fox News Voter Analysis, conducted in partnership with the Associated Press. Seculars in ANES defined as respondents who identified as something other than Catholic, Jewish, or Protestant and responded "none" and "no preference"

But if one stares long enough at the tea leaves a few things seem to be safe bets. Partisan polarization is likely to remain high for some time. It did not develop overnight and it will not decline that way either. Republicans and Democrats exhibit significant differences on important issues like climate change, systemic racism and racial justice, and economic inequality, to name but a few. Dramatically different perspectives on such fundamental matters would be difficult to reconcile even if levels of political civility were high and partisan animosity were low, which they most certainly are not. It is also unlikely that the high levels of partisan polarization in Americans' news consumption and other forms of political communication will shrink, at least in the near term.

Both parties have relatively large internal divisions, and while current commentary tends to focus more on the Republicans than the Democrats in this regard, both parties have serious work to do to keep their factions, and thus their coalitions, intact (Blake 2021; Pew 2019). Establishment-type Republicans for whom issues like free trade, reduced regulation, and fiscal conservatism were gospel increasingly find themselves at odds with a populist insurgent wing of the party that touts highly protectionist policies, an appetite to rein in big corporations, and appears indifferent (at least at times) on matters of taxing and spending. For Democrats, a moderate wing that trumpets the values of so-called 'Main St. America' and advocates for a gradual and bipartisan approach to problem solving faces growing pressure from a rising progressive faction within the party pushing a liberal agenda and seeking large scale change across the board. America's two party system means that each major party will always be marked by some degree of internal tension, but these pressures are quite high at present.

Finally, looking further at the matter of the parties' coalitions, it is difficult to envision the Republicans winning many future presidential elections unless they add to their current base of support. After all the GOP has only won the popular vote in one of seven presidential elections since 1992, and even that was a relatively close affair featuring an incumbent against an opponent who ran a poor campaign. While the electoral college will likely continue to give the GOP a structural advantage (Silver 2020), it is unclear that this will be enough to win presidential elections without attracting more voters from somewhere. Winning with a base of white, rural, evangelical, affluent voters will become increasingly difficult moving forward, as the percentage of the electorate represented by these voters continues to shrink. The GOP seemingly learned this lesson after the 2012 presidential election, when the party produced a post-election report stating its need to become more inclusive and attract greater support among women, voters of color, and LGBTQ+ voters. While the party did not move in this direction under Trump in 2016 and 2020, the fact remains that the Republicans need to attract more voters. The party's increased support among Latino and to a lesser extent African-American men in 2020 is one sign of a possible future avenue of growth, while coaxing suburban voters back into the fold might be an easier path. On the other hand, the Democrats appear to be poised for future success given their increasingly diverse coalition and support among groups that are growing in American society. But the party's decline among Latino men in 2020 is cause for concern, and there have long been voices within the Black community that Democrats take their support for granted and that it would benefit African-Americans to shop around politically. And, if progressive Democrats push the party too far to the left, it is easy to see suburban voters moving quickly back to the GOP and Democratic support further declining among the white working class. But the past is never certain prologue, and the future of both parties remains somewhat uncertain. What we can say with a high degree of confidence is that political parties will remain central to American politics and government.

References

Abramowitz, Alan I. 2010. *The Disappearing Center: Engaged Citizens, Polarization, and American Democracy*. New Haven, CT: Yale University Press.

———. 2013. *The Polarized Public? Why American Government is So Dysfunctional*. Boston: Pearson.

———. 2018. *The Great Alignment: Race, Party Transformation, and the Rise of Donald Trump*. New Haven, CT: Yale University Press.

Abramowitz, Alan I., and Steven Webster. 2016. The Rise of Negative Partisanship and the Nationalization of U.S. Elections in the 21st Century. *Electoral Studies* 41: 12–22.

Aldrich, John H. 1995. *Why Parties? The Origin and Transformation of Political Parties in America*. Chicago: University of Chicago Press.

American National Election Studies (ANES). 2019. *Time Series Cumulative Data File 1948–2016*. Ann Arbor, MI: Stanford University and University of Michigan. September 10.

Axelrod, Robert. 1972. Where the Votes Come From: An Analysis of Electoral Coalitions, 1952–1968. *American Political Science Review* 66 (March): 11–20.

Blake, Aaron. 2021. What GOP Civil War? Republicans Insist All is Well—Even as They Attack Each Other. *Washington Post*. March 2.

Brewer, Mark D., and Jeffrey M. Stonecash. 2007. *Split: Class and Cultural Divides in American Politics*. Washington, DC: CQ Press.

———. 2009. *Dynamics of American Political Parties*. New York: Cambridge University Press.

———. 2015. *Polarization and the Politics of Personal Responsibility*. New York: Oxford University Press.

Busch, Andrew E. 2005. *Reagan's Victory: The Presidential Election of 1980 and the Rise of the Right*. Lawrence, KS: University Press of Kansas.

Campbell, James E. 2018. *Polarized: Making Sense of a Divided America*. Princeton, NJ: Princeton University Press.

Castle, Jeremiah. 2019. New Fronts in the Culture Wars? Religion, Partisanship, and Polarization on Religious Liberty and Transgender Rights in the United States. *American Politics Research* 47: 650–679.

Dimock, Michael, and John Gramlich. 2021. *How America Changed During Donald Trump's Presidency*. Pew Research Center. January 29.

Edsall, Thomas B. 2006. *Building Red America: The Conservative Coalition and the Drive for Permanent Power*. New York: Basic Books.

Fiorina, Morris P., Samuel J. Abrams, and Jeremy C. Pope. 2011. *Culture War? The Myth of a Polarized America*, 3rd ed. New York: Pearson Longman.

Formisano, Ronald P. 1983. *The Transformation of Political Culture: Massachusetts Parties*, 1790s–1840s. New York: Oxford University Press.

Gerring, John. 1998. *Party Ideologies in America, 1828–1996*. New York: Cambridge University Press.

Hofstadter, Richard. 1968. *The Idea of a Party System: The Rise of Legitimate Opposition in the United States, 1780–1840*. Berkeley, CA: University of California Press.

Hunter, James Davison. 1991. *Culture Wars: The Struggle to Define America*. New York: Basic Books.

Huston, Reeve. 2015. Rethinking the Origins of Partisan Democracy in the United States. In *Practicing Democracy: Popular Politics in the United States from the Constitution to the Civil War*, eds. Daniel Peart and Adam I.P. Smith, pp. 46–71. Charlottesville, VA: University of Virginia Press.

Johnston, Ron, Charles Pattie, Kelvyn Jones, and David Manley. 2017. Was the 2016 United States Presidential Contest a Deviating Election? Continuity and Change in the Electoral Map—Or 'Plus ca change, plus c'est la meme geographie. *Journal of Elections, Public Opinion, and Parties* 27: 369–388.

Layman, Geoffrey. 2001. *The Great Divide: Religious and Cultural Conflicts in American Party Politics*. New York: Columbia University Press.

Levendusky, Matthew. 2009. *The Partisan Sort: How Liberals Became Democrats and Conservatives Became Republicans*. Chicago: University of Chicago Press.

———. 2013. *How Partisan Media Polarize America*. Chicago: University of Chicago Press.

Mason, Lilliana. 2018. *Uncivil Agreement: How Politics Became Our Identity*. Chicago: University of Chicago Press.

Martherus, James L., Andres G. Martinez, Paul K. Piff, and Alexander G. Theodoridis. 2021. Party Animals? Extreme Partisan Polarization and Dehumanization. *Political Behavior* 43: 517–540.

McGerr, Michael E. 1986. *The Decline of Popular Politics: The American North, 1865–1928*. New York: Oxford University Press.

Orr, Lilla V., and Gregory A. Huber. 2020. The Policy Basis of Measured Partisan Animosity in the United States. *American Journal of Political Science* 64 (July): 569–586.

Peart, Daniel. 2015. An 'Era of No Feelings'?: Rethinking the Relationship between Political Parties and Popular Participation in the Early United States. In *Practicing Democracy: Popular Politics in the United States from the Constitution to the Civil War*, eds. Daniel Peart and Adam I.P. Smith. pp. 123–144. Charlottesville, VA: University of Virginia Press.

Perlstein, Rick. 2001. *Before the Storm: Barry Goldwater and the Unmaking of the American Consensus*. New York: Hill and Wang.

Pew Research Center. 2014. *Political Polarization in the American Public: How Increasing Ideological Uniformity and Partisan Antipathy Affect Politics, Compromise, and Everyday Life*. June 12. Washington, DC.

———. 2019. *In a Politically Polarized Era, Sharp Divides in Both Partisan Coalitions*. December. Washington, DC.

———. 2020a. *2020 Election Reveals Two Broad Voting Coalitions Fundamentally At Odds*. November 6.

———. 2020b. *America is Exceptional in the Nature of its Political Divide*. November 13.

Rossiter, Clinton. 1960. *Parties and Politics in America*. Ithaca, NY: Cornell University Press.

Schattschneider, E.E. 2004 [1942]. *Party Government*. New Brunswick, NJ: Transactions Publishers.

Sides, John, Michael Tesler, and Lynn Vavreck. 2018. *Identity Crisis: The 2016 Presidential Campaign and the Battle for the Meaning of America*. Princeton, NJ: Princeton University Press.

Silbey, Joel H. 1991. *The American Political Nation, 1838–1893*. Stanford, CA: Stanford University Press.

Silver, Nate. 2020. Biden's Favored In Our Final Presidential Forecast, But It's a Fine Line Between a Landslide and a Nail-Biter. December 20, 2021. Available at: https://fivethirtyeight.com/features/final-2020-presidential-election-forecast/

Wood, B. Dan, and Soren Jordan. 2018. Presidents and the Polarization of the American Electorate. *Presidential Studies Quarterly* 48 (June): 248–270.

FURTHER READING

Readers wishing to delve further into the role and place of political parties in American politics and government would be well served by starting with three works cited in this chapter: E.E. Schattschneider's *Party Government* (2004 [1942], New Brunswick, NJ: Transactions Publishers); Clinton Rossiter's *Parties and Politics in America* (1960, Ithaca, NY: Cornell University Press); and John Aldrich's *Why Parties?* (2001, Chicago: Chicago University Press). These texts will provide a strong introduction to what parties do in the United States, and a solid foundation for future study.

In terms of the substance and history of partisan divisions in the United States, readers could turn to three additional works: *Dynamics of the Party System* by James L. Sundquist (1983, Washington DC: Brookings Institution Press); *Party Ideologies in America, 1828–1996* by John Gerring (1998, New York: Cambridge University Press); and *Dynamics of American Political Parties* by Mark Brewer and Jeff Stonecash (2009, New York: Cambridge University Press). These texts will provide readers a clear portrait of the nature and evolution of partisan conflict over time in the United States.

While it is often difficult for academics to fully make sense of current politics as they happen, readers interested in the current state of parties and partisanship in American politics could do worse than starting with Matthew Levendusky's *The Partisan Sort* (2009, Chicago: University of Chicago Press); Alan Abramowitz's *The Great Alignment* (2018, New Haven: Yale University Press); James Campbell's *Polarized* (2018, Princeton: Princeton University Press); and Lilliana Mason's *Uncivil Agreement* (2018, Chicago: University of Chicago Press). These studies will bring readers up to speed on the current scholarly discussions surrounding American political parties.

CHAPTER 6

Interest Groups and Money

Hye Young You

What do Google, the National Rifle Association, Harvard University, and the American Farm Bureau Federation have in common? They are all interest groups. Competition among interest groups lies at the heart of American democracy. Understanding why groups are organized and how they influence elections and policies is critical to the understanding of political representation in the United States.

Interest groups have played a central role in American democracy since the very beginning of the Republic. James Madison's *Federalist Paper* No. 10 famously discussed threats posed by factions—defined as 'a number of citizens, whether amounting to a majority or a minority of the whole, who are united and actuated by some common impulse of passion, or of interest, adverse to the rights of other citizens, or to the permanent and aggregate interests of the community'—and how to control them. Madison noted that forming factions is an inevitable part of human nature, therefore, a proper solution is not to remove its causes but to control for its effects. Madison believed that in a country as large as the United States, diverse interests would arise and compete against one another, thereby preventing domination by any one faction. Over time, as Madison predicted, the number of organized interests that are active in politics has increased.

H. Y. You (✉)
Wilf Family Department of Politics, New York University, New York, NY, USA
e-mail: hy21@nyu.edu

© The Author(s), under exclusive license to Springer Nature Switzerland AG 2022
G. Peele et al. (eds.), *Developments in American Politics 9*,
https://doi.org/10.1007/978-3-030-89740-6_6

83

However, the increasing number and diversity of organized groups does not necessarily lead to more equality in political participation and influence because some groups have louder voices than others (Schlozman et al. 2012). Therefore, a key issue concerning the role of interest groups in American democracy is the inequality of political voices expressed by different groups. The question of group influence on the political process and the distribution of unequal voices in American democracy is particularly important in this era of sharply increasing economic inequality. In addition, group conflicts by race, gender, generation, and income-level, and the lack of representation of certain interests has received unparalleled attention in recent political dialogues in the United States.

Why do different groups have unequal voices in the political process? The two most prominent channels that interest groups employ to influence political processes are campaign contributions and lobbying. These channels are designed to communicate information about individuals' and groups' preferences to policymakers and the main requirement for gaining participation in these channels is money. In recent years, an unprecedented amount of money has been spent on politics by individuals and groups. Although American democracy offers multiple venues for citizens and groups to participate in the political process, the importance of money in political participation could amplify the conversion of existing economic inequality into political inequality. The following section considers how the campaign finance system and the lobbying process allow unequal opportunities for different groups to influence political representation in the United States. It also analyzes why increasing the role of individual donors as opposed to corporate donors in financing elections—a tactic that campaign finance reformers touted as a way to empower citizen participation—does not necessarily lead to more desirable outcomes, such as electing fewer extreme candidates and producing less polarization.

CAMPAIGN FINANCE AND MONEY IN ELECTIONS

The structure of campaign finance in the United States allows interest groups and individuals to wield considerable influence in electoral processes. The cost of election campaigning has been increasing over time. In 2000, $1.41 billion was spent on the presidential race and $1.67 billion was spent on congressional races. Twenty years later, the 2020 election cycle was recorded as the most expensive election in the history of the United States: the presidential race cost $5.7 billion and congressional races cost $8.7 billion (Center for Responsive Politics 2021).

Modes of Campaign Financing: Public vs. Private

Where does the money to help candidates run for office originate? There are two modes of campaign financing and they are defined by their main sources of funding. The first mode is public financing, a system in which public funds—taxpayers' money—are provided to candidates who run for office. In 1971,

Congress passed the Federal Election Campaign Act (FECA), the first comprehensive campaign finance reform legislation in the United States. Congress authorized public financing for nominating presidential candidates when they amended the FECA in 1974 after the Watergate scandals, and the resulting Presidential Election Campaign Fund provides matching public funds to qualified candidates based on their records of donations from individual supporters (Briffault 2020). The main idea behind creating a public financing system for the presidential race was simple: to curb the influence of large and private contributions on the electoral process.

The public financing system played an important role in the nomination process of major political candidates from the 1976 presidential campaign onward. However, in 2008, Democratic presidential candidate Barack Obama announced that he would opt out of public financing as his campaign showed remarkable success in raising money. Because participating in public financing would impose a cap of $84.1 million on how much he could receive from private actors and how much he could spend on his general election campaign, Obama—who ultimately raised more than $750 million during his bid for the White House—chose to forgo public financing. No major party nominee has accepted public financing since 2008. The limited role of public financing in the United States implies that campaign finance through private actors has become the main source of financing for candidates and plays an important role in electoral success. To fully understand how campaign finance contributes to the current landscape of political representation, two key issues should be examined. First, we need to investigate who donates to campaigns. If donors and non-donors are significantly different in their political preferences and income levels as well as the types of candidates they prefer, the considerable influence of donors through campaign financing could generate a biased political system that tilts toward the donors' perspective. Second, we need to examine the motivation behind campaign contributions and whether campaign contributions facilitate donors' access to politicians and affect politicians' perceptions about public opinions and the types of policies that politicians enact.

Types of Donors

First, who donates to political campaigns? Broadly, there are two types of donors: individuals and groups. Individuals may make donations to candidates, political parties, and other political organizations, subject to some limitations. It is more complicated for groups to make campaign donations to candidates or parties. The Tillman Act of 1907 prohibited corporations and nationally chartered banks from making direct financial contributions to federal candidates. The Smith-Connally Act of 1943 and Taft-Hartley Act of 1947 extended the corporate ban to labor unions. However, in 1971 the FECA initiated fundamental changes in federal campaign finance laws and opened the door for groups to donate to political campaigns. The FECA mandated that organizations wishing to contribute to federal candidates and parties must create separate and segregated funds called Political Action Committees (PACs). Corporations and labor organizations are prohibited from making contributions to campaigns from their own treasury funds. However, PACs affiliated with corporations and labor organizations may raise voluntary donations from individuals, such as a corporate PAC raising money from its employees and a labor union PAC raising money from its members. For example, Google can contribute to candidates and parties as a company through its Google NetPAC and raises money from Google employees, but it cannot use money from the company's annual budget or revenues to support the Google NetPAC.

Contributions are subject to specific limits depending on donor types and recipient types. Figure 6.1 shows these specifications. An individual donor may contribute up to $2900 per election cycle to a campaign that a candidate organizes (*Candidate committee*) for the 2021–2022 election cycle. Individuals may also donate to PACs or party committees to support their political activities and the contribution limits are higher in this case. PACs may donate up to $5000 to a candidate's committee per cycle or $5000 per year to other PACs. PACs may also donate to party committees to support their activities, such as building party organizations and increasing election turnout.

Which type of donor plays a larger role in financing candidates? The left-hand panel in Fig. 6.2 shows the average candidate's fundraising portfolio (Barber and McCarty 2013). For all congressional candidates in each election cycle, the y-axis indicates the average percentage of three different sources

Donor		Recipient				
		Candidate committee	PAC† (SSF and nonconnected)	Party committee: state/district/local	Party committee: national	Additional national party committee accounts‡
	Individual	$2,900* per election	$5,000 per year	$10,000 per year (combined)	$36,500* per year	$109,500* per account, per year
	Candidate committee	$2,000 per election	$5,000 per year	Unlimited transfers	Unlimited transfers	
	PAC: multicandidate	$5,000 per election	$5,000 per year	$5,000 per year (combined)	$15,000 per year	$45,000 per account, per year
	PAC: nonmulticandidate	$2,900* per election	$5,000 per year	$10,000 per year (combined)	$36,500* per year	$109,500* per account, per year
	Party committee: state/district/local	$5,000 per election (combined)	$5,000 per year (combined)	Unlimited transfers	Unlimited transfers	
	Party committee: national	$5,000 per election**	$5,000 per year	Unlimited transfers	Unlimited transfers	

Indexed for inflation in odd-numbered years.

Fig. 6.1 Contribution limits for federal elections for 2021–2022 (Source: Federal Election Commission. Note: The numbers are based on the 2021–2022 election cycle. Some limits are subject to change, based on inflation)

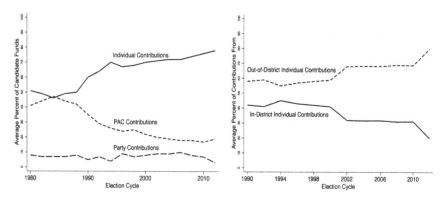

Fig. 6.2 Sources of congressional campaign funding, by type of donor and location (Source: Barber and McCarty, 2013)

in a fundraising portfolio. It is clear that, since the early 1990s, individual contributions have accounted for the greatest part of congressional candidates' fundraising portfolios. The same trend holds for Senate races and presidential campaigns.

Another interesting trend is shown in the right panel of Fig. 6.2. More than half of the contributions to candidates raised in congressional elections came from donors who lived outside the districts where the candidates were running for office. Donors who lived in big cities, such as New York City, Los Angeles, and Houston, donated heavily to political candidates across the nation. In the 2020 election cycle, Representative Alexandria Ocasio-Cortez of New York's 14th district received over $12 million in donations from people who lived outside of New York state; this accounted for more than 84 percent of her total campaign war chest. Less than 1 percent of Congresswoman Ocasio-Cortez's total contributions came from donors who lived in her district (Center for Responsive Politics 2021). This increasingly prominent role of out-of-district donors in financing campaigns raises a concern that politicians may become more responsive to the policy preferences of out-of-district donors. If out-of-district donors are more ideologically extreme than within-district donors, and out-of-district donors are especially vocal about partisan issues, such as abortion, a greater reliance on national donors could also lead to more polarized campaign platforms and legislative behaviors.

The Rise of Small Donors and Diversity in the Donor Class

Individual donors can be further divided into two categories depending on the dollar amount of their contributions. If an individual donor's aggregated contribution to a specific candidate or party committee in a given election cycle exceeds $200, it should be itemized by the recipient in their reporting to the Federal Election Commission (FEC) along with the donor's name, mailing

address, employer, occupation, the date of receipt and the size of the donation. Conventionally, contributors whose donations are itemized are called
'large donors.' Donors whose aggregated donation to a candidate or party
committee does not exceed $200, and, therefore, is not itemized, are referred
to as 'small donors.' In recent elections, the role of donors who make small
donations through the internet has received much attention, and candidates
often boast that their campaigns are supported by small donors. In the 2020
election, small donors played a prominent role in financing candidates. Republican Donald Trump raised 48.85 percent of his total campaign contributions
from small donors and small donors accounted for 38.94 percent of Democrat Joe Biden's campaign fundraising portfolio (Center for Responsive Politics
2021).

Large donations that are itemized with disclosed donor information give
more detailed information about the demographics of donors. Among those
who donated more than $200 in the 2020 election cycle, male donors
accounted for 55 percent of the total number of donors and 65 percent of
the total amount contributed. Female donors have increased their presence
over time. Whereas less than a quarter of donors who contributed more than
$200 in the 1990 election were women, that number rose to 45 percent in the
2020 election. During the 2020 presidential campaign, 48 percent of itemized
donations for Joe Biden and 36.6 percent of itemized donations for Donald
Trump came from female donors.

While female donors have made significant progress in their presence within
the donor class, the racial composition of donors has remained stable over
time with white donors being dominant. An analysis of itemized donations
shows that over 90 percent of donors are white, while only 67 percent of
the US voting age population is white (Grumbach and Sahn 2020). Although
Asians and Latinos have increased their participation in making contributions,
the total share of contributions from ethnic minorities for congressional and
presidential candidates is much smaller than their share of the US population.

Personal wealth is an important predictor as to whether an individual
contributes to political campaigns. Wealthy individuals participate extremely
actively in politics (Page et al. 2013) and the increased income inequality in
the United States has translated into political inequality. Although the number
of small donors has risen over time, a tiny fraction of donors from extremely
wealthy groups has increased their influence by spending large sums of money
on campaigns. In 1980, donations from individuals in the top 0.01 percent
of the income distribution among US adults accounted for 10 percent of
total campaign contributions. In 2018, donations from the wealthiest 0.01
percent of individuals made up over 45 percent of total campaign contributions (Database on Ideology, Money in Politics and Elections 2021). Overall,
the number of small donors and the diversity of the donor class have increased
over time, but a small fraction of wealthy donors still have a disproportionately
large presence in candidates' contribution portfolios.

PACs and Ideological Diversity

As the role of individual donors has increased in candidates' campaign financing, the role of PACs has decreased. But there are still many organizations and corporations that form PACs through which they donate to candidates, parties, and other PACs. Examples include the AT&T Inc PAC; the American Bankers Association PAC; and the Sheet Metal, Air, Rail, & Transportation Union PAC. In the 2020 election cycle, the National Association of Realtors (NAR) ranked at the top in terms of PAC spending by contributing $4 million to federal candidates. Of NAR's $4 million contribution, 52 percent went to Democratic candidates. NAR's contribution patterns show a partisan balance, but other PACs' contributions illustrate different scenarios. For example, the American Federation of Teachers Union PAC contributed $2.4 million in the 2020 election cycle and 99 percent of its contribution went to Democratic candidates. In contrast, the National Automobile Dealers Association also spent $2.4 million in the same election cycle but only 28 percent of their donations went to Democratic candidates (Center for Responsive Politics 2021).

PACs represent diverse interests and their contribution patterns are also diverse. Using information about the candidates to whom PACs and individuals donate, Bonica estimates the ideology of donors (Bonica 2013) and his work shows that there is substantial variation in donor ideologies. Individual donors are more ideologically extreme than PACs, and rarely split their donations between Democratic and Republican candidates. PACs associated with business interests show more moderate ideology than single-issue PACs, such as anti-abortion or gun-rights groups, but there is substantial variation among business-associated PACs. For example, the entertainment industry heavily donates to Democratic candidates, whereas the fossil fuel industry (oil, gas, and coal) mainly contributes to conservative candidates. Industries such as pharmaceuticals and finance show more bipartisan patterns of campaign donations.

Donors' Motivations

Why do individuals and groups donate to electoral campaigns and why do their donation patterns differ? Scholars have differentiated between the motivations of group donors and individual donors. The primary motivation for PACs is access to politicians. Corporations, trade associations, and other groups ultimately hope to influence policy outcomes and their campaign contributions are used as tools for gaining access to express their preferred policy positions to politicians. There is robust evidence that PACs' campaign contribution patterns follow the logic of access-seeking: PACs tend to contribute to incumbents, committee members who serve on the committees relevant to their interests, and majority party members who have strong agenda-setting power. For example, PACs formed by firms and associations in the finance industry donate more to politicians who serve on the House Financial Services Committee and Senate Finance Committee, which have direct jurisdiction over financial regulations. Politicians grant more access to donors than non-donors (Kalla and Broockman 2016) and PACs try to buy politicians' time through campaign contributions so legislators will prioritize the issues that PACs care about (Hall and Wayman 1990).

Individual donors demonstrate some motivational patterns that differ from those of group donors. Some scholars emphasize that individuals are motivated to contribute to campaigns by consumption value, which implies that individuals enjoy benefits from participating in the political process without expecting a return from politicians they support (Ansolabehere et al. 2003). Ideology is another factor cited as a motivation for individuals' donations. Studies show that a candidate's ideology is an important factor for many individual donors and individuals holding more extreme ideologies assign more weight to ideology than other factors when they decide to donate. In contrast to PAC donors, individual donors care less about the incumbency status or committee assignment of legislators when they choose to donate.

Given that individual donors show more ideological extremism, scholars have explored whether a larger role by individual donors, as opposed to PACS, is associated with electing more extreme candidates. Using variations in contribution limits imposed on individual and group donors at the state level, Barber (2016) shows that the increasing share of candidates' campaign money derived from individuals as opposed to PAC contributions leads to electing more extreme candidates. A recent surge in the number of small donors contributing to campaign fundraising through the internet has augmented the role of individuals financing political candidates. Although calls for eliminating the role of large money and business interests in politics often accompany a proposal to expand the role for small donors, empirical evidence suggests that a larger role for small donors in financing candidates' campaigns could lead to selection of more extreme candidates and polarization (Pildes 2020).

Citizens United and the Rise of Super PACs

Another noticeable trend in campaign finance is the rapidly increasing number of independent expenditures. An independent expenditure differs from a campaign contribution in the sense that it does not involve a direct transfer of money to candidates and parties. But individuals and groups can employ an independent expenditure to support or oppose specific candidates by running their own advertisements on various media platforms, such as TV and social media.

What types of groups engage in independent expenditure and what regulations apply to it? To understand the current practice of independent expenditure, it is important to understand how campaign finance laws have evolved over time. In 1974, immediately after comprehensive amendments to the FECA were passed in Congress, challenges were brought to the Supreme

Court regarding regulations on contribution and expenditure limits. The Supreme Court upheld the contribution limits as a safeguard for the integrity of elections, but the Court overturned the expenditure limits—the amount each campaign and party could spend—citing that the expenditure limits could restrict political speech. The Court's ruling in 1976 in *Buckley v. Valeo* established the idea that money counts as speech (Kang 2012). The Supreme Court's ruling that equates campaign spending with the first amendment constitutional right of free speech significantly limits the government's capacity to reform campaign finance since the constitutionality of the provisions in the reform agendas can be challenged easily through the judicial process. This, in turn, has produced the very complex and convoluted campaign finance systems in the United States.

Another major reform in campaign finance regulation was introduced in 2002 when two senators, John McCain and Russell Feingold, introduced the Bipartisan Campaign Reform Act (BCRA). The BCRA prohibited corporations and labor unions from using monies from their general treasuries for independent expenditures on political communications. The BCRA also prohibited corporations and labor unions from airing ads that explicitly supported or opposed a specific candidate within 30 days of a primary election or 60 days of a general election (activities referred to as 'electioneering communications'). Citizens United Inc., a conservative non-profit organization, sued the FEC during the 2008 presidential election cycle, arguing that the BCRA regulation was an unconstitutional burden on free speech.

In January 2010, the Supreme Court struck down BCRA's provision on electioneering communications, mentioning that the BCRA provisions discriminated against some individuals and groups by limiting their political speech. The *Citizens United v. FEC* decision did not change the regulations concerning how much corporations and unions could contribute directly to candidates and parties and which sources of funding they needed to use. However, the decision did make a change to allow corporations and labor unions to use their general funds to finance independent expenditures. Also, they are allowed to air advertisements that explicitly urge election or defeat of a candidate at any time.

After the ruling, a new kind of PAC—a Super PAC—that is exclusively devoted to independent expenditure has emerged. Super PACs cannot make direct contributions to candidates or parties. However, unlike traditional PACs, there is no limit on the size of donations that individuals and groups can contribute to Super PACs. Super PACs must disclose the names of their donors to the FEC but they can engage in an unlimited amount of independent spending. The major sponsors of Super PACs have been wealthy individuals. Since the *Citizens United* decision in 2010, the number of Super PACs has exploded and the dollar amount of independent expenditure has increased rapidly.

Although the rapid creation of Super PACs and their large expenditures are a driving force making elections more expensive in recent years, understanding Super PACs' impact on electoral politics requires further research. On one hand, Super PACs' spending on campaign advertisements could increase voters' knowledge about candidates, even though most of the ads are negative. Super PACs also make elections more competitive by reducing the financial advantages that incumbent politicians enjoy compared to their challengers. On the other hand, Super PACs provide another venue for a small group of wealthy individuals and well-resourced groups with highly polarized views to influence the political process. The ability to raise money from many individuals and groups during political campaigns provides a signal about a candidate's quality and competitiveness. However, if Super PACs substitute for candidates' traditional fundraising tasks, it suggests that those who finance Super PACs may have a disproportionate advantage in the selection of winning candidates.

Lobbying and Money in Policymaking

Lobbying is another important channel through which interest groups interact with policymakers in American politics. While the public holds skeptical and negative views about lobbying and lobbyists, lobbying serves as one of the key channels through which individuals and groups exercise their right to petition the government (Allard 2008). Although there are different perceptions about what constitutes lobbying activities, the Lobbying Disclosure Act of 1995 (LDA), which regulates lobbying activities by domestic interest groups, defines lobbying contacts as 'any oral or written communication to an executive or a legislative branch official that is made on behalf of a client with regard to the formation, modification, or adoption of federal legislation, rule, regulation, policy, or the nomination or confirmation of a person for a position of the United States government.'

Lobbying activities in the United States are extensive. Figure 6.3 presents the amount of total spending on federal lobbying recorded under the LDA for the period 1999–2019. Lobbying spending is divided into two types: expenditures by in-house lobbyists who are a group's employees and work in the group's lobbying arm within the organization (*In-House*), and expenditures by contracted lobbyists who work at lobbying firms (*Contract*). Both types of lobbying expenditures increased steadily until 2010 and, since then, almost $4 billion on average is spent on lobbying the federal government each year.

The numbers presented in Fig. 6.3 may underestimate how much money is actually spent on lobbying because the statutory definition of a lobbyist in the LDA and the subsequent reform bill, the Honest Leadership and Open Government Act passed in 2017, gives ample room for interpretation (Cain and Drutman 2014). The LDA defines a lobbyist as any individual (1) who is either employed by a client, (2) whose service includes more than one lobbying contact, and (3) whose lobbying activities constitute 20 percent

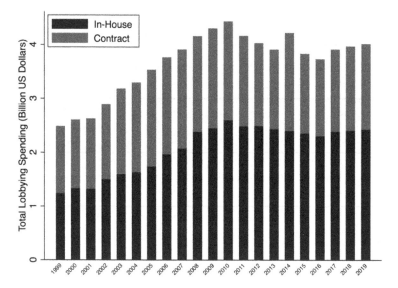

Fig. 6.3 Lobbying spending, 1999–2019 (Source: https://www.Lobbyview.org. Note: Numbers are inflation adjusted, in 2020 dollars)

or more of his or her time in service in a given quarter. Because lobbyists themselves determine whether they are required to register under the LDA, a significant number of individuals who carry out lobbying services are unregistered (Thomas and LaPira 2017).

There are over 10,000 lobbyists registered under the LDA every year. Lobbying reports most often cite budgetary issues as the subject of their lobbying activities followed by taxation, health, defense, and transportation. Among various interest groups who engage in lobbying activities, firms and business interests are ranked at the top in terms of lobbying spending and their expenditures on lobbying easily exceed their spending on campaign contributions. Other types of interest groups also have steadily increased their participation in the lobbying process; examples include universities, state and local governments, and foreign governments and businesses.

Theories of Lobbying

Why do groups spend copious amounts of their resources to lobby policymakers? There are three branches of theory that broadly categorize the motivations for lobbying. First, the exchange theory of lobbying argues that groups lobby to buy legislators' votes. Groups make campaign contributions to legislators and legislators deliver policy favors. Under this framework, lobbyists are passive agents who facilitate those exchanges through lobbying. If vote-buying is a key motivation for lobbying, groups need to target undecided legislators to maximize their utility. However, it is often observed that interest groups contribute to politicians who already agree with their policy preferences; thus, their votes are already secured in favor of the groups' preference.

The second theory of lobbying argues that lobbying aims to transmit information from interest groups to legislators. Groups have private information about how government policies would affect their interests and they attempt to convey this private information to persuade legislators. Politicians are generalists rather than experts on every issue, and therefore, they should be educated by various individuals and groups to produce informed policies. Interest groups can also transmit information on the political consequences of a politician's vote on a specific policy. Although the informational theory of lobbying is widely studied, some raise questions about its core argument. For example, there are sources other than a lobbying channel through which legislators can learn about the consequences of certain policies and public opinions. Also lobbying groups often contact politicians who are already the groups' closest allies and need the least persuasion to support their interests.

The third theory defines lobbying as legislative subsidies (Hall and Deardorff 2006). Based on the fact that lobbyists contact their allies in Congress, the legislative subsidy theory of lobbying argues that groups provide resources—policy information and legislative support—to their allies in Congress. The goal of lobbying is not to change legislators' minds. Instead, lobbying aids legislators who share preferences with groups to advance bills and agendas that matter to those groups. For example, the National Rifle Association (NRA) lobbies members of Congress who already agree with the group's position on gun rights. The NRA provides information about public opinion on gun-related issues or memos that summarize current gun-related issues to their allied politicians so the politicians can easily advance legislation that the NRA prefers or block advancement of legislative agendas that the NRA opposes.

Lobbying Targets

Theories of lobbying, and most media attention to lobbying, focuses on legislative lobbying: contacting politicians. However, a close examination of lobbying activities reveals that targets of lobbying are not limited to the legislative branch. Lobbying on a specific bill continues even after a bill becomes law and this 'ex post' lobbying, which targets specific provisions in the rules, demonstrates the importance of bureaucrats in implementing policies (You 2017). For example, in the aftermath of the 2008 financial crisis, Congress passed the Dodd-Frank Wall Street Reform and Consumer Protection Act (Dodd-Frank Act). Although the statute was 848 pages long, many important details were omitted and the statute mandated that federal agencies, such as the Securities and Exchange Commission (SEC), promulgate more than 300 rules to implement the Dodd-Frank Act.

During the rulemaking process, federal agencies invite individuals and groups to submit written comments containing their opinions to the agency formulating the rules. This is called the 'notice-and-comment' process. Federal agencies may respond to specific comments or incorporate the submitted comments in their final rulemaking. The bureaucratic rulemaking process provides another venue where groups influence government policies. From the passage of the Dodd-Frank Act of 2010 in Congress to the end of 2014, 2337 organizations submitted a total of 4405 comments on the 37 rules promulgated by the SEC (Ban and You 2019). The types of groups that engaged most frequently in the rulemaking process are corporations and trade associations, such as the Securities Industry and Financial Markets Association, which represents business interests.

Interest groups also actively lobby the judicial branch, especially when it concerns Supreme Court nominations. Some nominations for the Supreme Court's associate justice positions were politically contentious, such as President Reagan's nomination of Judge Robert Bork in 1987 or President Trump's nomination of Brett Kavanaugh in 2018. There is substantial group involvement in the nomination process to oppose or support these nominations. The number of groups involved in the Supreme Court nomination process has increased over time and the most active participants changed from groups such as the American Bar Association or labor unions to groups focusing on identity issues such as the National Association for the Advancement of Colored People (Cameron et al. 2020).

Role of Lobbyists and the Revolving-Door Phenomenon

Lobbyists, as intermediaries between interest groups and policymakers, play an important role in the process of lobbying and—despite the public's cynical views about lobbying as a profession—becoming a lobbyist has been one of the most popular options for former politicians and congressional staffers in their post-government careers. For instance, 26 out of 44 former members of Congress who served in the 115th Congress (which ended January 2, 2019) and left for jobs in the private sector became lobbyists in lobbying firms (Public Citizen). Revolving-door lobbyists—those who were government employees before moving to the lobbying industry—are paid better and receive the most media attention in the profession because prominent corporations and groups recruit them as their lobbyists. As the revolving-door phenomenon occurs more frequently, there is a growing concern that it could give a disproportionate advantage in the policymaking process to groups that can afford to hire revolving-door lobbyists.

Why are revolving-door lobbyists paid more than those without prior government service and why do groups hire them to represent their interests? There are two explanations for the wage premiums that revolving-door lobbyists enjoy. The first view considers revolving-door lobbyists as experts on issues and political procedures. Through work experience in government, these lobbyists accumulated knowledge on specific issues that may require technical information and complex policymaking processes. The second view argues that the main asset revolving-door lobbyists possess is not expertise on issues but connections they formed with politicians and other policymakers while they worked in government. Studies show that lobbyists' connections to politicians mainly determine the issues on which lobbyists work and their lobbying revenues (Blanes i Vidal et al. 2012; Bertrand et al. 2014). These results do not mean that lobbyists' issue expertise and institutional knowledge do not matter. Lobbyists who have personal connections to politicians may know the politicians' legislative priorities, and therefore may provide more tailored information to those politicians or screen the merits of clients who request access to the politicians whose time and resources are constrained. As the revolving-door phenomenon has expanded to bureaucrats moving into and out of government service, the role that prior employment in government plays in the lobbying process and the potential biases that can occur in policy outcomes by increasing numbers of revolving-door lobbyists require further research.

CONSEQUENCES OF UNEQUAL REPRESENTATION

Through campaign contributions and lobbying, interest groups that are active in politics have the opportunity to deliver their policy preferences and opinions to politicians and their staff members. However, if donors and lobbying groups hold policy preferences that differ sufficiently from those of ordinary citizens, frequent interactions with these interest groups and donors could influence politicians' understanding of their constituents' policy preferences and overshadow information reflecting the opinions that the majority of their constituents hold.

A recent study that surveyed state legislators and their constituents shows that politicians have consistent bias in their perceptions of constituents' policy preferences (Broockman and Skovron 2018). For example, in 2014, 84.3 percent of the public surveyed supported background checks prior to gun purchases. However, politicians significantly underestimated how much public support exists for universal background checks: on average, politicians assumed only 48.5 percent of the public support background checks. This suggests a significant misperception about the degree of public support for tightening regulations on purchasing guns. These misperceptions are also found in legislative staffers. Senior congressional staffers who have more frequent contacts with corporate donors hold more misperceptions about constituent preferences. The mismatch between actual and perceived constituency preferences is smaller if a member's office has more contact with groups that represent the mass public (Hertel-Fernandez et al. 2019).

A functioning democracy requires representation of diverse views to inform the government's decision-making process. The types of individuals and groups with whom politicians have most frequent contact can influence how accurately politicians perceive public opinions on most pressing issues that society needs to address, and campaign contributions and lobbying have profound impact on which individuals and groups have access to politicians. The tools that were designed to deliver opinions from diverse groups and individuals to politicians through the electoral process and policymaking in American democracy have, ironically, reinforced the unequal power and representation that individuals and groups experience in society. Although Madison's premise of the pluralism of diverse groups competing to influence political outcomes has been realized to some extent, a small fraction of individuals and groups have much louder voices than others. Each election cycle breaks the previous record of being the most expensive election in US history and lobbying has become an indispensable means for many powerful groups and large corporations in the political process. Increasing income inequality in the United States will give increasing advantages to wealthy individuals and well-resourced groups to exercise their political power through the role of money in American politics.

References

Allard, N. 2008. Lobbying is an Honorable Profession: The Right To Petition and The Competition To Be Right. *Stanford Law Review* 19 (1): 23–68.

Ansolabehere, S., J. de Figueiredo, and J. Snyder. 2003. Why is There So Little Money in U.S. Politics. *Journal of Economic Perspectives* 17 (1): 105–103.

Ban, P., and H. You. 2019. Presence and Influence in Lobbying: Evidence from Dodd-Frank. *Business and Politics* 21 (2): 267–295.

Barber, M. 2016. Ideological Donors, Contribution Limits, and the Polarization of American Legislatures. *Journal of Politics* 78 (1): 296–310.

Barber, M., and N. McCarty. 2013. *Causes and Consequences of Polarization*. American Political Science Association: Task Force Report.

Bertrand, M., M. Bombardini, and F. Trebbi. 2014. Is It Whom You Know or What You Know? An Empirical Assessment of the Lobbying Process. *American Economic Review* 104 (12): 3885–3920.

Blanes i Vidal, J., M. Draca, and C. Fons-Rosen. 2012. Revolving Door Lobbyists. *American Economic Review* 102 (7): 3731–3748.

Bonica, A. 2013. Ideology and Interests in the Political Marketplace. *American Journal of Political Science* 57: 294–311.

Briffault, R. 2020. A Better Financing System? The Death – and Possible Rebirth – of the Presidential Nomination Public Financing Program. In *The Best Candidate: Presidential Nomination in Polarized Times*, ed. Mazo, E., and M. Dimino. Cambridge University Press.

Broockman, D., and C. Skovron. 2018. Bias in Perceptions of Public Opinion among Political Elites. *American Political Science Review* 112 (3): 542–563.

Cain, B., and L. Drutman. 2014. Congressional Staff and the Revolving Door: The Impact of Regulatory Change. *Election Law Journal* 13 (1): 27–44.

Cameron, C., C. Gray, J. Kastellec, and J. Park. 2020. From Textbook Pluralism to Modern Hyperpluralism. *Journal of Law and Courts* 8 (2): 301–332.

Center for Responsive Politics. 2021. Accessed 01 Feb 2021 https://.opensecrets.org.

Database on Ideology, Money in Politics and Elections. 2021. Accessed 01 Mar 2021 https://data.stanford.edu/dime.

Grumbach, J., and A. Sahn. 2020. Race and Representation in Campaign Finance. *American Political Science Review* 114 (1): 206–221.

Hall, R., and A. Deardorff. 2006. Lobbying as Legislative Subsidy. *American Political Science Review* 100 (1): 69–84.

Hall, R., and F. Wayman. 1990. Buying Time: Moneyed Interests and the Mobilization of Bias in Congressional Committees. *American Political Science Review* 84 (3): 797–820.

Hertel-Fernandez, A., M. Mildenberger, and L. Stokes. 2019. Legislative Staff and Representation in Congress. *American Political Science Review* 113 (1): 1–18.

Kalla, J., and D. Broockman. 2016. Campaign Contributions Facilitate Access to Congressional Officials: A Randomized Field Experiment. *American Journal of Political Science* 60 (3): 545–558.

Kang, M. 2012. The End of Campaign Finance Law. *Virginia Law Review* 98 (1): 1–65.

Page, B., L. Bartels, and J. Seawright. 2013. Democracy and the Policy Preference of Wealthy Americans. *Perspectives on Politics* 11 (1): 51–73.

Pildes, R. 2020. Participation and Polarization. *Journal of Constitutional Law* 22 (2): 341–408.

Schlozman, K., S. Verba, and H. Brady. 2012. *The Unheavenly Chorus: Unequal Political Voice and the Broken Promise of American Democracy*. Princeton, N.J.: Princeton University Press.

Thomas, H., and T. LaPira. 2017. How Many Lobbyists are in Washington? Shadow Lobbying and the Gray Market for Policy Advocacy. *Interest Groups & Advocacy* 6: 199–214.

You, H. 2017. Ex Post Lobbying. *Journal of Politics* 79 (4): 1162–1176.

Further Reading

For those who are interested in the ideas behind campaign finance reform, La Raja and Schaffner's *Campaign Finance and Political Polarization* (2015, Ann Arbor: University of Michigan Press) provides a comprehensive account of the history of campaign finance in the United States and the concerns about ideas behind candidate-centered as opposed to party-centered campaign funding. Primo and Milyo's *Campaign Finance & American Democracy: What the Public Really Thinks and Why It Matters* (2020, Chicago: University of Chicago Press) provides an excellent survey on how public and political elites perceive campaign finance regulations and whether campaign finance reforms change public opinion about the quality of American democracy. An overview of the changes in campaign finance after the *Citizens United* ruling, such as the birth of Super PACs and legal constraints on the issue of coordination between Super PACs and candidates, can be found in Briffault's 'Super PACs' (2011, *Minnesota Law Review* 96: 1644) and Briffault's 'Coordination Reconsidered' (2013, *Columbia Law Review* 113: 88).

There are numerous studies that examine the motivations and behaviors of different kinds of donors. For access-seeking PACs, Fouirnaies and

Hall's 'How Do Interest Groups Seek Access to Committees' (2018, *American Journal of Political Science* 62.1: 132–147) examines how PACs change their donation patterns depending on politicians' congressional committee assignments. Li's 'How Internal Constraints Shape Interest Group Activities: Evidence from Access-Seeking PACs' (2018, *American Political Science Review* 112.4: 792–808) shows how donors to PACs strategically respond to donating behaviors of PACs. Barber, Canes-Wrone, and Thrower's 'Ideologically Sophisticated Donors: Which Candidates Do Individuals Contributors Finance?' (2017, *American Journal of Political Science* 61.2: 271–288) looks at how the ideological and policy positions of candidates affect individual donors' decisions to contribute. On the topic of the geography of donors, Gimpel, Lee, and Kaminski's 'The Political Geography of Campaign Contributions in American Politics' (2006, *Journal of Politics* 68.3: 626–639) and Gimpel, Lee, and Pearson-Merkowitz's 'The Check Is in the Mail: Interdistrict Funding Flows in Congressional Elections' (2008, *American Journal of Political Science* 52.2: 373–394) present excellent findings about how contributions from out-of-district donors shape the nomination process in the United States.

For lobbying, Drutman's *The Business of America is Lobbying: How Corporations Became Politicized and Politics Became More Corporate* (2015, New York: Oxford University Press) provides an excellent survey on the history of corporate lobbying and the reasons behind the rise of the political engagement of business interests. There are many papers that investigate the lobbying patterns of non-business interests. de Figueiredo and Silverman's 'Academic Earmarks and the Return to Lobbying' (2006, *The Journal of Law and Economics* 49.2: 597–625) examine how lobbying spending by universities affects academic earmarks. Goldstein and You's 'Cities as Lobbyists' (2017, *American Journal of Political Science* 61.4: 864–876) looks at lobbying activities of local governments at the federal level and Payson's 'Cities in the Statehouse: How Local Governments Use Lobbyists to Secure State Funding' (2020, *Journal of Politics* 82.2: 403–417) studies local governments' lobbying engagement at the state level.

CHAPTER 7

The Media and Politics

Philip John Davies

By the time Donald Trump entered the White House his impact on the media and the development of political communication in the US was already widely recognized. Trump's exceptional appetite for social media, especially Twitter, his apparently spontaneous and occasionally transgressive comments on policy, politics and society, his combative and often tasteless outbursts, and his incitements to violence against journalists and others who criticized him all ensured that his agenda was front and center across media platforms, regardless of the misinformation and vulgarity in many of his messages. In the words of Ezra Klein (**2020**), 'if it outrages, it leads', and Trump delivered outrage—his own, his supporters' and his critics'—regularly and with an unrivaled talent for engaging media attention.

Shifts in the landscapes both of political media and political ideology in the US may have created a unique opportunity for Donald Trump to seize the Republican nomination and then the presidency. Theda Skocpol sketched a twenty-first century history in which ultra-free-market political donors such as the Koch brothers and a GOP leadership that regularly mobilized voters with anti-immigrant and racially charged tropes stirred nativist populism within angry and resentful middle-class groups, shifting the Republican Party politically to the right. According to Skocpol (**2016**), 'the GOP became ripe for a Trump-style hostile takeover'.

P. J. Davies (✉)
Faculty of Business and Law, De Montfort University, Leicester, UK
e-mail: pjd@dmu.ac.uk

© The Author(s), under exclusive license to Springer Nature Switzerland AG 2022
G. Peele et al. (eds.), *Developments in American Politics 9*,
https://doi.org/10.1007/978-3-030-89740-6_7

This ideological shift did not go unresisted, but the communications tools available in society have also changed significantly. The range of media outlets for political information, debate, argument and assertion have multiplied, and the ability to use these emerging channels would be critical. Trump displayed media skills and charisma that appealed to a significant portion of Republican-leaning voters. Media vehicles that allowed increased targeting and broader unmediated access provided the means to reach those audiences most receptive to his message.

As the only president not previously to have served in any political or military role, Trump's rise to prominence was closely tied to his media presence. Most consistently, Trump's fourteen seasons from 2004 to 2015 starring in *The Apprentice* provided exposure and media experience. But Trump had been busy self-promoting on the American media scene for decades. From the 1980s he had taken multiple opportunities to appear, usually in a cameo role, in television series as well as documentary and entertainment films. The first of many Trump appearances in the *Doonesbury* cartoon series came in September 1987, when it was rumoured he might be contemplating a challenge for the presidency (Trudeau 2016). During the 2016 campaign there was talk of launching a Trump-branded television network, with Jared Kushner (Trump's son-in-law) exploring the idea, perhaps as part of the family's portfolio of business ventures. Top aides in the Trump campaign referred to the possibility that this kind of venture could help bolster Trump's political agenda (Haberman and Steel 2016).

The media has often enjoyed dealing with Donald Trump. His lifestyle of self-promotion and excess, his marriages to glamorous women, speculation over his wealth and his business deals all provided good copy. In 1989 an article in the *Chicago Tribune* tagged him 'The People's Billionaire' (Plaskin 1989). As his political ambitions shifted to the core of the Trump offer, verbal attacks on the mainstream media, or the 'lamestream media', became an integral part of the political rhetoric, and relations between Trump and the media became more strained.

Campaigning is only a partial test of the skills best suited to office holding. Presidents bring their own experience and expertise to the White House, but they also adapt, change and learn once in office. In 2017 there seemed a possibility that President Trump's relationship with the media might moderate, converging to a recognizable presidential norm. Likewise, Republicans unhappy with Trump's capture of the Party felt that, once in office, he might be more receptive to the benefits of their influence. Skocpol (2016) quotes a GOP voice opining that 'You're better off riding the beast than trying to ignore it'.

Any thoughts that President Trump would be more politically malleable once in office were challenged by an inaugural speech in which he promised to take the nation from 'American carnage' to 'America First,' and 'no longer accept politicians who are all talk and no action, constantly complaining but never doing anything about it.' Thoughts that having the intermediary of a

White House Press Office might smooth the President's relationship with the media faltered at the first appearance by White House Press Secretary Sean Spicer, where he falsely accused the media of minimizing the size of Trump's inaugural crowd. The President, meanwhile, had told an audience at the CIA headquarters that the news networks' reporting had been a lie, 'And I think they're going to pay a big price' (Hunt 2017).

Without the reliable or consistent support of a clear majority of the US electorate the Republican Party nevertheless accomplished significant political success in the early decades of the twenty-first century. The party's regionally based popularity, especially in medium sized states, combined with US constitutional provisions designed originally to avoid domination by the large states, magnified Republican potential in the US Senate and in the Electoral College, and provided the opportunity to gerrymander constituencies in the US House of Representatives and in state legislatures. As the signs increased that a diverse Democratic voting coalition might be emerging that would threaten Republican gains, the party leadership showed a natural inclination to maximize their chances to retain power: a willingness to use any technical advantages offered within the electoral system, including the exploitation of voter suppression methods.

Many Republican leaders who did not initially welcome Donald Trump's launch into presidential politics saw the benefits brought to the party's campaigns by his uninhibited populism and skill in connecting directly with Republican-leaning voters through the expanding array of lightly regulated media. His expertise in exploiting these media links to communicate with supporters also emphasized the potential primary election threat to their own political futures if they failed to keep in step. This chapter examines the political communication skills that Trump brought to Washington during his administration, and the ways those skills interacted with a changed landscape of media channels. The White House's media management during the coronavirus pandemic provides a case study of the classic Trumpian strategy of distraction. The over-optimistic predictions that the epidemic would be brief and small in impact, the scapegoating of China, the World Health Organization and various Democratic states, the advocacy of unverified treatments, and the negative portrayal of social distancing and mask wearing, all contributed to a political narrative that the coronavirus emergency was as an opportunity for unbridled government over-regulation, rather than a clear but catastrophic medical emergency. This in turn contributed to public confusion regarding the scientific evidence and undermined the governmental response to the pandemic. These misleading messages sit comfortably with consistent attacks by President Trump on the believability of any media source that questioned his actions, attacks that steadily elevated to underpin the Trump team's 'Big Lie' that the 2020 election was stolen and should be overturned, perhaps even to the point of violent insurrection.

The Trump Effect

In Donald Trump's bestselling book, *The Art of the Deal*, ghost writer Tony Schwartz invented the term 'truthful hyperbole' to encompass the cavalier exaggerations, misstatements and falsehoods habitually deployed in the then businessman's public communications (Trump and Schwartz 1987). Schwartz portrayed this as 'an innocent form of exaggeration—and … a very effective form of promotion.' Almost thirty years later in an interview prompted by Trump's political success, Schwartz made it clear that his opinion had changed: '"Truthful hyperbole" is a contradiction in terms. It's a way of saying, "It's a lie, but who cares?"' (Mayer 2016). 'The Art of the Lie' might have been a less attractive title for the book, but a more accurate indication of the media strategy that Trump would adopt during his administration.

Trump imported his rhetorical style into politics, despite some critics' expectation that his bombastic tone and aggressive language would not retain traction. Trump especially valued those in his team of advisers and counsellors who would defend his instinct to double down when challenged. Former Trump Campaign Manager and Presidential Counsellor Kellyanne Conway was unapologetic in defending the Trump style of political communications when, at the 2017 quadrennial Kennedy School Campaign Managers conference, she opined that Trump's supporters vote 'on things that affect them, not just things that offend them' (Keith 2016).

Conway also provided an early example of the Trump White House team's approach to media communications in January 2017, when on NBC's *Meet The Press* she defended the White House's demonstrably false claims about the size of the inauguration crowd as 'alternative facts'. Challenged by NBC's Chuck Todd saying, 'Alternative facts are not facts; they're falsehoods', Conway remained unmoved, later explaining, but hardly clarifying, her use of the phrase as meaning 'additional facts and alternative information … Two plus two is four. Three plus one is four. Partly cloudy, partly sunny. Glass half full, glass half empty. Those are alternative facts' (Blake 2017).

So surprised was the media establishment by the boldness of the Trump onslaught on what they perceived as the boundaries of the inflationary language normally expected from an administration that several attempts were made to record the misleading, mistaken and false statements. *The Washington Post* reported that 30,573 false or misleading claims had been made by President Trump during his four-year term. This stream of untruths and misdirections accelerated in the final year of the administration as Trump and his team delivered media messaging that consistently sought to undermine public trust in the reliability of major media outlets, to support the falsehood that the Black Lives Matter movement constituted an imminent violent threat to the nation, to dismiss the threat posed by the coronavirus pandemic and, perhaps most significantly, to erode public faith in the ability of the US system to deliver a fair and accurate result in the 2020 presidential election (Kessler 2021).

The traditional media appeared to consider this enormous deployment of misinformation as much more significant than did Trump's supporters. Many of the claims—made variously on Twitter and disseminated to the public through subsequent media coverage, at political rallies that gave the four-year Trump administration the appearance of a continuous election campaign, and at press conferences and other communications formats—were on matters not particularly significant to Trump-leaning voters.

Roderick Hart's research provides some support for Kellyanne Conway's 'alternative facts' argument, suggesting that Trump's supporters sifted through the political rhetoric for their truth, reacting to his accessible narrative of indignation on their behalf at feeling trapped, besieged and weary of policy and journalism that ignored the threats to their lifestyles. Trump's trademark style using small words, limited vocabulary and repeated narratives was delivered with emotion, anger, passion, energy and relentlessness. It spoke to voters' feelings that they were losing out to other groups in a changing world, and that Trump, who regularly told them how wonderful they were and how ill-served, understood their frustration and offered a different future.

The traditional media's interest in finding fault with the President's statements only emphasized the misfit between their journalistic output and the audience of Trump-leaning voters. Trump supporters were energized to find a leader willing to be transgressive on their behalf. The media criticism of Trump's utterances provided ammunition and opportunity for the President's attacks on the media as, among other things, incompetent, biased, failing and unpatriotic. A sense of anger widespread among conservatives in the electorate linked them to Trump, his rhetoric and his disdain for mainstream media. In that atmosphere the audiences attracted to the expanding spectrum of dedicatedly conservative media outlets grew.

Former Republican Governor of Massachusetts, Bill Weld, making a symbolic challenge for the Party's 2020 presidential nomination, referred in his campaign appearances to the frisson of excitement when a public figure pushes the boundaries of acceptable behavior in pursuit of objectives that an audience shares. This, in Weld's view, was understandable but did not excuse the president's role in eroding trust between the electorate, officeholders and the media. As George Packer (2021: 10) put it, 'To [Trump's] supporters, his shamelessness became a badge of honesty and strength. They grasped the message that they, too, could say whatever they wanted without apology'.

THE MEDIA AND THE MESSAGE

There has been a proliferation of news sources in the US while the media industry has simultaneously been losing substantial numbers of newsroom professionals. Consumption of print has declined most sharply, with a stark impact on the industry. Newspaper newsroom employment fell by 51 percent between 2008 and 2019, with 36,000 jobs lost. Over the same period radio newsrooms shed over 1000 staff, a fall of 23 percent. TV news-rooms (including cable) saw a modest five percent growth to just under 33,000 employees. Meanwhile digital newsrooms more than doubled in size, from 7400 employees to 16,090. Overall aggregate newsroom employment declined by 23 percent in this period while shifting especially sharply away from print and radio and toward digital sources (Grieco 2020).

Calculating accurately the American public's use of various news sources has become more complex with the emergence and recognition of sources beyond traditional print, broadcast TV and radio. The dominance of these formats has been upended by the spread of internet sources. In 1990 the internet was still predominantly a resource for research scientists, with a market penetration of about one percent. By 2018 it was used by 87 percent of the US population (Roach 2021).

Internet news content is sometimes generated by traditional news providers, but also offers the opportunity for multiple independent providers to create news and news-like commentary. Platforms created as entertainment providers have sometimes evolved to deliver this content. Delivery may be through personal computers, TV apps, laptops, smartphones, smartwatches and other portable devices. There are few if any measurement techniques that can accurately track news consumption, exposure to news or the intensity with which people consume news from these various sources (Barthel et al. 2020).

News consumers rarely rely on a single source, but they have their favorites. These favorites are changing as the spectrum of sources expands, and they vary between different demographic groups. A survey conducted shortly before the 2020 US elections found just over half (52 percent) of respondents preferred to receive news on digital platforms, with 86 percent getting news in that format at least sometimes. The figures for television were lower at 35 percent and 68 percent respectively, with radio (seven percent and 50 percent) and print (five percent and 32 percent) trailing as favorite sources, but still showing strongly as sources consulted occasionally. Digital sources appealed more to young voters (71 percent of 18–29 year-olds) than older ones (48 percent of over 65s), while those under thirty made much less use of television news (16 percent) than those over 65 (68 percent). The over 65s were the only group regularly to favor print (25 percent), a source that appears to have almost been eclipsed among the under 50s of whom less than four percent report frequent use of print for news (Shearer 2021).

Most Americans claim a considerable interest in the news, with almost two-thirds reporting that they look at the news several times daily, and four-in-ten claiming to follow stories in-depth at least once a day. Other surveys suggest that these self-reported figures are perhaps exaggerated. A recent conference report claimed that the proportion of the public regularly consuming news could be as low as ten percent, the same proportion of the public that US journalists believe read deeply into the details of stories (Media Insight Project 2018; Arroyo 2021).

Research conducted in the run up to the 2020 election found the political polarization of the American electorate was reflected in the mistrust that ideologically different groups felt toward different media outlets. Democrats expressed trust in a larger range of news sources than Republicans, but overall Democrats and Republicans were found to be living in separate media worlds. Conservative Republicans and liberal Democrats were especially distanced. Fox News, and radio hosts Sean Hannity and the late Rush Limbaugh were among the top five sources trusted by conservative Republicans and the top five distrusted by liberal Democrats. Inversely CNN, the *New York Times* and NBC News were in both liberal Democrats' top five trusted and conservative Republicans' top five distrusted sources. The constrained media bubbles trusted by competing political groups serve to eliminate challenges to the received wisdoms of those groups and reinforce antagonisms, especially between the most ideologically committed party political elements (Jurkowitz et al. 2020).

There has also been an increasing use of social media as a source for political news, with eighteen percent of all respondents reporting it as their primary source. Among those naming social media as their most likely source of political news 48 percent are in the 18–29 age group and a further 40 percent are aged 30–49. A survey of those most dependent on social media for their political news found them 'less aware and knowledgeable about a wide range of events and issues in the news'. This group was also more likely to have come across false or unproven claims, including conspiracy theories claiming that the Covid-19 pandemic was intentionally planned by powerful people. Furthermore, this group was less likely to express concern about the impact of false news (Mitchell et al. 2020).

While the media environment of US politics has expanded in recent years to offer many alternative sources and delivery methods, this growth has taken place in a relatively unregulated communications universe. This presents citizens with the opportunity to consult a wide variety of alternative media, but simultaneously allows the development of mutually supporting and ideologically driven webs of information providers.

Familiar television channels ABC, NBC and CBS have been joined not only by CNN and Rupert Murdoch's Fox, but also CNBC, MSNBC, and more recently dedicatedly conservative channels such as One America News Network, Newsmax and Right Side Broadcasting Network—generally available through cable or internet connections. Talk radio, while attracting a declining audience in recent years, still constitutes a network of hundreds of local stations. It has long been a strong field for conservative commentators and opinion leaders, who continue to attract an audience of millions.

Regarding social media, Donald Trump has personally shown the power of Twitter, using his account to communicate with tens of millions of followers with relative impunity until his account was closed in the wake of the attack on the Capitol on January 6, 2021. One competitor in social networking is the Parler app, which claims to be non-partisan, but has a significant right-wing user base. Telegram, Signal and MeWe are communications apps that have encryption options and have also proved popular with conservative groups. Each of these internet-based social media and communications apps offers the opportunity for groups to gather and share the news and information that interests them. For example, militant right-wing groups like Boogaloo and the Proud Boys (the latter labeled a terrorist organization by the Canadian government) have channels hosted on Telegram.

This variegated media environment is a relatively recent development. The opportunities and challenges that it brings will continue to change, channels will come and go, and matters like regulation and access are likely to be robustly debated. This growth in publicly available media has already had an impact on the conduct of US politics, but with the threat of a global health emergency the first port of call for many Americans was the traditional mass media.

PANDEMIC

Dr. Anthony Fauci, head of the National Institute of Allergy and Infectious Diseases, used a Voice of America broadcast on January 20, 2020, to speak of America's first recorded Covid-19 case, a 35-year-old man who had traveled recently from Wuhan, China. It became clear later that the virus had been present in the US since late 2019 and was already spreading rapidly in at least a dozen states. Over the following months the administration's media messaging became a core component of the nation's coronavirus crisis management.

The White House introduced daily coronavirus briefings in February 2020, where President Trump and administration officials took center stage in delivering news of the national response. The briefings exposed tensions that undermined the messages. The political leadership wished to play down the health threat and to avoid policy shifts that might derail economic growth in an election year. The medical experts were more wary of the virus. Their advice on social distancing, restriction of retail business, working at home and mask wearing adapted according to the increasing availability of research, generally becoming more unwelcome to the Trump White House as election day approached.

The televised and widely available media briefings provided the chance for Donald Trump to demonstrate his leadership in the face of a potential national disaster, but the President used the opportunity to say 'I don't take responsibility at all', to label the infection the 'China virus', 'Wuhan virus' and even 'Kung flu', to complain that the previous administration's crisis responses were worse, and to blame state governors for their states' infection rates. The briefings were abandoned in April after President Trump appeared to posit the utility of injecting disinfectant and beaming light into the body. His coronavirus adviser Dr. Deborah Birx's attempts to deflect these claims were made more difficult by the President's tendency to attack the messenger when he did not like the message.

Coronavirus briefings resumed in July, possibly in response to Trump's declining poll figures. Simultaneously, the US formally notified the UN of its intention to withdraw from the World Health Organization, which the President claimed had been proved by the pandemic to be under the control of China. Around the same time, Dr. Fauci felt it necessary to counter Trump's repeated claims on TV and through Twitter that the anti-malaria treatment hydroxychloroquine was also useful against coronavirus. On July 14 *USA Today* published an op-ed in which White House trade adviser Peter Navarro attacked Fauci, which the newspaper called 'misleading' and illustrative of an orchestrated White House media campaign against the government's senior medical adviser. Once the Trump administration had left office, both Birx and Fauci commented on the difficulties that scientific experts faced in a Trump White House determined to maintain a positive media message. They claimed that the response to Covid had been 'derailed', and that the resulting flawed strategy had 'very likely' cost lives (Leonard 2021).

The pandemic intersected with Donald Trump's re-election campaign in several ways, especially in threatening the long period of economic growth that had been inherited from President Obama. It is hard to find a balance between maintaining economic vitality and fending off an international health crisis that is acceptable to all, and various elements of the administration's Covid-19 response became weaponised in the election's confrontations. For many Trump supporters, business lockdowns and the wearing of masks became symbols of oppression and overbearing government control.

Trump wore a mask very rarely and used the forum of a televised presidential debate as one opportunity to mock Joe Biden for doing so, even though, as we now know, Trump was probably Covid-positive at that very moment. Trump's campaign and his White House organized large and extensively reported events with little social distancing. When Trump-aligned protestors, some carrying arms, threatened various state capitols his Tweets to 'LIBERATE MICHIGAN', 'LIBERATE MINNESOTA' and 'LIBERATE VIRGINIA' became a core talking point, and a motivation for his supporters, not just on Twitter but on all news platforms. Re-fashioned as issues of freedom and liberty basic to traditional American values, the wearing of masks, opening of schools and businesses and related matters became political lodestars rather than debatable matters of public health policy.

Trump's pandemic messaging was inconsistent in its detail and ignored or contradicted inconvenient evidence; and the President continued throughout to claim that the disappearance of the disease was imminent even while its attack on the country was accelerating. An internal report by Trump pollster Tony Fabrizio found that in ten key states where the pandemic was the top voting issue, voters supported a mask mandate, approved of Dr. Fauci, and felt that candidate Biden would deal with the health crisis more competently than President Trump. The Trump media campaign relating to the pandemic must be counted a failure (Dawsey 2021).

THE ENEMY OF THE PEOPLE

The impact of the pandemic on the 2020 presidential primary season was profound. Facing only token opposition, President Trump's progress to the GOP renomination was smooth, but in January 2020 there were still a dozen candidates in the race for the Democratic nomination, and a season of primaries and caucuses planned. Many of these contests had to be rescheduled, and voting arrangements altered to accommodate social distancing. For most candidates primary campaigning altered too, away from mass rallies and personal contact to even greater reliance on television, radio, telephone and internet in addition to traditional mailed materials.

In a move that emphasized and reinforced President Trump's dominance in the media, his administration had from its early days limited the variety of alternative official briefings that journalists had come to expect during previous administrations. According to the Committee to Protect Journalists, 'traditional briefings for the press disappeared for many months at a time at the White House and the State and Defense departments, and officials often refused to speak on the record' (Downie 2020). When reporters responded by cultivating their own sources, Trump attacked the resulting reports as 'fake news' and the sources as non-existent, and attacked the journalists personally as, among other things, 'corrupt', 'dishonest' and 'human scum'.

In the White House briefings on the Covid-19 pandemic, President Trump's instinct to react confrontationally to searching questions from journalists was not curbed by the severity of a world health crisis. He repeatedly labelled major media outlets such as CNN and *The New York Times* as 'failing' and as purveyors of 'Fake News.' He implied that MSNBC and other media outlets carrying critical analyses were colluding with the Democratic Party. 'The press is very dishonest,' he tweeted, and its journalists 'truly do hurt our country.'

Journalists were familiar with Trump's attack style, if not inured to it. He had revealed his intentions in a 2016 conversation with Lesley Stahl of CBS News which she went on to discuss the following year during an interview with Judy Woodruff of PBS. According to Stahl, when she asked why he continued his 'boring' attacks on the press after winning the election he responded, 'I do it to discredit you and demean you all so that when you write negative stories about me no one will believe you' (Mangan 2018).

He called the press 'THE ENEMY OF THE PEOPLE' repeatedly on Twitter, at campaign rallies and in other formats, as part of a long-term attempt to undermine public confidence in those channels of the media where he and his administration might be subject to critical analysis. President Trump regularly displayed his dislike of journalists in his White House press conferences and briefings, paying special attention to women. Jackson Katz and Jean Kilbourne writing in *Ms. Magazine* identified occasions on which Trump had reacted to pointed questions by calling women journalists 'nasty', 'horrid', accusing them of asking 'a lot of stupid questions' or 'not thinking – you never do', and telling them to be 'nice', 'relax' and 'keep your voice down'.

Trump constantly obsessed over his media ratings. He wanted attention and the mainstream media could not ignore his news value, however outrageous the basis of any story. After the November 2020 election, Margaret Sullivan, media correspondent of *The Washington Post*, considered her list of the media's failures during the Trump administration: normalizing an abnormal president, treating his deranged tweets as news, leaving his lies too often unchallenged, taking his propaganda events as live feeds, and falling into a trap identified by Mann and Ornstein of distorting reality by trying to create 'a balanced treatment of an unbalanced phenomenon' (Mann and Ornstein 2012).

It was rare that a journalist was able to respond in kind when President Trump was center stage, but there was a notable exception during the NBC Town Hall that replaced the second presidential debate. With the President defending his retweeting of QAnon conspiracy theories, the network's journalist Savannah Guthrie was moved to respond 'You're the president. You're not like someone's crazy uncle.' Even this kind of directness failed to have much impact either on Trump's strong supporters or on those more orthodox Republicans who had sympathy for some of his views and took pleasure in the difficulties that their Democratic competitors appeared to be facing on a political and media landscape transformed by Trump.

ELECTION, TRANSITION, INSURRECTION AND INAUGURATION

The 2020 election campaigns started in traditional style with the Iowa caucuses on February 3 and fell foul immediately of the vagaries of new technology and the demands of journalists across the spectrum of media. An app designed to collect and aggregate the results from almost 1700 simultaneous caucus meetings was overwhelmed, and the journalists who had descended on Des Moines with an expectation of instant news to report were disappointed. While the counting problems were quickly resolved, and results confirmed within a few days, the only media story was about 'chaos' in Iowa's electoral arrangements.

This tone of crisis segued neatly into later election coverage, as the threat of Covid-19 disrupted the primary season, the party conventions, the presidential debates and the general election campaign. Having won the nomination, Joe Biden adopted a style reminiscent of the 'front porch' campaigns of more than a century earlier, relying on news media coverage, advertising, volunteer phone banks and the like to communicate with voters. In contrast, after a brief pause, the Trump campaign moved back to mass audience events and rallies to maximize the President's media coverage.

The national anxiety in the face of pandemic may have provided more than usually fertile ground in which Donald Trump could seed, on multiple occasions, the idea that the US electoral system was susceptible to massive fraud. He claimed that the structures of the election, such as those for mail-in voting, were weak and open to corruption, that reporting of Biden's lead in the polls was due to bias in the mainstream media, that the only way he could lose the election would be as the result of an election theft, and that in the face of such potential injustice his supporters should be ready to fight to ensure his victory. With these sustained and unsubstantiated attacks on the integrity of the electoral system and on the media that reports US politics, Trump completed the journey from 'truthful hyperbole' to the 'Big Lie' that the 2020 election was corruptly stolen by the Biden campaign and its conspirators in the 'deep state.'

This was not a new theme. Roger Stone, the long-time Republican political consultant, Trump supporter and convicted felon, pardoned by Trump during his last month in the White House, had launched a 'Stop the Steal' operation in 2016 in preparation for a potential loss in that election, and the slogan resurfaced during the 2018 midterms. In November 2020, the Twitter hashtag #StoptheSteal was used to bring together Trump supporters, with the president's son Eric joining in the messages, and a 'Stop the Steal 2020' Facebook group attracted 300,000 members in one day before Facebook closed it down (Hayden 2020).

In the 2020 election Joe Biden gained 7.1 million more popular votes than Donald Trump. But the Trump campaign's strategy was never founded on winning a plurality of the popular vote. In 2016 he had won the Electoral College while losing the popular vote. That kind of victory looked possible again, and it proved close. Biden's 306 to 232 Electoral vote victory would have become a tie if Georgia, Arizona and Wisconsin had gone to Trump. In that case the selection of the next president would have been made by the House of Representatives, with each state delegation having a single vote. The Republicans controlled a majority of state delegations in the House and, especially in the confrontational atmosphere of 2020 politics, would almost certainly have returned Donald Trump to the White House. The total Democratic popular vote lead in these critically important states was less than 43,000 votes, or 28 thousandths of one percent of the total two-party popular vote. A swing of half that from Biden to Trump could have seen the president re-elected.

For the first time in US history, a president launched a vigorous post-election effort to overthrow the legitimate democratic outcome. Trump's legal team made a series of spurious challenges through the courts that ultimately failed, even before a US Supreme Court stacked with Trump appointees. He exhorted state officials and officeholders to challenge the public votes in their own states and alter the Electoral College tally regardless of the recorded public vote, and demanded that Vice President Mike Pence reject the Electoral College count on January 6, 2021, and declare the president re-elected (Rutenberg et al. 2021).

The morale of the president's supporters was massaged not just by his tweets. In the weeks after election day, White House press secretary Kayleigh McEnany made at least 23 appearances on Fox News' program 'Hannity,' pressing baseless claims of voter fraud and irregularities. In March 2021

McEnany was hired as a Fox News contributor. Conservative radio hosts Glenn Beck, Mark Levin, Bill Cunningham, Dan Bongino, Nick Fuentes and others whose audiences amount to millions spread unsupported claims that voting machines had been tampered with, regulations altered, and illegal voting taken place to give the Democrats a presidential victory. As January 6, 2021 came closer, they advised their listeners to 'go to war,' 'crush them' and 'occupy the Capitol' (Grynbaum et al. 2021b).

At the January 6 protest some participants spoke of their disenchantment with Fox News, which attracted their ire (as well as President Trump's) over its coverage of the election results. They had shifted allegiance to Newsmax and One America News Network (OANN). Some reported having already moved from Twitter to Parler, and when, in the wake of the Washington attacks, Parler temporarily lost its web base, they moved to other platforms such as Telegram, Signal, MeWe, Gab, 8kun and TheDonald.win. The audiences here are small, but intense and tightly clustered for targeting. Cross-messaging between ideologically sympathetic sources enables misinformation to spread widely and quickly as it is leveraged through the various outlets. A study of social media use from August to December 2020 identified a small number of individual accounts, including those of Donald Trump and two of his sons, that were particularly influential in spreading false information on the US election (Paul 2021).

The January 6 protest turned into a riot with injuries, fatalities, damage to the US Capitol, and threats from the Trump-supporting mob on lives of US Representatives, Senators, and Vice President Mike Pence. In a classic example of how the contemporary media world can operate, a tweet that speculated without evidence that 'Antifa or BLM … could be doing it disguised as Trump supporters' was repeated within minutes on Rush Limbaugh's national radio program. This lie was quickly repeated on Fox News and in *The Washington Times* online edition. In one hour the same afternoon the story 'was mentioned about 8700 times across cable television, social media and online news outlets' (Grynbaum et al. 2021a). Corrections and articles debunking this myth circulated less widely and less quickly. The narrative that the January 6 insurrection was not staged by Trump sympathizers but was an attack carried out by antifa provocateurs took firm hold among conservative Republicans.

Together with the inauguration of President Biden and the silencing of Donald Trump's Twitter account, there seemed an opportunity to move toward more moderation in America's many media channels. On the other hand, a report in the *Los Angeles Times* talked of a 'meme war' to recruit new members to right-wing groups on the internet, featuring images captured specifically for that purpose on January 6 (Hennessy-Fiske and Read 2021). Fox News announced a reorganization of its schedule that would increase its commentary at the expense of news content during peak viewing hours, in an apparent reaction to the audience gains made by OANN and Newsmax. And the 'Big Lie' that the election was stolen continued to have traction, providing the excuse in 43 states to introduce over 250 bills that would make voting more onerous (Wines 2021).

By the spring of 2021 Republicans such as Senator Mitch McConnell and Ambassador Nikki Haley, who had spoken severely about former President Trump's role in prompting the January 6 attacks on the US Capitol, were nevertheless affirming their commitment to support him should he achieve the party's presidential nomination for the 2024 race. Outrage about the attack on the US Capitol was fading among Republicans. The myth that the 2020 election was stolen retained its grip among most Republicans and continued to be circulated in some parts of the conservative media world.

There are always elections forthcoming in the USA, and attention moves quickly from an election that is finished to the campaign that is coming next. Candidates, parties and campaigners take lessons as they move on, including some of those outlined in this chapter. The tension between advancing the public good and electoral self-interest was highlighted by the partisan reactions to the coronavirus—both parties will be reflecting how a future crisis might be best managed. There was however little sign of reflection by the GOP on matters such as its use of voter suppression, gerrymandering and similar techniques. The party leadership has shown itself so concerned to gain and retain power that its commitment to democracy has been compromised. The experience of Trump's populist campaign rhetoric, his antagonism to and disdain of criticism, especially in traditional media sources, and the consistent and heavy use of ideologically oriented outlets, demonstrates well the viability of these weapons in the party armoury.

REFERENCES

Arroyo, J. 2021. Trust in the Media and Opportunities for Renewing the Relationship Between the Media and Citizens Following the US Elections. Key Point Summaries. *The Ditchley Winter Project*, February.

Barthel, M., A. Mitchell, D. Asare-Marfo, C. Kennedy, and K. Worden. 2020. Measuring News Consumption in a Digital Era. *Pew Research Center Journalism and Media*, 8 December.

Blake, A. 2017. Kellyanne Conway Says Donald Trump's Team has 'alternative facts.' Which Pretty Much Says It All. *The Washington Post*, 22 January.

Dawsey, J. 2021. Poor Handling of Virus Cost Trump His Re-election, Campaign Autopsy Finds. *The Washington Post*, 2 February.

Downie, L., Jr. 2020. *The Trump Administration and the Media: A Special Report*, 2020. New York: The Committee to Protect Journalists.

Grieco, E. 2020. U.S. Newspapers have Shed Half of Their Newsroom Employees Since 2008. Pew Research Center Fact Tank, 20 April.

Grynbaum, M., D. Alba, and R. Epstein. 2021. How Pro-Trump Forces Pushed a Lie About Antifa at the Capitol Riot. *The New York Times*, 1 March.

Grynbaum, M., T. Hsu, K. Robertson and K. Collins. 2021. How Right-Wing Radio Stoked Anger Before the Capitol Siege. *The New York Times*, 10 February.

Haberman, M., and E. Steel. 2016. Jared Kushner Talks of a Trump TV Network With a Media Deal Maker. *The New York Times*, 17 October.

Hart, R.P. 2020. *Trump and Us: What He Says and Why People Listen*. Cambridge: Cambridge University Press.

Hayden, M.E. 2020. Far Right Resurrects Roger Stone's #StopTheSteal During Vote Count. *Southern Poverty Law Center Hatewatch*, 6 November.

Hennessy-Fiske, M., and R. Read. 2021. Right-Wing Extremists Stage a 'meme war' to Compete for Trump Supporters. *Los Angeles Times*, 27 January.

Hunt, E. 2017. Trump's Inauguration Crowd: Sean Spicer's Claims Versus the Evidence. *The Guardian*, 22 January.

Jurkowitz, M., A. Mitchell, E. Shearer, and M. Walker. 2020. U.S. Media Polarization and the 2020 Election: A Nation Divided. Pew Research Center Journalism and Media, 24 January.

Katz, J. and J. Kilbourne. 2020. Trump and the 'Nasty', 'Horrid' Women Reporters, *Ms. Magazine*, 23 April.

Keith, T. 2016. Bitterness Overwhelms As Trump and Clinton Campaign Staffers Face Off At Harvard. *NPR: The Two-Way*, 2 December.

Kessler, G. 2021. Trump Made 30,573 False or Misleading Claims as President. Nearly Half Came in His Final Year. *The Washington Post*, 23 January.

Klein, E. 2020. *Why We're Polarized*. London: Profile Books.

Leonard, B. 2021. Fauci: Trump Administration's Covid Strategy 'very likely did' Cost Lives. *Politico*, 22 January.

Mangan, D. 2018. President Trump told Lesley Stahl He Bashes Press 'to demean you and discredit you so … no one will believe' Negative Stories About Him. *CNBC Politics*, 22 May.

Mann, T.E. and N.J. Ornstein. 2012. Let's Just Say It. The Republicans are the problem. *The Washington Post*, 27 April.

Mayer, J. 2016. Donald Trump's Ghostwriter Tells All. *New Yorker*, 25 July.

Media Insight Project. 2018. How Americans Describe Their News Consumption Behaviors. *American Press Institute*, 11 June.

Mitchell, A., M. Jurkowitz, J.B. Oliphant, and E. Shearer. 2020. Americans Who Mainly Get Their News on Social Media Are Less Engaged, Less Knowledgeable. *Pew Research Center Journalism and Media*, 30 July.

Packer, G. 2021. The Legacy of Donald Trump. *Atlantic*, Jan/Feb.

Paul, K. 2021. A Few Rightwingers 'fuelled bulk of election falsehoods'. *The Guardian*, 6 March.

Plaskin, G. 1989. Trump: 'The People's Billionaire'. *Chicago Tribune*, 12 March.

Roach, S. 2021. The Internet Versus Democracy. *Project Syndicate*, 20 January.

Rutenberg, J., J. Becker, E. Lipton, M. Haberman, J. Martin, M. Rosenberg and M.S. Schmidt. 2021. 77 Days: Trump's Campaign to Subvert the Election. *The New York Times*, 31 January.

Shearer, E. 2021. More than Eight-in-Ten Americans Get News from Digital Devices. *Pew Research Center Fact Tank*, 12 January.

Skocpol, T. 2016. Republicans Ride the Trump Tiger. *Project Syndicate*, 30 May.

Sullivan, M. 2021. The Media Never Fully Learned to Cover Trump. But They Still Might Have Saved Democracy. *The Washington Post*, 8 November.

Trudeau, G. 2016. *Yuge!* Kansas: Andrews McMeel.

Trump, D., and T. Schwartz. 1987. *The Art of the Deal*. New York: Random House.

USA Today. 2020. Opinion. 14 July.

Wines, M. 2021. In Statehouses, Stolen-Election Myth Fuels a G.O.P. Drive to Rewrite Rules. *The New York Times*, 27 February.

FURTHER READING

Marco Morini, in his book *Lessons from Trump's Political Communication: How to Dominate the Media Environment* (London, Palgrave Pivot, 2020), introduces the reader to Donald Trump the disintermediator, running as though in a permanent campaign, deploying rhetoric in similar ways to 1930s populist leaders and dictators, and exploiting contemporary media opportunities. Despite its title Jacob S. Hacker and Paul Pierson's *Let Them Eat Tweets: How the Right Rules in an Age of Extreme Inequality* (New York, Liveright, 2020) says almost nothing directly about the Twittersphere, instead concentrating on the shift of the Republican party to a strategy in which public policy increases the concentration of wealth in few hands while using the rhetoric of outrage to recruit voters to its cause. Trump's voice, mediated by Bob Woodward, can be found in *Rage* (New York, Simon and Schuster, 2020).

An analysis by Mark Thompson, *Enough Said: What's Gone Wrong with the Language of Politics?* (London, The Bodley Head, 2016) broadens the field of enquiry, including examples of shifts in the delivery and reception of political rhetoric from both sides of the Atlantic in recent decades. Addressing just the USA *Do Facts Matter: Information and Misinformation in American Politics* (Norman, OK, University of Oklahoma Press, 2015) by Jennifer L. Hochschild and Katherine Levine Einstein discusses several issues that retain long term significance in US politics, including the views of anti-vaxxers.

A good general background to the field is provided by Aeron Davis' *Political Communication: A New Introduction for Crisis Times* (Cambridge, Polity Press, 2019). An almost constant diet of newly published relevant research can be accessed from the Pew Research Center (https://www.pewresearch.org), especially its division dealing with Journalism and Media. The Brookings Institution (https://www.brookings.edu) and The Reuters Institute at Oxford University (https://reutersinstitute.politics.ox.ac.uk) can also carry useful contemporary reports and information. Detailed insights emerge in many academic journals, for example an early post-Trump administration piece is an article, 'Trump Trumps Baldwin? How Trump's Tweets Transform *SNL* Into Trump's Strategic Advantage,' *Journal of Political Marketing*, 19: 386–404, 2020.

CHAPTER 8

The Presidency

Jon Herbert

The Founding Fathers feared many things when they designed the US Constitution. Their most prominent concern, though, was a concentration of power that would overwhelm their hard-won freedoms. Their response was to construct a system that dispersed power and established incentives to keep it dispersed. They imagined particular threats. Perhaps a demagogue would inflame the passions of the people and concentrate power in the presidency? Perhaps factions—in modern-day terms, political parties—might take over the whole system?

Many observers believed Donald Trump was that demagogue. Declaring that his presidential 'authority was total', Trump did little to alleviate their worries. Political parties, too, were on the rise. A decades-long process of increasing partisanship made the parties a more prominent, even dominant, force. Many worried that the constitutional order faced an unprecedented stress test. The Constitution itself might change rarely, but had the constitutional system that operates in its shadow, buffeted by social, economic, and cultural changes, evolved in a way that jeopardized the survival of US democracy?

Optimists held on to the idea that the very design of the system would protect from such threats. An overly assertive presidency would be constrained by other institutions jealous to guard their prerogatives. Periods of intense

J. Herbert (✉)
School of Social, Political and Global Studies, Keele University, Staffordshire, UK
e-mail: j.n.herbert@keele.ac.uk

G. Peele et al. (eds.), *Developments in American Politics 9*,
https://doi.org/10.1007/978-3-030-89740-6_8

partisanship had passed without the collapse of the system. Furthermore, the tension between Trump, outsider populist rejecting the establishment, and the elites of the Republican Party that he criticized, suggested that each might restrain the other.

This chapter explains that that is not what happened during Donald Trump's presidency. Instead, Trump and the Republicans established a working relationship based on familiar patterns of presidential-party cooperation, titled here as 'the partisan presidency'. Elected Republicans sustained and protected Trump's presidency, making significant gains from doing so.

The Partisan Presidency

The Presidency and the Rise of Partisanship

The presidency confronts a more partisan environment than it did fifty years ago. The changes have occurred in virtually every location in the political system, impinging on most aspects of presidential leadership. The US population is more partisan, institutions in Washington are more partisan, and so are the institutions bridging the gap between the two.

Voters have 'sorted' into the two parties since the 1980s. They hold more coherent views on ideology and policy which correlate more closely to one of the party's positions. More people identify strongly with one political party. In a phenomenon of 'negative partisanship', people loathe the other party more strongly than they used to. Partisanship appears wrapped up in a more affective, identity-driven politics (Mason 2018). Social media has created partisan echo chambers on left and right, reinforcing, not challenging, the views of those inside. These communities are developing different rhetorics and views of reality, encouraging dispute over even basic facts.

Party mechanisms have changed. Activists and donors are more ideologically committed and more extreme in their policy positions. A tighter network of interest groups has developed around each party, touting their specific policy positions. Media outlets with more partisan identities have emerged.

Increasingly, institutions of government are shaped by battles for partisan control. Congress is now dominated by each party's pursuit of advantage. Mechanisms limiting partisan control are being stripped back. Congressional voting patterns are more partisan. Increasingly, decisions are a function of how each party can maximize its chances of winning majorities in the next set of elections (Lee 2016). This battle is infecting other venues including the courts and the executive branch. Most US states, and their policies, are witnessing similar shifts. Every political arena is now an opportunity for partisan gain so the sharpened contest influences every institution.

Conflict over party ideologies and policy agendas, at both public and elite level, has deepened. Ideological distance between the parties has grown and contrasting issue positions, strongly held and backed by opposing publics and interest groups, are significant parts of the battle. New issues, as they emerge, quickly become subjects of conflict. Party divisions over 'mask politics' in 2020 demonstrated the process: a basic public health issue in a pandemic allowed the major parties to stake out opposing positions on masks, either as a vital social responsibility to protect fellow Americans or a crass infringement of personal liberty. Each party perceives incentives to create division over an emerging issue. Once parties have staked out conflicting positions in public, scope for compromise between them is reduced, as the party's position cannot be sacrificed.

Parties are more coherent, in policy, identity, and ideological terms. Hence, elections are now intense contests for partisan dominance between two party tribes with sharply contrasting understandings of the world. That has been reinforced by structural changes, such as gerrymandering and shifting residential patterns which create more safe seats for each party. This tightened vertical integration of parties from voters through media, interest groups, and party structures to elites seems to overwhelm many forces that fragmented the US and its politics, such as geographical sectionalism and ideological diversity. Elections are now national and contested between tribes that perceive extraordinary stakes in each election. Partisan polarization has significant implications for the operation of the political system and presidential leadership within it at public and congressional levels.

The present-day, more partisan, public perceives and judges the presidency differently. Presidential approval numbers are influenced by growing partisanship. Presidents might now realistically expect approval ratings from their own party in the 90–95 percent range while receiving 5–10 percent approval from the opposition party. Partisan-tinted glasses shape people's judgments of other political issues; for example, partisans are far more likely to judge the performance of the US economy favorably under a president of their own party.

The presidency now has more impact upon all US elections, even in midterms when they are not on the ballot. Elections are now fought between national-level party images, rather than over local considerations and the presidency is crucial in shaping those party images (Jacobson 2019). Parties' performances in elections reflect, to a degree, levels of presidential success in the preceding Congress (Lebo and O'Geen 2011). This situation makes the performance of the presidency a vital consideration for the party: legislators' fate, in winning re-election or not, is shaped more by the presidency than in previous decades, so they have increased incentive both to support a president of their own party and to impede an opposition president. Lee (2008) shows how presidents taking a public position on an issue encourages legislators to vote with their own party, arguing that this polarizing effect is because presidents, by taking public positions, add new partisan considerations into legislators' decision-making processes. The presidency, therefore, is now an integral part of partisan contests in Congress, rather than an outsider looking in and attempting to influence proceedings, as if above partisanship.

The Centrist Presidency

The above represents a change in how presidential leadership operates. Sixty years ago, Neustadt's (1960) understanding of the constitutional system—with powers distributed and a presidency with little command but some vantage points and leverage—emerged amid discussions of American pluralism. The separated system provided a venue for competition among interests in a society of many and diverse groups, based on sectionalism, race, religion, economic interests, and more forms of fragmentation. Parties, then neither too ideological nor unified, were merely one further form of division. Neustadt did not emphasize party, instead portraying the presidency more generally working with whoever the relevant players were. He was never ignorant of party's significance, but it did not warrant a central place in his understanding of leadership. Instead, Neustadt's model outlined a presidency attempting to move various power players around the board to further policy goals by building consensus, implying a center ground as the main locus of presidential activity.

Presidents trying to lead took strategic decisions to concentrate on the center ground. In Congress, theories focused on how presidents tried to win support from moderates in the center. Debates over presidential influence often focused on 'party switchers' and 'cross-pressured' legislators who might be swayed by presidential attention. Major reforms were achieved by constructing bipartisan coalitions that represented at least some two-party consensus. Electoral politics also demanded action at the center. Campaigning and commentary focused on swing voters, ideological moderates, and independents. Even as partisanship began to sharpen, presidential candidates performed ideological and rhetorical contortionism to portray themselves as centrists through devices such as the 'third way' or 'compassionate conservatism'. Elections were to be won by picking up marginal voters in the center ground. In the legislature and in public, presidents built compromises: ideological purity was a luxury rarely afforded if elections were to be won and policy reforms achieved.

Centrist leadership, however, has a poor record in the twenty-first century. In his second term, George W. Bush could not achieve bipartisan immigration or social security reforms. Obama promised 'post-partisanship' but when governing struggled to build bipartisan coalitions in Congress. Centrist strategies failed because the environment in which they were deployed became less favorable. The ideological poles of each party became more attractive to legislators, as reflected in partisans voting with their own party more regularly and greater ideological distinction between the parties' policy agendas. This attraction is a function of institutional and electoral changes that imposed revised incentive structures. Most congressional districts are safely in the hands of one party; the leading threat to a legislator's career is being 'primaried', that is, being beaten in a battle for their party's nomination, not in the subsequent contest between the parties. Primary challenges usually come from the party's extreme wing; party voters seem to reward ideological purity, statements of absolutes, and appeals to identity. The greater role of ideological interest groups and individual donors in funding campaigns reinforces this effect. Compromising in Washington is seen as betraying the party agenda. Tighter party discipline in Congress, as party leaderships gained more powerful sanctions since the 1990s, also tie legislators closer to their party. Equally, individual and collective rewards might come from party loyalty. Rewards for ideological purity might include career advancement or access to party and donor funding to support campaigns. Under the 'shared fate' argument, these legislators saw potential electoral gains from inflicting defeats on the other party's president. Hurting the power of the other party's brand by associating its president with defeat was very appealing. The enhanced power of the partisan core generates congressional parties with contrasting policy agendas and heightened strategic incentives for legislators to back their party.

These changes make centrist presidential strategies less successful. In ideological terms, there are simply fewer moderate legislators for presidents to appeal to. In partisan terms, bipartisan strategies depend upon members of the other party supporting a president despite party labels, which those legislators are more reluctant to do. The subjects of presidential persuasion were less persuadable, so both Bush and Obama confronted determined and unified resistance from the party that opposed them. Where the compromise and consensus needed to achieve reform might have been possible in times of less ideological dispute and tempered partisan incentives, the current system layers an intense, more rigid partisanship over that constitutional system (Mann and Ornstein 2012).

A similar argument applies to the public. Public views of a policy or president might influence policy decisions taken in Washington, meaning that a president's capacity to influence those public views is a source of power (Kernell 1997; Edwards 2003). However, public partisanship is now more coherent, rooted in greater sharing of policy positions, ideologies, identity, and even views of reality. That coherence may make it harder to attract a partisan to support presidents of the other party. If more of the public are resistant to influence by a president due to partisanship, the potential for presidential leadership is reduced.

The Partisan Presidency

Presidents, therefore, have less incentive to follow centrist strategies. Wanting to achieve change, they have searched out alternative means. Some scholars understand presidents' frequent use of executive power in this light (Rudalevige 2005). Others highlight presidents' tendency to rely on party more in dealings with public and Congress. The flip side of growing opposition partisanship is that presidents may expect more loyalty from their own party, encouraging presidents to pursue a partisan presidency.

The 'partisan presidency' is an alternative to centrist strategies. It is a president's decision to work with their own party to the exclusion of the opposition. It rejects bipartisanship or post-partisanship and instead embraces partisan conflict and the president's role within it. It accepts the desirability of partisan control by the president's party and a committed presidency–party cooperation to win elections and control institutions. Presidents use this strategy more because it has enhanced chances of success; both among public and Congress, own-party audiences are more receptive to presidential appeals, so presidents hunt where the ducks are.

In Congress, there are two primary rules of the partisan presidency. First, the opposition party is likely to eschew cooperation and attempt to undermine the incumbent. Second, the president's party has incentives to work with the chief executive. These rules determine that the partisan governing strategy can play out in two different ways, depending on the status of the president's party in Congress. The president's prospects are bright if his party has majorities in both houses of Congress (even better, a super-majority in the Senate), but a president facing a Congress with majorities of the other party is disadvantaged. Note that recent scholarship suggests presidents have limited capacity to improve their strategic situation in Congress; they must accept their role as 'facilitators', that is, taking opportunities available to them given the constraints of their governing environment (Edwards 2009).

Presidents with majority party support in Congress and who choose to work with their own party are presented with ready-made mechanisms to assist their efforts. Interests, ideas, and institutions may all be aligned to support a prepared agenda, presenting a party caucus ready to support the president. Of course, the picture is not always that clear: parties still have divisions over policy, ideology, and strategy, but they share many basic principles. The challenges of presidential leadership lie in holding their party together. Particularly, presidents are likely to work closely with their party's leadership in Congress as they build party coalitions in support of the agenda. The strategy offers the prospect of substantial achievements and a long-term policy legacy, as reflected in partisan votes that sustained the major legislative achievements of recent presidents, such as Obama's healthcare reform and Trump's tax cuts.

Presidents who lack party majorities in Congress face a gloomy outlook. Under divided government, the opposition party can block the presidency. Little legislative achievement can be expected and instead, each party pursues partisan conflict, looking for strategic advantage in hope of victory at the next election. The party base must be rallied, often through symbolic votes to demonstrate commitment to issue positions and the opposition must be discredited and fragmented. The situation promises only a tedious grind of conflict with limited success, except in conditions of extraordinary crisis (Franklin and Fix 2016).

The partisan presidency has a public dimension. After the 2004 election campaign, Republican strategist Karl Rove was accredited, although he subsequently denied it, with developing a new strategy for winning presidential elections (Rove 2010). He believed there were enough Republican voters among the electorate, if they voted, to win re-election for George W. Bush. Rather than worrying about moderates and independents, Rove targeted his strategy on maximizing Republican turnout. This '50 percent plus one' strategy revolved around appeals to motivate Republican partisans. Much messaging was negative campaigning, focusing on threats that Democrats posed, especially on social issues such as gay marriage. Milkis and Rhodes' concept of the 'New American Party System' also noted a more public partisan role for presidents. They describe the presidency's increased commitment to pronouncing party doctrine and expanding its appeal, raising campaign funds for the party and campaigning on behalf of partisan brethren (Milkis et al. 2012). Political parties expect presidents to promote the party actively in public. The president is now expected to be a partisan warrior.

The logical extension of this electoral strategy is to concentrate presidential communication on the party when governing. The opposition party is predisposed to resist presidential persuasion, so communicating with them does not warrant consumption of scarce resources. Crafting awkward messages compromising between party core and center is less likely to satisfy either audience. Instead, the president should 'go partisan' (Rottinghaus 2013), concentrating on their own, more receptive party supporters. Presidents can play to fellow partisans' rhetoric and realities, cues more readily triggered in the partisan environment. Partisan-leaning media outlets and social media make this possible.

This combination of congressional and public dimensions of the partisan presidency effectively marks out a new locus of presidential activity. Rather than an ideologically moderate center as a place to build consensus, presidents choose a partisan strategy revolving around the locus of their party. Presidents make these choices because the changed levels of receptiveness to presidential leadership guides them toward their own parties.

Qualifiers: The Two Loci of Presidential Action

The above is a highly stylised account stressing basic patterns in strategy and power. The real picture is more nuanced and the presidency is not suddenly, exclusively, and unyieldingly partisan. The center has not disappeared completely. It may be less well represented in Congress and fewer members of the public may be persuaded to occupy it, but it can still provide the margin between winning and losing, so presidents still focus some energy there.

In the electoral arena, there are still highly contested states in presidential elections. In 2020, Biden won Pennsylvania by 1.2 percent and three states, Wisconsin, Arizona, and Georgia, by less than a single percentage point. Candidates still scramble for every vote in swing states. The public has not taken parties so firmly to their hearts: parties are deeply unpopular with those not affiliated to them, and have not even become more popular with their own identifiers in recent decades. The most distinct change is that partisans loathe the other side more (Abramowitz and Webster 2018).

Equally, in Congress, the difference between presidential victory and defeat in high-profile battles is often down to votes at the center. The most liberal Republican and the most conservative Democrat are still the votes at the margin that presidents often have to pursue. Not everything in Congress is partisan. Curry and Lee (2019) describe 'non-party government' to capture still high levels of bipartisan voting and continuing limits to majority parties' capacity to pass their chosen agendas.

It is better to conceive the twenty-first-century presidency as working at both center and party core, but with more emphasis on the partisan pole than their predecessors of the mid-twentieth century. Presidents juggle demands of the two loci and leadership is often about finding devices to reconcile sharply enhanced tensions between the two in a manner that allows a presidency to achieve its goals.

In electoral politics, presidents try to combine the needs to mobilize the party faithful and to win over independents skeptical of partisanship. The result is a trend of major party nominees running with the party label but pitching themselves as 'above party' or post-partisan. In Congress, presidents see the problem reflected in internal party divisions. Obama worked with a tranche of moderate midwestern Democrats, the so-called 'Blue Dogs', on his party's right while taking criticism from the liberal core of his party. Trump lost his proposed 'repeal and replace' reform of healthcare in 2017 as first the Freedom Caucus on his party's right, and then moderates on the left, refused to accept his proposal. Biden too must manage the conservatism of West Virginia Senator Joe Manchin and the liberalism of 'The Squad' led by Representative Alexandria Ocasio-Cortez.

The constitutional order has not changed, but presidents' strategic calculations within it have. Partisanship has changed the incentives attached to different strategies of leadership, making partisan strategies more likely to reap rewards.

President Trump

Into this partisan environment thundered Donald Trump. In 2016, his populist rhetoric seemed to promise the antithesis of a partisan presidency. He described a US divided between a corrupt elite in Washington and a massed, wronged populace and declared himself the one person who could represent that populace against the elite. Both parties in Washington were labeled as part of the problem. When Trump won office, therefore, a fight with Republican elites was expected. His 'plague on all your houses' rejectionism of the establishment was just one cause of tension. Trump was not, it appeared, committed to the Republican Party, having changed party affiliations regularly before 2016. His commitment to the party's conservative ideology was highly questionable. Promises of large spending programs in healthcare and infrastructure, tariff protection for American workers and a US foreign policy motivated by a narrow 'America First' conception of US interests all flew in the face of stated Republican Party principles. Trump's previous statements on some social issues, such as gay rights and gun control, plus his immigration proposals, also worried establishment Republicans. Furthermore, Trump won the party's presidential nomination in a hostile takeover. Trump declared his loathing of elites, including those in the Republican Party and 'Never Trumpers' provided concerted resistance. He won the nomination by mobilizing the mass of the party to win primary elections despite the elite party's skepticism. The stage was set for conflict between Trump and his party in Washington.

Trump arrived in Washington to adopt an unconventional governing style that reflected his populist, outsider appeal. His performance of the office in public and his conduct of it in the Oval Office were both highly personalized. Neither suggested anything but further conflict. He did not, though, break with many conventions of the partisan presidency. Trump and the Republicans developed a functional interaction rather than unleashing disastrous bouts of internecine squabbling. While that was ultimately unsuccessful when it came to re-election, Trump and the Republicans achieved significant policy reforms, and, despite his unconventional behavior and its consequential scandals, kept him in office for four years.

Trump: The Performance

For Trump, much of presidential leadership was communication. Compared to his predecessors, he spent more time consuming and trying to influence the media. While his Twitter habit drew attention because of his tweets' perceived influence, this was an element in a broader Trump operation to dominate news coverage. Using tweets, phone calls, and public comments, he produced a deluge of news stories and provided those stories in enticing, if familiar, forms to make sure they won maximum attention. Trump was media catnip, offering a personal narrative (easy to cover and relatable for audiences) full of personal beefs (conflicts make for good stories) and bad behavior (shock value takes headlines). The impact of every controversial tweet was multiplied many times by mainstream media attention. Interventions were timed carefully to distract from unfavorable stories. Trump understood the system and instituted a program of remorseless self-promotion.

There were consistent themes to the president's propagation of the Trump brand. He offered a public persona with distinctive characteristics. He reinforced his populist message and he performed leadership.

Trump's public persona was, in many respects, distinctly unpresidential. He displayed unusual emotions on the stump: presidents are not usually incandescent with rage, nor prone to braggadocio. His performances were often rant-laden, sometimes rambling and virtually incoherent. Rather than portraying himself as president of all the people, he threw abuse at various target groups, whether institutions of federal government, the media or individuals with high profiles in politics, sport or media. Speaking his mind, and sometimes *whatever* was on his mind, Trump's breaches of presidential etiquette helped him to project authenticity. He was a break from the polished, measured politicians, refusing to be standardized or compromised by Washington, presenting as true to himself and the people he represented.

This authenticity fitted into a broader populist message. Trump had a clear sense of the reason for his election and worked diligently to communicate it. As an outsider, he rejected the Washington establishment repeatedly and vociferously, in a manner echoing many Tea Party messages of the preceding decade. He was against the system and the 'deep state'. This was part-conspiratorial as he gave voice to ludicrous claims to reinforce the message that his, and the people's, enemies were evil and that only he could defeat them. Trump disregarded the facts, peddling falsehoods and producing remarkable inconsistencies in his statements. His claims of great achievements were often simply untrue as were many other statements, germane to politics or not; the *Washington Post* (Fact Checker 2021) recorded 30,573 lies. A blend of political rejectionism, marketing chutzpah and a tolerant right-wing media allowed him to operate as though unbound by the rest of the world's reality.

Trump also performed leadership. With inflated claims of his own brilliance, Trump communicated how his leadership was different. First, he had to appear to lead, exerting power in the name of the people he claimed to represent. Trump engineered many opportunities to be seen giving orders. Ceremonies to issue executive orders, apparently—but not actually—untrammeled expressions of raw presidential power, served the purpose particularly well. Second, he also had to be seen to win. This was not a process of consensus building. Instead, he performed conflicts to be resolved by his vanquishing of the enemy. Trump lived out public battles selecting suitable targets for his anti-establishment rhetoric. He personalized conflict, choosing individuals to symbolize his preferred issues. Obama, Hillary Clinton, and Nancy Pelosi represented the evils of liberalism in a fairly standard, if more brutally stated and personalized, Republican format. Trump, though, generated new enemies. For example, his combative, if often illogical and ill-informed, press conference performances provided visuals of him shouting down a media that he labelled 'enemy of the people' and 'fake news' for their liberalism and their questioning of his leadership. Finally, Trump performed popularity. Rallies of cheering, MAGA-hat wearing supporters allowed Trump to portray a popular president serving the people.

Trump honed the performance of power, demonstrating his role as the bringer-of-change and rule-breaker. He presented himself as an independent, anti-establishment leader representing the people. Nor was this all performance: he brought a different style of governing to his duties as Chief Executive.

Trump in the Oval Office

Each president brings a personal skill set and a particular approach to office, but Trump was a genuine outlier. Having both developed his own style in business and decided that his predecessors in the Oval Office had failed, he was dismissive of previous presidential practices. Most of all, he personalized the presidency, relying on his own capacities rather than acknowledging the ability of the institution of the presidency to support and protect him.

Achieving constructive change in Washington demands the president's energy, time, expertise, strategy, and coordination. Trump's primary focus was, as established, communication, but beyond that, he was inclined to engage with other areas of presidential leadership inconsistently.

Policy detail and the processes of policy-making did not absorb Trump. He was not predisposed to listen to briefings carefully, tending to draw out only points that reinforced his established convictions. He rejected expert advice, preferring his own gut instincts and taking decisions regardless of his limited expertise. Details he evaded might include what would be legal or what the political or policy repercussions of his actions might be. This absence of responsibility to policy-making systems and the support they provide freed the president to issue decisions, sometimes by tweet, when he wished. Nor did Trump work particularly closely with Congress. His involvement in supporting his legislative agenda was sporadic and sometimes destructive because he did not understand the politics of the issues and deals he discussed. He did not deliver the classic administrative leadership of the managerial presidency. Presidents must follow up their orders to make sure they are implemented, keeping the administration concentrated on the president's goals. Trump would explode with fury at failures to execute his orders, apparently interpreting them as personal slights, but he could also raise an issue, demand action, and then forget about it for months. The notorious incident in which White House staffer Gary Cohn simply removed paperwork on trade policy toward South Korea from the president's desk was a clear example (Woodward 2018). Actors within his administration mounted a 'resistance' to outmaneuver what they considered Trump's most eccentric and dangerous decisions (Anonymous 2019). Many of his frustrations were derived from clashes between conceptions of the presidency. Trump believed that he had been elected to give the orders, while those versed in government administration felt they could not implement those orders if they were against the law or, to them, self-evidently detrimental to US interests.

Trump did not recognize that he was working within a larger organization that he could use productively to magnify his impact as president, whether through careful policy planning, accessing legal expertise, coordinating communication or liaising with other institutions. The institutional presidency had developed to support leadership over nearly a century; Trump's personal style isolated him from many of its useful features, diminishing his impact. Rather than helping to launch preferred policies into the public sphere in the most favourable manner, White House communications specialists were often left rushing to catch up with impacts of the president's latest tweet. Perhaps more seriously, so were congressional liaison staff, who had to handle fallout from Trump's impetuous behavior on Capitol Hill. Trump's personalisation of the office suspended the operation of the presidency as an institution and weakened his leadership by doing so. His refusal to be constrained by its demands also created liabilities.

Trump's leadership style produced serious policy failures. Policy was poorly planned, leading to unnecessary waste of scarce presidential resources and, worst of all, self-inflicted defeats. Perhaps due to the willingness to ignore the law, or at least push its interpretation beyond reasonable bounds, the administration frequently found its actions challenged in court. The inability to factor political consequences into decision-making led to embarrassing climb downs on positions such as separating immigrant families on the border, a scandal complete with images of young children in cages. Trump's failure to handle the Covid-19 pandemic, pretending that it did not present a serious threat and then denying any responsibility for it (entitled the 'state authority hand-off' within the administration) will feature centrally in assessments of his legacy (Shear et al. 2020). Trump's belief that he could define reality with his rhetoric proved phenomenally dangerous. He could have guided public behavior to enhance safety. Instead, his rhetoric created partisan division in defiance of scientific advice on masks and social distancing. His refusal to engage federal leadership took a national crisis and guaranteed a fragmented, ill coordinated response. States ended up in bidding wars against one another for PPE, for example. Expert advice was available: Trump's exaggerated personalisation of the presidency encouraged him to ignore it.

Trump's disdain for the law and personalisation of the office also produced an unprecedented range of scandals. He was the first president to be impeached twice, but his administration's conduct is perhaps best captured by the idea that the scandals can be presented by category. First, Trump was accused of jeopardizing national security, for example by discussing national security secrets in a meeting with the Russians. Second, conflict of interest scandals haunted the administration. Stories emerged on how the Trump campaigns and administration enriched the president and his family, whether through direct payments to his businesses from the federal government or through foreign governments trying to curry favor by spending money with Trump businesses. Separate scandals broke on the self-enrichment of Trump's cabinet officers, most notably Scott Pruitt at the Environmental Protection Agency. Third, the administration manipulated information for political advantage, such as editing federally funded scientific reports to downplay the threat of climate change. Trump's verbal innovations combined with more systematic attempts to misinform. Fourth, the administration strove to render itself unaccountable for its actions, such as sacking inspectors general responsible for auditing and reporting on the activities of federal agencies. Trump appeared to obstruct justice, for instance, firing James Comey as FBI Director to hinder investigation of his 2016 campaign's ties to Russia. Finally, the administration persistently undermined election processes. Trump threatened to withhold foreign aid to Ukraine unless their government helped investigate the Biden family's financial and political conduct. He launched a coordinated campaign to overturn the 2020 election results, including pressuring Republican election officials in key states to find more Trump votes and culminating in the January 2021 insurrection. These activities provided a barrage of news throughout Trump's term, supplemented by scandals from before he won office, such as his exploitation of his charitable foundation for personal gain, his tax arrangements and hush payments from campaign funds used to buy silence from former lovers.

While Trump dismissed accusations against him as establishment conspiracies, they were a perpetual burden on the administration, sapping resources and compromising focus. Policy failures and scandals demonstrated how Trump's personalisation of the presidency denied him the sustenance and protection of the institution.

TRUMP AND THE PARTISAN PRESIDENCY

The partisan presidency and Trump's personalized presidency present very different versions of the office. The partisan presidency suggests a presidency constrained by, and choosing governing strategies in response to, its institutional context. Trump's style calls on the 'great man' school of history, where the individual alone provides transformative leadership through astute decision-making and rhetoric—or at least through a phone to tweet and a pen for signing executive orders. Yet Trump, for all the performance and expected tensions between himself and his party, did not ignore or outmaneuver constraints of the partisan presidency. Instead, he played key partisan roles for Republicans and in turn, earned the elite party's tolerance and support despite his unconventional behavior.

The Republican elites in Washington sustained Trump in office with their power. In Congress, Republicans provided high levels of support for legislation that Trump supported (FiveThirtyEight.com 2021). Amid the blizzard of scandals, Trump's misconduct was often tolerated and sometimes not even investigated. Most notably, his party protected him through two sets of impeachment proceedings, refusing to remove him from office. His executive actions sometimes instigated Republican resistance, but most were allowed to stand. Public criticism of Trump from his own party was scarce. Many were willing to spread Trump's alternative facts, even his fantasies on the supposed theft of the 2020 presidential election. There are two differing explanations of Republicans backing their president, although each is rooted in the president's base strategy.

Trump's Base Strategy

Trump prioritized communication and chose the messages; he also focused on a particular audience. The 2016 election appeared to mark the emergence of the so-called 'base' of Trump voters. Trump was initially thought to have connected with large groups of voters inspired by him personally, a theory used to explain his insurgent victory in the 2016 primaries and his surprising success in midwestern states. Trump embraced this interpretation, claiming the base as the source of his legitimacy as president and making it intrinsic to his populist narrative. Hence, he took a strategic decision on assuming office to focus communication on them. Using right-wing media and his Twitter account, he maintained a steady stream of messages to his target group to express his persona, leadership, and achievements.

The 'base', though, turned out to be remarkably Republican. Some analysts suggested Trump had done much to attract white working-class Americans to the party, but later analyses contested this interpretation. Trump was, by targeting the base, following the partisan strategy and judging by his high approval ratings among Republican identifiers, pursuing it effectively.

Trump's theory of presidential power was simple. This rank-and-file Republican support was his leverage to influence Washington. Various theories have suggested that presidents can use public support to shape legislators' behavior. Kernell's 'Going Public' (1997) argues that legislators will hesitate to cross a popular president. Trump, however, pursued a partisan version of this strategy. He did not try to widen his presidency's appeal, instead believing that Republican politicians would respond to the views of their Republican voters. He used his messaging to criticize elected Republican officials who opposed him, making sure that voters in their district would register the president's displeasure and pressure the recalcitrant legislator. Trump believed he had to encourage and trade on 'a little fear' among his fellow Republicans. Commentators argued that Trump used this popularity to achieve dominance of the Republican Party. Cowed legislators would not defy the will of the president and their district. Trump also undertook a systematic capture of the party's commanding heights, installing loyalists at the Republican National Committee and capturing state party mechanisms. References to 'Trump's Party' abounded.

In this reading, Trump arrived in Washington and did what he wanted, but this account has two flaws. First, presidents find it very difficult to communicate effectively with publics, even within their party and through social media (Christenson et al. 2021; Edwards 2016). Second, thinking of elite Republicans as under political siege from their own leader and voters ignores what they gained from their tolerance. Trump survived within the constitutional system because his party had incentives to sustain him in return for concrete gains in policy, in institutional power and, until 2020, in the electoral arena.

Trump, Partisan Warrior

Trump decided to work with Republicans in Congress. After a Trump Tower meeting with Republican Speaker Paul Ryan during his transition, a legislative agenda was agreed that committed Trump to party priorities of repealing and replacing Obama's healthcare reforms and then tax cuts. The former foundered amid internal Republican disagreements, but Trump had bowed to party priorities. Tax cuts became the signature legislative achievement of his term. He also cooperated in nominating social conservatives to the judiciary, including three justices to the Supreme Court. Republicans were delighted, although, tellingly, insiders tended to give leading legislators credit rather than Trump. Trump won power and Republicans used it.

Not only did Republicans achieve these tangible policy gains, but Trump's apostasies, while causing friction, rarely led to major legislative action. His major proposal for immigration reform, revealed in January 2018, received some congressional discussion and was quietly shelved by the party leadership who considered it divisive. Big-spending infrastructure reform never emerged. Substantial funding for the border wall was not forthcoming, whether during unified Republican government or during 2019 when, in pursuit of it, Trump engineered the longest government shutdown in history. Trump articulated the occasional socially liberal policy, but his administration almost always took resolutely conservative positions on hot button issues such as gun control, abortion, and LGBTQ+ rights. In Congress, at least, much of Trump's radical agenda was contained and dismissed. His legislative achievements were distinctly 'ordinary' in both volume and ideological character (Herbert et al. 2019).

Instead, Trump resorted to executive action to pursue his new policies. The limited progress made on the wall was largely funded by a combination of declaring a national emergency and re-allocating Department of Defense funding on grounds of national security. Changes to immigration policy were pursued through the 'administrative presidency', shaping implementation of the laws directly. Trump began a trade war with China using powers, again in the name of national security, delegated to the presidency by Congress in decades-old legislation. Occasionally congressional Republicans resisted these innovations, for example pressuring Trump to implement sanctions imposed on Russia as punishment for their interference in the 2016 election. Largely, though, Republican elites recognized the presidency's advantages when shaping policy by executive power. Executive action is difficult to resist, but from legislators' perspectives they also have the advantage of plausible deniability if the president's initiatives failed. Also, many of Trump's executive actions were well received among Republicans. His deregulatory and anti-bureaucratic agendas were in line with conservative ideology. As Rudalevige (2021) argues, executive action is not always a hostile presidential assault on others' authority; bureaucrats, legislators, and party interests may all advocate the use of presidential authority for their own purposes. Trump's 2016 victory provided Republicans with access to presidential power and in many respects, it was used for Republican goals. This power was not purely used for policy. By influencing electoral processes and the bureaucratic agencies and procedures that shaped them, Republicans, via Trump, could advantage themselves in the electoral arena, whether by trying to shape census results, implementation of civil rights legislation or Post Office delivery of mail-in votes. Trump assisted in the institutionalization of party influence, not just through court appointments but through politicization of the federal bureaucracy. Republicans countered elements of Trump's agenda and tolerated others, but saw substantial gains from his conduct of executive power.

The president was also a useful party leader in public. First, in 2016 Trump won the election and Republicans won majorities in both houses of Congress, despite his unconventional campaigning. Second, he decided not to attempt a purge of elected establishment Republicans. He attacked those who criticized him openly, thus demonstrating his power and imposing his 'fear' to increase his leverage. However, as the 2018 mid-terms approached he rejected former White House advisor Steve Bannon's proposal to select Trump-style firebrands to back in Republican primaries against elected establishment figures. Trump supported the party in the 2018 campaign. He attended fund-raisers and party events. Third, Trump sounded like a partisan warrior. He spoke directly to the Republican base with partisan-style negative campaigning. He articulated the threat of liberal politicians and policies, promising they would bring chaos and collapse. The issue set was familiar to observers of Republican politics: crime, law, and order which he connected to race; economics; nationalism and patriotism tied to strength in foreign policy; faith and the threat to it posed by the federal government. There were innovations here, such as integrating race, law and order, security and economics in his immigration messaging and the power of his trade message. The main strength, though, was Trump's capacity to express the threat in direct and often vitriolic terms that triggered an emotional response rooted in identity. Trump was very effective at undermining the legitimacy of his rhetorical targets, whether Democrats, liberals or the federal government. In many Republicans' eyes, Trump 'owned the libs'. Meanwhile, his self-promotion provided positive, if often wildly exaggerated, claims of Republican achievements. In an era of presidential image doing so much to shape party image, Trump made big, positive claims for the party. Trump was, in public, an effective partisan. Even after the 2020 election defeat, most Republicans accepted Trump's bizarre 'stolen election' narrative, recognizing that a furious Republican base would be a supportive one and that Trump was weakening Democrat Biden's legitimacy.

There were, of course, substantial qualifiers to this cosy picture for Republicans. Trump threatened to change the party. While his policy innovations were contained in Congress, he was still advocating anti-internationalist and immigration policies that traditional conservatives disliked. His tribalism extended to denigrating key institutions of liberal democracy in ways that extended conservative attempts to reduce the size and reach of government to a type of nascent anarchism based in absolute resistance to the state. His disrespect for the rule of law threatened to mutate into an authoritarian assault on the system. Party strategists worried about divisions that Trump's approach encouraged; the future electoral prospects of an avowedly whites-only party seemed dim. As dramatically demonstrated in the Capitol Hill insurrection, some supporters inspired by Trump's rhetoric held extreme views that others in the party were not ready to embrace. Yet, in aggregate, Trump's was a deeply partisan presidency and one that Republicans saw good reasons to sustain. When the majority party in Congress, up to January 2019, they were slow to investigate scandals or resist Trump's initiatives. Even as Republican legislators contemplated how to cast their votes during his first impeachment in early 2020, they encountered a presidency that was stunningly popular with its own partisans, coasting to renomination and, with a healthy economy, had a good chance of re-election. 'Shared fate' calculations suggested that any response other than rallying around in support of Trump would be profoundly damaging, especially as he delivered many benefits.

Trump, like his predecessors, provided a presidential narrative that placed him above party. While more dramatic, his populist claims served the same function as Clinton's third way or Obama's post-partisanship in obscuring partisanship and presenting the president as an independent operator. In many senses, though, Trump was even more partisan than his predecessors. In Congress, he worked with Republicans under a unified government. His communication focused on his party base and he played his role as a partisan warrior. That partisanship kept him in office as, despite his misconduct, the services he provided to Republicans insulated him from investigation and impeachment.

Conclusion: Biden and the Partisan Presidency

The changing structures of US politics have bound presidents and their parties closer together. Even a president as unconventional as Trump operated within the strictures of, and benefitted from the advantages of, the partisan presidency. As Biden took office in 2021, he inherited the same office within the same institutional structure.

Biden campaigned as a less divisive figure than Trump. Ideologically, he was seen as a moderate Democrat. Experienced in the cross-partisan comity of the Senate, his record suggested that he would search out cooperation between the parties. Lacking Trump's love of public combat, Biden's personality and concept of politics as public service pointed to a less divisive approach (Osnos 2020). He came to office with Democratic party majorities in Congress, but the slender margins suggested a need to work with Republicans. There were many reasons to expect a centrist presidency.

Biden adopted a bold agenda. He signed his first major legislative achievement, the 'American Rescue Plan' (ARP), in March 2021. The coronavirus relief package was a distinctly liberal measure, not just because of its $1.9 trillion price tag, but in its substantial stimulus cheques to citizens, enhanced aid to the unemployed, increase in food stamp benefits, expanded child tax credits, and subsidies for individuals' health insurance premiums. Republicans did not cooperate and attacked the legislation as unnecessary and expensive. The legislation passed with Democratic votes alone; every single Republican voted against the package in House and Senate. The new president followed up his first achievement with pledges to act on infrastructure, climate change, and racial equality in his 'American Jobs Plan' and promised a further 'American Families Plan'. Republicans condemned the plans to increase corporate taxes to pay for boosted federal research and infrastructure spending and labelled them 'nonstarters for bipartisan negotiations' (Tankersley 2021). The rules of partisan conflict asserted themselves from the start of Biden's presidency.

Where Obama had, in 2009, built a compromise stimulus package to woo Republican support that never materialized, Biden acknowledged the partisan nature of his governing environment. Speaking during negotiations over the passage of ARP, he reflected on the prospects of bipartisanship declaring: 'I've told both Republicans and Democrats that's my preference: to work together. But if I have to choose between getting help right now to Americans who are hurting so badly and getting bogged down in a lengthy negotiation or compromising on a bill that's up to the crisis, that's an easy choice'. He chose a partisan strategy from the start.

References

Abramowitz, Alan I., and Steven W. Webster. 2018. Negative Partisanship: Why Americans Dislike Parties But Behave Like Rabid Partisans. *Political Psychology* 39 (S1): 119–135.

Anonymous. 2019. *A Warning*. London: Little, Brown.

Christenson, Dino P., Sarah E. Kreps, and Douglas L. Kriner. 2021. Going Public in an Era of Social Media: Tweets, Corrections, and Public Opinion. *Presidential Studies Quarterly* 51 (1): 151–165.

Curry, James M., and Frances E. Lee. 2019. Non-Party Government: Bipartisan Lawmaking and Party Power in Congress. *Perspectives on Politics* 17 (1): 47–65.

Edwards, George C. III. 2003. *On Deaf Ears: The Limits of the Bully Pulpit*. New Haven: Yale University Press.

———. 2009. *The Strategic President: Persuasion and Opportunity in Presidential Leadership*. Princeton, NJ: Princeton University Press.

———. 2016. *Predicting The Presidency: The Potential of Persuasive Leadership*. Princeton, NJ: Princeton University Press.

FiveThirtyEight.com. 2021. Tracking Congress in the Age of Trump. https://projects.fivethirtyeight.com/congress-trump-score/.

Franklin, Daniel Paul, and Michael P. Fix. 2016. The Best of Times and the Worst of Times: Polarization and Presidential Success in Congress. *Congress and the Presidency* 43 (3): 377–394.

Herbert, Jon, Trevor McCrisken, and Andrew Wroe. 2019. *The Ordinary Presidency of Donald J. Trump*. London: Palgrave Macmillan.

Jacobson, Gary C. 2019. *Presidents and Parties in the Public Mind*. Chicago, IL: University of Chicago Press.

Kernell, Samuel. 1997. *Going Public: New Strategies of Presidential Leadership*. Washington, DC: CQ Press.

Lebo, Matthew J., and Andrew J. O'Geen. 2011. The President's Role in the Partisan Congressional Arena. *Journal of Politics* 73 (3): 718–734.

Lee, Frances E. 2008. Dividers, Not Uniters: Presidential Leadership and Senate Partisanship, 1981–2004. *Journal of Politics* 70 (4): 914–928.

———. 2016. *Insecure Majorities: Congress and the Perpetual Campaign*. Chicago, IL: University of Chicago Press.

Mann, Thomas E. and Norman J. Ornstein. 2012. *It's Even Worse Than It Looks: How the American Constitutional System Collided with the New Politics of Extremism*. New York: Basic Books.

Mason, Lilliana. 2018. *Uncivil Agreement: How Politics Became Our Identity*. Chicago, IL: University of Chicago Press.

Milkis, Sidney M., Jesse H. Rhodes, and Emily J. Charnock. 2012. What Happened to Post-Partisanship? Barack Obama and the New American Party System. *Perspectives on Politics* 10 (1): 57–76.

Neustadt, Richard E. 1960. *Presidential Power: The Politics of Leadership*. New York: John Wiley.

Osnos, Evan. 2020. *Joe Biden: American Dreamer*. London: Bloomsbury Publishing.

Rottinghaus, Brandon. 2013. Going Partisan: Presidential Leadership in a Polarized Political Environment. Brookings Institution Report. https://www.brookings.edu/research/going-partisan-presidential-leadership-in-a-polarized-political-enviro nment/.

Rove, Karl. 2010. *Courage and Consequence: My Life as a Conservative in the Fight*. New York NY: Threshold Editions.

Rudalevige, Andrew. 2005. *The New Imperial Presidency: Renewing Presidential Power After Watergate*. Ann Arbor, MI: The University of Michigan Press.

———. 2021. *By Executive Order: Bureaucratic Management and the Limits of Presidential Power*. Princeton NJ: Princeton University Press.

Shear, Michael D. et al. 2020. Inside Trump's Failure: The Rush to Abandon Leadership Role on the Virus. *New York Times*, September 15. https://www.nytimes.com/2020/07/18/us/politics/trump-coronavirus-response-failure-leadership.html.

Tankersley, Jim. 2021. Biden Details $2 Trillion Plan to Rebuild Infrastructure and Reshape the Economy. *New York Times*, April 15. https://www.nytimes.com/2021/03/31/business/economy/biden-infrastructure-plan.html.

Washington Post: Fact Checker, 2021. In Four Years, President Trump Made 30,573 False or Misleading Claims. *Washington Post*. https://www.washingtonpost.com/graphics/politics/trump-claims-database/?itid=lk_inline_manual_4. Last Accessed April 2, 2021.

Woodward, Bob. 2018. *Fear: Trump in the White House*. London: Simon & Schuster.

FURTHER READING

There are many books on partisanship (see Brewer's recommendations in this volume) but Darrell M. West's *Divided Politics, Divided Nation: Hyperconflict in the Trump Era* (2019, Washington DC: Brookings Institution Press) is a neat, personalized introduction to the subject. On parties and the presidency specifically, Sidney M. Milkis' corpus of work is vital, starting with *The President and the Parties: The Transformation of the American Party System since the New Deal* (1993, New York: Oxford University Press). B. Dan Wood's *The Myth of Presidential Representation* (2009, Cambridge: Cambridge University Press) and Daniel J. Galvin's *Presidential Party Building: Dwight D. Eisenhower to George W. Bush* (2010, Princeton: Princeton University Press) are both excellent and Gary C. Jacobson's *Presidents and Parties in the Public Mind* (2019, Chicago: University of Chicago Press) is a groundbreaking study on the relationship between candidates, presidents, party and the public. Jeffrey E. Cohen's *The President on Capitol Hill: A Theory of Institutional Influence* (2019, New York: Columbia University Press) suggests the congressional dimensions of the partisan presidency have long been prominent.

There is a proliferation of insider accounts on Trump's presidency and more will emerge. Anonymous' *A Warning* (2019, New York: Little, Brown) did not offer too many new revelations but it provides a good overview of Trump's style. Bob Woodward's accounts of presidencies are always informed by insider access: *Fear* (2018) and *Rage* (2020) and, with Robert Costa, *Peril* (2021, all London: Simon and Schuster). Evan Osnos' short book, *Joe Biden: American Dreamer* (2020, London: Bloomsbury) has won much attention as a considered portrayal of the new president.

CHAPTER 9

Congress

James M. Curry

Plus ça change, plus c'est la même chose
Jean-Baptiste Alphonse Karr

In some ways, Congress has changed a great deal over the past several decades. Its legislative processes have changed. Its methods of communication with the public have evolved. Most of all, party conflict and party discipline have dramatically increased. At the same time, much has remained the same. Since the founding, most laws have passed Congress with broad bipartisan support and that remains the case, and those laws are still developed by drawing on the specialized knowledge and expertise of lawmakers and their staff.

This chapter takes stock of the contemporary Congress, providing an overview of what has and has not changed on Capitol Hill in recent decades, focusing on Congress's two primary functions: *policymaking* and *representation*. What emerges is a portrait of a dynamic institution that evolves, but in many ways remains the same. On policymaking, we see a legislature that goes about its business in very different ways from the past, but the outcomes of the policymaking process are very similar. On representation, we see an institution that looks dramatically different—it is far more diverse than it was a generation ago—and that communicates with the public in a far more partisan manner. However, representation remains grounded in lawmakers' attentiveness to their specific districts and states.

J. M. Curry (✉)
Department of Political Science, University of Utah, Salt Lake City, UT, USA
e-mail: james.curry@poli-sci.utah.edu

Evolution has been a constant feature of Congress. It has rarely operated in precisely the same manner for any meaningful period. Elected officials of every generation change the institution to adapt to an evolving country and address the challenges facing it. But evolution does not mean congressional politics are completely changed. Nor are the changes necessarily good or bad. Recent, especially partisan, changes to Congress have often been a focal point of criticism of the institution. Lawmakers are seen as too beholden to their parties and too partisan in their rhetoric. Intense two-party conflict is seen as the cause of inaction and gridlock. In the concluding section of this chapter, the changes witnessed in Congress are considered against contemporary concerns that Congress is 'broken,' failing the American public, or in desperate need of reform. In the final analysis, Congress has always been maligned by the American citizenry, but it has always performed better than its greatest detractors believe.

POLICYMAKING

Congressional policymaking is different in many ways than it was a half-century ago. That itself is not terribly surprising. A lot about the world has changed in that time. However, the specific changes that have occurred on Capitol Hill are in many ways more about how Congress goes about its business and less about the outcomes it produces.

What Has Changed?

Changes in membership to the House and Senate, and to the chambers' rules and procedures, have produced a legislature that in many ways looks and operates differently than it did in the 1940s or 1950s. More than anything, Congress is more partisan and party-led in its tenor and its processes.

The first, and perhaps most obvious change, is that Congress is a far more partisan place than it was a half-century ago. Throughout much of the twentieth century, both parties were beset by internal ideological and sectional divides. The Democrats, in particular, were deeply divided into northern and southern factions, representing distinctly liberal and conservative wings of the party. Today, both parties are far more cohesive. The Democratic Party is more uniformly liberal and the Republican Party more uniformly conservative (McCarty 2019). Party divides have been further reinforced by intensified competition for control of the House, Senate, and White House (Lee 2016). Since the 1980s, party majorities in Congress have been historically small and fleeting, with control of the chambers up for grabs in every election. This atmosphere heightens the partisan implications of everything happening on Capitol Hill.

As a result, partisan divides are now readily observable in Congress. They are perhaps no more apparent than in patterns of roll-call voting. Figure 9.1 shows the share of roll-calls on the House and Senate floors that united at

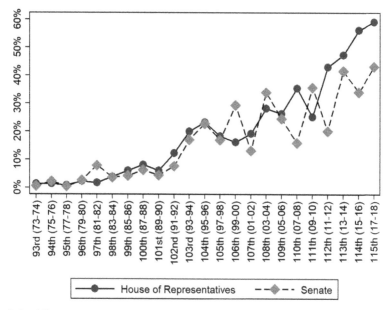

Fig. 9.1 Ninety percent party votes, 1973–2018 (Source: Brookings Institution, 2021. *Vital Statistics on Congress: Data on the US Congress*, Updated February 2021)

least 90 percent of one party against 90 percent of the other, over-time. In the 1970s, votes of this nature were virtually nonexistent. Today, Democrats and Republicans are far more likely to vote in lockstep against each other. During the 115th Congress (2017–2018), for instance, 59 percent of roll-call votes in the House and 43 percent in the Senate pitted 90 percent of one party against 90 percent of the other.

Secondly, Congress has also become more party-centric in how it organizes itself. For much of the twentieth century, from the 1920s through the 1960s, congressional decision-making was dominated by its committees. After a revolt in the House of Representatives against the domineering Speaker Joseph G. Cannon in 1910, committees, and in particular their chairpersons, became centers of power on Capitol Hill (Cooper and Brady 1981). Two strong norms of deference bolstered the power of committees and their chairs during this period. First, legislators largely deferred to the policy decision made by committees. Secondly, within committees, there was a strong deference to seniority. The most senior majority party member of the committee automatically became the chairperson, and the chairperson was delegated authority over the committee's agenda.

During this period committees dominated congressional policymaking. The influence of parties and party leaders was secondary. As Speaker John W.

McCormack (1962–1971) advised new members of Congress at the time, 'Whenever you pass a committee chairman in the House, you bow from the waist. I do.'

In the 1970s, Congress began to make changes (Rohde 1991). First, House Democrats adopted a number of reforms aimed at making committees and their chairs more responsive to the party, requiring chairs to be selected by a secret ballot vote in the party caucus, giving the party caucus the power to assign members to each committee, and reducing the power of committee chairs over subcommittees. House Republicans also adopted reforms, and in some ways went even farther in the 1990s, requiring Appropriations subcommittee chairs—who oversee the writing of spending bills—to pledge to execute the party's plan. Today, obtaining a committee leadership post, or a seat on a powerful committee, requires demonstrating sufficient loyalty to the party as well. Parties are now the most consequential institutions on Capitol Hill.

Congress has also altered its legislative processes. Fifty years ago, Congress typically operated using what are now referred to as 'regular order' processes. There is no standard definition of regular order, but it is what we often think about as the textbook 'how a bill becomes a law' way of doing business on Capitol Hill: bills are introduced and referred to a committee where they are scrutinized in hearings and amended in freewheeling 'mark-ups.' Subsequently, bills are only scheduled on the floor if the committee approves of them at the end of this process. On the House and Senate floors, bills are again debated, and lawmakers have more opportunities to amend. If a bill passes on the floor, it is sent to the other chamber, where this process repeats itself.

This textbook approach was once the norm on Capitol Hill. Today, these processes have been replaced in many cases by centralized, party leadership-led, and behind the scenes approaches labeled as 'unorthodox lawmaking' (Sinclair 2016). Today, committee processes are often truncated or even bypassed entirely during the legislative process. Party leaders are now the central players on Capitol Hill, setting the legislative agenda, and taking the reins developing and negotiating the substance of policy proposals behind the scenes (Curry 2015; Hanson 2014). Curry and Lee (2020) estimate that about half of the important legislation passed by Congress in recent years was considered using at least some unorthodox procedures.

One observable consequence of these changes is that a lot of lawmaking is now accomplished in what congress-watchers call 'omnibus legislation'—massive legislative packages that combined dozens of bills in order to build support for passage. These massive bills are compiled and negotiated with party leaders taking the lead. Indeed, laws enacted by Congress are much longer today than they were a few decades ago. In the 1950s, for instance, the average length of new laws passed by Congress was less than 2.5 pages. Between 2010 and 2018, that average was more than 15 pages (Brookings Institution 2021). Major legislation is often 100s or even 1000s of pages in length, as evidenced by the Coronavirus Aid, Relief, and Economic Security (CARES) Act at 335 pages and the omnibus government spending and Covid-19 relief package enacted by Congress in December 2020 at almost 5600 pages long.

The use of budget reconciliation, a procedure by which Congress can sidestep Senate filibusters to pass some major legislation, is another observable change (Reynolds 2017). Reconciliation has been used by congressional majorities during periods of unified party government in recent years, including most recently to pass the Democrats' American Rescue Plan in March 2021 and the Republicans' Tax Cuts and Jobs Act in December 2017. These reconciliation packages tend to be centralized legislative efforts with party leaders in each chamber taking the lead on negotiations and traditional committee processes side-stepped along the way.

In short, Congress has evolved from a decentralized institution that empowered committees and experienced muted party conflict to a highly partisan and centralized institution. The steps today's Congress takes to make policy certainly look different than they did a generation ago.

What Has Remained the Same?

A lot has changed in how Congress conducts its business, but a lot has also stayed the same. While Congress is organized differently, and conducts its business differently, than in the past, the legislative outcomes it produces appear strikingly similar.

First, and despite all the change that has occurred to the levels of party conflict and to the empowerment of parties and party leaders throughout the legislative process, *policymaking* remains overwhelmingly bipartisan. In other words, while the parties are more internally cohesive, more divided from one another, and more central to legislative decision-making, lawmaking continues to require the building of broad bipartisan support.

Figures 9.2 and 9.3 show the percentage of House and Senate voting in support of new laws on final passage votes from the early 1970s to the late 2010s. Each gray dot is the level of overall chamber support for passage of every law enacted by Congress. The dashed line is an over-time trend. The most striking feature of these figures is how little change is apparent. From 1973 through 1980, bills becoming law were supported on the floor by 89 percent of House members and 88 percent of senators, on average. From 2011 to 2018, bills becoming law were supported by 93 percent of House members and 80 percent of senators, on average. Generally, bills becoming law receive overwhelming support in Congress. Those that do not are rarities.

The high levels of party conflict apparent on roll-call votes generally, shown in Figure 9.1, reflect a rise in the number of messaging votes (discussed below) that Congress takes in order to clarify lines of conflict between the parties. It also reflects the large number of procedural votes taken on the floors of the

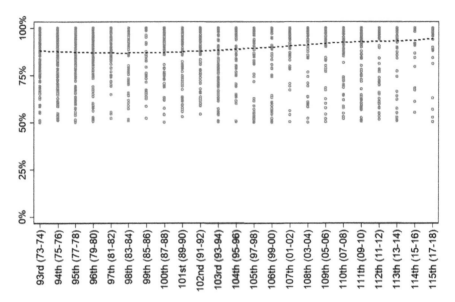

Fig. 9.2 Percent supporting new laws on final passage in the House, 1973–2018 (Source: Data compiled by the author)

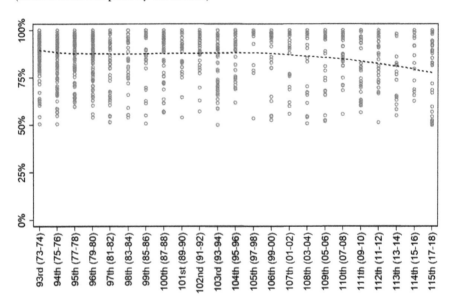

Fig. 9.3 Percent supporting new laws on final passage in the Senate, 1973–2018 (Source: Data compiled by the author)

House and Senate in recent years that divide the parties. What it does not reflect is any rise in the levels of partisanship on things that actually become law.

Congress remains less partisan than it seems in another way as well. As described above, the parties have gained more control over congressional organization and processes. However, neither these newfound powers nor their increased levels of ideological cohesion have translated into clear policy gains. This lack of change is apparent in a study by Curry and Lee (2020). Taking stock of the stated legislative priorities of congressional majority parties from the 1980s through the end of the 2010s, they find that the parties achieve some success on what they set out to achieve about 50 percent of the time. However, there are no discernable over-time patterns in rates of success or failure. Parties are not any better or worse than they were a generation ago at realizing their policy goals through the legislative process. Parties also achieve most of their successes through compromise. In other words, most successes involve backing down on the most controversial aspects of a party's legislative proposals in order to build bipartisan support for passage. Single-party legislative victories, like the Affordable Care Act or the Republican's 2017 Tax Cuts and Jobs Act, were always rare and have not become more common.

How can it be that Congress has become so much more partisan, generally, while lawmaking remains bipartisan? One reason is the disruptive force of the separation of powers system for the parties' ambitions. Parties seeking to enact their policy agendas need to win enough support for passage in the House of Representatives and Senate and earn the signature of the president. This is easier said than done. It has been rare in contemporary American history for all three institutions to be controlled by the same party. Since 1955, the federal government has been under divided control between the parties two-thirds of the time. Since 1981, divided government has been the reality 75 percent of the time. Most of the time, the parties share power in Washington.

However, even unified control of government does not guarantee success for a party. One reason is that the Senate is typically not governed by majority rule. Senate rules require that at least 60 senators agree to end debate on a bill before it can be considered for passage. In the contemporary Congress, this means that legislation needs at least 60 votes in the Senate for passage. Since 1981, however, a Senate majority party has only controlled 60 or more of the chamber's 100 seats just once—when the Democrats held 60 seats for five months in 2009. Otherwise, for more than 39.5 of the last 40 years, getting 60 votes in the Senate has meant reaching across the aisle to build bipartisan support.

Disagreements within the parties also play an underappreciated role in the parties' inabilities to realize dramatic policy gains. In other words, a party's failure to achieve its policy goals is not just the result of a divided government and filibustering. On about half of their stated policy goals since the 1980s, congressional majority parties came up short because they were unable to build enough support for specific legislative proposals from among their own ranks.

Examples of majority party disunity on major legislative proposals are readily apparent. In 2017, the Republicans' efforts to repeal and replace the Affordable Care Act came to an end when three Republican senators refused to back the plan. In 2010, the Democrats were unable to enact their ambitious cap-and-trade proposal to address climate change due to disagreements within their ranks. Forty Democrats opposed the bill on the House floor, and Senate Democrats were split among two competing proposals. In 2005, President George W. Bush's ambitious Social Security reform effort never got off the ground as congressional Republicans were unable to unify enough to even introduce a bill. President Bill Clinton's health care reform efforts went up in flames in 1993–1994 due to divisions among Democrats about how, and how much, to reform federal health care policy.

Congressional productivity has also changed less than most people think. While Congress is an institution that is often beset by gridlock and stalemate, it is not entirely clear that Congress has become less productive in recent decades as party conflict has increased.

By some metrics, Congress appears less productive. Sarah Binder (2014) takes stock of the productivity of Congress by assessing the issues on the national agenda in each year and seeing whether or not Congress took action (passed a law) addressing each issue. She finds that between 1947 and 2012 the share of issues left unaddressed by Congress has increased. Another common metric of congressional productivity is how many laws it passes. Judged by this metric, Congress has become far less productive in recent years. The congresses of the 1950s and 1960s passed between 600 and 1000 new laws every two years. In recent years, those numbers have been much lower. Four of the five congresses that enacted the fewest laws since the late 1940s have taken place since 2010: the 112th (283 laws), the 113th (296 laws), the 114th (329 laws), and the 116th (344).

In contrast, by other measures, Congress appears to have remained far more productive. For instance, while Congress has been passing fewer laws, it continues to pass many pages of law. Figure 9.4 shows the number of pages of new statute enacted by each Congress since the late 1940s. Overall, by this metric, Congress has become *more* productive over the years, not less, increasing its output fourfold. At the very least, it has become neither more nor less productive since the 1980s, even as party conflict has sharply increased in the subsequent decades.

Other fundamental aspects of congressional policymaking have remained important, as well. One of these is the importance of knowledge and expertise on the issues. Developing and writing policy proposals and legislation requires that Congress has a sufficient degree of expertise at its disposal. The congressional committee system formed, in part, to enable Congress to divide labor and develop specialization among its membership on a growing number of issues (Gamm and Shepsle 1989). In the contemporary Congress, the role of committees in harboring and utilizing policy expertise has only grown.

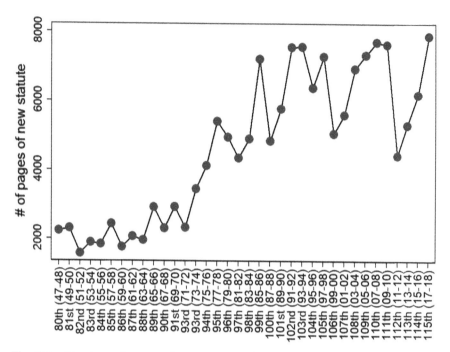

Fig. 9.4 Number of pages of statute enacted by Congress, 1947–2018 (Source: Brookings Institution, 2021. *Vital Statistics on Congress: Data on the US Congress, Updated February 2021*)

Members continue to specialize in issues related to their committee assignments. Committees continue to hire and retain dozens of expert staffers to aid in the writing of legislation. Especially in the House, the quantity and quality of legislative staff employed by congressional committees is unmatched and has helped to maintain the important role of committees in developing legislation in Congress.

The knowledge and expertise of members also continue to shape the building of coalitions and support for legislation in Congress. Having specialized in only one or two issues, lawmakers must nevertheless cast votes on bills and amendments addressing other issues on which they have little expertise or background. In recent years, the extent to which members of Congress cast votes with only limited information has been exacerbated by leadership-led processes that speed up the consideration of large omnibus packages and leave many members in the dark about the full contents and implications of the items on which they are voting (Curry 2015).

Needing information, lawmakers routinely seek cues from colleagues they view as knowledgeable and trustworthy to decide what to support and how to vote. Committee leaders—chairs and minority ranking members—are a major source of these cues. In both the House and Senate, there is evidence that statements and voting cues given by committee leaders and committee members shape the votes of their colleagues and the likelihood that floor amendments pass or fail (Curry 2019; Fong 2020).

Policymaking in Perspective

In short, while Congress has changed, much about congressional policy-making remains the same. Despite increased party conflict and party power on Capitol Hill, most laws continue to be passed with overwhelming bipartisan support, and majority parties achieve their policy goals mostly through bipartisan compromises. Despite concerns about growing gridlock, there is mixed evidence that Congress has become less productive since the mid-twentieth century. Despite legislative processes that are more party-centric, the policy knowledge and expertise of committees, committee members, and committee staff continue to play an important role in policymaking.

REPRESENTATION

In some ways, Congress has changed more in how it represents the American public than in policymaking. Today, Congress is far more representative of the diversity of the American populace than at any time in its history. It is also in some ways more effective at reflecting and communicating the political disagreements that exist in the country, and at communicating with constituents. Of course, some things remain the same. Members of the House and Senate still build support among voters by cultivating a personal vote in their districts and states. It may be harder in today's partisan environment for lawmakers to develop loyal bases of voter support independent of partisanship, but it is still possible.

What Has Changed?

Three big changes have permeated congressional representation in recent decades. First, Congress has become more descriptively representative of the American public. It is often noted that Congress does not look like America. That is correct—it does not. As a representative institution it remains heavily white, wealthy, and male. However, in recent decades Congress has become far more diverse in almost every way. The 117th Congress (2021–2023) is the most diverse in history on gender, race, and ethnicity.

Gender representation has seen dramatic gains in recent years (Center for American Women and Politics 2021). Seventy years ago, at the start of the 82nd Congress (1951–1952), there were just eight women in Congress—seven in the House and one in the Senate. Thirty years later, at the start of the 1980s (97th Congress, 1981–1982), women's representation had improved only marginally, with 23 women (21 representatives and two senators) on

Capitol Hill. Today, women's representation is far more apparent. At the start of the 117th Congress (2021–2022), there were 143 women in Congress— 27 percent of the body's membership—including 119 in the House and 24 in the Senate. These numbers are still a long way from gender-parity, but there are differences in that regard between the parties. Most of the women on Capitol Hill, almost 75 percent, are members of the Democratic Party. House Democrats are almost evenly split between the genders—49 percent of House Democrats are women compared to 14 percent of House Republicans. In the Senate, one-third of Democrats are women compared to 16 percent of Republicans.

Congress has become more racially and ethnically diverse as well. Seventy years ago, Congress was almost entirely white. At the start of the 82nd Congress (1951–1852), for example, there were just two Black Americans, three Latinos, and one Native American in the House. The U.S. Senate was 100 percent white. At the start of the 117th Congress (2021–2022), in contrast, almost one-quarter of the Congress was racially or ethnically diverse (Schaeffer 2021). This diversity is most apparent in the House, where 14 percent of lawmakers are Black—a proportion almost identical to the share of Black Americans in the general public. Another nine percent identified as Hispanic, three percent as Asian-American or Pacific Islander, and one percent as Native American. These percentages are lower than in the American public but are closer to that benchmark than they were a generation ago. In the Senate, diversity is far less apparent, where 89 out of 100 senators were white in 2021.

Representation of other historically underrepresented groups has also reached new highs. The 117th Congress (2021–2022) had a historic number of openly LGBTQ members: ten in total, with eight in the House and two in the Senate. These numbers remain small, but prior to the 1980s, there had not been any openly LGBTQ individuals in the House or Senate. Congress has also become less overwhelmingly Christian in recent years, though Christians are still over-represented in the House and Senate relative to the American public (Pew Research Center 2021). In the 1960s, 93 percent of members of Congress identified as Protestant or Catholic. At the start of the 117th Congress (2021–2022), that share had dropped somewhat to 85 percent. The shares of Jews, Muslims, Hindus, Buddhists, and Mormons now either meet or exceed their shares of the U.S. population. The most underrepresented religious group on Capitol Hill are those who do not affiliate with any religion. These individuals comprise roughly one-quarter of the public, but less than one percent of lawmakers.

Much of the growing diversity on Capitol Hill has been concentrated in the Democratic Party. Not only are most women in Congress Democrats, so are most Blacks, Latinos, Non-Christians, and every LGBTQ member. In the 117th Congress (2021–2022), 92 percent of Republicans were white,

85 percent were male, 99 percent were Christian, and none were openly LGBTQ. There are also some dimensions on which Congress has not become more representative relative to the public. Congress remains overwhelmingly wealthy. It is also much older than the general adult population. But still, recent decades have witnessed dramatic improvements in diversity.

The growing diversity of Congress matters. Political scientists have found a number of substantive consequences of so-called 'descriptive representation.' For one, there is substantial evidence that lawmakers from historically under-represented groups are more attentive to the interests and needs of those who share their identities. In other words, women lawmakers are generally more attentive to issues of importance to women (Swers 2013), BIPOC (Black, Indigenous, and People of Color) lawmakers are more attentive to issues of importance to BIPOC Americans (Rouse 2013; Tate 2018), and LGBTQ lawmakers are more attentive to issues of importance to LGBTQ lawmakers (Hansen and Treul 2015). Adding diversity to the rolls of representatives in Washington helps give voice and attention to more classes of Americans.

There are also differences in the legislative effectiveness of lawmakers from varying backgrounds and identities. One consistent finding is that women representatives are more effective lawmakers than men (Anzia and Berry 2011). Because it is harder for women to get to Congress, those who make it tend to be exceptionally skilled and qualified, more-so than their male counterparts, on average. Evidence on the success found by BIPOC legislators is more mixed, and most of that research is focused on legislative action in state legislatures. Women of color, in particular, face barriers that can undermine their influence on Capitol Hill (Hawkesworth 2003).

Nevertheless, diversity on Capitol Hill likely improves Congress's responsiveness to different people. Legislators often have skewed perceptions of their constituents and are generally more responsive to constituent outreach and opinion coming from people they perceive to be like them. In other words, white legislators are more likely to respond to constituency requests from constituents they perceive as white, while black legislators are more likely to respond to constituents they perceive as black (Butler and Broockman 2011). Similarly, women legislators are more likely to respond to requests from women (Lowande et al. 2019).

Altogether, while the faces of Congress do not fully reflect the diversity of America, that diversity has improved. Those improvements have had important benefits for the representation of women, racial and ethnic minorities, LGBTQ Americans, and more.

A second change regards congressional communications. Today's Congress is better than those of past eras at communicating and clarifying the lines of disagreement between the parties. A generation ago, many in the public complained that the parties were insufficiently distinct, and many could not adequately ascertain the differences between the parties on many issues. Scholars and reformers advocated more 'responsible parties' that would advocate clear and divergent platforms to present as options to the public. Today, the wishes of party reformers have been realized in many ways. Voters are far better able to identify differences between the parties compared to the past (Hetherington 2001).

In addition to the growth of party cohesion described above, improved party messaging has also played a role in this new reality. Democrats and Republicans in both chambers have invested heavily in communications and public relations operations. Fifty years ago, just five percent of the staff to congressional party leaders had job titles related to communications. By 2015, more than 40 percent of Senate leadership staff and 30 percent of House leadership staff worked in communications (Lee 2016). These staff help the parties develop, communicate, and coordinate public relations campaigns for the parties.

The parties have also taken advantage of their expanded procedural control over the House and Senate floors to set up so-called 'messaging votes.' These are largely symbolic bills and amendments that are not designed to impact public policy, but instead to communicate party differences via provoking party divisions on roll-call votes. These votes enable parties to demonstrate solidarity with groups of voters in their party's coalition and show voters what they would do if they could make policy all on their own. These votes can also help draw contrasts with the other party which can be useful come election season.

Messaging votes are often maligned, and they undoubtedly have costs, allowing members of Congress to pander to constituents without having to acknowledge the real-world trade-offs of their specific policy proposals. However, these activities also serve an educational function, helping today's voters better understand the differences between the parties, and to make informed choices at the ballot box.

Individual members of Congress have found their communications capacities improved in recent years as well, owing to advancements in communications technology in the twenty-first century. Members of Congress have quickly adapted to social media, using Twitter, Facebook, and other platforms to communicate directly with their constituents and the broader public. During the 116th Congress (2019–2020), members of the House and Senate tweeted more than 1.5 million times and some lawmakers have millions of followers on Twitter.

Social media has allowed more lawmakers more opportunities to communicate with national audiences without a filter. No longer must they wait to be invited to speak on national news outlets, or to be recognized to speak on the House or Senate floors. They can now communicate whatever messages they prefer, whenever they wish. This has given voice to perspectives and constituencies that in the past might have been sidelined by party leaders. New media outlets may afford increased prominence to more extreme voices on both sides of the aisle. Good or bad, it means that more voices than ever are reflected and projected by members of the House and Senate.

What Has Remained the Same?

Not everything about congressional representation has changed. Adjustments to congressional demographics, messaging, and media technology have not altered one of the most fundamental aspects of congressional representation: the geographic basis of congressional apportionment. Unlike the elected legislatures in most other modern democracies, Congress continues to elect its members from single-member geographically separate districts and states. This structure ensures that since 'each representative is beholden to a specific geographical area, issues that are important to a particular neighborhood or region are sure to have a champion' (Amy 2000).

Representatives and senators in Congress continue to allocate substantial times and energy into cultivating a personal vote among their constituents—one that is sometimes separate from their party affiliation. The typical member of Congress dedicates about half of their professional staff to what is called 'constituent service'—that is, responding to requests from constituents for help. Large numbers of citizens report having this kind of contact with their representatives, receiving help resolving problems with their Social Security checks, veterans' benefits, citizenship status, and more.

Lawmakers also seek to cultivate a personal vote by 'bringing home the bacon.' Whether called 'congressionally directed spending,' 'earmarks,' or something else, members of Congress are able to direct federal spending for projects in their districts and state, including fixing roads, improving schools, building community centers, purchasing firefighting equipment, and more. Often derided as 'pork,' these federal projects can make a big difference in communities throughout the country. The geographic basis of representation in Congress ensures that every community has a local advocate fighting to direct funds to them, rather than elsewhere (Lee 2003). Members of Congress, in turn, are happy to talk about their efforts on the campaign trail in order to cultivate voters.

Beyond constituent service and pork, geographic representation also ensures different communities and regions across the country, with different interests and opinions, have an advocate as policy is being made. It ensures that both parties in Congress are at least somewhat geographically diverse, representing varied parts of the country. Consequently, the parties are responsive to less narrow interests than they might otherwise be as they develop legislation.

Democrats, for instance, have to consider more than just urban and coastal areas when they develop climate change legislation. Though most of their representatives come from these parts of the country, enough also represent districts and states from the interior of the country, including from coal and gas producing areas. Republicans must consider the interests of citizens in varied parts of the country, as well. In their drive to replace the Affordable Care Act in 2017, Republicans ran into resistance from members of their own party representing states that had benefited from the generous Medicaid expansion included in the law. In their effort to reform the tax code later that year, they encountered opposition to the proposed elimination of the SALT (state and local tax) deduction from Republicans representing states with higher tax rates. The geographic basis of representation in Congress ensured that these interests were heard, rather than ignored.

In short, the ties geographic representation creates between members of Congress and their constituents benefit Americans across the country. It ensures every community in America has an advocate, seeking to support local concerns and interests, and helping citizens in that part of the country get what they need from the federal government. The increased partisan loyalty of voters and the decline of 'split' districts and states (those that vote for a congressional candidate from one party and a presidential candidate from another) has certainly created new challenges for lawmakers as they seek to cultivate a personal vote. It is harder for members of one party to win reelection in places that lean toward the other party. Nevertheless, lawmakers like West Virgina Democrat Joe Manchin, Maine Republican Susan Collins, and Montana Democrat Jon Tester show that it is still possible.

Conclusions

Congress has often been a focal point of criticism. Today it is derided as a dysfunctional 'broken branch,' incapable of dealing with the country's challenges. Some of that derision focuses on how Congress has *changed* over the last half-century. Intense two-party conflict is blamed for gridlock and inaction on Capitol Hill. Congress is seen as a place where either one party steamrolls the other or nothing happens at all, and where legislative considerations reflect nothing but partisan calculations. The quality of representation from members in Congress is also seen as suspect. Lawmakers are seen as too beholden to their parties today to provide their constituents with adequate representation.

The analysis here indicates that while Congress has changed quite a bit, and become unmistakably more partisan, not all of these supposed negative consequences are apparent. Congressional parties are far more powerful institutions on Capitol Hill than they were a generation ago, and congressional processes are far more centralized and managed by party leaders. However, laws continue to be enacted with the same levels of bipartisan support that they earned in the 1970s, and the parties have not become any better (or worse) at achieving their legislative goals. Nor is it the case that congressional productivity has ceased—it is passing just as much statute (in total pages) as it was 40 years ago. Moreover, all of the partisan change has not erased the important role of knowledge and expertise in legislative politics, either. Members of Congress still specialize in their efforts and develop expertise on a small number of issues. Committees continue to be central nodes of expertise on their issues, drawing on the experience of committee members, and the technical knowledge of their staffs, to develop policy proposals, and to sway the votes of their colleagues.

Congressional representation, though changed, has not entirely changed for the worse, either. Members of Congress clearly behave in more partisan ways. That may frustrate many citizens, but it is also the case that lawmakers remain attentive champions for their districts and states. Efforts to bring home the bacon, and provide service and policy representation to constituents, remain hallmarks of Congress. Recent efforts to bring back earmarks (which designate funds for a specific purpose) are a testament to that fact. It is also hard to deny the clearly positive changes to descriptive representation on Capitol Hill. Congress is far more reflective of the American public than at any other time in the past. This, along with advances in communication technologies, has enabled Congress to speak on behalf of a more diverse array of constituencies than ever before. While still a long way from reflecting all of the rich diversity in the country, the level of diversity in Congress today is an unmistakably positive change.

Congress is far from perfect. There remains much to dislike about the institution and many reasons to be concerned. Not all the changes we have observed on Capitol Hill are desirable, by any means. But it is also not the case that Congress has experienced wholesale change or change entirely for the worse. Congress is an ever-evolving institution, but it is also an institution in which much remains the same.

References

Amy, D.J. 2000. *Behind the Ballot Box: A Citizen's Guide to Voting Systems*. Praeger.

Anzia, S.F., and C.R. Berry. 2011. The Jackie (and Jill) Robinson Effect: Why Do Congresswomen Outperform Congressmen? *American Journal of Political Science* 55 (3): 478–493.

Binder, S.A. 2014. Polarized We Govern? *Brookings Institution Press.* https://www.brookings.edu/wp-content/uploads/2016/06/BrookingsCEPM_Polarized_figRep lacedTextRevTableRev.pdf.

Brookings Institution. 2021. *Vital Statistics on Congress.* https://www.brookings.edu/multi-chapter-report/vitalstatistics-on-congress/.

Butler, D.M., and D.E. Broockman. 2011. Do Politicians Racially Discriminate Against Constituents? A Field Experiment on State Legislators. *American Journal of Political Science* 55 (3): 463–477.

Center for American Women and Politics. 2021. History of Women in the U.S. Congress. https://cawp.rutgers.edu/history-women-us-congress.

Cooper, J., and D.W. Brady. 1981. Institutional Context and Leadership Style: The House from Cannon to Rayburn. *American Political Science Review* 75 (2): 411–425.

Curry, J.M. 2015. *Legislating in the Dark: Information and Power in the House of Representatives*. Chicago: University of Chicago Press.

———. 2019. Knowledge, Expertise, and Committee Power in the Contemporary Congress. *Legislative Studies Quarterly* 42 (2): 203–237.

Curry, J.M., and F.E. Lee. 2020. *The Limits of Party: Congress and Lawmaking in a Polarized Era*. University of Chicago Press.

Fong, C. 2020. Expertise, Networks, and Interpersonal Influence in Congress. *Journal of Politics* 82 (1): 269–284.

Gamm, G., and K. Shepsle. 1989. Emergence of Legislative Institutions: Standing Committees in the House and Senate, 1810–1825. *Legislative Studies Quarterly* 14 (1): 39–66.

Hansen, E.R., and S.A. Treul. 2015. The Symbolic and Substantive Representation of LGB Americans in the US House. *Journal of Politics* 77 (4): 955–967.

Hanson, P. 2014. *Too Weak to Govern: Majority Party Power and Appropriations in the US Senate*. New York: Cambridge University Press.

Hawkesworth, M. 2003. Congressional Enactments of Race-Gender: Toward a Theory of Raced-Gendered Institutions. *American Political Science Review* 97 (4): 529–550.

Hetherington, M.J. 2001. Resurgent Mass Partisanship: The Role of Elite Polarization. *American Political Science Review* 95 (3): 619–631.

Lee, F.E. 2003. Geographic Politics in the U.S. House of Representatives: Coalition Building and Distribution of Benefits. *American Journal of Political Science* 47 (4): 714–728.

———. 2016. *Insecure Majorities: Congress and the Perpetual Campaign*. Chicago: University of Chicago Press.

Lowande, K., M. Ritchie, and E. Lauterbach. 2019. Descriptive and Substantive Representation in Congress: Evidence from 80,000 Congressional Inquiries. *American Journal of Political Science* 63 (3): 644–659.

McCarty, N. 2019. *Polarization: What Everyone Needs to Know*. Oxford University Press.

Pew Research Center. 2021. Faith on the Hill: The Religious Composition of the 117th Congress. https://www.pewforum.org/2021/01/04/faith-on-the-hill-2021/.

Reynolds, M.E. 2017. *Exceptions to the Rule: The Politics of Filibuster Limitations in the U.S. Senate*. Washington, DC: Brookings Institution Press.

Rohde, D.W. 1991. *Parties and Leaders in the Postreform House*. Chicago: University of Chicago Press.

Rouse, S.M. 2013. *Latinos in the Legislative Process: Interests and Influence*. New York: Cambridge University Press.

Schaeffer, K. 2021. *Racial, Ethnic Diversity Increases Yet Again with the 117th Congress*. FactTank: PEW Research Center.

Sinclair, B. 2016. *Unorthodox Lawmaking: New Legislative Processes in the US Congress*. Thousand Oaks, CA: CQ Press.

Swers, M.L. 2013. *Women in the Club: Gender and Policy Making in the Senate*. Chicago: University of Chicago Press.

Tate, K. 2018. *Black Faces in the Mirror: African Americans and Their Representatives in the U.S. Congress*. Princeton: Princeton University Press.

FURTHER READING

There are many good books about what has changed, and what has not, in congressional policymaking. On what has changed, Barbara Sinclair's (2016) *Unorthodox Lawmaking: New Legislative Processes in the U.S. Congress* (Washington, DC: CQ Press) provides a thorough overview of changes to congressional processes; David Rohde's (1991) *Parties and Leaders in the Postreform House* (Chicago: University of Chicago Press) covers the party reforms of the 1970s and their consequences; and Frances Lee's (2016) *Insecure Majorities: Congress and the Perpetual Campaign* (Chicago: University of Chicago Press) details how the tactics of congressional parties have become more confrontation in recent decades. On what has remained the same, David Mayhew's (2017) *The Imprint of Congress* (New Haven, CT: Yale University Press) provides an insightful historical account of the performance of the U.S. Congress and its impact on American society; and James Curry's and Frances Lee's (2020) *The Limits of Party: Congress and Lawmaking in a Polarized Era* (Chicago: University of Chicago Press) shows how congressional policymaking has remained largely bipartisan despite rising partisanship in American politics.

Many books and readings cover the evolution of congressional representation, as well. Michele Swers's (2013) *Women in the Club: Gender and Policy Making in the Senate* (Chicago: University of Chicago Press) and Dittmar's, Sanbonmatsu's, and Carroll's (2018) *A Seat at the Table: Congresswomen's Perspectives on Why Their Presence Matters* (New York: Oxford University Press) examine the influence and importance of women's representation. Stella Rouse's (2013) *Latinos in the Legislative Process: Interests and Influence* (New York: Cambridge University Press) and Katherine Tate's (2018) *Black Faces in the Mirror: African Americans and Their Representatives in the U.S. Congress* (Princeton, NJ: Princeton University Press) examine descriptive representation among Latinx and Black Americans, respectively. Nicholas Carnes's (2013) *White-Collar Government: The Hidden Role of Class in Economic Policy Making* (Chicago: University of Chicago Press) and Kristina Miler's (2018) *Poor Representation: Congress and the Politics of Poverty in the United States* (New York: Cambridge University Press) highlight representation of the poor and working classes in Congress. Hansen's and Treul's (2015), 'The Symbolic and Substantive Representation of LGB Americans in the US House' (*Journal of Politics* 77:4, 955–967) examines LGBT representation in Congress.

CHAPTER 10

The Politics of the Courts

Emma Long

The four years of the Trump Administration saw significant changes within the US federal court system. Trump appointed almost a quarter of all lower federal court judges, an opportunity afforded by several years of Senate Republicans' refusal to hold hearings for President Obama's nominees. These judges serve for life and their influence is likely to stretch well into the future. Trump also found himself with the opportunity to appoint three new Supreme Court Justices. While appointing a third of the nation's highest court would be significant enough, the nature of those appointments had outsized importance, providing the first chance in decades to shift decisively the balance on the Court to the conservatives. The combination of life tenure and his appointees' relative youth means Trump's impact on the Court will remain current even as historians look to write their first assessments of his Administration.

But perhaps more significant than the impact of new personnel on the work of the courts is Trump's impact on the culture of the judiciary. The lasting legacy of the Trump Administration may well be the deepening politicisation of the courts. Trump and his supporters, more than any previous administration, treated the courts as the spoils of electoral victory, another branch of government over which they could expect control and from which they expected cooperation. The two Supreme Court appointments which bookended his presidency revealed this clearly. But at the same time, when rulings

E. Long (✉)
School of Art, Media and American Studies, University of East Anglia, Norwich, UK
e-mail: emma.long@uea.ac.uk

© The Author(s), under exclusive license to Springer Nature Switzerland AG 2022
G. Peele et al. (eds.), *Developments in American Politics 9*,
https://doi.org/10.1007/978-3-030-89740-6_10

did not go his way, Trump attacked individual judges and their courts and interpreted their actions as challenges to his own personal power and authority. In this he echoed other areas of his presidency where dissent was considered disloyalty and challenges were interpreted as the work of the political forces ranged against him. In relation to the courts, Trump exacerbated, although he did not create, a growing trend to see judges as political actors and their rulings primarily in the context of their significance for policy questions. Such perception of the work of the courts, especially of the Supreme Court, is dangerous to the institutional legitimacy on which the Court relies for its authority. The long-term significance of this politicisation, however, may rest in the actions of Democrats and the administration of President Joe Biden.

The Politics of Judicial Appointments I: The Political Spoils

Treating the Supreme Court as part of the political spoils associated with winning the election campaign was one of the ways in which Trump and the Republicans deepened the politicisation of the federal judiciary. Although using language which sought to distance themselves from obvious partisanship, a comparison of the events of 2016 and 2020 reveals the politics behind their actions.

In 2016, following the death of conservative icon Justice Antonin Scalia, Republicans, determined to prevent President Obama making a third appointment to the Court, announced that they would not hold hearings on any nominee put forward by the Administration. The election was then nine months away and they duly did as they promised: they delayed holding hearings on Obama's nominee, Judge Merrick Garland, for a record-breaking 293 days until his nomination lapsed with the end of the 114th Congress. In contrast, Scalia's successor, Justice Neil Gorsuch, moved from nomination to appointment in 66 days. In 2020, when liberal icon Justice Ruth Bader Ginsburg died less than two months before the election, Trump and Senate Republicans moved to appoint Amy Coney Barrett to the Court in under six weeks. When she took office on 27 October 2020, the presidential election was two weeks away. The contrast between the inaction in 2016 and the subsequent speedy response in 2020 highlights the fact that, regardless of the political rhetoric, the different approaches were about ensuring Republicans the opportunity to fill the vacancies on the Supreme Court.

Leading Republicans supported and defended their actions in terms which treated Court appointments as simply one more benefit of winning at the ballot box, although they wrapped it in the language of deference to the will of the people. 'The American people shouldn't be denied a voice,' declared Chair of the Senate Judiciary Committee Senator Chuck Grassley in March 2016 (Desjardins 2020). More than 20 Republican Senators defended the refusal to hold hearings on Garland on the grounds of the people's right to have a say in the direction of the Court by waiting until after the election. Then only a candidate, Trump also played his part, using tweets and speeches to emphasize the importance of the Court to the election and to the nation. 'Hopefully the Republican Party can come together and have a big WIN in November, paving the way for many great Supreme Court Justices!' he tweeted in March 2016. Four years later Trump repeated the message: 'We were put in this position of power and importance to make decisions for the people who so proudly elected us, the most important of which has long been considered to be the selection of United States Supreme Court Justices. We have this obligation, without delay!' Senate Majority Leader, and architect of all three of Trump's Court appointments, Mitch McConnell agreed, arguing: '… Americans reelected our majority in 2016 and expanded it in 2018 because we pledged to work with President Trump and support his agenda, particularly his outstanding appointments to the federal judiciary' (Desjardins 2020).

Federal judicial appointments are, of course, inherently connected to electoral outcomes. Under the terms of Article 2, Section 2 of the Constitution, candidates are nominated by the president and appointed with the advice and consent of the Senate, inextricably linking appointments to election results. So the actions of Trump and the Republicans connecting the two vacancies on the Court at either end of his term of office to the respective elections were, in some ways, a simple recognition of the reality: the party and individual who holds office has control over appointments. But the unprecedented refusal to hold hearings in 2016, and then the speed with which hearings took place four years later, spoke more of a deliberate attempt to manipulate the timeline to achieve desired outcomes. Trump and McConnell's decision to ignore the fact that the 2018 elections had returned the House to Democratic control, and thus somewhat muddied the waters when it came to the 'will of the people,' spoke to similar intent. Republicans were blatantly playing politics with the Court while denying doing anything of the sort.

The politics of both appointments occasionally leaked out in Republican comments about the respective nominations, however. Ironically Republicans in 2016 offered the Biden Rule in defense of delaying hearings. In a 1992 Senate speech, Biden had stated: 'once the political season is under way … action on a Supreme Court nomination must be put off until after the election campaign is over.' The purpose of this, Biden made clear, was to avoid partisanship creeping into a nomination process already under scrutiny after the bitter hearings over the nomination of Clarence Thomas. The absence of Republican discussion of this element of Biden's speech was important in changing the context of the Biden Rule: far from avoiding divisive partisanship, quoting the sitting Vice President while obstructing President Obama seemed designed to deepen such divisions. Similar partisan sentiments were evident elsewhere. 'The Senate Republican majority was elected to be a check and balance to President Obama,' declared Senator John Thune, echoing indirectly McConnell's widely quoted 2010 declaration that 'the single most important thing we want to achieve is for President Obama to be a one-term president' (Desjardins 2020; Kessler 2017). In 2020, President Trump warned his supporters that Joe Biden and 'far-left lunatics' would be in charge of the Supreme Court should Republicans not turn out to vote: 'Biden will destroy the United States Supreme Court. Don't let this happen!' Indirectly, then, the president and other leading Republicans made clear that their actions regarding the appointments of Gorsuch in 2016 and Barrett in 2020 were deeply motivated by the very partisan politics Joe Biden had spoken of trying to avoid.

In 2020, however, Democrats also linked election results and the Court vacancy. Biden, now Democratic candidate for the presidency, and Senate Minority Leader Chuck Schumer echoed Republicans' arguments about democratic legitimacy and argued the voice of the American people 'should be heard.' Such arguments carried equally little weight to those offered by Republicans: both parties were looking for the opportunity to fill the vacancy. But the Democrats' arguments in 2020 suggest that the explicit linking of the Court and electoral politics may have become a widespread trend. Even if the battles of 2016 and 2020 were unusual in offering two election-year vacancies so close together, and allowing that election year nomination battles heighten the connections of the Court to the election in ways not seen at other times, the willingness of both parties to make the connections is a potentially worrying development for the institutional legitimacy of the Court. If the Court is increasingly seen as filled by justices appointed via unfair practices or packed with politically motivated appointees, the legitimacy of their rulings may well also come into question.

The Politics of Judicial Appointments II: Shaping the Court

The second way in which the Trump Administration and leading Republicans risked deepening the politicisation of the judiciary's work was in the nature of the appointments themselves. In this, the historical moment played a significant role. On a Court finely balanced between liberals and conservatives for decades, each new appointment held the possibility of shifting the balance decisively one way or the other, heightening the political tensions around each Court vacancy.

It is widely accepted by scholars and commentators that presidents seek to appoint justices to the Supreme Court whose ideology broadly aligns with theirs (Nemacheck 2008). This phenomenon is not new. In 1800, President John Adams appointed Chief Justice John Marshall to the Court in large part because, as a Federalist, Adams hoped Marshall might act as a restraint on the incoming Republican Administration of Thomas Jefferson. Justices are often assessed by how closely or not their opinions over their careers aligned with the ideologies of the presidents who appointed them. So there has long been an understanding that presidents may, broadly, seek to shape the ideological makeup of the Supreme Court through the nomination process.

Two factors raised the stakes for Trump's appointees. First, it has become increasingly common among scholars, politicians, and the media to discuss the Court more explicitly in partisan terms. In 1993, Jeffrey Segal and Harold Spaeth asserted that justices were policymakers who, more often than not, voted for results in cases that aligned with their personal political views. The justices themselves have consistently resisted this portrayal of their work. Then-nominee for Chief Justice John Roberts commented in 2005 in testimony before the Senate Judiciary Committee: 'Judges and justices are servants of the law, not the other way around … Judges are like umpires. Umpires don't make the rules; they apply them' (US Committee on the Judiciary 2005). More than a decade later, lamenting the partisan nomination process, Justice Elena Kagan argued, 'it makes the world think we are sort of junior varsity politicians. I think that's not the way we think of ourselves, even given the fact that we disagree' (Ehrlich 2018). While scholars have suggested the influence of, among others, public opinion, the need for institutional balance, and pragmatism on judicial decision-making, the justices themselves argue the overriding factors are the law, legal interpretation, and precedent. But Segal and Spaeth's theory has proved consequential, shaping not only scholarly work on the Court but public discussions too. Thus references to 'liberal' or 'conservative' justices, which once meant the broad judicial philosophies and approaches of the members of the Supreme Court, have increasingly (and misleadingly) come to be shorthand for rulings and approaches which appear to favor Democrats or Republicans. Discussions among scholars, commentators, the media, and politicians have in recent decades thus deepened this perception of justices as partisan political actors, despite repeated denials from justices on both sides of the political sphere that this is how they operate.

The ideological balance on the Court in 2016 only heightened the significance of this understanding. Following Earl Warren's retirement as Chief Justice in 1969, the very liberal Court slowly became more conservative, the legacy of more appointments by Republican presidents. By the 1980s, the Court was balanced between liberals and conservatives with Justice Sandra Day O'Connor in the center. Following O'Connor, Justice Anthony Kennedy and then, after 2018, Chief Justice John Roberts occupied the role as 'swing justice': judicially conservative but willing, on occasion, to vote with the Court's liberal members to determine the outcome of cases. On abortion, gay rights, and Obamacare, each had, in turn, disappointed political conservatives. Now the opportunity to appoint new justices offered Trump and Senate Republicans the chance to fundamentally shift the ideological balance on the Court to the right, fulfilling a decades-long project to establish a decisive, dependable conservative majority (Teles 2008; Bennett 2017).

In this light, the battles over Court vacancies in 2016 and 2020 were mirror images of each other. In 2016, a Democratic president sought to replace a leading conservative jurist with a (moderate) liberal; in 2020, a Republican president had the opportunity to replace a leading liberal jurist with what, most suspected, would be a deeply conservative jurist. Either would tilt the balance on the Court. The delay in the former case and the hurry in the latter indicated that control of the Court's ideological makeup was crucial to the actions of Republicans and the Trump Administration and to the outrage felt by Democrats who accused their political opponents of 'stealing' the nominations. Such motives were reflected in their language. 'We cannot afford to lose the Supreme Court for generations to come,' stated then-presidential hopeful Ted Cruz in March 2016. 'President Obama,' echoed Senator Richard Shelby, 'is attempting to solidify his liberal agenda by drastically changing the direction of the Court for decades to come.' Eschewing the overt politics, McConnell and Grassley also made references to 'change' on the Court if Garland was appointed. In 2020, Cruz again warned the nation was, 'one vote away from losing our fundamental constitutional liberties,' while Senator Kelly Loeffler declared, 'Our country's future is at stake' (Desjardins 2020). Both appeared to have taken cues from the President who tweeted frequently about the threat to the Court and to American liberties, offering the outlandish prediction on 21 October that 'The first thing Washington Democrats will do if Biden is elected is pack the Supreme Court with radical left judges who will eliminate your 2nd Amendment.' Democrats also drew on the political consequences of Barrett's appointment, emphasizing threats from a conservative Court to the availability of abortion, marriage equality, and federal healthcare provision. Perhaps most obviously, Democratic members of the Senate Judiciary Committee boycotted the committee vote on Barrett, which they could not win, instead leaving pictures of those they claimed had been aided by the now-threatened Affordable Care Act.

This was not, of course, the first time the Supreme Court had been made a political issue. President Nixon's 'law and order' campaign in 1968 was a barely concealed attack on the criminal justice rulings of the Warren Court while President Reagan's promise to appoint only 'strict constructionists,' or those who would interpret the law narrowly, was a coded message for seeking conservative judicial appointments. But Trump and leading Republicans employed the politics more directly and blatantly than in any previous election, tying judicial appointments more deliberately and explicitly to partisanship. At the same time, Democrats' willingness to engage in similar kinds of rhetoric, linking appointees explicitly with preferred legal and jurisprudential outcomes, is deeply concerning as it suggests a new norm. The battles over both Gorsuch and Barrett reinforced the sense of Supreme Court Justices as political actors by debating their appointments in explicitly political terms. The risk is that their rulings come to be seen in the same light. Polls already suggest the American public see the Court as making political decisions (*Pew Research Center* 2015; Hartig 2020). If that continues, exacerbated by debates like those of 2016 and 2020, the risk is a shift from seeing judicial opinions as political to seeing them as illegitimate.

Aware of the heated political battles surrounding them, Gorsuch and Barrett were the models of judicial impartiality through the nomination and hearing processes. Both refused to be drawn on questions with political impli-cations. Barrett in particular was criticized for being evasive and failing to answer even basic questions about her understanding of the law and the Constitution under the guise of remaining politically neutral. In his 2018 nomination hearings, by contrast, Brett Kavanaugh took a very different approach.

Kavanaugh's nomination avoided the electoral politics which dogged those of his colleagues, but was deeply enmeshed in the politics of the Court's ideo-logical balance. Having sat at the Court's center for more than a decade, Kennedy's retirement was a major blow to Democrats who had hoped he would remain on the bench until Trump left office. Permitting Trump to appoint his successor would shift the balance on the Court further to the right and, without a Senate majority, Democrats were unable to block his appointment. Beyond this, however, the politics came from the nominee himself.

The catalyst for an unprecedented outburst of partisan politics from a judi-cial nominee was a leaked story that Kavanaugh had been accused of sexual assault. Initially intended to be private information, eventually Professor Chris-tine Blasey Ford's name became public and, on 27 September 2018, she testified before the Senate Judiciary Committee that while they were both in high school, Kavanaugh had sexually assaulted her. In a lengthy opening statement, Kavanaugh denied the allegations. But in doing so he brought party politics to bear from the start. Referring to the investigation which had followed the initial leak of the allegations, he argued: 'This whole two-week effort has been a calculated and orchestrated political hit, fueled with apparent pent-up anger about President Trump and the 2016 election, fear that has been unfairly stoked about my judicial record, revenge on behalf of the Clintons and millions of dollars in money from outside left-wing opposition groups' (*New York Times* 2018). Kavanaugh's statement brought presidential politics directly into the nomination hearings.

Using attack as a method of defense, Kavanaugh echoed the approach of his now-colleague, Justice Clarence Thomas who faced allegations of sexual harassment in 1991. Then, Thomas also criticized the hearings, all but daring the all-white Senate Judiciary Committee to find him unfit for the post: 'It is a national disgrace. And from my standpoint, as a black American, as far as I am concerned, it is a high-tech lynching for uppity-blacks who in any way deign to think for themselves, to do for themselves, to have different ideas ...' (US Committee on the Judiciary 1991). Where Thomas drew on race, Kavanaugh drew on partisan politics, accusing his critics of opposing him for political reasons. Most surprising about his statement was how closely it echoed the sentiments frequently expressed by President Trump, character-ising critics as opponents motivated by little more than political and personal animus. Allying himself so closely with the president's methods, Kavanaugh eschewed the more common approach of claiming judicial independence and drew directly on the politics of the debates around him as a defense strategy.

Although Barrett's clear avoidance of such politics suggests that Kavanaugh did not start a trend, his actions nevertheless represented another way in which politics and the judiciary became more deeply intertwined in the era of Trump.

MAKING IT PERSONAL: TRUMP AND THE FEDERAL JUDICIARY

Trump's linking of the judiciary and legal rulings to electoral outcomes and partisan politics extended well beyond the Supreme Court nominations and appointments process. The federal judiciary generally was a target for both the president's ire and praise. Successes for the Administration's position were frequently claimed by Trump as political wins in language which implied the wins were for him personally or, at the very least, for him and his supporters. In contrast, decisions which went against Trump or the Administration were deemed 'unfair,' 'ridiculous,' and 'disgraceful.' Even the Supreme Court, to whom Trump frequently claimed the Administration would appeal, did not avoid claims of anti-Trump bias. After the Court in summer 2020 ruled that the Administration had offered insufficient justification for ending DACA, Trump tweeted, 'Do you get the impression that the Supreme Court doesn't like me?,' accusing it not only of making decisions to oppose Trump on personal grounds but also of making 'horrible & politically charged decisions.'

This pattern of praise and criticism extended to individual judges and justices. On the former, sometimes Trump recognized them by name: for example, Judge Robert Payne of the District Court for the Eastern District of Pennsylvania, whose ruling on Virginia election laws was widely interpreted as a defeat for the Never Trump movement in the 2016 election, and Megan King, whose 2019 campaign for Superior Court Judge in Pennsylvania received 'Full and Total Endorsement' from Trump. Others were simply declared 'highly respected.' For those who ruled against the president or the Administration, Trump's favorite approach was to claim political or personal bias. When Judge Gonzalo Curiel of the District Court for the Southern District of California ruled against Trump University during the 2016 campaign, Trump used campaign rallies to attack him: 'I have a judge who is a hater of Donald Trump, a hater,' he told a San Diego rally in May 2016. 'His name is Gonzalo Curiel and he is not doing the right thing' (Stracqualursi and Struyk 2017). More common, however, was to associate those ruling against his interests with his political opponents. Curiel and others were labeled simply as 'Obama judges.' Such a November 2018 criticism of Jon S. Tigar, of the United States District Court in San Francisco, to whose ruling on the administration's immigration policy practices Trump objected, earned a rare rebuke from Chief Justice Roberts.

Roberts' retort to the President's criticism was important. 'We do not have Obama judges or Trump judges, Bush judges or Clinton judges,' he said: 'What we have is an extraordinary group of dedicated judges doing their level best to do equal right to those appearing before them' (Liptak 2018). Implicitly reasserting the position taken by many judges that they decide each case based on the specific facts and the law before them, Roberts challenged what had become, and ultimately remained, a common trend in Trump's formal and informal responses to the judiciary: that rulings reflected, and judges acted based on, nothing more than personal or political opinions about the individuals who brought the cases before the court. Taken together we see that Trump's approach to the judiciary differed little from that taken toward the other political branches. Judges, courts, and rulings in his favor received praise and were aligned with him, his supporters, and their interests. Those who ruled against him could be nothing other than aligned with his political opponents, working to undermine Trump and his supporters. Either way, Trump's comments were designed to paint the judiciary in political colors.

Arguing that judges make decisions as political actors was nothing new. But the barrage of Trump's attacks is important for the judiciary in the longer term. Studies have shown that political messaging over time has cumulative and long-term effects on the public (Gotlieb et al. 2017). Whether received by Trump supporters who hung on every word and tweet, or liberals fundamentally opposed to everything Trump stood for, the constant accusation of political decision-making by the courts feeds into public consciousness and a general sense of the work of the judiciary. In combination with politically charged nomination hearings and a culture increasingly willing to see judges and justices as making political decisions, Trump's assault on the US judiciary represents a long-term risk to the judiciary generally and to the Supreme Court in particular.

THE TRUMP APPOINTEES AND SUPREME COURT RULINGS

There is no doubt that the conservative activists who have made control of the Supreme Court their mission and target for the last three decades or more hope that Trump's legacy will be a stream of rulings in closer accord with their political positions than current precedent on issues such as gun rights, abortion, free speech, religious liberty and church-state relations, and LGBTQ rights. And the result of Trump's appointees is that the current Supreme Court is the most conservative since the early 1930s when the so-called 'Four Horsemen' (Justices Pierce Butler, James McReynolds, George Sutherland, and Willis Van Devanter) were supporting the doctrine of liberty of contract over Progressive-era employment reforms and striking down FDR's earliest New Deal legislation. Today Justices Clarence Thomas, Samuel Alito, Neil Gorsuch, Brett Kavanaugh, and Amy Coney Barrett, as well as Chief Justice Roberts, all adhere, in the main, to conservative judicial approaches, although importantly they differ on what those are, while Justices Stephen Breyer, Elena Kagan, and Sonia Sotomayor constitute the Court's liberal-leaning bloc. Conservatives hope, liberals fear, and most commentators expect that the clear 6:3 conservative majority will mean a raft of decisions supporting conservative policy positions.

Despite the headlines and discussions of divided Courts, however, the bulk of the work done by the Court does not reveal ideological divides. In some areas, then, the impact of the new justices is likely to be less significant than anticipated. For example, in *City of Chicago v. Fulton*, decided in January 2021, the Court ruled 8:0 that Chicago did not have to return residents' impounded cars under a reading of the Bankruptcy Code. Such cases, perhaps unsurprisingly, hardly hit the national headlines. But the larger point is that a significant number of cases each year are decided unanimously or by large majorities. As Fig. 10.1 shows, although the percentage has fallen in the last few years, roughly half of the Court's cases are decided unanimously or by large majorities. Equally, not all 5:4 decisions divide along ideological lines. *Salinas v. US Railroad Retirement Board*, decided in February 2021, saw the Court split narrowly on a jurisdictional question of the Board's authority. The majority comprised liberals Sotomayor (who wrote the opinion), Breyer, and Kagan, and conservatives Roberts and Kavanaugh. Both types of cases often involve technical legal issues and are more often a question of legislative interpretation than constitutional questions, but they are the bulk of the Court's work and are largely, although not exclusively, non-ideological. When discussing the Court and politics, it is important to remember that a large part of the Court's work is not dominated by ideological divisions. As such, the impact of Trump's appointees in these areas is likely to be less dramatic.

That said, a small number of cases can have an outsized influence on people's lives and on public perception of the Court. Those cases disproportionately involve questions of constitutional interpretation and attract significant, and usually divided, political attention. And it is here where we can understand why, in particular, Republicans worked so hard to ensure Barrett's

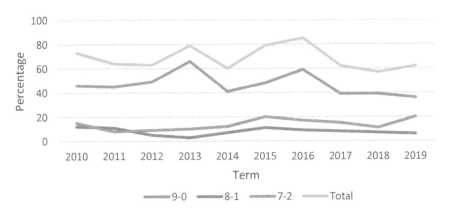

Fig. 10.1 Percentage of each term's cases decided by unanimous or large majority vote, 2010–2019 (Source: Data adapted from SCOTUSBlog Stat Pack, October 2019 Term, p. 17)

appointment before the 2020 election and why that appointment could be so important.

Months before the 2020 election, conservatives had reason to cheer. In the previous two terms the Court had upheld a version of the president's travel ban (*Trump v. Hawaii*, 2018), refused to uphold the finding of discrimination against a baker who refused to bake a wedding cake for a gay couple (*Masterpiece Cakeshop, Ltd. v. Colorado Civil Rights Commission*, 2018), declined to intervene in instances of political gerrymandering (*Rucho v. Common Cause*, 2019), and held that a war memorial in the shape of a cross on government land did not violate the separation of church and state (*The American Legion v. American Humanist Association*, 2019). The 2019 term also saw the Court increase protections for religious organizations from otherwise generally applicable laws in cases involving contraception provision (*Little Sisters of the Poor Saints Peter and Paul Home v. Pennsylvania* and *Trump v. Pennsylvania*, 2020), employment discrimination (*Our Lady of Guadalupe School v. Morrissey-Berru*, 2020), and scholarship programs (*Espinoza v. Montana Department of Revenue*, 2020).

But summer 2020 brought a number of unpleasant surprises for those who had argued that Trump's Court appointees were a major achievement of his administration and would help reshape the law in a conservative direction for generations. Within the space of a couple of months the Court refused the opportunity to significantly expand gun rights (*New York State Rifle & Pistol Association v. City of New York*), expanded legal protections for LGBTQ workers (*Bostock v. Clayton County*), rebuked the administration over its handling of DACA (*Dept. of Homeland Security v. Regents of the University of California*), struck down one of the nation's most restrictive abortion regulations in Louisiana (*June Medical Services v. Russo*), and rejected the president's claims to keep private all of his financial information (*Trump v. Vance*). Perhaps most disheartening for the president's supporters was that Gorsuch and Kavanaugh joined Roberts to require the president to release some of his financial information, and, of all people, Gorsuch had written the opinion (for a 6:3 majority) that expanded application of Title VII of the 1964 Civil Rights Act to protect gay and transgender employees from employment discrimination.

As the 2020 election campaign moved from primary season into the general election, the Court, which had been such a success for Trump in 2016, and which Republicans had, quite reasonably in light of two new appointments, hoped to make a key part of the 2020 campaign, thus appeared a more difficult issue on which to make a claim of 'success.' In light of this, it is hardly surprising that many Republicans greeted a third vacancy on the Court with barely concealed glee: a third conservative appointment offered the possibility of shifting the 'unreliable' Roberts from his spot at the center and actually solidifying the Court's conservative majority.

While the full impact of Barrett's appointment on such topics will remain unclear for some time, two issues which arose shortly after her appointment provide some hint of what might be to come.

The first controversies involved Covid-19 restrictions and churches. This was a contentious topic from the introduction of restrictions on group gatherings in March 2020. Many religiously conservative churches claimed that laws which treated them like other mass gatherings, such as concerts and sports events, were tantamount to religious discrimination. That summer, with Ginsburg still serving, the Court largely upheld these state restrictions where there was no clear evidence that churches were actually being treated more harshly than similarly placed groups or individuals (*South Bay United Pentecostal Church v. Newsom*; *Calvary Chapel, Dayton Valley v. Sisolak* et al.). But in late 2020 and early 2021, the Court struck down similar restrictions (*Roman Catholic Diocese of Brooklyn, New York v. Cuomo*; *Agudath Israel of America v. Cuomo*). Justice Alito, at the same time, in a speech to the conservative Federalist Society, lamented that religious liberty 'is fast becoming a disfavored right' (Golde 2020). Despite Alito's alarmist rhetoric, greater protection for religious conservatives has been a feature of the Court for at least a decade. But the difference between the Ginsburg era and the Barrett era suggests the possibility of even more protection to come in this area.

The second highly watched area was the issue of abortion. When the Covid pandemic began, many states closed down abortion service providers, arguing they were not essential services. Pro-choice campaigners, not without reason, argued that such closings were simply abortion prevention by another name. On 12 January 2021, the Court, over the dissent of Sotomayor and Kagan, upheld an FDA regulation requiring women seeking an abortion drug to collect that prescription in person rather than permitting virtual prescription (*Food and Drug Administration v. American College of Obstetricians and Gynecologists*). With Roberts supporting the FDA, it is likely that the same result may have come even with Ginsburg still on the Court, but liberals are concerned that this too is a signal of what is to come.

It is important to note, though, that none of these cases was decided after full briefing and oral argument, but via emergency orders and applications. They thus do not have the same long-term legal weight. But as insights into the impact of Ginsburg's replacement with Barrett, they suggest liberals' concern is not misplaced, on these issues at least.

Gateway to the Supreme Court: Trump's Impact on the Lower Federal Courts

Trump's impact will also be felt for some time on the lower federal courts—the 94 US District Courts and the 13 US Circuit Courts of Appeal which sit below the US Supreme Court. Although discussed less often than the Supreme Court, the lower federal courts are important for understanding the work of the Supreme Court. During his term in office, Trump appointed 54 federal appeals court judges or 30 percent of the total number. To give some sense of scale, that number compared to 55 for Obama and 62 for George W. Bush in eight years of their respective presidencies (Gramlich 2021). Trump regularly boasted about the number of appointments. Other Republicans also emphasized their success in appointing judges. In July 2020, as Congress adjourned for the summer recess, McConnell declared, 'When we depart this chamber today, there will not be a single circuit court vacancy for the first time in at least 40 years' (Johnson 2020). As many commentators noted, however, Trump's ability to appoint judges came in large part because of Republican success in blocking President Obama's nominees for years, leaving vacancies of which Trump was able to take advantage.

The significance is not just in the number of appointments but the placement. Trump strengthened the number of Republican appointments on key appeals courts while his appointments also switched the balance on three from a majority of Democrat-appointed judges to a majority of Republican appointments: the Atlanta-based Eleventh Circuit, the Manhattan-based Second Circuit, and the Philadelphia-based Third Circuit. On the Ninth Circuit, described by Trump as 'a complete and total disaster' and a 'big thorn in our side,' the Democratic majority reduced from 18–7 to 16–13 (Wheeler 2020). Trump's appointees have then strengthened the conservative presence within the federal judiciary.

All of this is significant because of the role that the federal appeals courts play as gatekeepers to the Supreme Court. When deciding whether to accept a case on a particular issue, one of the Court's guiding principles is whether there is a lower court split. Before accepting the cases on marriage equality, which became *Obergefell v. Hodges* in 2015, the Court had previously turned down a series of challenges to state marriage laws. While the justices did not provide explanation for their subsequent acceptance of *Obergefell* and companion cases, in the interim the Sixth Circuit had, in contrast to the other appeals courts, held that laws restricting marriage to one man and one woman did not violate the Constitution. This constituted a circuit split and the Court subsequently accepted the case. With the influence of Trump's conservative appointees, circuit splits, even on politically controversial issues, may become rarer, making issues less likely to reach the Supreme Court.

The Court refusing to hear a case, known as 'denying cert,' is also important. Although the denial does not create legal precedent, it does leave the lower court ruling in place. In effect, the more conservative justices could avoid wading into politically controversial issues while still ensuring the operation of conservative legal reasoning by simply refusing to hear cases and leaving the lower court rulings in place. The Court avoids having to make controversial decisions which put it in the spotlight, while the practical reality is that a more conservative judicial reading of issues is in operation in parts of the country. In whichever way, Trump's appointment of so many federal appeals court judges is likely to have significant, if less widely commented upon, effects on the federal judiciary.

Recognizing a judiciary less favorable to their understandings of the law, more liberal activists and lawyers may simply avoid bringing lawsuits at all. In the 1980s and 1990s, anti-abortion campaigners, cognisant that the Supreme Court was increasingly unlikely to overturn *Roe v. Wade*, especially after its 1992 ruling in *Planned Parenthood v. Casey*, turned instead to state legislatures. They sought legislation which, while keeping to the letter of the law as set out in *Roe* and *Casey*, nevertheless worked in the gray areas around the edges of the rulings, making abortion access harder while never abolishing it outright. So-called TRAP laws (targeted restriction of abortion providers), almost all offered by state legislators as protection for women's health, in reality have been designed to restrict access to abortion providers. Anti-abortion campaigners have achieved enormous success in this. Liberal campaigners, fearing adverse rulings from lower courts or even the Supreme Court, which would be difficult to eventually overturn, may then choose simply to bypass the courts and focus on legislatures instead. For those who argue that the courts should remain out of the business of making decisions on issues of political controversy, this result might represent the restoration of democratic debate and control and the limitation of a judiciary which has become too powerful and overstepped its role. But for heirs of the Civil Rights and Women's Rights Movements, for whom Supreme Court rulings helped pave the way and protected hard-won gains, the loss of the courts as a potential venue to fight for rights is a significant one.

The Biden Administration and the Trump Legacy

Although Biden's presidency is likely to see a reduction in the personal attacks on judges, there is a very real risk that Democrats' retaliation against Republicans over their treatment of the Supreme Court could further damage the Court's legitimacy and entrench the politicisation of its work. The liberal movement to pack the Supreme Court gained momentum during the 2020 primary campaign. Long before the appointment of Justice Barrett, several leading liberal advocacy groups signed an open letter criticizing 'the Republican theft of the Supreme Court' and calling for an expansion in the number of justices 'to restore our democracy and protect the rights of all Americans' (Otterbein 2020). After the push to get Barrett appointed to the Court before the election, such claims gathered pace.

Democratic advocates of Court packing genuinely risk doing similar damage to the legitimacy of the Supreme Court as Republicans did under Trump. They risk, in Biden's words, 'turn[ing] the Supreme Court into just a political football, whoever gets the most votes gets whatever they want' (CBS *60 Minutes* 2020). The liberal groups' open letter to Democratic candidates in summer 2020 framed the issue in relation to political and policy outcomes on reproductive freedom, LGBTQ rights, and gun control. Others spoke about the nomination in the same terms. Current Vice President Kamala Harris called the Barrett hearings 'a sham' which 'shows how Republicans will stop at nothing to strip health care from millions of Americans with pre-existing conditions.' Openly gay, former presidential hopeful Pete Buttigieg commented: 'My marriage might depend on what is about to happen in the Senate with regard to this justice' (Luscombe 2020). Likely intended to encourage Democratic voters to the polls in November, the barrage of comments along these lines served only to reinforce the deepening politicisation of the Court under Trump. Democrats argued for a right to retaliate in the face of Republicans' perceived outrageous treatment of the Court. They had associated Barrett and potential future nominees with desired issue-based outcomes, and based their arguments on the assumption that the Court is part of the political spoils that comes with electoral success. All echoed comments made by Trump and McConnell, and if they continue, from whichever party, they risk fundamentally damaging the Court's ability to do its job.

President Biden has, however, resisted these calls so far. As Chairman or ranking member of the Senate Judiciary Committee for 17 years, including presiding over the contentious nominations of Robert Bork and Clarence Thomas, Biden has long experience of dealing with the politics surrounding the Court. In late January 2021 he did what he said he would in an October 2020 interview with CBS *60 Minutes* and began appointing a bipartisan commission to consider, within a 180-day window, questions of court reform. That commission, and Biden's resistance to dramatic changes to the courts, may ultimately prove to be the bulwark against further damage to the Court's legitimacy.

REFERENCES

Bennett, D. 2017. *Defending Faith: The Politics of the Christian Conservative Legal Movement*. Lawrence: University Press of Kansas.

CBS *60 Minutes*. 2020. Joe Biden: The 60 Minutes 2020 Election Interview. Available at: https://www.youtube.com/watch?v=kSAo_1mJg0g.

Cruz, T. 2016. Statement on the President's Supreme Court Nomination. In *The American Presidency Project*, ed. G. Peters and J. Woolley, March 16. https://www.presidency.ucsb.edu/node/314766.

Desjardins, L. 2020. What Every Republican Senator Has Said About Filling a Supreme Court Vacancy in an Election Year. *PBS*, September 22. https://www.pbs.org/newshour/politics/what-every-republican-senator-has-said-about-filling-a-supreme-court-vacancy-in-an-election-year.

Ehrlich, J. 2018. Kagan: Confirmation Gridlock Makes Supreme Court Look Like 'Junior Varsity Politicians'. *CNN*, July 25. https://edition.cnn.com/2018/07/25/politics/kagan-kavanaugh-junior-varsity-politicians/index.html.

Golde, K. 2020. At Federalist Society Convention, Alito Says Religious Liberty, Gun Ownership Are Under Attack. *SCOTUSBlog*, November 13. https://www.scotusblog.com/2020/11/at-federalist-society-convention-alito-says-religious-liberty-gun-ownership-are-under-attack/.

Gotlieb, M., R. Scholl, T. Ridout, K. Goldstein, and D. Shah. 2017. Cumulative and Long-Term Campaign Advertising Effects on Trust and Talk. *International Journal of Public Opinion Research* 29: 1–22.

Gramlich, J. 2021. How Trump Compares with Other Recent Presidents in Appointing Federal Judges. *Pew Research Center*, January 13. https://www.pewresearch.org/fact-tank/2021/01/13/how-trump-compares-with-other-recent-presidents-in-appointing-federal-judges/.

Hartig, H. 2020. Before Ginsburg's Death, a Majority of Americans Viewed the Supreme Court as 'Middle of the Road'. *Pew Research Center*, September 25. https://www.pewresearch.org/fact-tank/2020/09/25/before-ginsburgs-death-a-majority-of-americans-viewed-the-supreme-court-as-middle-of-the-road/.

Johnson, C. 2020. Wave of Young Judges Pushed by McConnell Will Be 'Ruling for Decades to Come'. *NPR*, July 2. https://www.npr.org/2020/07/02/886285772/trump-and-mcconnell-via-swath-of-judges-will-affect-u-s-law-for-decades.

Kessler, G. 2017. When Did Mitch McConnell Say He Wanted to Make Obama a One-Term President? *Washington Post*, January 11. https://www.washingtonpost.com/news/fact-checker/wp/2017/01/11/when-did-mitch-mcconnell-say-he-wanted-to-make-obama-a-one-term-president/.

Liptak, A. 2018. Chief Justice Defends Judicial Independence After Trump Attacks 'Obama Judge'. *New York Times*, November 21. https://www.nytimes.com/2018/11/21/us/politics/trump-chief-justice-roberts-rebuke.html.

Luscombe, R. 2020. Buttigieg to Fox News Sunday: Barrett Nomination Puts My Marriage in Danger. *The Guardian*, October 18. https://www.theguardian.com/us-news/2020/oct/18/pete-buttigieg-amy-coney-barrett-supreme-court-nomination-same-sex-marriage.

Nemacheck, C. 2008. *Strategic Selection: Presidential Nomination of Supreme Court Justices from Herbert Hoover Through George W. Bush*. Charlottesville, VA: University of Virginia Press.

New York Times. 2018. Brett Kavanaugh's Opening Statement: Full Transcript. *New York Times*, September 26. https://www.nytimes.com/2018/09/26/us/politics/read-brett-kavanaughs-complete-opening-statement.html.

Otterbein, H. 2020. Liberal Groups Back Plan to Expand Supreme Court. *Politico*, June 11. https://www.politico.com/news/2020/06/11/liberal-groups-expand-supreme-court-plan-313037.

Pew Research Center. 2015. Negative Views of Supreme Court at Record High, Driven by Republican Dissatisfaction, July 29. https://www.pewresearch.org/politics/wp-content/uploads/sites/4/2015/07/07-29-2015-Supreme-Court-release.pdf.

SCOTUSBlog. 2020. Final Stat Pack for October Term 2019. SCOTUSBlog, July 20. https://www.scotusblog.com/wp-content/uploads/2020/07/Final-Statpack-7.20.2020.pdf.

Segal, J., and H. Spaeth. 1993. *The Supreme Court and the Attitudinal Model*. New York: Cambridge University Press.

Stracqualursi, V., and R. Struyk. 2017. President Trump's History with Judge Gonzalo Curiel. *ABC News*, April 20. https://abcnews.go.com/Politics/president-trumps-history-judge-gonzalo-curiel/story?id=46916250.

Teles, S. 2008. *The Rise of the Conservative Legal Movement: The Battle for Control of the Law*. Princeton: Princeton University Press.

US Committee on the Judiciary, US Senate. 1991. *Hearings on the Nomination of Clarence Thomas to be Associate Justice of the Supreme Court of the United States, October 11–13, 1991.* Washington, DC: Library of Congress. https://www.loc.gov/law/find/nominations/thomas/hearing-pt4.pdf.

———. 2005. *Hearings on the Nomination of John G. Roberts, Jr. to Be Chief Justice of the Supreme Court of the United States, September 12–15, 2005.* Washington, DC: US Government Publishing Office. https://www.govinfo.gov/content/pkg/GPO-CHRG-ROBERTS/pdf/GPO-CHRG-ROBERTS.pdf.

Wheeler, R. 2020. Judicial Appointments in Trump's First Three Years: Myths and Realities, January 28. Washington, DC: Brookings Institution. https://www.brookings.edu/blog/fixgov/2020/01/28/judicial-appointments-in-trumps-first-three-years-myths-and-realities/.

FURTHER READING

The best overview and coverage of the contemporary work of the Supreme Court is provided by SCOTUSBlog (https://www.scotusblog.com/). Run and written by legal scholars and practitioners, it offers non-partisan, real-time coverage of the Court, its cases, and the issues surrounding it. Among the most useful resources are the summaries of main cases and their oral arguments, the regular symposia on key issues to which leading scholars and practitioners contribute, and their 'daily read' which links readers to coverage of the Court in a range of other online publications. For discussion of the legal and constitutional issues addressed by the Court, both contemporary and historical, the National Constitution Center provides a wealth of resources including blog posts, podcasts, interviews, and live events (https://constitutioncenter.org/).

A good introduction to the workings of the Court is Linda Greenhouse, *The US Supreme Court: A Very Short History* (Oxford: Oxford University Press, 2012). The Supreme Court reporter for the *New York Times* for three decades, Greenhouse packs all her experience into a relatively brief 126 pages. David O'Brien, *Storm Center: The Supreme Court in American Politics* (New York: W. W. Norton & Co., 12th ed., 2020) and Robert McKeever, *The United States Supreme Court: A Political and Legal Analysis* (Manchester: Manchester University Press, 2nd ed., 2016) both offer more detailed explorations of how the Court works and the links between the Court and US politics. For an historical overview, a good starting point is Robert McCloskey and Sanford Levinson, *The American Supreme Court* (Chicago: University of Chicago Press, 6th ed., 2016).

Thoughtful studies of the various ways in which legal and political conservatives have focused on the courts since the 1960s include Daniel Bennett, *Defending Faith: The Politics of the Christian Conservative Legal Movement* (Lawrence: University Press of Kansas, 2017), Ann Southworth, *Lawyers of the Right: Professionalizing the Conservative Coalition* (Chicago: University of Chicago Press, 2008), and Steven Teles, *The Rise of the Conservative Legal*

Movement: The Battle for Control of the Law (Princeton: Princeton University Press, 2008). These actions provided the foundation on which President Trump was able to build to reshape the Court during his presidency. For a journalistic take on the impact of these developments on the Court itself see Jan Crawford Greenburg, *Supreme Conflict: The Inside Story of the Struggle for Control of the United States Supreme Court* (London: Penguin Books, 2008).

Most of the coverage of the nominations and appointments of Justices Gorsuch, Kavanaugh, and Barrett has, to date, been published by journalists rather than academics and so often reflects the politics of the moment. Examples include David Kaplan, *The Most Dangerous Branch: Inside the Supreme Court in the Age of Trump* (New York: Broadway Books, 2018) and Ruth Marcus, *Supreme Ambition: Brett Kavanaugh and the Conservative Takeover* (New York: Simon & Schuster, 2019). Attempts to provide early scholarly responses to contemporary events include Todd Ruger, *American Justice 2018: The Shifting Supreme Court* (Philadelphia: University of Pennsylvania Press, 2018) and Mark Joseph Stern, *American Justice 2019: The Roberts Court Arrives* (Philadelphia: University of Pennsylvania Press, 2019).

CHAPTER 11

The Federal Bureaucracy

Bert A. Rockman

This chapter explores the evolution of the federal bureaucracy and assesses the relationship between it and presidents especially in regard to differences between Democratic and Republican presidents in its management. It then explores some of the most salient aspects of the Trump Presidency's relationship between the bureaucracy and the federal executive as well as between Trump and his appointees. Trump's policies and attitudes toward the bureaucracy were a combination of his own temperament and experience as well as the political need to build and solidify what he believed to be a viable electoral and governing coalition. In Trump's case, the objective was less to cultivate an expansive coalition than to intensify a narrow but highly committed one.

THE ADMINISTRATIVE BACKGROUND

Until the early twentieth century the US federal government was relatively weak. Government, such as it was, largely centered around local communities and states. However, by the time of the second industrial revolution that developed in the period after the Civil War, the need for more regulation of commerce emerged as various interests (agriculture versus railroads, for instance) were pitted against one another. Most staffing of the very limited administrative state of the day was done through political patronage. By 1883,

B. A. Rockman (✉)
Department of Political Science, Purdue University, West Lafayette, IN, USA
e-mail: barockma@purdue.edu

© The Author(s), under exclusive license to Springer Nature Switzerland AG 2022
G. Peele et al. (eds.), *Developments in American Politics 9*,
https://doi.org/10.1007/978-3-030-89740-6_11

Congress had enacted the Pendleton Act which provided a professional merit system of career civil servants to staff the federal government's departments and agencies. While the positions affected were limited at first, their number rapidly expanded over the next decade. Over several decades, government regulations over food safety, child labor, and other labor conditions came into being as well as a central banking overseer (the Federal Reserve system).

The New Deal policies of President Franklin D. Roosevelt (1933–1945) brought a massive expansion of the federal establishment to Washington which was further generated by the growth in a national defense and intelligence apparatus induced by the World War and subsequently bolstered by the Cold War. Additionally, the new welfare-warfare state provided significant expansion of federal functions, including, for example, veterans' benefits and new educational, scientific, and transportation infrastructure. Additional executive departments and agencies as well as an emerging institutional presidency came into being. These trends of growing federal power and bureaucratic expansion continued through the Cold War period and, especially, through the Great Society programs of the Lyndon Johnson administration (1963–1969). And they persist as federal regulations derive or are perceived to derive from prior statutes through the doctrine of delegation which gives deference to administrative agencies to interpret statutes (*Chevron* 1984). This doctrine means that administrative agencies are empowered to interpret and mandate regulatory rules that they understand to derive from provisions of the underlying legislative statute.

With this significant expansion of federal jurisdiction and interpretation of law, the quest for political control over the federal bureaucracy has become increasingly prominent (Aberbach and Rockman 1976; Moe 1985; Potter 2019). One reason for this search lies in the competitive structure of American governing institutions. The term 'separation of powers' implies a clear demarcation of authority across these institutions. The reality is anything but, as one scholar of American public administration put it succinctly, the fundamental question of American government is 'who is boss'? (Long 1949).

The textbook triadic separation of powers system is not simply the executive led by the presidency, the legislative, and the judicial branches of government. It is really a quartet that includes the agencies and departments of government that issue regulations and thereby make policy as well. From that standpoint, there are two elements of executive discretion. One element is *presidential discretion* that is exercised through Executive Orders, Presidential Memoranda, and other instruments of presidential control that conditionally permit the chief executive to alter existing interpretations of statutory law or even to avoid enforcing them as in President Obama's decision to not enforce the Defense of Marriage Act (DOMA). The other element is *agency discretion* operating especially through legislative delegation to the executive and the expertise of the bureaucracy and, thereby, the issuance of rules surrounding an agency's interpretation of a legislative statute. Presidents want to make agency discretion conform with the policy and political objectives of their presidencies, although they may vary in the degree of intensity with which they pursue that desire. Therein lies an inevitable clash between the permanence, continuity, and expertise of the bureaucracy on the one hand and the political needs and policy responsiveness of the president and, sporadically, the legislature on the other.

The Partisan Divide

Since the New Deal administration of Franklin Roosevelt, the lines between the political parties with respect to the growth of the federal government had become clear and largely reversed much of their historic positions. From this point forward, Republicans have been especially skeptical of governmental growth outside of defense and criminal law enforcement. Democrats, on the other hand, generally have pushed for more state intervention which usually brings with it a growth in bureaucracy. At times these differences have varied in their intensity reflecting each party's internal coalition, the nature of the issues involved, and the temperament and experience of each president. But the trend has been clear. Democrats have generally been pro-government and, thus, more favorable in general to the bureaucracy. Alternatively, Republicans have generally been for smaller governments. Not surprisingly, the tensions between the permanent government and the president have tended to be greater under Republican presidents than under Democrats.

Since the Ronald Reagan era (1981–1989), the parties also became more internally coherent ideologically and increasingly divided between rural/exurban vs. urban/suburban constituencies (Cramer 2016; Rodden 2019) and, accordingly, the differences between them grew stronger. However, while many of the attitudes toward the bureaucracy and career officials are governed through an ideological frame and, therefore, a party frame, politicians also crave power and loyalty. Politicians generally want agencies to favor constituencies that are part of their support base. Moreover, the demand for loyalty to the political superior is omnipresent. The cardinal rule is to avoid embarrassing the political leaders and to be responsive to their priorities. When that pressure becomes too great and the independence of the career officials is threatened, experience, continuity, and expertise are endangered (Resh 2015). Trump would certainly not be the first president to create that risk but his frequent references to his 'absolute power' and his disdain for the governmental establishment and its procedures arguably raised this risk to unparalleled levels. Referring to the Constitution's provisions, Trump boldly and wrongly proclaimed that 'I have an Article II where I have the right to do whatever I want as president. But I don't even talk about that' after he just had (Brice-Saddler 2019).

Two other characteristics of the US political system are worthy of note. The first in this regard is the legal culture that surrounds the bureaucracy. The second is the political culture which promotes individualism and skepticism toward government.

THE LEGAL CULTURE

It is hardly surprising that bureaucratic actions have to be grounded in legal procedures. As Max Weber (1958), the great theorist of bureaucracy, observed early in the twentieth century, bureaucracy is a system of administration that is a concomitant of the legal rationalization of authority. Administrative actions need to be legally justified as they are likely to end up in litigation when they are politically divisive. The tendency to litigate administrative actions (or inactions) is a consequence of the harshly divisive political climate that has arisen in American politics in recent decades, and especially during the presidencies of Barack Obama and Donald Trump. Both were inclined to use executive initiatives to substitute for statutory authorization, especially when legislative action seemed unachievable.

Obama recognized that there were constraints on presidential authority, having taught constitutional law and having articulated the limits of presidential power. But that did not deter him after Republicans gained control of the House of Representatives in 2011 and the Senate in 2015 and used every legislative tactic to frustrate his ambitions. Consequently, Obama turned out to be a frequent initiator of unilateral executive action. These actions included, for example, expansive interpretations of existing law (limiting greenhouse gas emissions based upon the Clean Air Act of the 1970s) and others which ignored enforcement of prior legislation (the Defense of Marriage Act) and the similar exercise of discretionary non-enforcement with respect to undocumented immigrants brought to the country as children (DACA—Deferred Action for Childhood Arrivals).

Over time, presidents have utilized discretionary authority connected to their responsibilities as executors of laws and as commanders-in-chief of the armed forces to generate authority as first movers. Congressional opposition to such presidential initiatives has been usually toothless and unenforceable (Devins 2009). Notably, litigants filing complaints often have been other executives, especially attorneys general in the states: Republican ones opposing the Obama administration and Democratic ones in opposition to the Trump administration.

As a result of litigated political conflict displacing more conventional forms, the courts have become the dominant political authorities in the American political system. The 'jurocracy' is a consequence of the lack of congressional capacity for action that, in turn, is largely a function of a combination of political divisiveness, archaic institutional rules, narrow majorities in the Senate, and party leaders protecting their members from having to take unpopular votes. Understandably, this makes the courts a prime prize for whichever party can gain control of the judicial appointment processes.

THE POLITICAL CULTURE

Hyper-individualism is a significant element of American popular culture, and that can have adverse consequences for respecting authority, especially of experts and scientists. A significant minority of the public, for example, refuses to abide by relatively minimal public health recommendations such as wearing a mask, practicing social distancing, or even accepting inoculation under conditions of global pandemic. One may be allowed to bring risk upon oneself even though there is implicit moral hazard by virtue of burdening the health care system. However, unwillingness to undertake minimal precautions to prevent dangers to others is an explicit moral hazard. Of course, most Americans do abide by these precautions. But a minority that is largely, if imperfectly, a reflection of the Trumpian core support base has been overtly resistant and reflects, as John Hibbing (2020) puts it, less of an authoritarian bent than an anarchistic one.

As a candidate for the presidency from 2015, Donald Trump aligned himself with the right-wing populist notion of 'the deep state' actually governing the United States against the popular will or interest, one manifestation of a distrust of government. The 'deep state' meant the permanent government of civil servants, foreign service, and intelligence officers, and even senior military officers. From that perspective, Trump was a president in opposition to his government rather than a partner or leader of it.

THE REPUBLICAN ROAD TO TRUMP

Although Trump was an outlier among recent Republican presidents in his personal conduct and his abundant ignorance of governmental institutions, his hostility to the bureaucracy was largely in line with those of his party's recent presidents including Richard Nixon (1969–1974), Ronald Reagan (1981–1989), and George W. Bush (2001–2009). Both Richard Nixon and Ronald Reagan made revamping the bureaucracy a priority as did two Democratic presidents, Jimmy Carter and Bill Clinton, but in different ways. For the Democratic presidents, structural reforms were pursued to compensate for the vulnerability of Democrats on issues surrounding the efficiency of performance and administrative accountability. Consequently, Carter engineered a significant overhaul of the senior civil service system through legislation that was designed to provide greater prestige by incentivizing career officials to achieve status in their person rather than in their particular position as well as to allow them to take sabbaticals to upgrade their knowledge. The downside was that it also made them more vulnerable to political manipulation from above.

Clinton's big idea, mostly a project of his Vice-President, was to emphasize efficiency, streamlining, and cutting red tape. The initiative was called *Reinventing Government* and was inspired by a set of ideas loosely known as *New Public Management* (NPM) which was popular in neo-liberal circles in the 1980s and 1990s. The idea was to make government as nimble as the private sector supposedly was, or at least to sell the idea that the Clinton Administration cared more about the end product than the process. The government of laws, however, is about process and many of the proposed reforms ran counter to processes of accountability that were in place and which were unlikely to be surrendered.

Barack Obama, the last Democratic president before Biden, was greatly interested in policy but less so in administration. His major contribution was to emphasize 'evidence-based' policymaking (Haskins and Margolis 2015). It is remarkable, in retrospect, to observe how otherwise unremarkable this idea was. As matters turned out, Obama's presidency and perhaps his party's fate in the 2014 midterm elections were affected by the troubled roll-out that year of the President's signature health care plan (Kamarck 2016). Later, when the benefits of the Affordable Care Act (ACA) actually came into being and the technical issues for enrollment were resolved, it became more popular. By then, however, it was too late for the Democrats to reap the benefit in the 2014 and 2016 elections.

Nixon and Reagan had different ideas. Nixon began by creating more agencies early in his administration and more regulations with an active policy agenda; but he then transitioned as electoral concerns loomed and as disloyalty within the bureaucracy became an obsession. Nixon sought to cover up illegal operations and to discredit those who challenged the administration's version of events as occurred over the conduct of the Vietnam War and the Pentagon Papers revelations of 1971. Nixon also fired his own appointees who had criticized the administration's lackluster efforts to enforce school desegregation in the South as part of a Southern political strategy. In the end, Nixon sought to build a bureaucracy that would be exclusively loyal to him and his political interests (Nathan 1983; Heclo 1975).

From the outset, the Reagan presidency wanted a bureaucracy that would be loyal to its policy objectives—objectives that were remarkably transparent in contrast to those of most of his predecessors. Except for defense and law enforcement, Reagan wanted a reduction in government everywhere (Rockman 1995). The administration cut budgets, instituted Reductions-in-Force (RIFs) at the agencies they targeted, and ensured that ideological hard-liners be appointed in charge of policies they most wanted to affect. Among other things, they were startlingly successful in ensuring that the civil servants who were to work most closely with political appointees were carefully vetted for policy reliability (Aberbach and Rockman 1995). Of course, not everything worked out according to the grand design. Some of the administration's appointees got into legal difficulties and their replacements were less doctrinaire.

In sum, Nixon came in creating new programs for government to do and new agencies to implement them but ultimately was brought down by his abuses of presidential power. Reagan, by contrast, came to office intending that policy would follow his conservative ideas, and he was largely successful in doing so, though he could never get control of the mandated expenditures part of the federal budget. By the time George W. Bush took office in 2001, the Republican Party had been moving substantially farther to the right. Although George W. Bush's father had notably emphasized 'prudence' as the key to managing government, George W. Bush was in spirit closer to Reagan and more closely aligned with the rightwards trend of his party though it had not yet reached its current state of disrespect for the processes and institutions of governance.

The Bureaucracy and the Trump Administration

It is often noted that there are three key components of administrative control: personnel, procedure, and money. But there is also a fourth—the corruption of institutions for purely political objectives. Trump's knowledge of American governing institutions and traditions, of public policy, and of law was meager. Other presidents, of course, vary in their degree of policy wonkiness. But usually they understood that they could consider the perspectives of those they had chosen to advise them and to do so for more than three minutes without going off subject. Some even read their briefing papers— or at least parts of them—before meeting with their advisers. Not so Trump (Rucker and Leonnig 2020; Barnes and Goldman 2020; Miller and Nakashima 2020). Rather, he seemed possessed by an extraordinary confidence in his instincts which, as instincts typically are, were untethered to any larger conceptions. Serious people found him to be a difficult person to work for and usually before they could say, 'I quit', were put out of their misery by Trump having fired them which was often followed by a presidential denunciation of their intelligence, mental balance, and/or character. Studies conducted through The Brookings Institution (Tenpas 2021) have noted an extraordinarily high level of departures of Trump appointees. More than 92 percent of Trump's 'A' team White House staff positions turned over more than once. Frequent departures were also notable among Trump's cabinet-level positions as was evidence of more than normal departures discovered among senior civil servants (Lim 2020).

Another way of vitiating bureaucratic influence, while simultaneously clearing out existing personnel, was to move bureaus out of Washington to far away destinations. These included, among others, the Bureau of Economic Research in the Department of Agriculture and the Bureau of Land Management in the Department of the Interior. The moves had two objectives. One was to sever ties to Washington-based media and congressional staff; the second was to incentivize senior civil servants to leave rather than uproot themselves. In all likelihood, both objectives were accomplished, but we know for sure that the second one was (Magill and Boyanton 2020).

To reiterate a critical point, however, Trump's bombast and distaste for being restrained by legal procedure and expert advice were not out of line with the emergent tendencies in his adopted party. An increasingly dominant wing of the GOP, especially in the states but also in the House of Representatives, saw the permanent government as an enemy in cahoots with the Democrats when they controlled the executive branch and in opposition to the Republicans when they controlled the executive. The notion of neutral competence had largely become irrelevant. The legion of permanent government officials in whatever service—civil, foreign, or intelligence—was, as Trump's (briefly) trusted adviser Steve Bannon claimed 'the deep state,' a notion that conjured up a subversive array of officials on the prowl to sabotage the Trump Presidency.

Personnel

At the political level, many of Trump's appointees, much like their boss, were ethically challenged and found themselves in a swirl of scandal leading to their departures. These included his first Secretary of Health and Human Services (Tom Price), his first Administrator of the Environmental Protection Agency (Scott Pruitt), his first nominee to be Secretary of Labor (Andrew Puzder), and ultimately also his first confirmed Secretary of Labor (Alexander Acosta), and his initial Secretary of the Interior (Ryan Zinke). Other lesser scandals consumed sub-cabinet appointees and those of 'acting' officials as well, for example, the acting Secretary of Defense (Patrick Shanahan) who replaced Trump's initial appointment, General James Mattis. These acting officials could avoid the perils of Senate confirmation hearings.

Trump defended his volume of 'acting' officials who were supposed to be standing in for those to be confirmed by the Senate by noting that he liked it that way (Samuels 2019). That designation gave him great flexibility in that he could show them the door more readily. He valued exclusive loyalty to him and wanted to keep everyone on edge and paying fealty to him. What he also did not want was public exposure of nominees before Senate hearings. That in itself may be a good indication of the caliber of nominee that Trump was seeking. But it also meant that no one was secure in their job. Rather, they were like contestants on Trump's pre-presidency reality show, 'The Apprentice'—easily hired, easily fired. It should also be noted that with some frequency Trump's 'acting appointments' were not made according to the existing procedures, thereby raising issues around the legality of their decisions in office (*Los Angeles Times* 2020).

It did not help one's prospects by appeasing (or agreeing with) Trump 99 percent of the time if the remaining one percent made Trump feel threatened. Such was the case of Trump's first Attorney General, Jeff Sessions, who was also the first senator to endorse Trump in 2015 and whose views coincided with Trump's desires on immigration and almost everything else. Because of a potential conflict of interest, however, he recused himself from the investigation of Russian government influences in Trump's 2016 election. Trump never forgave Sessions for that and publicly humiliated him with considerable frequency before firing him after the 2018 midterm elections.

When Sessions ran to reclaim his former Senate seat in 2020 in the Republican primary, Trump endorsed his opponent who, subsequently, won the party nomination and the general election. For Trump, loyalty was a one-way street. Notably, Trump's successor to Sessions, William Barr, was about as pliant an attorney general as can be had, acting as though his client was Donald Trump rather than the United States. Being more politically astute than Sessions, Barr jumped from the sinking Trump ship on December 23, announcing that he would do so on December 14 while Trump was doubling down on his insistence that he won the 2020 election and raising doubts about whether he would actually leave the White House voluntarily.

Loyalty—complete and absolute—was the main criterion by which Trump chose to staff his administration. Most presidents want loyalty in the mix but loyalty was usually one of the ingredients, not the exclusive one. When Trump came to Washington, his connections were few and so he initially relied upon those who looked the part, as he often put it with regard to 'his generals,' who turned out not to be sufficiently pliant. He also relied upon those who seemed to belong to the segment of the party willing to do the bidding of the interests that Trump needed for election financing and to satisfy his electoral coalition. By the time his presidency ended his appointees were even more frequently acting and anonymous. He even fired his Secretary of Defense in the interregnum between his re-election loss and the inauguration of his successor. While Trump advertised that he would appoint only the smartest people to be in his administration, his appointments were slow to occur and were regarded by career officials as being inferior to those who had served under the previous Republican administration (Lewis and Richardson 2021).

Trump's vengeance against those who failed his tests of absolute loyalty was unremitting. Trump was first impeached under charges arising from his phone call to the President of Ukraine regarding a proposed investigation of Joe Biden's son in return for releasing already congressionally appropriated military assistance funding. After being acquitted by the Senate on a nearly straight party line vote, Trump took his revenge against those who had done what the law required them to do. The Inspector General of the intelligence community who was required to pass on a whistle blower complaint to the Director of National Intelligence was fired less than two months after Trump's acquittal as were other Inspectors General whose independence provoked Trump's ire. Similarly, Army Lieutenant-Colonel Alexander Vindman who testified at the request of the House Intelligence Committee about Trump's phone call was unceremoniously ousted from his assignment at the White House and was visibly removed from the White House grounds by security personnel. Vindman's brother, Yevgeny, also an Army Lieutenant-Colonel and assigned to a different role in the White House was ousted from his job there despite not being on Trump's call nor being called to testify.

To be sure, all presidents use the 'spoils system' to reward significant donors and bundlers of donors as well as loyalists who can be relied on to implement the president's wishes. But Trump made extraordinary use of this option where he could. Ambassadorial appointments to destination capitals usually go to those who have helped the president get elected on the supposition that they will also help the president get re-elected. Presidents usually set aside about one-third of ambassadorial posts for non-career appointments. Under Trump that figure was closer to one-half (Kelemen 2020). Many of these non-career ambassadors had little to no experience in the country to which they had been assigned and nearly all were ones to whom the sitting president owed a political debt. This form of incompetence pervades all presidential administrations and not all such nominees are confirmed by the Senate. However, Trump not only made more of these nominations, they were more apt to create significant controversy. Trump's ambassador to Germany, Republican political activist Richard Grenell, for example, began his tenure by *publicly* proclaiming that Germany should cut off its economic ties to Iran evoking a strong response from the German media.

As a parting shot, the Trump administration issued an executive order transferring civil servants at the Office of Management and Budget (OMB) to a newly created status called Schedule F. The idea behind Schedule F was to turn previously civil service protected budget analysts into unprotected and more readily uprooted officials serving at the pleasure of the president. The executive order was designed to go into effect on January 19, 2021 (one day before President-Elect Biden's inauguration); but it was executed in a way that did not comply with the required procedures, demonstrating the usual level of procedural (in)competence, and thus failed the test of legality (Eagan 2021).

Procedures

A rationalized legal system generates an abundance of codified procedures as to how things are to be done. That would matter little, however, to a president disdainful of governmental procedures. Trump's leading adviser was apparently his gut. As he put it, 'I have a gut, and my gut tells me more sometimes than anybody else's brain can ever tell me' (Sullivan 2018). But when things went top-side down, he was quick to blame others, especially judges, for overruling him. In Trump's world, there were friends and enemies, the latter inevitably being discounted as partisan. The equation with 'friends' did not equilibrate. More was expected of them than was returned.

As Trump had just settled into office, he instituted a Muslim travel ban concocted by his White House policy adviser, Stephen Miller, without it being properly vetted by the relevant enforcement agencies or legal counsel. People already aboard aircraft headed to the US were denied permission to enter including permanent (green card) US residents. Chaos—a Trumpian trademark—ensued. A federal judge in the state of Washington, in the face of a lawsuit brought by that state's attorney general, then ordered an injunction to the ban. Predictably, Trump referred to him as an 'Obama judge.' Ultimately, on a third try, a more carefully crafted travel ban was designed affecting many but not all Muslim majority countries and one non-Muslim country, thereby making it less likely that discrimination could provide the basis for a winning lawsuit against the action.

When Obama was president, Republicans frequently attacked his resort to unilateral authority. Trump, however, deployed such authority even more frequently. He took great pride in publicizing all the executive orders he had issued to deregulate interpretations of previous administrations (Khimm 2017). Trump's successor though, Joseph Biden, has set a record number of executive initiatives by reversing those of his predecessor (Koslof 2021).

Why is this contemporary resort to unilateral executive authority flourishing? The answer mainly lies in the incapacity of Congress to legislate and the impatience of the president to achieve something. In the Senate, the extraordinary majority requirement (the so-called filibuster option) now exists as a minority party tool (whichever party happens to be in the minority at any given time) to thwart the majority unless the majority party has an extraordinary majority to begin with. Consequently, legislation has a long shelf life because of the difficulty in revoking it or amending it. It becomes easier, if likely more transient, to make changes through administrative interpretation (Moe 2012; Howell 2003; Huber and Shipan 2002). Given the frequency of legislative gridlock and the demands from a president's political constituency, the need to do something is understandably tempting, even if its durability is limited.

Trump was fond of announcing his 'absolute right' to undertake some unilateral action or other. While he had no such privilege, of course, he did intuitively understand that he had the capability to be a first mover and that it would take a substantial coalition to defend successfully against his initiatives. He also understood that litigation requires a long game from his opponents when the time horizons for action are short. Presidential action is often served by this strategic advantage, as Trump well understood. Moreover, by seeding the courts with his nominees, he may have believed that as his actions eventually went through the court system he would be advantaged. That premise was based on his flawed transactional view of life, namely that judges should act on his behalf because he nominated them to their positions.

Money

A theme that Trump played on during his campaign for the presidency that began effectively after his formal announcement in 2015 was that he would build a wall to keep out immigrants to the US and that Mexico would pay for it. While the Trump base ate this pledge up, it was inconceivable that this would come to pass. The former Mexican president, Vicente Fox, with a strong command of English colloquialisms responded publicly to Trump's quite astonishing claim proclaiming that 'I'm not going to pay for that f......g wall.' With the US Congress also unwilling to appropriate funds for its construction, Trump forced a lengthy shutdown of much of the federal government in 2018. The wall was a powerfully symbolic centerpiece of the Trump Presidency.

As Congress failed to appropriate new funding for the wall beyond maintenance for the existing fencing and a small appropriation beyond that, Trump declared that he would move funding previously allocated in the defense budget for other purposes to be used toward the construction of the wall. Despite majority opposition in Congress to Trump's move (which essentially violated Congress's constitutional responsibility to appropriate funds), it could not override Trump's veto of the congressional resolution. This inability of Congress to control its own appropriations process reflected two things about the US political system. One is that since overriding a presidential veto requires a concurrent two-thirds majority in each chamber, presidents have considerable advantages in rearranging how appropriated monies can be distributed. The second thing it revealed was that, while there were some Republican defectors from Trump's raiding other Defense Department funding for constructing the wall, the great majority of Republicans in Congress stood by him reflecting his now firm control of the party base.

Trump's first budget proposed a significant increase in the Defense (hard power) budget and a thirty percent decrease in the State Department (soft power) budget. That reflected the perspective of Mick Mulvaney, Trump's first budget director, and also that of Trump himself. Trump's first Secretary of State, Rex Tillerson, a former CEO of Exxon Mobil, was tasked with diminishing the State Department's footprint which made him highly unpopular with the professional foreign service. His successor, Mike Pompeo, proved to be even more unpopular.

The Corruption of Institutions

Trump's disdain for institutions was fueled by personal animus against key actors whom he could not control, such as the former director of the FBI, James Comey, and his subsequent acting director, Andrew McCabe. In fact, this was one of the most characteristic features of Trump's behavior—the demand for total loyalty to him and the disdain for institutions and institutionalized practices. These traits had intensified as the 2020 election came into view. Two examples will suffice to demonstrate these traits.

The first of these concerned the decennial census, the outcome of which defines the allocation of governmental benefits as well as representation in Washington and the state capitals. The administration first decided that it would count only citizens in the 2020 census despite there being no such legal provision or precedent to do so. They also sought to limit the count by hastening the deadline for its reporting. The Supreme Court allowed an earlier cutoff date (Bahrampour 2020) but deferred judgment on the exclusion of non-citizens to a later but indefinite date, while holding that the traditional count should prevail in the 2020 census (Totenberg and Wang 2020).

Trump also sought to use the US Postal Service (USPS) to hold up and thus discourage the use and, above all, the counting of mail-in ballots which he believed would be unfavorable to his re-election. The USPS is a public corporation and not a governmental agency as such. A board (whose members were all appointed by President Trump) approved of his appointment of Louis DeJoy as the Postmaster General. DeJoy was a major Republican and Trump fundraiser and his efforts to cutback service at the USPS was widely perceived as reflecting Trump's desire to discourage mail-in voting which had been instituted in many states in the face of the Covid-19 pandemic. DeJoy issued a controversial warning to the effect that mail-in ballots might not be counted in time in view of the service cutbacks being instituted at USPS. On the same day that this warning was issued, Trump claimed that mail-in ballots would likely prevent an accurate count (Corasaniti et al. 2020). That DeJoy followed a strategy consistent with Trump's urging does not necessarily mean that he willfully was trying to fulfill Trump's demands. But there was little doubt that Trump was doing what he could to ensure that the USPS would comply with his desire to restrict the electorate to favor his followers—a strategy now much in use among Republican legislators in the states.

The Durability of Trump's Influence on the Bureaucracy

How durable or transient will Trump's influence be on the bureaucracy and what does it mean for governance? One indication may be the number of Trump's executive orders that Biden reverses, though Biden's own orders themselves must meet procedural criteria. When presidents undertake unilateral actions to make policy, these can be reversed with more ease than can statutory enactments. Even so, the prior administrative regulations will hold until the procedural criteria are fulfilled by the current administration. The rule of law frustrates impatience. But for presidents, they can at least point to something they did even if it takes longer to come to fruition.

When there are changes in presidential administrations, personnel changes are typically sharp, reflecting not only each party's stock of possible personnel but also each president's. In that sense, transience is the watchword. The Biden administration has emphasized expertise and science in stark contrast to Trump's disdain for them (Lewis 2018). The larger question, however, has to do with what kind of party the Republican Party will be. There is, after all, a team of Republican policy experts as well. But those were not the kind of people the Trump branch of the party exhibited much interest in. And if the right retains its current dominance in the Party, with or without Trump, it is quite possible that the hollowing out of government, its loss of expertise, and of scientific knowledge will be long term (Eagan 2021).

Senator Lindsay Graham of South Carolina claimed that Trump was a consequential president. Consequences imply at least some measure of durability though nothing as to whether they are good or bad. Perhaps the most consequential outcome of all has been the ability of Trump to gain dominance in a party that is part of a duopoly in American politics. That means that this party has at least a 0.5 probability of being in power at any given point in time. It may not require Trump himself to be in power to have a longstanding effect on the country's institutions including the bureaucracy.

REFERENCES

Aberbach, J., and B. Rockman. 1976. Clashing Beliefs Within the Executive Branch: The Nixon Administration Bureaucracy. *American Political Science Review* 70: 456–468.

———. 1995. The Political Views of U.S. Senior Civil Servants. *Journal of Politics* 57: 838–852.

Bahrampour, T. 2020. What the Supreme Court's Rulings Mean for the 2020 Census and Trump's Attempt to Exclude the Undocumented from the Count. *The Washington Post*, October 18. washingtonpost.com/local/social-issues/what-the-supreme-courts-rulings-mean-for-the-2020-census-and-trumps-attempt-to-exclude-the-undocumented-from…

Barnes J., and A. Goldman 2020. For Spy Agencies, Briefing Trump Is a Test of Holding His Attention. *The New York Times*, May 21. nytimes.com/2020/05/21/us/politics/presidents-daily-brief-trump.html.

Brice-Saddler, M. 2019. While Bemoaning Mueller Probe, Trump Falsely Says the Constitution Gives Him 'the Right to Do Whatever I Want'. *The Washington Post*, July 23. washingtonpost.com/politics/2019/07/23/trump-falsely-tells-an-auditorium-full-teens-constitution-gives-him-right-do-whatever-i-want/.

Chevron U.S.A. Inc. V. Natural Resources Council, Inc. 1984. 467 US 837.

Corasaniti N., K.P. Vogel, L. Broadwater, and H. Fuchs 2020. As Courts Back Broad Mail-in Voting, DeJoy Apologizes for Missteps. *The New York Times*, September 17. https://www.nytimes.com/2020/09/17us/politics/usps-louis-dejoy.html.

Cramer, K. 2016. *The Politics of Resentment: Rural Consciousness in Wisconsin and the Rise of Scott Walker*. Chicago: University of Chicago Press.

Devins, N. 2009. Presidential Unilateralism and Political Polarization: Why Today's Congress Lacks the Will and the Way to Stop Presidential Initiatives. *Williamette Law Review* 45:395: 395–414.

Eagan E. 2021. Trump Has Quietly Hollowed Out the Government. *Slate*, January 19. https:slate.com/news-and-politics/2021/01/trump-civil-service-government-html?sid=5388f31edd52b8e41100253&utm_medium=email&utm_source….

Haskins, R., and G. Margolis. 2015. *Show Me the Evidence: Obama's Fight for Rigor and Results in Social Policy*. Washington: Brookings Institution Press.

Heclo, H. 1975. OMB and the Presidency: The Problem of Neutral Competence. *The Public Interest*, Winter, 80–98. nationalaffairs.com/storage/app/uploads/public/58e/1a4/bdd/58e1a4bdd8829631104296.pdf7.

Hibbing, J. 2020. *The Securitarian Personality: What Really Motivates Trump's Base and Why It Matters for the Post-Trump Era*. New York: Oxford University Press.

Howell, W. 2003. *Power Without Persuasion: The Politics of Direct Presidential Action*. Princeton, NJ: Princeton University Press.

Huber, J., and C. Shipan. 2002. *Deliberate Discretion? The Institutional Foundations of Bureaucratic Autonomy*. New York and Cambridge: Cambridge University Press.

Kamarck, E. 2016. *Why Presidents Fail and How They Can Succeed Again*. Washington: The Brookings Institution.

Kelemen, M. 2020. Under Trump, More Big Donors Have Been Named Ambassadors—And Controversies Have Followed. *NPR*, August 18. npr.org/2020/08/18/903199848/under-trump-more-big-donors-are-named-ambassadors-and-controversies-have-followed/.

Khimm, S. 2017. Trump Cuts Red Tape at White House Event Touting Deregulation. *NBC News*, December 14. NBCNews.com/politics/white-house/trump-cuts-red-tape-white-house-event-touting-deregulation-n829851.

Koslof, E. 2021. Yes, President Biden Signed More Executive Orders in His First Week Than Any Past President. *VERIFY*, January 27. executive-orders-in-his–first-week-than-any-past-president/65-06d6cad9-3027 ....

Lewis, M. 2018. *The Fifth Risk*. New York: W. W. Norton.

Lewis, D., and M. Richardson. 2021. The Very Best People: President Trump and the Management of Executive Personnel. *Presidential Studies Quarterly* 51 (3): 51–70.

Lim, D. 2020. Federal Work Force Attrition Under the Trump Administration: Unusually High Attrition Among Senior Civil Servants Undermines the Federal Workforce, A New Analysis Shows. *Government Executive*, December 28. govexec.com/management/2020/12/federal-workforce-attrition-under-trump-administration/171045/.

Long, N. 1949. Power and Administration. *Public Administration Review* 9 (Autumn): 257–264.

Los Angeles Times Editorial. 2020. Trump's Troubling Preference for 'Acting' Appointees. *Los Angeles Times*, September 6. latimes.com/opinion/story/2020-09-06/trumps-acting-appointees/

Magill, B., and M. Boyanton. 2020. Trump's Agency-Gutting Relocations are Ripe for a Biden Reversal. *Bloomberg Law*, November 24. news.bloomberglaw.com/environment-and-energy/trumps-drain-the-swamp-agency-moves-ripe-for-biden-reversal.

Miller, G., and E. Nakashima 2020. President's Intelligence Briefing Book Repeatedly Cited Virus Threat. *The Washington Post*, April 27. washingtonpost.com/national-security/presidents-intelligence-briefing-book-repeatedly-cited-virus-threat/2020/04/27/ca66949a-8885-11ea-ac8a-fe9b8088e101.

Moe, T. 1985. The Politicized Presidency. In *The New Direction in American Politics*, ed. J. Chubb and P. Peterson. Washington: The Brookings Institution.

———. 2012. Delegation, Control, and the Study of Public Bureaucracy. *The Forum* 10 (2). https://doi.org/10.1515/1540-8884.1508.

Nathan, R. 1983. *The Administrative Presidency*. New York: Wiley.

Potter, R. 2019. *Bending the Rules: Procedural Politicking in the Bureaucracy*. Chicago: University of Chicago Press.

Resh, W. 2015. *Rethinking the Administrative Presidency: Trust, Intellectual Capital, and Appointee-Careerist Relations in the George W. Bush Administration*. Baltimore: Johns Hopkins University Press.

Rockman, B. 1995. The Federal Executive: Equilibrium and Change. In *The New American Politics: Reflections on Political Change*, ed. B. Jones. New York and London: Routledge.

Rodden, J. 2019. *Why Cities Lose: The Deep Roots of the Urban-Rural Divide*. New York: Basic Books.

Rucker, P., and C. Leonnig. 2020. *A Very Stable Genius: Donald J. Trump's Testing of America*. New York: Penguin Press.

Samuels, B. 2019. Trump Learns to Love Acting Officials. *The Hill*, April 14. thehill.com/homenews/administration/438660-trump-learns-to-love-acting-officials/.

Sullivan, K. 2018. Washington Post: Trump Says His 'Gut' Can Tell Him More Than 'Anybody Else's Brain Can Ever Tell Me'. *CNN Politics*, November 27. cnn.com/2018/11/27/politics/washington-post-trump-gut/index.htmls.

Tenpas, K. 2021. *Tracking Turnover in the Trump Administration*. brookings.edu/research/tracking-turnover-in-the-trump-administration/.

Totenberg, N., and H.L. Wang. 2020. Supreme Court Punts Census Case, Giving Trump an Iffy Chance to Alter Numbers. *NPR*, December 18. npr.org/2020/12/18/94687596/supreme-court-punts-in-census-case-says-its-premature-to-decide-the-issue.

Weber, M. 1958. Bureaucracy. In *From Max Weber: Essays in Sociology*, trans. and ed., H. Gerth and C.W. Mills. New York: Oxford University Press.

FURTHER READING

The administrative state is frequently referred to as the permanent government. It persists through the comings and goings of people who hold elective office. It is composed of a variety of agencies tasked with a problem or, more likely, responsibilities for some aspects of a problem. The bureaucracy is in theory an agent of the principals who have the political responsibility for leading the government. To be responsive and accountable, in principle, the bureaucracy must obey the orders of the elected governors. However, detailed knowledge of past precedents and the machinery of government provides the bureaucracy with some advantages in its relationships with elected officials. It also has experience as to what has worked in the past and what has not. In many instances bureaucracies also represent special expertise well beyond the capabilities of most elected officials. Inevitably, therefore, there are tensions between administrative responsibility, on the one hand, and accountability and responsiveness to the political principals on the other. This tension is further complicated by the American system of separated powers, which are actually separated principals (the president, the Congress, and the judiciary) who may be in conflict with one another.

A classic textbook that covers these issues from a general standpoint is Donald F. Kettl, *The Politics of the Administrative Process*, 8th edition (2021, Washington DC: CQ Press). Another is Steven J. Balla and William T. Gormley, Jr., *Bureaucracy and Democracy: Accountability and Performance*, 4th edition (2018, Washington DC: CQ Press). A further effort to examine issues of administrative responsiveness can be found in Joel D. Aberbach and Bert A. Rockman, *In the Web of Politics: Three Decades of the U.S. Federal Executive* (2000, Washington DC: The Brookings Institution).

Some further notable works that examine why presidents are driven to put their stamp on the federal bureaucracy are Richard P. Nathan, *The Administrative Presidency* (1983, New York: John Wiley and Son), Terry M. Moe, 'The Politicized Presidency' in *The New Direction in American Politics* (eds.)

John Chubb and Paul Peterson (1985, Washington DC: The Brookings Institution), William G. Howell, *Power Without Persuasion: The Politics of Direct Presidential Action* (2003, Princeton: Princeton University Press). Two notable studies of the adverse effects of efforts to tighten central political control over the federal executive are David E. Lewis, *The Politics of Presidential Appointments: Political Control and Bureaucratic Performance* (2008, Princeton: Princeton University Press) and William G. Resh, *Rethinking the Administrative Presidency: Trust, Intellectual Capital, and Appointee-Careerist Relations in the George W. Bush Administration* (2015, Baltimore: Johns Hopkins University Press).

Finally, two recent and notable works demonstrate the repertory of bureaucratic responses to resist unilateral presidential control: Rachel Potter, *Bending the Rules: Procedural Politicking in the Bureaucracy* (2019, Chicago: University of Chicago Press) and Andrew Rudalevige, *By Executive Order: Bureaucratic Management and the Limits of Presidential Power* (2021, Princeton: Princeton University Press).

CHAPTER 12

Federalism

Ursula Hackett

The United States is federal: national, state, and local governments divide and share policymaking power. There are fifty state governments and about **90,000** local governments such as townships, municipalities, school districts, and parishes. In his seminal *Federalism: Origins, Operation, Significance*, William Riker (1964) wrote: 'Federalism is a precisely definable and easily recognizable constitutional artefact'. Students of federalism owe a great debt to Riker, who considered the legal framework of federalism and how federalism affects the operation of political power. But federalism is neither 'precisely definable' nor a mere 'constitutional artefact.' Riker's definition fails to capture the dynamism and variety of American federalism, in which policymakers at local, state and federal level exploit both constitutional and extra-constitutional resources strategically in pursuit of their goals.

The United States is the archetypal model of a federal system. Indeed, as Kenneth Wheare (1967) argues, 'the federal principle has come to mean what it does because the United States has come to be what it is.' In other words, scholars often look to the American model as a vision of how federalism is and should operate. But from a cross-national perspective American federalism is extraordinary in many ways: all states have equal legal standing and

U. Hackett (✉)
Department of Politics and International Relations, Royal Holloway, University of London, London, UK
e-mail: Ursula.hackett@rhul.ac.uk

© The Author(s), under exclusive license to Springer Nature
Switzerland AG 2022
G. Peele et al. (eds.), *Developments in American Politics 9*,
https://doi.org/10.1007/978-3-030-89740-6_12

authority, and the system has also been comparatively elastic in adapting to enormous changes in physical size, population, race, economy, and culture. Recent partisan polarization threatens to fragment it further. This is not just a 'constitutional artifact,' but a dynamic, living political ecosystem.

Federalism is a system of multiple spheres of constitutional authority, geographically defined political-administrative units, and a strategic arena in which policymakers and advocates angle for advantage. Martha Derthick (2001) said that federalism is a choice about 'how many communities to be.' In this chapter we will examine not only the constitutional architecture that underpins American federalism, but also the dynamic exercise of political power within—and sometimes beyond—these constitutional bounds.

American federalism can be characterized in both collaborative and competitive ways. States and localities share information and come together to achieve common purposes, but they also compete with one another to attract businesses and win federal funding. The priorities of local, state, and federal governments do not always align, so national and sub-national governments are sometimes allies (for instance, when the federal government offers funding to expand state capacity) and sometimes enemies (as when liberal and conservative administrations clash over policy).

Policymakers can collaborate, horizontally (between states) and vertically (between national and sub-national levels of government), through formal and informal mechanisms. Organizations such as the National Governors Association (NGA) and the National Conference of State Legislatures (NCSL) speak for the nation's state executives and legislatures respectively, coordinating action between states and communicating state imperatives to the federal government. Informally, policymakers in each state learn about what is happening around the country and share best practices, enabling policy to diffuse between states, especially between neighbors and states with similar policy challenges and political cultures.

Federalism affects the prosperity, the security, and the many everyday services available to each person living in the United States. Especially during periods of extreme partisan polarization and legislative gridlock at the federal level—as we see today—state governments make many consequential decisions. During the coronavirus pandemic, the role of states became still more important.

OVERVIEW OF RECENT DEVELOPMENTS

This chapter emphasizes three key characteristics of American federalism in recent years. First, American federalism remains a dynamic system with a high degree of flexibility. Conservative and liberal states have innovated in a variety of ways, including LGBTQ+ protections and restrictions, environmental standards, abortion access, and schools policy. Secondly, some state innovations prompt retribution from the federal administration. Federal policymakers have been willing to pursue punitive strategies against their political enemies at state level in an attempt to achieve their goals. There have been aggressive federal moves in the fields of environmental policymaking, taxes and spending, and the pandemic response. Thirdly, changes to state election law and court appointments confirm the truth of the fact that American federalism is an arena of strategic partisan maneuvring for political advantage.

In a federal system sub-national governments enjoy important policymaking power and authority, making policy innovation possible. Amidst growing partisan polarization, liberal states launched lawsuits against the Trump administration and pushed for policies such as LGBTQ+ protections and climate mitigation, while conservative states moved to expand private school choice, reduce union power, and restrict abortion access. Policy innovations such as school vouchers and recreational cannabis decriminalization spread across multiple states, as policymakers learned from their neighbors. Some state policy changes were met with enthusiasm from the federal administration; others prompted a more aggressive response.

American federalism has recently become more punitive. The federal government used its formal powers to punish sub-national jurisdictions when policy differences arose between local, state, and federal level. The Trump administration denied billions of dollars in federal grant money to 'sanctuary cities,' jurisdictions that withhold information from federal authorities about undocumented immigrants in their jails. During the pandemic, the federal government varied its response to state needs depending upon the political allegiance of the state leadership, with the Republican regime in Florida receiving all of the medical supplies it wanted from the federal stockpile while Democratic-led states such as Michigan, Colorado, and Massachusetts received only a fraction of their requests.

American federalism is an arena in which strategic policymakers deploy multiple tools to reach their goals, adhering to different visions of the federal–state relationship according to political expediency. For instance, Scott Pruitt, who served as President Trump's Environmental Protection Agency (EPA) Administrator from February 2017 until July 2018, identified the principle of 'cooperative federalism' as central to his approach as Administrator, claiming that state governments should be partners with the federal administration rather than passive instruments carrying out federal goals. After Pruitt was confirmed, however, the federal administration changed tack, pulling a variety of legal and financial strings in an attempt to prevent states such as California from pursuing more stringent environmental standards in vehicle emissions.

As they maneuvre for partisan advantage within the federal system, governments utilize many different tools to achieve their goals in different policy areas. The Trump administration used *waivers*—that is, granting special permissions for individual jurisdictions to bypass certain federal requirements—in order to influence healthcare policy when interacting with state governments, but often relied on eliminating or modifying federal rules and regulations in the field of climate and environmental policy (Thompson et al. 2020). As this chapter will detail, American federalism stands fragmented at the outset of the Biden administration, with partisan polarization pushing liberal and conservative states further apart, not only on questions of policy but also on political procedure, as states restrict access to voting, and redistrict for partisan advantage.

FEDERALISM AND PARTISANSHIP

The oldest theories of federalism are of the 'dual federalism' type, which is the idea that each government has a separate domain and sphere of policymaking authority. Like a cake with clearly defined layers, the federal government is responsible for national priorities such as defence; state governments handle state-level priorities and administer elections; and localities deal with municipal and neighborhood-level issues such as local education and policing. Such theories were displaced by more complex metaphors, such as 'marble-cake federalism,' where policymaking responsibilities are intermingled and there is no rigid delineation of authority between different levels of government (Grodzins 1966). This intermingling of policymaking responsibilities means that the latitude for action enjoyed by federal and state governments cannot be stipulated according to policy type. Policymakers favor federal or state action when it suits their policy priorities, with the degree of collaboration between federal and state governments a function of political will.

Across a range of public policy areas—whether environmental protection, education policy, healthcare, or social welfare—Democrats tend to favor national level control, whereas Republicans tend to prefer state-level control. This is the straightforward story of partisanship and federalism, but in practice both Republican and Democratic policymakers have sought to increase states' latitude of action, or expand federal power, only when and to the extent that it suits their policy priorities and electoral goals. Republicans are more likely to limit state authority through 'ceiling preemptions' that cap the amount of regulation states can enact on a certain issue, for instance by preventing states from setting new emissions standards for a particular industry. By contrast, Democrats tend to limit state power through 'floor preemptions,' which set minimum standards that states can exceed if they want to, but must at least match.

A Republican administration committed to the principle of state autonomy may nevertheless favor federal directives if such directives help it achieve its policy purposes. This instrumental approach to federalism was clearly in evidence in the Trump administration's approach to federal student loans. As the federal government dialed back oversight of student loan servicers, more than a dozen states sought to protect student borrowers by tightening their regulation of loans providers and creating a 'borrower bill of rights,' but Education Secretary Betsy DeVos argued that such states' moves were pre-empted by federal law. When DeVos unveiled an interpretation of the law arguing that only the federal government—not states—has the power to oversee student loan servicers, the National Governors' Association (NGA) issued a warning: 'We are concerned the department is heading in a direction that runs counter to the principles of collaborative federalism governors presented to Congress' (National Governors Association 2018). Governors urged the federal department to collaborate with states to protect students.

By contrast, in other educational policymaking arenas, such as schools policy, the federal Education Department favored a state-centered approach. The federal government lent rhetorical support to the push for private school choice, a core Republican priority, but it lacked the votes in Congress to pass a federal voucher program, a policy offering money to parents to spend on a private education for their children. So instead, the focus remained upon encouraging state efforts. This perspective was articulated forcefully by Education Secretary Betsy DeVos in a speech in New York City in May 2018.

> A top-down solution emanating from Washington would only grow government ... a new federal office to oversee your private schools and your scholarship organizations. An office staffed with more unelected and unaccountable bureaucrats tasked to make decisions families should be free to make for themselves. Just imagine for a moment how that might impact you under an administration hostile to your faith! So, when it comes to education, no solution—not even ones we like—should be dictated by Washington, D.C. (Klein 2018)

Secretary DeVos and her wealthy husband, Dick DeVos, came to political prominence as donors and advocates in Michigan. Over three decades, they donated millions of dollars to groups seeking to create vouchers in the state. Their efforts in Michigan never succeeded, spiked (in part) by a strict state constitutional prohibition against aid programs for religious schools, but the voucher cause has had rapid recent victories in other states, particularly Ohio, Wisconsin, Arizona, Florida, and Louisiana (Hackett 2014). In 2000 there were just eight school voucher programs in the American states; by the end of 2020 there were 61. The issue is highly partisan; Republican victories at state level made the expansion of private school choice possible.

Electoral change can substantially affect the dynamics of federalism. Extraordinary Republican success in the 2010 midterms, the first of Barack Obama's presidency, saw the GOP gain 680 seats in state legislatures and flip 20 chambers. In contrast to the federal Congress, where efforts to reauthorize the federal education law failed repeatedly between 2007 and 2015, state legislatures with trifecta Republican control could pursue their agenda much more easily. A trifecta is a situation in which a single political party controls both chambers of the state legislature and the governorship. Under the Trump administration, when Republican priorities aligned at state and federal level, the federal government encouraged state action on issues such as private school choice or Right to Work legislation, which prohibits agreements requiring union membership as a condition for employment. In an increasingly polarized country, partisan alignment between state and federal level paves the way for cooperation, but partisan differences often prompt conflict.

FEDERALISM AND POLICY INNOVATION OR REBELLION

States have enacted many measures that innovate and challenge federal policies, occasionally passing laws that deliberately conflict with federal statutes. According to the principle of 'uncooperative federalism,' states are sometimes the allies and other times enemies of the federal government (Bulman-Pozen and Gerken 2009). For instance, during George W. Bush's presidency, some states charged with carrying out the 2001 Patriot Act, a law which strengthened law enforcement's capacity to counter terrorism, refused to enforce portions they deemed unconstitutional. Some Republican states rebelled against the Affordable Care Act by refusing to expand Medicaid eligibility.

Since the founding of the American republic, states have jealously guarded their prerogatives and rebelled against federal mandates they perceived as onerous. In 1842 the Supreme Court decided not only that state officials were *not* required to enforce the Fugitive Slave Act of 1793, but also that states could legally prohibit government officials from apprehending runaways. In other words, the federal government was prohibited from forcing states to carry out federal requirements, an 'anti-commandeering' doctrine further elucidated in *New York v United States* (1992) and *Printz v United States* (1997). American federalism today is rife with state resistance to federal directives, through such means as 'sanctuary' cities which refuse to cooperate with federal immigration enforcement, and state lawsuits challenging federal policy.

In addition to their role as challengers to the federal government, the states are powerful arenas of policy innovation in a variety of fields, from drug legalization to social welfare reforms. According to Justice Louis Brandeis's famous dissent in the 1932 Supreme Court case *New State Ice Co. v. Liebmann* (1932):

> It is one of the happy incidents of the federal system that a single courageous state may, if its citizens choose, serve as a laboratory; and try novel social and economic experiments without risk to the rest of the country. (Brandeis [dissent] 1932)

Brandeis's concept of states as laboratories is an influential one because the metaphor captures the range of innovative activity at state level. For instance, in the field of LGBTQ+ protections, state innovation proceeds on both the left and right, with many conservative states considering policies such as 'bathroom bills' limiting public toilet use based on birth sex, or banning LGBTQ+ sex education in public schools. On the liberal side, other states have considered enacting non-discrimination protections and permitting recognition of a range of gender identities on government documents.

Yet at a time of heightened 'affective polarization'—the sort of tribalism that views members of the opposing party as hated enemy rather than respected opponent—partisans would dispute the second part of Brandeis's statement that policy experimentation is 'without risk to the rest of the country.' The Supreme Court held in 2015 in *Obergefell v Hodges* that states must recognize the marriages of same-sex couples from other states, but the decision provoked a backlash in conservative states, and some counties in Alabama, Texas, and Kentucky refused licences to same-sex couples. State innovations—either restricting or relaxing LGBTQ+ protections, for example—can prompt furious responses from partisans in other states.

FEDERALISM AND PUNISHMENT

During the Trump administration, some state policy differences prompted a punitive response from the federal government, which used its formal powers to punish the states. In environmental policymaking, for example, the Trump administration's Environmental Protection Agency (EPA) clashed with California over EPA proposals to weaken greenhouse gas and fuel economy standards for cars and light trucks.

This assertion of federal authority stands in stark contrast to the typical pattern of partisanship in environmental policymaking, whereby Democratic regimes (such as President Obama's administration) tend to shift the balance of authority from the states back toward the federal government while Republican ones (as under President George W. Bush) encourage more state-led efforts. It also stands in contrast to the approach the Trump administration took elsewhere in environmental policy, where the EPA, Department of Interior, and other agencies initiated a comprehensive rollback of federal rules and pledged to work closely with states. At his confirmation hearing before the Senate Committee on Environmental and Public Works, President Trump's first EPA Administrator, Scott Pruitt, stated:

> [C]ooperative federalism must be respected and applied by the EPA with regard to our environmental laws. Congress has wisely and appropriately directed the EPA through our environmental statutes to utilize the expertise and resources of the States to better protect the environment, and for the States to remain our nation's frontline environmental implementers and enforcers. If we truly want to advance and achieve cleaner air and water the States must be partners and not mere passive instruments of federal will. (Pruitt 2017)

Despite Pruitt's insistence that the federal administration would respect state prerogatives, the federal administration pursued a punitive approach with California.

For the past fifty years, the state of California has carved out a leadership role on auto emissions by enacting strict standards. The passage of the Clean Air Act (CAA) of 1963 granted the EPA the authority to regulate air pollution from motor vehicles, but at the time the CAA was passed California was already experimenting with new laws and standards to address its own pollution problems. Congress created an exemption for the state, requiring the EPA to grant California a waiver so that the state could apply its own emissions regulations. As long as California's standards were at least as stringent as the federal ones, the state was permitted to set its own strict standards—standards currently adopted by twelve other states and the District of Columbia.

When the Trump administration decided to relax fuel economy rules, ostensibly on grounds of consumer cost, disputes about California's special status reached a crisis point. The *New York Times* reported that President Trump was 'enraged' as California reached an informal agreement with four car manufacturers (BMW, Ford, Honda, and Volkswagen), which voluntarily committed the companies to California's stricter standards (Davenport and Tabuchi 2019). Other companies, including Toyota, Fiat Chrysler, and General Motors, sided with the federal administration.

In an unprecedented maneuvre, the EPA retaliated against California's actions by withdrawing its waiver. No previous administration had ever revoked a state's authority to regulate its own air quality. Andrew Wheeler, Head of the EPA after Pruitt, said:

> We embrace federalism and the role of the states, but federalism does not mean that one state can dictate standards for the nation. (Wheeler 2019)

The Trump administration also opened an antitrust investigation into the companies who had reached the voluntary agreement with the state, threatened to cut off federal highway funding to the state, and served several Californian cities for alleged violation of the Clean Water Act. The Department of Justice filed a lawsuit against the state's cap-and-trade program for regulating greenhouse gas emissions.

The Trump administration's EPA sought to accelerate the development of fossil fuel extraction and infrastructure, rescinding the Obama administration's Clean Power Plan (CPP) in June 2019 and replacing it with its own, much more modest, Affordable Clean Energy (ACE) rule. CPP was an effort to transition state electricity portfolios away from coal and toward renewables and 'cleaner' fossil fuels such as natural gas. Following the principle of cooperative federalism, the Obama administration established individual state-by-state emissions targets tailored to each state's existing energy mix, allowing states to choose among different compliance options, such as increased coal plant efficiency, switching to natural gas, or more renewables.

The Obama plan was ambitious—producing an estimated 32 percent reduction in CO_2 emissions below 2005 levels by 2030—but states had discretion about how to meet federal targets. The Trump administration's replacement ACE rule was far less ambitious, estimated to produce only a 0.7 percent reduction in emissions within the same time frame (Goelzhauser and Konisky 2020). The Trump administration's actions in environmental policymaking were aimed squarely at weakening standards and punishing liberal states, such as California, which sought to toughen them. This is punitive federalism at its most obvious.

More subtly, Republicans in Congress pursued policies aimed at benefiting Republican-leaning states and penalizing Democratic-leaning ones. For example, the 2017 Tax Cuts and Jobs Act—one of the 115th Congress's few legislative accomplishments—capped at $10,000 the federal deductibility of state and local taxes: taxpayers' ability to reduce their federal tax bill according to the amount they pay in state and local taxes. Democratic states such as California and New York, where taxes are highest, were hardest hit. With Democrats taking control of Congress and the White House after the 2020 elections, House Speaker Nancy Pelosi and Senate Majority Leader Chuck Schumer called for repeal of the cap, although the Biden Administration is opposed in part because of the budgetary implications: allowing taxpayers to make deductions reduces the amount the federal government can take in tax revenue.

FEDERALISM AND TARGETED FUNDING

When it seeks to compel states to adopt a particular position, the federal government might provide funding to states. For instance, under the Affordable Care Act the federal government offered to pay 100 percent of the costs of Medicaid expansion for people with incomes up to 138 percent of the federal poverty level for the first few years, dropping to 90 percent by 2020 and beyond. By February 2021, 38 states plus DC had adopted the Medicaid expansion and 12 states had not done so.

State governments' ability to withstand or redirect federal interference depends in part upon their financial position. The pandemic caused state revenues to drop precipitously, with tax collections for March-August 2020 on average 6.4 percent lower than the same months in 2019 (Center on Budget and Policy Priorities 2020). Budgetary difficulties force states to plead for federal relief, petitions to which the Trump administration was notably reluctant to accede, especially for Democratic states. The Biden administration indicates that it is willing to spend more in federal aid to states in order to help them weather the pandemic.

But Democratic administrations have also leveraged state budgetary challenges to compel states to adopt federal priorities. For instance, when responding to the financial crisis, the 2009 stimulus bill included a program called Race to the Top, a $4.35bn competitive grant program that encouraged states to bid for money by aligning themselves with the Obama administration's policy priorities on curriculum reforms, technology, standards, and charter schools. In three successive rounds the federal administration invited states to demonstrate their commitment to these priorities and awarded funds accordingly. Delaware and Tennessee won the first round, nine states plus DC received money in the second round, and seven further states received smaller awards in the third round.

Eighteen states and DC eventually received money through the competition, yet 14 states made bids in every round of the competition but received no federal money. Despite the tiny size of the federal investment in the program (less than $5bn from a stimulus package worth more than $800bn), the Obama administration leveraged wide-ranging educational reforms across its five priority areas. Even states that never received money were induced to align their education preferences with the administration's because the three-round competition awarded states points based on their accomplishments prior to applying as well as their plans for further reforms. Moreover, the continuing fiscal crises in the states, exacerbated by the recession, meant the money was needed urgently. The federal government gained leverage over the states by exploiting the latter's weakened financial position.

FEDERALISM AND THE COURTS

To enhance their leverage with other levels of government, policymakers can also utilize the constitutional framework setting out the relationships between states and federal government. National power is bolstered by the fact that the federal Constitution asserts its supremacy (Article VI, Clause 2) and by the Interstate Commerce Clause (Article I, Section 8, Clause 3) which grants Congress the power to 'regulate commerce' among the several states. States are constrained by the Privileges and Immunities Clause of the Fourteenth Amendment, which asserts that 'No State shall make or enforce any law which shall abridge the privileges or immunities of citizens of the United States.' When opposing the federal government, states rely upon the capacious Tenth Amendment's Reserved Powers: 'The powers not delegated to the United States by the Constitution, nor prohibited by it to the States, are reserved to the States respectively, or to the people.'

According to the Tenth Amendment, then, all powers not expressly granted to the federal government in the Constitution are the preserve of the states. Given that the Constitution makes no mention of local government, political parties, or policies such as education, healthcare, and welfare, the Tenth Amendment seems to grant considerable latitude to the states and to limit the power of the federal government, as Antifederalists demanded. But when applied in court, this Amendment and the other sections of the Constitution admit a range of interpretations. Litigants utilize competing considerations, and courts adjudicate.

The Supreme Court has weighed in on the proper relationship between federal and state governments. In *South Dakota v Dole* (1987), the Court found that the federal government can constitutionally attach conditions to funding grants to states as long as the conditions are 'reasonable,' but states must be able to reject or accept those conditions (and the associated money) knowingly and voluntarily. The Court has been called upon to adjudicate when the use of federal conditional grants crosses the line from persuasion to coercion. Only once has the Court determined that a federal grant crossed that line: the Affordable Care Act (ACA)'s expansion of Medicaid eligibility in *National Federation of Independent Business v Sebelius* (2012). Medicaid is a jointly administered federal and state program that helps pay healthcare costs for low-income Americans, and the ACA was the Obama administration's signature healthcare law. The Court determined that the ACA represented a 'gun to the head' of states because it threatened them with a loss of all federal Medicaid funding should they decline the ACA's terms.

Although the Court's *Sebelius* decision struck down the 'coercive' ACA Medicaid expansion, it narrowly saved the constitutionality of the 'individual mandate'—the requirement that individuals purchase health insurance—as a valid exercise of Congress's taxing power. Chief Justice John Roberts provided the pivotal fifth vote in the 5–4 decision. As the Court tacked further to the right over the course of the Trump presidency, the Chief Justice found himself in the position of swing justice in a variety of cases—including those implicating federalism.

Of the judges and justices deciding federalism cases in recent years, a disproportionate number were appointed by Republican executives—a function of Republican political success in capturing state government since 2010, combined with Senate Majority Leader Mitch McConnell's success at denying a hearing to President Obama's nominees and fast-tracking President Trump's. Trump left office having appointed 226 federal judges in a single term, as many as his predecessor appointed in twice the time. The political affiliation of a judge or justice's elected appointer—governor or president—is a good predictor of his or her stance in legal cases (Hackett 2020). Constitutional provisions define the divisions of authority between state and federal governments only loosely, and partisanship matters more than many justices like to admit publicly for the outcome of federalism cases.

Given this favorable legal environment, conservative states have recently enacted policies that are specifically designed to enable the courts to overturn certain liberal precedents. For example, pro-life policymakers passed numerous laws restricting reproductive choice, hoping that the ensuing legal challenges would allow a conservative Court to overturn the landmark 1973 pro-choice ruling, *Roe v Wade*. From January 2017 to November 2020, 88.7 percent of abortion-related laws enacted by states sought to restrict access to abortion services (Hubbard 2021).

In two razor-thin 5–4 decisions, *Whole Woman's Health v Hellerstedt* (2016) and *June Medical Services, LLC v Russo* (2020), the Supreme Court struck down, respectively, Texas and Louisiana policies requiring abortion doctors to obtain admitting privileges at local hospitals—policies that reduce the availability of abortions by making it more difficult for clinics to operate. But with Justice Ruth Bader Ginsburg's death in September 2020 allowing President Trump a third Supreme Court pick, Amy Coney Barrett, conservative states anticipate a more sympathetic response to cases involving abortion restrictions in the near future.

The Court has also made a number of recent decisions pertaining to the conduct of American democracy and the relationships between federal and state governments. In its landmark 2013 decision *Shelby County v Holder* the

Court effectively undermined Section 5 of the Voting Rights Act (VRA) of 1965 which had required some states and localities to obtain federal preclearance before making changes to their voting laws or practices. Congress enacted the VRA to tackle entrenched racial discrimination in voting, with Sections 4 and 5 covering jurisdictions—mostly in the South—that made it particularly difficult for racial minorities to vote. The 2013 Court held that the offending sections were 'a drastic departure from basic principles of federalism' and 'the principle that all states enjoy equal sovereignty' because they required certain jurisdictions to obtain federal permission in electoral matters. Liberated from the preclearance requirements, previously covered states started to enact a variety of measures that restrict voting, from photo ID laws and the elimination of same day voting to the purging of voters from state rolls.

Racial gerrymandering—redistricting boundaries to limit the political influence of particular racial groups in violation of the Equal Protection Clause of the Fourteenth Amendment—has received a mixed response from the federal Court in recent years. In *Rucho v Common Cause* (2019) the conservative majority on the Court held 5–4 that partisan gerrymandering claims are 'nonjusticiable,' meaning such claims are political and not part of a court's sphere of judicial authority. But in *Virginia House of Delegates v. Bethune-Hill (2019)* the Court upheld a federal district court ruling that 11 of Virginia's voting districts were racially gerrymandered, and thus unconstitutional. Given high levels of polarization among elites across the United States, state efforts to create partisan advantage will likely continue under the Biden administration.

Federalism and the Covid-19 Pandemic

The Covid-19 pandemic laid bare the collective action problems inherent in a federal system. In disasters such as forest fires or tornadoes, a crisis typically affects just one or a handful of states. State governments regularly offer mutual aid. For instance, when wildfires ripped through California in August 2020, ten other states—from Texas to Washington—sent equipment to help battle the blazes. A formal process called the Emergency Management Assistance Compact sets out the structure for deployment and payment for services from other jurisdictions. Crisis response is designed to be 'locally executed, state-managed, and federally supported,' with local governments taking operational control of the situation, aided by outside resources and assistance as required (Kayyem 2020).

But the Covid-19 pandemic affected all fifty states at once, and the rising toll of the virus set off a series of bidding wars over medical equipment between states. In March 2020 Andrew Cuomo, Governor of New York—one of the worst hit states, and an early epicenter of pandemic in the United States—complained:

You have 50 states competing to buy the same item...We all wind up bidding up each other and competing against each other, where you now literally will have a company call you up and say, 'Well, California just outbid you.' It's like being on eBay with 50 other states, bidding on a ventilator. (Smith 2020)

Desperate for aid, California sought to contract with Chinese face mask manufacturers directly, Illinois had the state assistant comptroller hand over a cheque for millions of dollars to a mask-selling middleman in the parking lot of a McDonald's restaurant, and Massachusetts even deployed an American football team's plane to fly to China for supplies.

The Trump administration was strikingly indifferent to states' appeals for relief. In a March 2020 conference call with the nation's governors about the pandemic, President Trump said: 'Respirators, ventilators, all of the equipment—try getting it yourselves' (Kayyem 2020). Jared Kushner, President Trump's son-in-law and senior advisor, was widely ridiculed when he claimed that the medicines and supplies in the Strategic National Stockpile were not really for sub-national jurisdictions. He said: '...the notion of the federal stockpile was it's supposed to be *our* stockpile...It's not supposed to be states' stockpiles that they then use' (Blake 2020).

Congress allocated funds to states for affected sectors, including childcare, education, and law enforcement. In March 2020 Congress passed its first stimulus package, the $2.2 trillion Coronavirus Aid, Relief, and Economic Security Act (CARES Act), providing cash payments for adult Americans, alongside increased unemployment benefits and loans for corporations and states. That same month, the Federal Reserve lowered target interest rates to 1.25 percent, loaned $500 billion to state and local governments, and resumed large-scale quantitative easing—that is, buying up bonds and other financial assets in order to increase the money supply. In December the lame-duck session of Congress passed an additional $900 billion stimulus relief as part of the Consolidated Appropriations Act of 2021, including loans and grants for small businesses, another stimulus cheque for low-income individuals, further increases in federal unemployment benefits, and aid to state and local governments for rental assistance programs.

Officially, the White House encouraged local officials to take the lead in determining when and how quickly to ease restrictions and reopen their economies during the pandemic. After all, the Tenth Amendment reserves powers not specifically enumerated in the Constitution—including public health and law enforcement—to state governments. In practice, however, and against the guidance of its own officials and experts, the Trump administration pressured states to reopen as quickly as possible. In defiance of state-imposed stay-at-home orders in Democrat-led jurisdictions, the President tweeted 'LIBERATE MINNESOTA!' 'LIBERATE MICHIGAN!' and 'LIBERATE VIRGINIA.'

The federal government lacks the constitutional authority to implement a 'national lockdown.' Yet in April 2020 President Trump falsely claimed that whether 'to open up the states' and restart the economy 'is the decision of the President,' not state governors. He told reporters: 'When somebody is the president of the United States, the authority is total and that's the way it's got to be. … It's total. The governors know that.' Local leaders, the President asserted, 'can't do anything without the approval of the president of the United States.' These claims are categorically false and betray the President's ignorance of federalism and the Constitution. White House guidelines were theoretically aimed to facilitate the nation's states in responding to the virus effectively, but decisions about whether and how quickly to open up actually belonged to state governors.

CONCLUSION: THE IMPORTANCE OF FEDERALISM TODAY

William Riker ultimately came to the conclusion that federalism is a minor institution with little impact upon policy outcomes (Riker 1964). But federalism has always affected the prosperity, security, and wellbeing of every person in the United States. As partisan polarization paralyzes the federal Congress, with even unified Republican or Democratic governments stymied by institutional checks and balances, the locus of law-making shifts to the states. State governments have innovated in myriad policy areas—from student loans and vehicle emissions to private school choice, right-to-work laws, abortion access, and LGBTQ+ protections.

During the pandemic, as states and localities pursued different approaches and the virus laid bare deep racial and geographical inequalities in health and wellbeing, federalism became even more consequential. State governments relied upon their vertical relationships with the federal government for desperately needed funding, but were forced into horizontal competition with fellow states for supplies. The deeply partisan nature of federalism under conditions of heightened polarization was laid bare by partisan differences in the federal administration's responses to state appeals.

Far from being a 'precisely definable constitutional artifact,' American federalism is a dynamic system in which policymakers adopt different visions of the federal–state relationship according to political expediency. When it suits their purposes, both liberal and conservative policymakers have favored a greater (or lesser) role for state governments. Strategically utilizing constitutional language, and exploiting partisan advantages built up since their 2010 midterm breakthroughs at state level, Republicans have recently scored successes on elections, taxes, education, and union regulation. At the outset of the Biden administration, with a Democratic federal government facing 23 Republican state-level trifectas (compared to 15 Democratic trifectas) and a federal judiciary dominated by Republican appointees, this uncooperative, fragmented, and polarized partisan dynamic is set to continue.

References

Blake, A. 2020. Analysis|The Trump Administration Just Changed Its Description of the National Stockpile to Jibe with Jared Kushner's Controversial Claim. *Washington Post*, April 3.

Brandeis, L. (dissent) 1932. *New State Ice Co. v. Liebmann*, 285 U.S. 262. United States Supreme Court.

Bulman-Pozen, J., and H.K. Gerken. 2009. Uncooperative Federalism. *Yale Law Journal* 118: 1256–1310.

Center on Budget and Policy Priorities. 2020. States Grappling with Hit to Tax Collections. Center on Budget and Policy Priorities, November 6. https://www.cbpp.org/research/state-budget-and-tax/states-grappling-with-hit-to-tax-collections.

Davenport, C., and H. Tabuchi. 2019. Trump's Rollback of Auto Pollution Rules Shows Signs of Disarray. *New York Times*, August 20.

Derthick, M. 2001. *Keeping the Compound Republic: Essays on American Federalism.* Washington, DC: Brookings Institution Press.

Goelzhauser, G., and D.M. Konisky. 2020. The State of American Federalism 2019–2020: Polarized and Punitive Intergovernmental Relations. *Publius: The Journal of Federalism* 50 (3): 311–343.

Grodzins, M. 1966. *The American System: A New View of Government in the United States.* Chicago, IL: Rand McNally.

Hackett, U. 2014. Republicans, Catholics and the West: Explaining the Strength of Religious School Aid Prohibitions. *Politics and Religion* 7 (3): 499–520.

———. 2020. *America's Voucher Politics: How Elites Learned to Hide the State.* New York: Cambridge University Press.

Hubbard, K. 2021. In States, Abortion Legislation Frequent in Recent Years. *US News & World Report*, February 25.

Kayyem, J. 2020. Trump Leaves States to Fend for Themselves. *The Atlantic*, March 17.

Klein, A. 2018. DeVos: State Bans on Public Money to Religious Schools Should Go to "Ash Heap of History". *Education Week*, 16 May.

National Governors Association. 2018. Governors Voice Concerns Over New Student Borrower Proposal. National Governors Association (blog), March 12.

Pruitt, S. 2017. Environmental Protection Agency Designate E. Scott Pruitt Attorney General, State of Oklahoma Senate Confirmation Hearing Opening Statement. Washington, DC.

Riker, W. 1964. *Federalism: Origin, Operation, Significance.* Boston: Little, Brown and Company.

Smith, D. 2020. New York's Andrew Cuomo Decries 'EBay'-Style Bidding War for Ventilators. *The Guardian*, March 31.

Thompson, F.J., K.K. Wong, and B.G. Rabe. 2020. *Trump, the Administrative Presidency, and Federalism.* Washington, DC: Brookings Institution Press.

Wheare, K. 1967. *Federal Government*, 4th ed. London: Oxford University Press.

Wheeler, A. 2019. *Administrator Wheeler Addresses National Automobile Dealers Association.* Environmental Protection Agency.

FURTHER READING

Read *Publius: The Journal of Federalism* for the latest scholarship on American (and comparative) federalism. This journal publishes an annual review issue, *The State of American Federalism*, offering an informative round-up of developments in American federalism over the past year.

William Riker and Martha Derthick are key starting points for scholars of American federalism. Riker's *Federalism: Origins, Operation, Significance* (1964, Boston: Little, Brown and Company) remains the classic text in federalism scholarship. Riker describes the political logic behind the formation of federal systems and argues that the United States was a politically centralized federal system from the founding. Martha Derthick's many distinguished contributions to the study of federalism were honoured by a special issue of *Publius* in Spring 2017 (Volume 47, Issue 2). Her 2001 book, *Keeping the Compound Republic* (Washington DC: Brookings Institution Press), explores the changes made to American federalism by Progressivism, the New Deal, and the civil rights revolution.

Beyond the classic 'layer cake' and 'marble cake' visions of federalism, Paul Manna's *School's In: Federalism and the National Education Agenda* (2006, Washington DC: Georgetown University Press) introduces a model of federal-state relations based upon 'borrowing strength': leveraging the capacities possessed by other governments in the federal system. John Dinan's *State Constitutional Politics* (2018, Chicago: University of Chicago Press) shows how state constitutional amendments have served as instruments of governance. Ursula Hackett's *America's Voucher Politics* (2020, New York: Cambridge University Press) explores state policymakers' use of innovative policy designs to avoid legal challenges at both state and federal level.

From the Founding compromises, to Civil War, to slow progress on Civil Rights, American federalism has always been about race. Lisa Miller's *The Perils of Federalism* (2018, New York: Oxford University Press) explains how the American system structures representation on crime and violence in ways that disadvantage low-income racial minorities. Jamila Michener's *Fragmented Democracy: Medicaid, Federalism, and Unequal Politics* (2018, New York: Cambridge University Press) demonstrates that the federal nature of America's largest public health insurance program negatively affects the political participation of low-income racial minorities.

CHAPTER 13

Immigration Policy

Andrew Wroe

'Who are we?' asked political historian Samuel Huntington of his fellow Americans. It is a question that has fascinated academic scholars, media commentators, and ordinary Americans for more than two centuries. It speaks to further questions of individual and collective identity and to the stories that the nation tells about itself—in particular about who is and can be an American and what the US stands for and indeed means.

One story, which can be thought of as America's semi-official narrative and is found in school textbooks and national hagiographies, is that America is a nation of immigrants, having welcomed and integrated around 100 million newcomers across several hundred years from all over the world with relatively few problems. It is built on the notion that anyone can become an American regardless of race, ethnicity, religion or even place of birth because, ultimately, being American is about subscribing to a set of ideas and values that include liberty, individualism, democracy and equality of opportunity, and a related sense that the US offers unparalleled social mobility and economic opportunities free from class-based constraints and other hidebound social and cultural restrictions. America is like a melting pot in which new arrivals' distinct cultures, races, and ethnicities are blended to form a new and unique American culture. In this narrative, America is exceptional, a shining city on a hill,

A. Wroe (✉)
School of Politics and International Relations, University of Kent, Canterbury, UK
e-mail: a.j.wroe@kent.ac.uk

G. Peele et al. (eds.), *Developments in American Politics 9*,
https://doi.org/10.1007/978-3-030-89740-6_13

offering hope and refuge to the ambitious and persecuted wherever they may be.

A darker narrative challenges this rosy view. Often told in academic analyses, it is the story of a nation that has fought to exclude 'bad' immigrants based on their specific religious (non-Protestant), racial (non-white), and ethnic identities, while keeping the door ajar to favored groups of 'good' migrants, specifically White Anglo-Saxon Protestants (WASPs), who are perceived to be more assimilable, more authentically American. It emphasizes the xenophobia and racism directed at each new wave of immigrants, whether Germans in the eighteenth century, Irish Catholics in the mid-nineteenth, Chinese laborers at the century's end, southern and eastern Europeans in the early decades of the twentieth century, and Latinos, especially Mexicans, across the whole of US history. To this must be added the genocide of the continent's first peoples, Native Americans, and the sorry histories of slavery and racial segregation.

Erika Lee (2019) argues that while the semi-official narrative may acknowledge the existence of episodes of xenophobia, it characterizes them as abnormal, infrequent, un-American events. For Lee, in contrast, xenophobia—the fear of and prejudice toward foreigners—is a constant feature of American history. America is in her words 'a nation of xenophobia' and xenophobia is a part of its national ideology.

While seemingly irrevocably opposed, the semi-official 'America as a nation of immigrants' narrative and Lee's alternative 'America as a nation of xenophobia' narrative are in fact not mutually exclusive. They can be seen as competing traditions. Both have been and continue to be powerful forces in American history, and at any particular point one may be more influential than the other. The US through its history has oscillated between broadly welcoming and repelling immigrants depending on the number arriving, their origin, the strength of the American economy and the demand for labor, whether America is at war or peace, and the ability of opportunistic politicians to whip up nativist sentiment. Both narratives are true and present even at the same time. Each is a permanent feature of the nation's history, although at any particular time one or the other may be in ascendance or relative decline. They both have a long history.

Huntington's answer to his own question would not surprise Lee. He argued that Americans are defined by 'Anglo-Protestant culture, traditions, and values' (2004: xviii). Whether Huntington's arguments are racist, as his critics allege, remains a matter of contention. What is clear is that the historian mirrored the wider concerns of a sizeable proportion of white Americans about the country's changing demographic profile as the twentieth century bled into the twenty-first. America is becoming less white, and many in the white majority worry about losing their dominant political, economic, and cultural status. Trump tapped into these fears during his presidential campaign and White House tenure with a relentless focus on the dangers of immigration. This message appealed especially to less educated and lower income white voters, who were also attracted by Trump's anti-globalization and America First appeals.

This chapter's primary focus is, unsurprisingly, President Trump and his immigration agenda. It tells the story of how he thrust immigration policy center-stage and leveraged it to win the keys to the White House. Immigration was the *sine qua non* of Trump's presidency. It sparked his candidacy to life when he descended the gilded escalator at Trump Tower to claim that Mexico was deliberately sending rapists, criminals, and drug dealers to the US, and it subsequently provided direction, focus, motivation, and urgency to Trump's White House years. And yet, despite the sound and fury and bombastic rhetoric dripping with nativism, President Trump had relatively limited success in reforming America's immigration laws and architecture. Most notably, Trump largely failed to deliver on his central promise to build a 'big, beautiful wall' between the US and Mexico, never mind getting Mexico to pay for it. To be sure, Trump did have other policy wins on immigration issues, some of real significance. By the end of his presidency, refugee and asylee numbers were significantly down, green card applicants were subject to significantly stricter 'public charge' rules, and the novel coronavirus helped push down undocumented entry on the southern border and opened up an opportunity to revoke international students' visas and bar temporary workers. But nearly all Trump's wins were achieved via executive actions, and subsequent presidents will find them easy to overturn. They will not constitute a significant legacy of policy reform.

As well as setting out the gap between Trump's soaring anti-immigration rhetoric and the constrained reality of his concrete policy achievements, the chapter also seeks to account for that gap. In brief, some of the reasons for Trump's limited success are familiar to all students of American politics: the system was designed to be slow and cumbersome, resistant to ambitious and unprincipled leaders. And Trump unearthed resistance across the system: in the legislature, the courts, the federal bureaucracy, the states, and his own White House. But another important part of the story is Trump's own failings of leadership. His mismanagement of key personnel and advisers, absence of a clear and coherent policy narrative, outrageous antics and words, and misguided and ineffective legislative and communications strategies all undermined his efforts to reform America's immigration policy. The chapter finishes with an analysis of President Joe Biden's alternative immigration reform agenda and discusses his chances of success. It begins, though, by placing recent developments in their party political context.

The Political Parties and Immigration

The Republican Party is more internally divided on immigration than the Democratic Party, but neither party has a clearly defined position. The Republican Party flirted seriously with an anti-immigration agenda in the 1990s, especially on illegal immigration, but returned to its liberal, pro-immigration position in 2000, at the elite level at least (Wroe 2008). President George W. Bush believed that Latinos and Asians were natural Republicans—conservative on moral and cultural issues, hard-working and suspicious of big government—and thought that he could make the GOP the majority party by driving a pro-immigration wedge into the Democratic Party's coalition and breaking off substantial proportions of its minority voters. To do so, he championed a so-called pro-immigration 'comprehensive' reform bill, which entailed legalizing, either temporarily or permanently, the status of millions of undocumented immigrants and possibly offering them a path to American citizenship. It is known as 'comprehensive' because it also seeks to deal with the enforcement side of the immigration problem, which means removing undesirable aliens, especially violent criminals, already resident in the US and stemming the arrival of future undocumented persons via enhanced border security and employer and welfare sanctions. Most versions of comprehensive reform also allow for guest-worker programs while leaving America's generous legal immigration provisions strictly untouched. The prospects for comprehensive reform worsened dramatically in 2001 when the Al Qaeda attacks on New York City and Washington DC securitized the immigration issue and opened two old immigration wounds: religion and race.

The GOP's 2008 presidential candidate, Senator John McCain, was also a long-time proponent of comprehensive immigration reform, but he tacked to the right in order to win the Republican nomination, taking a harder line than he had as a legislator. This was largely due to a rightward shift in the GOP base—that is, party activists and its most tuned-in supporters—on cultural and moral issues generally and immigration specifically, which in turn is pulling the party elite to the right. There is a firestorm on talk radio, Fox News and right-wing websites such as Breitbart whenever a senior Republican or, worse, president nods even vaguely in the direction of liberal immigration reform. At the same time, the GOP's traditional business wing remains staunchly pro-immigration. The schism is reflected in Congress, where a significant albeit shrinking minority of Republican members of Congress support comprehensive reform.

A more conservative group takes what is usefully called an 'enforcement first' position. Its proponents first demand strong action on the border and interior enforcement before they will consider legalization. In practice, some enforcement firsters' benchmarks are so unrealizable—demanding, for example, a completely secure and impregnable border—that the humanitarian or liberal aspects of the reform program would never be triggered. It is, in practice, an 'enforcement only' position masquerading as 'enforcement first.' The 'enforcement only' group is large and growing and rejects any form of legalization as an amnesty for lawbreakers, and will not support any policy proposal that even hints at giving any form of legal protection to illegal immigrants regardless of how secure the border is.

On the other side of the aisle, Democrats are more unified around a pro-immigration position, although this is a relatively recent innovation.

Historically, labor unions, who for the most part are aligned with the Democratic Party, were hostile to immigration, because of the perception that firms would use immigrant labor to undercut domestic workers' wages and job security. But service sector unions, increasingly drawing their membership from minority workers, became more sympathetic to the pro-immigration position and thus so did the Democratic Party. In addition, the party has shed its historic association with slavery and racial segregation in the south and embraced multiculturalism and minority rights. Its broad rainbow coalition, which includes African Americans, Latinos, Asians and more highly educated white liberals, is a natural fit with the pro-immigration position. Nonetheless, the Democratic Party in Congress is far from united on the details of immigration reform. Some members adopt a zero tolerance position on any perceived threats to immigrants' and refugees' rights, and are less likely to support the comprehensive-type reforms that require trade-offs and compromises. More moderate members, though, are willing to negotiate with Republicans and make concessions on, say, border security and interior enforcement.

In sum, the key division in the Republican Party today is between anti-immigration cultural conservatives and pro-immigration economic conservatives—and cultural conservatives are on the rise. Divisions in the Democratic Party are less pronounced in part because the party does not divide as neatly along cultural and economic lines. Such intra-party divisions mean that immigration reform is replete with unholy alliances: unions align with big business, liberal intellectuals with free-market economists, and civil-rights organizations with pro-family Christians in favor of more generous immigration policies, albeit for differing ideological and pragmatic reasons. Yet, comprehensive immigration reform is often killed by an ideologically incoherent alliance of Congress's most conservative Republicans and most liberal Democrats.

The overall trend, though, is that both parties are becoming more internally united on immigration while the gap between the parties' positions is growing. Like many other issues in American politics, immigration has joined the partisan culture wars. This was evident in the 2012 presidential contest.

Mitt Romney, who followed McCain as the Republican Party's presidential candidate, was a relatively liberal Republican governor of Massachusetts, but like McCain ran to the right of his established position in order to capture the party's nomination in 2012. While running against Obama in the general election, Romney maintained his more hostile anti-immigration posture, arguing that he would make life so unpleasant for undocumented immigrants that they would choose to 'self-deport.' His defeat at the hands of President Obama triggered some soul searching by the Republican establishment. Could the party win by pursuing hard-line immigration policies? Its answer, outlined in a post-mortem publication called the Growth and Opportunity Project, was no. Not only was the party's support among Asian and Latino voters in decline, but these groups were the fastest growing segment of the electorate. While demography is not destiny, the report concluded that 'We must embrace and champion comprehensive immigration reform. If we do not, our Party's appeal will continue to shrink to its core constituencies only.' However, neither Trump nor the party activists who dominate the primary selection process appeared to have got the memo.

TRUMP

Becoming President

Trump fancied himself a political heavyweight several decades before finally trying for the biggest prize in American politics, and dipped his toe in the water periodically, often whipping up racial animosity—for example, by claiming America's first and only black president, Barack Obama, had not been born in the US and was therefore ineligible to be president. Trump stopped dancing around the political fringes and finally announced his entry into the race to become the 2016 Republican presidential nominee with an incendiary and now infamous speech in Trump Tower, New York City, on June 16, 2015. He told the modest crowd, which included paid actors playing at being Trump supporters, that Mexico was sending criminals, rapists, drug dealers—and some nice people, he assumed—into the US. His solution: a big, beautiful border wall. That is well known. What is less well known, is that Trump stumbled by accident on the idea of making a border wall the heart of his campaign and, later, the central obsession of his presidency (Davis and Shear 2019). His first political advisors, Sam Nunberg and Roger Stone, were concerned that Trump always went off script and would forget to talk about immigration, even though it got a good response when he did. According to Davis and Shear's reporting, Nunberg hit on a solution:

> Nunberg called up Stone with what he thought was the perfect mnemonic. Trump loves two things: boasting about himself and talking about building things. Let's have him promise to build a wall on the southwestern border with Mexico. And tell him to say he'll cut foreign aid to Mexico to pay for the construction. Trump fancied himself above all else a master of the construction trade. He wouldn't be able to resist talking about building a giant edifice as only he could, and from there it would be easy. He would promise to crack down on illegal immigration, lament the problems at the border, and warn of the threat of violence and disease from migrants swarming into the US.... The crowd loved it. Trump loved their reaction even more. (Davis and Shear 2019: 24)

Nunberg and Stone were later joined as advisors by Stephen Bannon, chair of alt-right media company Breitbart News, Alabama Senator Jeff Sessions and his young aide Stephen Miller. Bannon went on to become Trump's chief strategist and senior counsellor in the White House and Sessions his first Attorney General. But it was the indefatigable Miller, the only one of the original advisors to stay in the White House for the whole of Trump's term, who would become the driving force behind Trump's attack on the American immigration system. Miller also became Trump's main speechwriter, giving him a unique opportunity to influence the president's rhetoric and policy positions. Miller, his boss Sessions, and Bannon had a radical, populist anti-immigration blueprint and realized that Trump was the ideal 'vessel' to carry it (Davis and Shear 2019: 21).

The wall specifically and angry anti-immigrant rhetoric more generally were compelling for Trump for many reasons. With few ideological moorings— a registered Democrat until 1987, long-time pro-choice, and a supporter of universal healthcare and a ban on semi-automatic weapons in 2000—they gave him credibility among the party's most culturally conservative supporters but also had the potential to reach a wider audience. Nunberg knew he couldn't run on the Obama Birther conspiracy—it was both false and racist—but the wall and immigration on the other hand were racialized without necessarily being racist. They offered plausible deniability to accusations of racism, while sending strong signals on issues such as race, ethnicity, identity, and belonging, and tied in with Trump's other themes on globalization, trade and America First to appeal to the white working-class voters who felt threatened by economic and demographic change. It was not exactly an ideology but it was an internally coherent package of ideas. It set him apart from establishment conservatives like Marco Rubio and Jeb Bush who were in favor of comprehensive immigration reform. It burnished his outsider image as someone who said it as he saw it, a truth-telling disruptor unbound by political correctness or cancel culture, unlike the establishment politicians who carefully polled and parsed every word. And it created the impression that Trump was a man with solutions to the most intractable policy problems.

The Muslim Travel Ban

On December 2, 2015, Syed Rizwan Farook, an American-born citizen of Pakistani descent, and his wife Tashfeen Malik, a Pakistani-born permanent legal resident, killed 14 people and seriously injured many more in a terrorist attack in San Bernardino, California. With the first presidential primary contests only two months away, Trump doubled down on his already harsh anti-immigrant messaging by calling 'for a total and complete shutdown of Muslims entering the United States until our country's representatives can figure out what the hell is going on.' The anti-Muslim attack was widely criticized as blatantly racist and impermissible speech, including by other Republican presidential hopefuls. But it reprised old fears of race and religion from 9/11, solidified Trump's support, helped him to victory in the party's primaries and became the foundation of one of his first actions as president.

One week into his presidency, Trump signed Executive Order 13769, better known as the Muslim travel ban, to exclude citizens of seven Muslim-majority countries (Iran, Iraq, Libya, Somalia, Sudan, Syria, and Yemen) from entering the US on the grounds of protecting national security. But the EO was sloppily written, caused immediate chaos and confusion at the nation's airports and ports of entry, and was quickly challenged and enjoined in multiple courts pending a full review.

The law gives the president considerable leeway to act unilaterally on many immigration issues, without Congress's explicit approval. The 1952 Immigration and Nationality Act states:

> Whenever the President finds that the entry of any aliens or of any class of aliens into the United States would be detrimental to the interests of the United States, he may by proclamation, and for such period as he shall deem necessary, suspend the entry of all aliens or any class of aliens as immigrants or nonimmigrants, or impose on the entry of aliens any restrictions he may deem to be appropriate.

But while the courts had traditionally interpreted the act to give presidents substantial scope to regulate who enters the US, no law is absolute. In addition to protections offered by the US Constitution, the subsequent 1965 immigration act explicitly prevented migrants from being denied a visa on grounds of race, sex, nationality, or place of birth. As the travel ban looked very much like a Muslim ban, it was on a precarious legal footing. After a federal appeals court upheld the lower federal court's decision, the White House cut its losses and rewrote the order rather than face a protracted legal battle that would end in a probable defeat in the Supreme Court.

Trump unhappily signed the second and weaker executive order on March 6, 2017, but it too was quickly blocked in the courts even before it became effective. The US Supreme Court was due to hear the case, when it was rendered moot on publication of the third effort at a travel ban in the form of a Presidential Proclamation on September 24. It was declared unconstitutional by a Hawaii-based federal judge in September but went into effect in December 2017 after the intervention of the Supreme Court pending a full hearing in Spring 2018. The third iteration removed some of the seven original majority-Muslim countries and added several non-majority-Muslim ones. The Court upheld the travel ban on June 26, 2018. Trump extended it to six more countries in February 2020.

It had taken over a year for the travel restrictions to go into effect and in a much watered-down form. Trump's White House team lacked governmental experience. Key advisors like Bannon and Miller believed that the federal bureaucracy was part of a deep state conspiracy to cripple Trump's presidency rather than a source of institutional strength. An executive order in a more ordinary White House would receive input from multiple federal agencies and departments, including the government's top lawyers, as well as key members of Congress and friendly pressure groups. Bannon and Miller, however, were determined to circumvent these players and recruited a small team of similarly minded political appointees, led by Gene Hamilton, another former Jeff Sessions' aide, to write the executive orders in secret. A fuller process that brought in rather than excluded key bureaucrats, experts, lawyers, and stake-holders could have quickly produced an order more likely to withstand the inevitable legal scrutiny. Trump's White House, however, was disorganized, even chaotic, and so thus was the policy it generated.

DACA and Dreamers

If Trump could at least claim a partial win on the travel ban, his efforts on the Obama-era program called Deferred Action for Childhood Arrivals (DACA) and the group of immigrants known as Dreamers were a failure. Dreamers is the colloquial name given to children brought into the US by their parents or others without the correct authorization. Because the children did not choose to come to the US and did not break the law of their own volition, they are regarded by many on both sides of the partisan divide as a special case and elicit sympathy. Created via an executive memorandum signed by Obama in June 2012, DACA allowed eligible Dreamers to live, study, and work in the US without threat of deportation, but it did not give them permanent legal status or a route to citizenship.

DACA enraged Stephen Miller. It was an amnesty program in his view because it shielded from deportation persons who had entered the country illegally. Further, it had been enacted via executive fiat rather than congres-sional statute, which he thought a clear violation of the law. It was near the top of Miller's hit list, but Trump was conflicted. He hated it simply because it was a successful Obama initiative, but also because Miller, Sessions, and Bannon were feeding him the line that it was an amnesty. He knew that amnesty was a red line for his more fervent supporters, alt-right and Fox News commentators, and restrictionist pressure groups. DACA was thus one of the many things that Trump promised to stop on 'day one' of his presidency. On the other hand, Trump was uncharacteristically sympathetic to the Dreamers' cause. He publicly said on multiple occasion that Dreamers were great kids and that he 'loved the Dreamers.' Trump did not really understand the details of immigration reform generally or DACA specifically, but he knew he faced a dilemma. He quickly signed EOs on sanctuary cities, refugees, Muslim trav-ellers, and the wall, but hesitated on ending DACA, even though an EO was written and waiting.

After much debate inside the White House, Jeff Sessions finally announced on September 5, 2017 that DACA would be terminated effective March 5, 2018. The Trump administration hoped that delaying the end of the program for six months would spur action in Congress on a Dreamers-for-wall deal. Democrats would fund the wall in order to protect Dreamers, and Republi-cans would finally accede to protecting Dreamers in return for wall funding. However, the hope they would force Democrats to the negotiating table by signing DACA's death warrant but delaying its execution was undermined by the courts. Like the travel ban, the order was poorly written and the adminis-tration failed to follow the correct procedure for ending the program. A federal court quickly ruled against the administration, requiring it to keep DACA open, at least temporarily. A further effort by Miller to restrict DACA's reach by closing it to new applicants was struck down in Federal District Court in April 2018. Judge John D. Bates was especially scathing of the administration's case, noting its 'meagre legal reasoning.' The Supreme Court finally weighed in June 2020 in *Department of Homeland Security v. Regents of the University of California*. While it did not make a judgment about the constitutionality of the DACA program, it agreed with the lower courts that the process by which it was rescinded by the Trump administration was 'arbitrary and capricious.'

Using an executive order to end a federal program initiated via a previous president's executive order would normally be a relatively straightforward task if the rules were followed and the order properly crafted by knowledgeable policy and legal experts. Not in Trump's White House.

The Art of No-Deal: Trump's Border Wall

Less than one week into his presidency on January 25, 2017, Trump signed Executive Order 13767, directing the construction of 'a physical wall along the southern border.' The order could not allocate any funds for the wall, and so was in effect just an aspirational collection of empty words. Congressional legislation was required to provide the money to build the wall and would prove yet another huge frustration for the president.

As noted in the previous section, DACA and wall were entwined, and the most likely route to success for both was via a Dreamers-for-wall deal. Some of Trump's more ambitious advisors thought they could even leverage DACA to win major changes to legal immigration. Miller put together a four part plan and briefed the press in late January 2018 ahead of the president's state of the union address on January 30. The 700,000 people currently in DACA, plus another 1.1 million who were eligible but had not applied, would be protected from deportation immediately and could apply for citizenship a decade or more down the line. The White House wanted three things in return: border security in the form of $25 billion to build the wall; an end to chain migration, by restricting family-reunification visas to petitioners' spouses and minor children, not adult children or other extended family members such as siblings and parents; and scrapping the diversity visa lottery, which awarded 50,000 green cards to underrepresented immigrants, and redirecting them to 'merit-based' immigrants.

Despite Miller's ambitious wish-list, the reaction from conservative commentators and media was brutal. Breitbart headlined its story 'Amnesty Don' and Ann Coulter, a prominent conservative author and one of the few people Trump followed on Twitter, called the deal 'impeachable.' Inside Congress, the Freedom Caucus in the House and Ted Cruz in the Senate expressed opposition. They were not prepared to accept a limited amnesty as part of any deal, even one as stuffed full of restrictionist goodies as Miller's. Democrats and immigrant-rights groups were equally unimpressed, in part because the deal was lopsided 3 to 1 in favor of the conservative position, but also because the changes to the composition of legal migration crossed a liberal red line. They would not curtail family reunification even in return for protecting Dreamers.

Even after being ambushed by both conservatives and liberals, the four part deal stayed in Trump's state of the union address, where Trump tried to portray it as a 'down-the-middle compromise.' Democratic leader Nancy Pelosi thought otherwise: 'The president presents himself as generous toward Dreamers, but he's holding them hostage to the most extreme anti-immigrant agenda in generations.' Senator Bob Menendez called it a 'compromise between the far right and the alt-right. Consider it Dead on Arrival.' It was.

Trump felt under pressure. He couldn't strike a deal to fund the border wall, and apprehensions at the border were increasing quickly (see Fig. 13.1). A radical intervention was required, thought Miller and Sessions. They hatched a zero tolerance policy that would subsequently turn into one of the lowest points of the Trump presidency. Officially beginning on May 7, 2018, it mandated the prosecution of all adults who crossed the border illegally, and the end of so-called 'catch and release' whereby undocumented persons were caught, processed, and released into the community to await a court date. However, zero tolerance required separating parents from their children when families crossed together, with parents incarcerated in one institution, children in another. They could not be held together for any length of time because of a court ruling that limited children's confinement to twenty days. Prosecuting parents meant separating families.

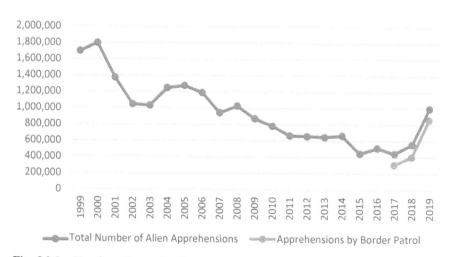

Fig. 13.1 Number of apprehensions
(*Source* Table 33, 'Aliens Apprehended: Fiscal Years 1925 to 2019', *2019 Yearbook of Immigration Statistics* [https://www.dhs.gov/immigration-statistics/yearbook/2019/table33])

When audio and then video emerged in early June 2018 of distraught children, including toddlers, in chain-link cages crying out for their absent parents, there was uproar in the US and around the world. The administration's justification was that they were just enforcing the law, but no immigration law required separating child and parent, and no previous post-war administration had done so. The unspoken hope of Miller and Sessions was that word of the tough new zero tolerance policy would filter southward, and families would make the decision not to risk crossing the border for fear of being split up. The other hope was that the family separation policy would force members of Congress to the negotiating table. While taking Dreamers hostage had not worked, perhaps wall funding would be forthcoming in exchange for ending family separation.

After two more weeks of unrelenting and universal criticism Trump backtracked and ended the policy via executive order on June 20, not because it was inhumane, but because the optics were 'nasty.' 'The crying babies doesn't look good politically' he told congressional Republicans (Davis and Shear 2019: 277). It was a wholly avoidable political disaster. But it was also a humanitarian disaster. The pain inflicted on the estimated 4000 separated families was incalculable. Worse, because of poor record keeping by federal agencies, many were never reunited.

Shocked by the family separation disaster, Republican leaders in Congress quickly put together a compromise bill in late June 2018. It was designed to attract moderates horrified by the family separation policy by requiring families to remain united in custody while offering a path to citizenship for Dreamers. It hoped to win over conservatives by cutting chain migration and ending the diversity visa program, along with $25 billion for the wall. It failed in the House 121–301. Trump endorsed it at the last minute, but made no serious effort to lobby on its behalf. Indeed, he tweeted only a week earlier that Republicans should 'stop wasting their time' on immigration legislation until after the 2018 midterms, thus cutting the legs out from under the GOP leadership in its efforts to build support for the bill among representatives. He was ranting wildly in the White House rather than reaching out to his fellow partisans to persuade them to take a tough vote in support of his wall. In the event, and largely abandoned by their president, only half of Republicans voted yes, most unable to swallow the poison pill of an amnesty for Dreamers without political cover from Trump. The other half joined the solid Democratic bloc in voting no. Trump was unable to unite his party on his signature policy. The Democrats were unified in opposition by the threat to legal immigration and Trump's increasingly eccentric efforts to force a deal.

Republicans lost control of the House in the November midterms in part because white women in the suburbs were turned off by his hostile anti-immigrant message. With the Democrats now in control, the administration would have to make more concessions to strike an immigration deal. In an effort to strike a bipartisan immigration deal, he met with Congress's top two Democrats, incoming House Speaker Nancy Pelosi and Senate Minority

Leader Charles Schumer, in the White House on December 11, 2018. In front of the TV cameras, which Trump invited into the meeting, Schumer goaded Trump into saying he would 'proudly' shut down the government in order to force Congress to pay for his border wall: 'So I will take the mantle. I will be the one to shut it down. I'm not going to blame you for it.' Republicans were aghast and Democrats delighted. With not enough votes in Congress to support a funding bill that included just $5 billion for the wall, the US government ran out of money and shut down on December 21, 2018. After five weeks, the longest shutdown in history, and amid mounting pressure, Trump caved and agreed to sign a temporary funding bill to end the shutdown. In the funding bill proper, he got $1.4 billion for border security, none of which could be used to build new wall.

On the same day, February 15, 2019, when he signed the funding bill into law, Trump declared a national emergency at the border. While ridiculed by Democrats as a political stunt and immediately challenged in the courts, it allowed the administration to redirect money from the Department of Defense budget to wall projects, circumventing Congress. Together with money that the government had collected itself, from service fees and asset forfeitures for example, the government amassed about $10 billion (Pierce and Bolter 2020: 32), in addition to the $4.5 billion allocated by Congress in various budget bills to repair existing sections of wall. So how much wall did Trump build in four years? The US–Mexico border is 2000 miles long. Much of it is uninhabited, inhospitable, or has a natural defense (such as the Rio Grande). When Trump entered office, fencing at the border totalled just under 700 miles. When Trump left office fencing at the border totalled just over 700 miles. Yet his administration claimed to have built 452 miles of new wall. The mathematical discrepancy is accounted for by the fact that nearly all the 'new wall' was actually repaired or enhanced existing fencing. According to US Customs and Border Protection (CBP) estimates, only 47 miles of new primary barriers were built where none stood before (Giles 2021). Whether the additional 400 miles of reconditioned fencing can be defined as 'new' or not is debatable, but it seems unlikely that it is what Trump or his avid supporters envisaged when he promised to build a 'big, beautiful' wall which Mexico would pay for.

Interior Enforcement and Sanctuary Cities

While running for president, Trump promised to create a 'deportation force' to find and expel the roughly eleven million unauthorized aliens estimated to reside permanently in the US. He later scaled this pledge back to a 'deportation taskforce' that would focus its attentions on criminal aliens. Trump maintained that all unauthorized persons were subject to arrest and deportation, however, even if it looked as if the nine million non-criminal aliens were no longer a priority.

However, the actual likelihood of being deported under Trump was low, and much lower than under Obama. The Obama administration deported upwards of 200,000 individuals in each of his first four years in office. Trump's administration never deported close to 100,000 in any of his four years. Put differently, Trump deported only one-third as many as Obama over the same timeframe (Chishti and Pierce 2020). Deportations did drop dramatically during Obama's second term, in part because the president was stung by liberal criticism of him as the 'deporter-in-chief.' Trump would gladly have embraced the label but was unable to increase deportations to anything like the level of Obama's peak or even average years. That is in good measure a consequence of the resistance of sanctuary cities to his interior enforcement agenda.

In the first week of his presidency and on the same day that he signed the impotent executive order requiring the building of a border wall, Trump also signed EO 13768. It expanded the criteria for deporting undocumented residents from Obama's focus on criminal aliens to 'all removable aliens,' and withheld federal funds from 'sanctuary cities.' The term sanctuary city is not a legal term but is widely understood to refer to jurisdictions that refuse to cooperate with federal immigration enforcement agencies—for example, by not informing Immigration and Customs Enforcement (ICE) that they have a suspected undocumented person in custody on suspicion of committing a crime, and by refusing a 'detainer' notice to hold the individual until ICE arrived. As with most of Trump's executive actions on immigration issues, the EO was immediately blocked in several courts and then subjected to a series of defeats in the US district and appeals courts.

Humanitarian Programs: Refugees, Asylees and TPS

The US had long had the most generous refugee program in the world before Trump's presidency. In the last two decades of the twentieth century, it regularly took upwards of 100,000 refugees per year, and in 1980 over 200,000. The official ceiling in the twenty-first century was usually between 70,000 and 80,000, although actual numbers admitted were sometimes much lower, especially after 9/11, as Fig. 13.2 shows. In Obama's last year in office, the official ceiling was 85,000 and the administration admitted only six fewer refugees than the ceiling allowed. The ceiling is under the control of the executive branch, although it must follow the correct procedures and consult with Congress.

The program had long been framed by Republican and Democratic administrations alike as a humanitarian response to overseas crises, and one that simultaneously promoted US soft power abroad. Refugees apply and are vetted outside of the US, and pre-approved for entry before they travel, unlike asylum seekers who claim asylum on reaching the US, and then must wait while their claim is processed. Post-9/11 fears of inadvertently admitting terrorists via the refugee program mean they are the most extensively vetted of any immigrants. Yet Trump and Miller insisted that they were potential terrorists, especially Muslim refugees from the Middle East, and those that were not terrorists

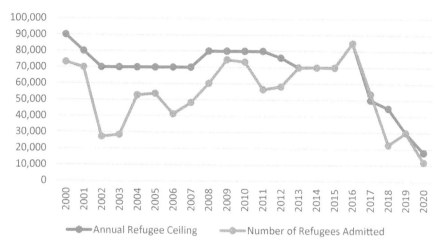

Fig. 13.2 Refugee numbers
(*Source* Table 13, 'Refugee Arrivals: Fiscal Years 1980 to 2019', *2019 Yearbook of Immigration Statistics* [https://www.dhs.gov/immigration-statistics/yearbook/2019/table13])

would be a welfare burden and commit crime. In the 2010s, the world's primary source of displaced people was Syria. As the civil war spiralled out of control, Trump declared his intention to bar Syrian refugees from entering the US. It was accomplished by putting his signature in January 2017 on the travel ban executive order (EO 13769), which indefinitely suspended the entry of Syrian refugees, but also paused the refugee admissions program for 120 days and slashed the overall refugee ceiling to 50,000. Miller's goal however was to reduce the number toward zero but also to switch the source and type of the few successful refugees from the Middle East and Muslim to Africa and Christian. The latter goal was achieved in part by enhanced vetting requirements for potential refugees in eleven 'high risk' countries. While Miller never achieved his zero goal, in 2020 the ceiling was pushed down to a historic low of 18,000 and only 12,000 arrived for resettlement.

As well as offering a historically generous welcome to refugees, the US grants asylum to tens of thousands of people each year who can demonstrate they have a well-founded fear of persecution in their home country. Numbers requesting and being granted asylum were quite steady for most of the twenty-first century, but spiked as Trump came to office (see Fig. 13.3) in response to a wider increase in people trying to cross the border and border interceptions (see Fig. 13.1). As per refugees, the Trump administration wanted to cut the number applying for and being granted asylum. One problem, as Trump and Miller saw it, was that migrants could present themselves at the US–Mexico border or another port of entry and claim asylum or enter the country illegally and claim asylum once intercepted by the immigration authorities. Having done so, it was illegal under US and international law to turn them away or

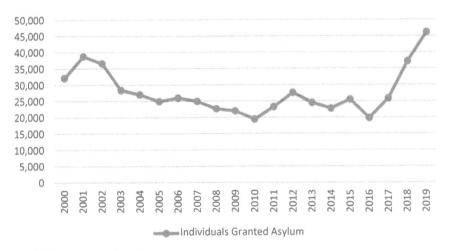

Fig. 13.3   Grants of asylum
(*Source* Table 16, 'Individuals Granted Asylum', 2019 Yearbook of Immigration Statistics [https://www.dhs.gov/immigration-statistics/yearbook/2019/table16])

deport them without due process. Asylum seekers' claims had to be processed and adjudicated.

We saw above how the Trump administration went so far as to separate children from their parents in its effort to dissuade migrant families from claiming asylum. When this failed due to the public outcry, Trump narrowed the criteria for asylum to exclude gang and domestic violence, pushed part of the asylum processing bureaucracy back into Mexico and Central America (under threat of economic sanctions if they refused), and introduced 'metering' to let only very limited numbers of asylum seekers cross the border. And when Covid-19 struck, the administration used a 75-year-old public health statute to temporarily suspend the processing of asylum claims. In combination, these actions effectively closed off asylum applications at the southern border by April 2020. However, the number crossing the border rose thereafter (see Fig. 13.6) and asylum applications correspondingly increased as Trump's tenure neared its end.

Another important humanitarian program in Miller's sights was Temporary Protected Status (TPS), established in 1990 by George H.W. Bush to provide refuge to Salvadorians who had fled the civil war, and since used many times by subsequent presidents. While they cannot apply for permanent legal residency, each set of beneficiaries saw its temporary status constantly extended to become a de facto permanent residency. After much bureaucratic in-fighting, Miller eventually won the day, and TPS status was withdrawn from or not extended to nearly all beneficiaries. But it was a pyrrhic victory. In a now very familiar pattern, a federal court issued an injunction in October 2018 to suspend the program's termination.

Legal Immigration

Trump sent mixed signals on legal immigration, sometimes supporting cuts and other times appearing to resist them. For Miller and many of the restrictionist pressure groups, cutting legal immigration and changing its composition from family-based, or 'chain migration' in their language, to 'merit-based' was at least as important as reducing illegal immigration and much more important than building a border wall. The administration, however, did not have the legal authority to switch visa allocation from family-based to merit-based or to reduce the upper limit of visas available in each category. That would require congressional action, which would never be forthcoming with the Democrats implacably opposed. Miller therefore strove to find ways to apply existing law more vigorously.

While the administration could not legally lower the number of green cards available for family reunification, it sought to reduce the number awarded by tightening eligibility. One way to do so was via the 'public charge' rule. Numerous immigration statutes sought to bar the entry of, or to deport, immigrants who put a strain on the public purse by using any number of welfare and health programs. But the rule was rarely enforced. Moreover, precisely what constituted a public charge was ill-defined in those laws and was left to the immigration bureaucracy to determine. Miller wanted the public charge rule defined as broadly as possible to include immigrants who received even the most meagre forms of financial assistance and to be applied systematically to remove those who became a public charge. The rules were tightened in August 2019, but their application was interrupted by various legal challenges.

Another way to reduce legal immigration was to make the application process more onerous and to gum up the immigration bureaucracy by requiring ever more arduous and detailed checks on applicants. Miller put pressure on the US Citizenship and Immigration Services, the DHS agency responsible for processing work permits, travel visas, green cards, and naturalization requests. For example, application times for both employment-based green cards doubled over the four years of the Trump administration from seven to fourteen months. The number of rejected applications also increased. Via a myriad of policy and rule changes, Miller succeeded in making coming to America more difficult. But the effect on applications for permanent legal status and citizenship was fairly minor, as Figs. 13.4 and 13.5 show. Moreover, the fall only returned the numbers back to the average for the previous ten years after a spike in the last year of Obama's presidency. One reason that Miller's innovations had little effect on the hard numbers is that they will take time to feed through the system, if indeed they are allowed to stand, which is unlikely. Another is that the determination of applicants to get a green card and citizenship overcomes all hurdles put in their way. America, during Trump's presidency, was still awarding green cards to one million immigrants each year, and citizenship to nearly as many.

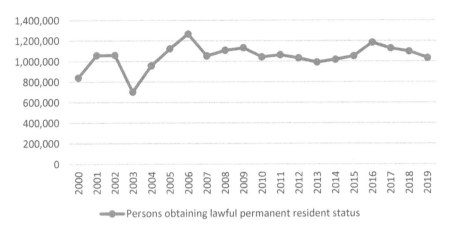

Fig. 13.4   Persons obtaining lawful permanent resident status
(*Source* Table 1, 'Persons Obtaining Lawful Permanent Resident Status: Fiscal Years 1820 to 2019, 2019', Yearbook of Immigration Statistics [https://www.dhs.gov/immigration-statistics/yearbook/2019/table1])

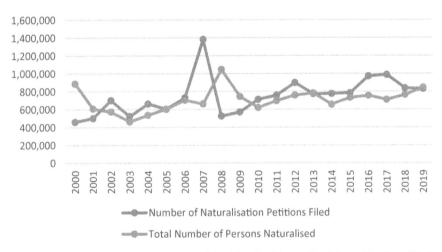

Fig. 13.5   Naturalisations (*Source* Table 20, 'Petitions for Naturalization Filed, Persons Naturalized, and Petitions for Naturalization Denied: Fiscal Years 1907 to 2019', *2019 Yearbook of Immigration Statistics* [https://www.dhs.gov/immigration-statistics/yearbook/2019/table20])

Covid-19

Rahm Emanuel, President Obama's first chief of staff, once famously said that you 'should never let a serious crisis go to waste' because they provide opportunities to leaders to do things that might otherwise prove impossible. As a once-in-a-century health crisis, Covid-19 presented an opportunity to

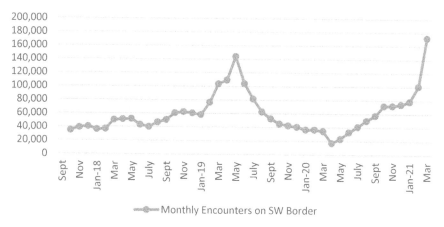

Fig. 13.6 Monthly border patrol 'encounters' with migrants on SW border (*Source* 'CBP Southwest Land Border Encounters' [https://www.cbp.gov/newsroom/stats/southwest-land-border-encounters])

the Trump administration to make good on many unfulfilled immigration promises, but would the president and his advisors be wily enough to make good use of it?

One view is that the pandemic 'supercharged the president's immigration agenda' (Pierce and Bolter 2020). A more restrained view is that the pandemic provided both opportunities and obstacles to the Trump administration's agenda and ultimately facilitated only some of its restrictionist goals. Further, the pandemic-facilitated reforms were accomplished via executive fiat rather than congressional legislation, making them vulnerable to unilateral action by the Biden administration. It is also the case that some of the changes in migration flows, which look like wins for Trump, are in fact the effect of the pandemic rather than actions taken by the administration itself. These flows will therefore trend back to the status quo ante when the pandemic ends.

Like most countries, the US put restrictions on international business and leisure travel, but it also suspended many of its immigration programs. Most dramatically, it stopped accepting asylum claims at the US–Mexico border. Despite Trump's longstanding demands that the border 'be closed,' his administration had little success pre-Covid, with asylum claims peaking in 2019. Claims dropped dramatically thereafter, however, in part because travel northwards through Central American and Mexico became more difficult under pandemic conditions, but also in part because the administration issued a March 2020 rule, effective initially for 30 days but later extended indefinitely, to expel asylum seekers without processing their claims. The rule was justified with reference to a 1944 act which gives the director of the Center for Disease Control and Prevention (CDC) the power to bar foreign nationals who posed a health risk. While the rule and the pandemic seemed to have an immediate effect in pushing down asylum claims and unauthorized entries, the numbers quickly rose to pre-pandemic levels later in 2020.

A presidential proclamation on April 22, 2020 temporarily suspended for 60 days the issuance of most family-reunification and diversity lottery visas and most types of temporary worker visas. Other orders extended the bar on employment visas, suspended refugee resettlement and barred foreign students. Many of these visas and programs had long been top targets of Stephen Miller, but again the restrictions were only temporary.

Further, the pandemic undermined the administration's already underwhelming efforts to remove unauthorized immigrants, especially criminal aliens, from the country's interior. It interfered with operations to locate and take into custody suspected aliens and slowed the immigration courts' ability to process cases.

BIDEN

Joe Biden entered office with an ambitious plan to overturn most of his predecessor's immigration reforms and to introduce some important reforms of his own. In his first 100 days alone, Biden took nearly 100 executive actions on immigration, three times as many as Trump during the same period (Chishti and Bolter 2021). More important than the raw numbers is that Biden's executive actions unpicked a good proportion of the reforms that Trump and especially Stephen Miller worked so feverishly for over four years.

Trump expanded the scope of immigration enforcement to include all persons in the US without authorization. Biden narrowed it to criminal aliens and national security risks, and ICE arrests quickly fell by two-thirds. Trump imposed travel bans and visa restrictions targeted at thirteen predominantly African and majority-Muslim countries. Biden scrapped them on his first day in office. Trump placed the lowest ever ceiling on refugee admissions and slowed resettlement to a trickle. Biden raised the ceiling more than three-fold. Trump tried to decimate the TPS program, closing it for almost all beneficiaries. Biden reinstated the protections and additionally made upwards of 300,000 Venezuelans eligible for temporary protected status. Trump introduced a 'public charge' rule to exclude poorer legal immigrants. Biden killed it. Trump stopped issuing visas to new immigrants, temporary workers, and foreign students in April 2020. Biden reinstated the visas one month into his presidency. Trump was obsessed with building a big, beautiful border wall. Biden downed tools.

All-in-all, half of Biden's executive actions on immigration in his first 100 days were specifically designed to undo Trump's (Chishti and Bolter 2021). But in some ways, the Biden administration has fallen short and faces some serious tests. Like two of his recent predecessors, Presidents George W. Bush and Barack Obama, Biden promised a comprehensive immigration reform bill that would address humanely the issue of the eleven million unauthorized persons residing in the US while also striving to curtail the future entry of millions more. Like Bush and Obama, Biden is likely to be disappointed by the partisan dynamics in Congress, and instead pursue piecemeal reform on the few issues on which the public is strongly in favor, such as protecting Dreamers. Whether Biden can persuade enough Republicans to come on board to make up the sixty Senators needed to overcome the filibuster rule is unknown. But so long as the Republican Party remains in thrall to Trump and continues its drift to the right, the likelihood of a bipartisan pro-Dreamer coalition looks increasingly remote.

Another testing issue for Biden, which has taxed policymakers for decades, is asylum and the southern border. Granting asylum to persons fleeing persecution is part of a humanitarian package that also includes refugee resettlement and the temporary protected status program. But it does not enjoy the same public and political support. The policy problem is that the US abuts Mexico which in turn is close to several Central American nations where tens of millions of people live in destitution and desperation, in fear of their lives from marauding and heavily armed drug gangs and, indeed, sometimes even from government itself. A ready supply of potential immigrants and a network of smugglers parked on the border of the world's most successful economy is a problem enough, but domestic and international law means that immigrants who present themselves at the border and make an asylum claim cannot be simply turned away. The first three months of Biden's presidency saw the number of 'encounters' as they are officially known between Border Patrol agents and migrants on the southwest border jump from 79,000 in January 2021 to 172,000 in March 2021, a twenty-year high (see Fig. 13.6). And with the rise came endless media coverage, and growing pressure to act.

The border situation is particularly perilous for Biden because he has rejected both Trump's get-tough rhetoric and his disregard for the humanitarian aspect of the migration issue. The rising numbers may have enraged Trump, but he could at least leverage the desperate border situation for political advantage, arguing that it demonstrated the urgent need to 'build the wall' or introduce other extreme measures. Biden's solutions are more nuanced and less amenable to three word soundbites, and his instinct is to consider the humanitarian implications of any decisions. As such, he quickly ended the programs which pushed asylum processing away from the border and into Mexico and Central America. And Vice President Kamala Harris has been tasked with tackling the deep and complex causes that spur the large supply of migrants from Central America. Biden also attends to a very different political base and interest-group community than Trump, but they watch him equally carefully. He quickly backtracked in the face of a torrent of criticism from immigrant-rights and refugee advocacy groups after wobbling on the 62,500 ceiling on refugee admissions. While Trump had to watch his right flank, Biden must watch his left. Tackling the difficult border situation while keeping key political constituencies on-board will be an extraordinarily difficult task.

CONCLUSION

The presidency of Donald J. Trump was defined by its effort to cut immigration and reform the wider immigration architecture, including its laws and bureaucracy. Did it succeed? The hard data suggest not. Both legal and unauthorized immigration levels remained largely unchanged through most of his four years in office, whether of permanent or temporary legal immigrants or asylum seekers. It is true that permanent and temporary legal immigration declined in late 2020, but this was more a Covid-19 effect than a Trump effect. Undocumented entry followed a similar trajectory.

The Trump administration did manage effectively to stop immigration from a small number of countries named in the third iteration of its travel ban, and it slashed refugee resettlement by 80–90 percent. It also oversaw an important change to the 'public charge' rule for legal immigrants that could stop the entry of immigrants from poorer families. But none of these changes were effected via statute law. Trump, even though he enjoyed unified government for the first two years of his presidency, was unable to persuade his fellow partisans in Congress of the merits of his reform program. Even though he had lambasted his predecessor for using executive actions, Trump himself relied exclusively on executive orders, memorandums, proclamations, and changes to bureaucratic rules, issuing more than 400 by one estimate (Chishti and Bolter 2020). Biden moved quickly to undo many of these.

Trump did not even succeed on his single most prominent policy promise to build the wall. 'Partially repair the border fence' was a chant rarely heard at his rallies. Ironically, a wall—whether made of concrete, steel, or huge pointed bollards, sharpened at the top and painted black to get hot in the sun (all favored designs of Trump at one point or other)—would have been one of the least effective ways of curbing illegal immigration. It was an absurdly simplistic solution to a devilishly difficult policy problem that had stumped serious policymakers for decades. Resolute migrants would fairly easily be able to go over, through, around or under it. Most would simply approach an official entry point in the wall and claim asylum. Kevin McAleenan, head of CBP and a favorite of Trump's, estimated a wall may be about 20–25 percent effective, while closing legal loopholes would cut entry by 75–80 percent (Davis and Shear 2019: 370).

The politics that had undone so many presidents' immigration reform plans were alive and well, but Trump made an already-difficult situation worse. He played his hand poorly. His hardball tactics and inflammatory language further politicized the issue, making it almost impossible for Democrats to sign onto a compromise deal that included significant funding for a new wall. Any doing so would face intense hostility from colleagues and activists and the risk of being primaried. Trump was also a poor negotiator. He lacked message discipline, was unaware of important and critical details and was prone to attack those whose support he needed if he felt slighted. Perhaps worse, his word could not be trusted. On multiple occasions during his presidency, congressional Republicans and those working for him in government thought they had nailed Trump down on a controversial policy position only for Trump to change his mind—usually after watching criticism of his original position on Fox News. Trump was so unreliable that other political actors stopped taking risks for him.

Trump could have obtained more money to build the wall than he did and could have avoided two government shutdowns. $25 billion was on the table early in his presidency in exchange for protecting Dreamers. Other times when a deal looked likely, Trump refused to publicly and strongly support it for fear of a backlash from conservative media and his base. Without the president's political cover, his own partisans would be risking their careers by voting for any deal that legalized, or amnestied, unauthorized residents, even on a temporary basis. Trump always liked to portray himself as the strongest and the toughest leader, but at key moments he refused to expose himself to the political risk that controversial policy changes always engender. He was not prepared to spend the political capital he had built up with his base on a compromise deal, but without a compromise no deal was available. It was a failure of leadership. Furthermore, policymakers in Congress most of the time simply did not know where Trump stood on the key issues, or what legislation he would sign. Trump did not understand the policy details or even the politics of immigration reform, yet it was and remains one of the most complex and incendiary of all policy issues in the American political system. The structural and political impediments to reform are of course also part of the explanation for Trump's failure. Biden will therefore also struggle to effect his own reforms, but his political skills suggest he may have a better chance than Trump. One thing is sure: Biden began his term vigorously and successfully using his executive powers to turn the clock back on Trump's reforms.

REFERENCES

Chishti, Muzaffar, and Jessica Bolter. 2020. The "Trump Effect" on Legal Immigration Levels: More Perception than Reality? Migration Policy Institute.

———. 2021. Border Challenges Dominate, But Biden's First 100 Days Mark Notable Under-the-Radar Immigration Accomplishments'. Migration Policy Institute.

Chishti, Muzaffar, and Sarah Pierce. 2020. *Trump's Promise of Millions of Deportations Is Yet to be Fulfilled*. Migration Policy Institute.

Davis, Julie H., and Michael D. Shear. 2019. *Border Wars: Inside Trump's Assault on Immigration*. New York: Simon and Schuster.

Giles, Christopher. 2021. Trump's Wall: How Much Has Been Built During His Term? *BBC*, January 12.

Huntington, Samuel. 2004. *Who Are We? The Challenges to America's National Identity*. New York: Simon and Schuster.

Lee, Erika. 2019. *America for Americans: A History of Xenophobia in the United States*. New York: Basic Books.

Pierce, Sarah, and Jessica Bolter. 2020. Dismantling and Reconstructing the U.S. Immigration System: A Catalog of Changes under the Trump Presidency. Migration Policy Institute.

Wroe, Andrew. 2008. *The Republican Party and Immigration Politics: From Proposition 187 to George W. Bush*. New York: Palgrave Macmillan.

FURTHER READING

There are hundreds of books on America's immigration history, some of them astonishingly impressive. Favorites include John Higham, *Strangers in the Land: Patterns of American Nativism, 1860–1925* (New York: Atheneum, 1965), Louis DeSipio and Rodolfo de la Garza, *Making Americans, Remaking America: Immigration and Immigrant Policy* (Boulder, Colorado: Westview Press, 1988), David Reimers, *Unwelcome Strangers: American Identity and the Turn Against Immigration* (New York: Columbia University Press, 1998). Erika Lee's *America for Americans: A History of Xenophobia in the United States* (New York: Basic Books, 2019), which is referenced in this chapter is particularly worth seeking out for both its historical scope and beautifully observed details.

There are also already hundreds of books on Donald Trump, with hundreds more still to be published, no doubt. Some of those written by journalists on America's most serious newspapers (the *Washington Post* and the *New York Times* stand out for their coverage of Trump), whose day job was observe and chronical this most extraordinary president, offer real insights into the chaos and dysfunction in the White House. The *Post*'s Bob Woodward's two books, *Fear* (New York: Simon and Schuster, 2018) and *Rage* (New York: Simon and Schuster, 2020) stand out, the second one in particular because he interviewed Trump himself multiple times for it. The *Times*' Julie Hirschfeld Davis and Michael D. Shear's *Border Wars: Inside Trump's Assault on Immigration* (New York: Simon and Schuster, 2019) offers a superb account of the intersection of Trump and immigration reform.

Finally, there are a multitude of pressure groups and think tanks and institutes working on immigration issues. The information and reports they produce are useful but often written from a particular ideological perspective. Always take care with your sources. But a couple stand out for their independence and objectively. The Migration Policy Institute offers a constant stream of excellent commentary on all aspects of American immigration. And the Pew Research Center is a valuable source of good quality data on immigration trends and public opinion. It also runs a special Hispanic Trends section, which offers a trove of fascinating reports and data.

The only problem with these two literatures—on immigration and on Trump—is the sheer volume. It is more than a lifetime's work to read what already exists, and more is published every week.

CHAPTER 14

The Economy, Environment, Regulation, and Trade

Gregory L. Rosston

'Make America Great Again' was an economic success, a continuation of the Obama recovery, or a failure based on your point of view, and possibly all three depending on which parts of the Trump economic policy you examine.

In 2016, Donald Trump ran on a promise to bring back American jobs, to save the coal industry, and create 4–5 percent annual GDP growth, among other things. By the time of Covid-19's devastating impact, beginning in March 2020, America had a very low unemployment rate and steady growth. The President was running for reelection based on his record on the economy and judicial appointments. About half of the US electorate thought that economic record was sufficient for reelection and about half did not.

American economic policy over the four years of the Trump administration does not fit neatly into a stereotypical Republican mold of free market views leading to the repeal of the previous administration's more regulatory Democratic positions. Instead, economic policy was based on a short-term transaction-based approach with some governing principles, but ones that differed depending on the type of policy. President Trump relied on the aura of his business sense to push for policies that would show him as scoring 'wins' for the American public without highlighting potential costs. As a result, the underlying Trump administration's traditional conservative philosophy of lowering taxes and reducing regulation was very different from its positions

G. L. Rosston (✉)
Stanford Institute for Economic Policy Research, Stanford
University, Stanford, CA, USA

© The Author(s), under exclusive license to Springer Nature
Switzerland AG 2022
G. Peele et al. (eds.), *Developments in American Politics 9*,
https://doi.org/10.1007/978-3-030-89740-6_14

Fig. 14.1 US unemployment rate (percentage), 2000–2021 (Source: Federal Reserve Bank of St. Louis)

on trade, where government became a key player, and its position on spending where deficits were not important.

The Trump administration's economic policy positions need to be viewed not only for their philosophical economic basis, but also through the lens of what was feasible to accomplish. As for all administrations, constraints depended on the laws, on Congress, and on court actions. In some areas Congress was most important, in some it was the courts, and in some areas the president acted alone without express support. In addition, economic policy during the Trump administration, just as nearly every other policy in the world, needs to be analyzed pre-Covid and during Covid.

When President Trump took office in January 2017, the economy was relatively strong. As Fig. 14.1 shows, unemployment was 4.7 percent and on a downward path.

GDP growth was 2.3 percent. While it was not at record breaking levels (nor at the promised 5 percent), Fig. 14.2 shows that it had been mostly in the 2–3 percent range since the depths of the Great Recession and was higher than comparable areas like the European Union through the end of 2019.

President Trump promised to reduce taxes and was not concerned about budget deficits (and stated during the campaign that he was the 'King of Debt'). Before the economic ravages of Covid, his philosophies of tax reduction, not worrying about spending, reducing or eliminating government regulation, and negotiating deals himself with other countries seemed to be pushing a strong aggregate economy.

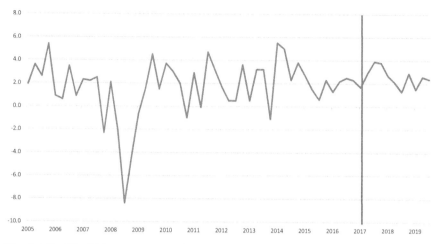

Fig. 14.2 US GDP, percentage change, 2005–2020 (Source: Federal Reserve Bank of St. Louis)

Fiscal Policy

Taxation

Traditional Republican orthodoxy is that the Federal Government is too large and needs to be reined in. Some conservatives claim limiting revenues by reducing taxes ('starving the beast') will naturally reduce the role of government. However, there is no evidence that revenue cuts lead to spending reductions in either Republican or Democratic administrations. In a different justification for tax cuts, some politicians, such as Senator Ron Johnson (R-WI), claim tax cuts pay for themselves because lower taxes will turbo-charge economic growth leading to higher tax revenues despite the lower rates. However, most economists, including conservative scholars such as Niskanen (2006), realize that tax cuts alone do not increase federal revenue.

Regardless, Republican politicians combined 'starving the beast' with the ideological power of tax-cut led growth to justify cutting taxes. The 2017 Tax Cuts and Jobs Act (TCJA) required congressional legislation and presidential approval. Most congressional actions, with the exception of Supreme Court nominations and budget reconciliation, are subject to filibuster in the Senate, which requires 60 votes to overcome. In 2017, the Republican Party had majority control of both the House and the Senate, but the Senate majority was not enough to overcome a Democratic filibuster. As a result, Congress passed the TCJA as a 'reconciliation' with only 50 Senate votes, all Republican, but its rules constrained the scale of the legislation—the personal tax cuts are scheduled to expire after ten years. The corporate tax cuts do not expire as their budgetary impact was assessed differently with the expectation

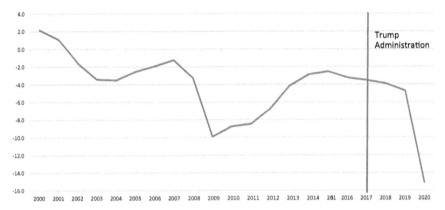

Fig. 14.3 US federal budget surplus (deficit) as a percentage of GDP, 2000–2020 (Source: Federal Reserve Bank of St. Louis)

that the cost would not be as great due to repatriation of funds and expanded business activity.

As a result of these taxation measures, federal deficits increased by nearly 50 percent as a share of Gross Domestic Product (GDP). Figure 14.3 shows the federal deficit increased from 3.1 percent of GDP in 2016 to 4.6 percent of GDP in 2019, before any impact from Covid-19.

The most visible piece of the TCJA was a decrease in federal tax rates for most individual taxpayers and it also cut the top corporate marginal rate from 36 to 21 percent to be closer to the rates charged in other countries. The previous tax differential caused US companies to retain trillions of dollars overseas rather than repatriating them, as repatriation would subject the income to the US corporate income tax, whereas leaving it overseas meant that taxation could be delayed or possibly avoided.

The individual and business tax cuts show in part the Trump administration's focus on claiming a victory to curry favor with the traditional Republican base that cares greatly about tax rates.

Spending

While conservatives talk about reducing the size of government, there have been little to no cuts to government spending in Republican administrations in the past forty years, and the Trump administration did not change that record, largely due to the fact that it is politically difficult to cut programs. Government expenditures are generally categorized as 'discretionary' or 'non-discretionary.' Discretionary spending requires legislative authorization each year to continue, whereas non-discretionary spending requires legislation to stop it. The major non-discretionary spending programs include Social Security, Medicare, and Medicaid. Defense accounts for about half of discretionary spending with myriad other programs such as education, homeland security, transportation, scientific research, food safety, and many others making up the rest (Gale 2019).

Pre-Covid, neither Congress nor President Trump made attempts to follow Republican orthodoxy by reducing federal spending. President Trump proposed to increase defense spending and not to decrease Social Security or Medicare. Without the ability (or desire) to reduce non-discretionary spending and with a promise to restore spending on the military, only 15 percent of spending (Nondefense Discretionary in Fig. 14.4) was available for cuts.

Without substantial cuts to this small portion of the budget (which would likely cause significant political fights given the disparate nature of the remaining programs, each with its own constituency), overall spending would increase, and the administration did not prioritize spending cuts. As a result, President Trump's proposed budgets had large and increasing deficits.

In addition, there were controversial political features of the budget that delayed congressional approval. The fights over Deferred Action for Childhood Arrivals (DACA) and funding for 'The Wall' meant to span the US-Mexico border, both of which were small in budget terms ($5.7 billion requested for 'The Wall' out of a budget of about $4.5 trillion or about 0.1 percent), caused government shutdowns of three days and 30 days.

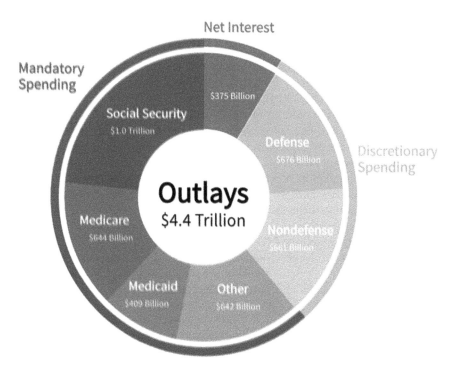

Fig. 14.4 Fiscal year 2020 federal budget (Source: Congressional Budget Office 2020)

In addition, despite numerous pronouncements about large infrastructure bills that likely would have received at least some bipartisan support, the Trump administration never brought forward a concrete proposal nor did the Republican-controlled Congress pass any such initiatives for his signature.

Overall fiscal policy in the Trump administration implemented traditional conservative views favoring tax cuts and accepting the fact that it is hard to rein in spending. The hard reality of spending cuts is not a new Republican problem—while many traditional conservatives hail the Reagan presidency as the hallmark of conservatism, federal outlays increased nearly six percent per year over his two terms (Office of Management and Budget 2021). Similarly, the Trump administration did not cut spending or worry about deficits. While many Republicans had been concerned about deficits during the Obama administration and were very vocal about it, there was little Republican pushback against increased deficits during the Trump administration until the Covid crisis (discussed more below); and even then Republican deficit worries were muted because they had achieved their main fiscal policy goal of reducing taxes. In addition to tax reduction, the administration focused on enacting a more business-friendly environment through regulatory policy.

REGULATION

Regulatory policy affects nearly every part of the economy and probably affects most people more than changes to the tax code. Many conservative commentators blamed excessive regulation for the slow economic recovery during the Obama presidency. President Trump, with his business background, embraced the traditional pro-business Republican philosophy that minimizing regulation will let businesses thrive leading to greater American prosperity and increased jobs and wages. Again, like tax cuts, removing regulations, especially environmental regulations, have near-term benefits and long-term costs, and the latter seemed less important to a short-term focused president.

Government regulation prevents people and businesses from doing things that hurt themselves and hurt others (including the environment). The Trump administration held the view that government involvement hampers the working of market forces and restricts individual liberty. Less than two weeks after his inauguration, President Trump instituted a 'Regulatory Cap,' whereby whenever an agency 'publicly proposes for notice and comment or otherwise promulgates a new regulation, it shall identify at least two existing regulations to be repealed' (Executive Order No. 13771, 2017). Such a simple 'two for one' tradeoff sent a signal that regulatory rollbacks were a priority.

However, the executive branch does not have free rein to repeal regulations as most are derived from federal law. The Trump administration was not timid about rescinding regulations and various groups challenged the basis for these regulatory changes. As a result, the administration lost a high percentage of cases in court review. Courts ruled for the Trump administration in fewer than 15 percent of the cases compared to about 70 percent in previous administrations (Davis Noll 2020).

Despite some court losses, the Trump administration as well as its opponents agree that the administration was successful in its deregulation agenda, still proving able to repeal a relatively large number of regulations. The January 2020 Economic Report of the President claimed significant success, resulting in substantial benefits to consumers through increased competition for a variety of products including prescription drugs, health insurance, and telecommunications. In addition, it pointed out the benefits to small businesses that then faced reduced regulation and less need for relatively expensive regulatory compliance. The Office of Management and Budget (OMB) also claimed significant success: 'Fiscal Year 2020 witnessed record success under EO 13771, as agencies achieved regulatory cost savings of more than a hundred billion dollars' (Office of Information and Regulatory Affairs [OIRA] 2020).

Opponents of many of the actions would agree that the Trump administration was successful in its mission to deregulate but would disagree with many of the administration's calculations because they claim benefits from the repealed regulations had not been counted and that removal of regulations caused more harm than good.

Environmental Regulation

The Trump administration took a large number of actions to reduce environmental restrictions on business: it changed the calculation of the social cost of carbon, withdrew from the Paris Climate accord, rolled back Obama increases in corporate average fuel economy standards, challenged California's authority to impose separate vehicle emission requirements, and replaced the Clean Power Plan (CPP) with the Affordable Clean Energy (ACE) plan.

Social Cost of Carbon

Because burning carbon harms the environment, its social cost is higher than the direct or private cost of extraction and use. The extra social cost above the private cost is an 'externality.' However, the total economic harm over time is unknown. Estimating the social cost of burning carbon (SCC) requires assuming levels of key inputs such as the long-term discount rate (because damage may last for centuries), the amount of damage, and the ability for humans and the economy to adapt to climate change. With these assumptions, models calculate ranges of the present value of the long-term SCC. That is important because the SCC can be used in cost-benefit analyses for regulatory review, such as determining the net social benefits of requiring scrubbers on power plants to reduce or remove carbon emissions.

In 2010, the Obama administration issued its first report on the SCC (Inter-agency Working Group on Social Cost of Carbon 2010). The report calculated a range of $5 to $65 per ton of carbon and a central global cost estimate of $50 per ton in 2007 dollars. It also noted that the SCC would increase over time and updated its estimates through 2016. The Office of Management and Budget requires analysis of costs and benefits using a domestic perspective and allows for optional consideration of a global perspective (OMB 2003). The Obama administration used the global SCC because carbon emission creates global externalities and because reducing carbon requires global cooperation (Interagency Working Group on Social Cost of Carbon 2010).

President Trump's EO 13783, 'Promoting Energy Independence and Economic Growth,' promoted domestic energy production of all types, disbanded the Interagency Working Group, and withdrew the technical supporting documents 'as no longer representative of governmental policy.' In this executive order, the Trump administration considered only domestic damages and used a higher discount rate (reducing the calculated harm from long-term damage). These two choices reduced the SCC in 2020 from $50 per ton to $7 per ton (US Government Accountability Office [GAO] 2020). Then the Trump Administration used the lower SCC in cost-benefit analyses to justify changes in various environmental programs. In essence, the Trump administration was willing to discount harm to the environment in exchange for short-term economic growth.

Paris Climate Agreement

The Paris Climate Agreement requires signatory countries to submit plans to help limit long-term global warming to less than 2 degrees Celsius and preferably 1.5 degrees. Every five years, countries must submit increasingly aggressive plans to reduce their emissions of greenhouse gases. In addition to providing plans for carbon reduction, countries voluntarily provide funding for low-income countries to help them comply with their goals. The Agreement is purely voluntary—there are no binding restrictions for action and no require-ments to provide funding. Leaving (and rejoining) the Agreement is relatively easy (except for the three-year delay to leave). Because it is an executive agree-ment rather than a treaty, entry and exit do not require Senate approval. In addition, there is no judicial review of entry or exit decisions. As a result, the President alone has the power to join or leave.

On June 1, 2017, President Trump announced that the US would be leaving the Paris Climate Agreement:

I will work to ensure that America remains the world's leader on environmental issues but under a framework that is fair and where the burdens and respon-sibilities are equally shared among the many nations all around the world. No responsible leader can put the workers and the people of their country at this debilitating and tremendous disadvantage. The fact that the Paris deal hamstrings the United States while empowering some of the world's top-polluting countries should dispel any doubt as to the real reason why foreign lobbyists wish to keep our magnificent country tied up and bound down by this agreement. It's to give their country an economic edge over the United States. That's not going to happen while I'm president. I'm sorry. (Trump White House 2017)

The US withdrew from the Paris Climate Agreement on November 2, 2020 following through on President Trump's announcement. President-elect Biden announced that one of his first actions as President would be to re-enter the Paris Agreement and he did so on his first day in office.

Fuel Standards and California

Corporate Average Fuel Economy (CAFE) standards require each auto manufacturer to meet an overall weighted average fuel economy standard across the vehicles it sells. Congress first enacted CAFE standards in 1975. The Obama administration increased the CAFE standards in 2012 to 54 miles per gallon (MPG) for cars by 2025. Major auto manufacturers agreed to this standard at the time (possibly in part due to government 'bailout' funding during the 2008 Great Recession). In addition, California has generally been able to set its own auto emission standards under an exemption from the 1970 Federal Clean Air Act since it had its own standards in place at the time. California has imposed tougher emission standards, but because of the size of the California auto market and the economies of scale of producing similar cars nationwide, auto manufacturers have generally complied with California standards.

The Obama-era increases in mileage requirements threatened to increase the cost of automobiles. As a result, with the election of President Trump, some auto manufacturers pushed to limit the rule changes. The Trump Environmental Protection Agency (EPA) and Department of Transportation (DOT) relaxed the rules, claiming that not only would laxer rules save consumers money; they would also lead to more new car purchases and thus safer cars on the road. In part, they justified their calculations because the lower SCC discussed above reduced the benefits of reduced carbon emissions. In addition, the Trump administration tried to rescind the ability of California (and other states) to set more stringent standards. These actions did not require congressional approval and became effective in 2020.

Clean Power Plan (CPP)

In *Massachusetts v. Environmental Protection Agency* (2007), the Supreme Court ruled that the EPA is required to regulate carbon dioxide once it concludes that greenhouse gases are a threat to public health. In 2009, the EPA found that carbon dioxide and other emissions did, indeed, threaten public health. In response, the Obama administration enacted the Clean Power Plan (CPP) in 2015 to regulate emissions from electric utilities.

West Virginia, along with several other states, challenged the CPP and the Supreme Court temporarily blocked implementation in 2016 until legal challenges could be resolved (*State of West Virginia et al. v. Environmental Protection Agency* 2016). The court challenges continued into the Trump administration, which then decided not to pursue the CPP. However, because of *Massachusetts v. Environmental Protection Agency* in 2007, the Trump administration could not abdicate its responsibility to regulate, so it proposed the Affordable Clean Energy (ACE) rule in 2019. The ACE rule set more lenient emission standards, reduced the EPA's power, and delegated more power to state regulators.

The stricter Obama rules had relied on the 'co-benefits' of reducing other particulate matter. Reducing mercury emissions alone did not pass a cost-benefit test, but the reductions in other particulate matter substantially increased health benefits so the overall restrictions easily passed a cost-benefit test. The Trump EPA focused only on the specific benefits and did not account for possible co-benefits, allowing them to justify the reduction in standards.

The Trump administration's rollback of environmental regulations reflected its view that short-term, business-friendly wins were important. In addition, they showed a focus only on damages that had an impact on the US and ignored the impacts on other countries and the long-term effects US actions had on environmental policies elsewhere. While it suffered some losses in court, the Trump administration delivered many of its deregulatory goals, lowering the cost to businesses and reducing government involvement in individual decisions, not only in the environmental arena, but also in other areas such as relaxing payday lending rules. Because of the Congressional Review Act's (CRA) prohibition on instituting substantially similar regulations to those struck down by Congress, those changes will not be undone unless Congress changes substantially.

TRADE

Free trade has long been a Republican lodestar. Economists generally believe in the potential of trade to benefit all parties and increase overall welfare. It is well-known that the general economic model of overall benefits from trade relies on flexibility to respond to differential prices, to retrain workers to produce different goods and services, and to redeploy capital or the ability to provide payments to those displaced. However, such transfers are difficult to effectuate.

President Trump campaigned on the more populist view of trade as a zero-sum game and vowed to pull out of deals and renegotiate others where he felt that the US was getting a bad deal. His background in real estate and other business dealings led him to believe that everything was negotiable and that he was the consummate negotiator. He brought this philosophy into trade negotiations where he wanted 'better deals' for the US and to protect and increase US jobs. He was equipped with the power to pursue this agenda. The president has the power to negotiate trade agreements and then send them to Congress for approval. For agreements that have yet to be signed, the President has the power to withdraw unilaterally without congressional approval and has the ability to issue tariffs and to block trade in the name of national security.

Trans-Pacific Partnership (TPP)

The easiest trade change that President Trump made was to exit from the TPP negotiations since it had yet to be approved by Congress. The TPP was a proposed trade agreement between Australia, Brunei, Canada, Chile, Japan, Malaysia, Mexico, New Zealand, Peru, Singapore, Vietnam, and the US. President George W. Bush led the US to join TPP negotiations in 2008. President Obama continued the negotiations throughout his term and signed the trade deal in 2016.

The politics of trade, however, seemed to be changing. Congress did not vote on TPP during the election year. Both Republican and Democratic presidential candidates opposed at least parts of the TPP, as did House and Senate members. UC Berkeley Professor and former economist in the Clinton administration Bradford DeLong brings together many of the 2016 campaign's anti-trade statements:

> Such agreements will leave, or have left, "millions of our workers with nothing but poverty and heartache" (Trump), have "lost [us] ... manufacturing jobs" (Trump), and created "catastrophe" (Trump). The agreements amount to "the death blow for American manufacturing" (Sanders), they "undermine our independence" (Trump), and they "forced American workers to compete against desperate and low-wage labor around the world" (Sanders), all while causing "massive job losses in the United States and the shutting down of tens of thousands of factories". (Sanders)

> And what did we hear from the center establishment? We had popular vote–winning (but Electoral College–losing) Democratic Party presidential nominee Hillary Rodham Clinton. She stated: "I will stop any trade deal that kills jobs or holds down wages, including the Trans-Pacific Partnership. I oppose it now, I'll oppose it after the election, and I'll oppose it as president. ...". (DeLong 2017)

President Trump was concerned that the reduction in tariffs would move manufacturing jobs overseas and increase the trade deficit, in part by allowing other countries to devalue their currencies to promote sale of their goods to the US at low dollar prices and to reduce demand for US products because of high relative prices for US exports. President Trump was able to pull out of the TPP before Congress voted, and therefore there was no treaty for the

Senate to vote on. The remaining TPP countries signed a similar agreement, the Comprehensive and Progressive Agreement for Trans-Pacific Partnership (CPTPP). The revised agreement had many of the same provisions, but less protection for intellectual property that the Obama administration had pushed for.

North American Free Trade Agreement (NAFTA) and United States-Mexico-Canada Agreement (USMCA)

The second important trade agreement for the Trump Administration to address was NAFTA (Villarreal and Fergusson 2017). President George H.W. Bush negotiated NAFTA and signed it in 1992. Congress then approved it and President Clinton signed the final version in 1993. It became effective on January 1, 1994. The US and Canada had a bilateral free trade agreement prior to NAFTA but wanted to increase trade with Mexico as it was liberalizing its economy and growing rapidly. The provisions of NAFTA were primarily directed at trade liberalization but did not address the flow of immigration.

President Trump campaigned heavily on the issues of illegal immigration and trade. Relations with Mexico have an impact on both. By using the construction of 'The Wall' and also promising to be 'tougher' on trade with Mexico by threatening to withdraw from NAFTA, he was able to appeal to those people who felt that either Mexico or Mexicans in the US had taken their jobs.

There is debate about the impact of NAFTA on US manufacturing jobs. Total trade with Mexico was about $600 billion in 2020, about 15 percent of US foreign trade. Mexican imports accounted for only about 2 percent of GDP (International Trade Administration 2020). As a result, it is more likely that the loss of manufacturing jobs in the US was due to overall global trade (including China) and automation than an increase in imports from Mexico.

Nevertheless, at Trump's behest, the US, Canada, and Mexico negotiated USMCA in 2018. President Trump pressured Congress to ratify the agreement by threatening to pull out of NAFTA unilaterally if Congress did not approve. He signed the new agreement in January 2020. Many parts of the USMCA are similar or the same as NAFTA (Amadeo 2021). There are some changes to value-added requirements and minimum wages in auto manufacturing, rules on trucks, dairy, intellectual property (similar to the provisions that the CPTPP removed from the TPP draft after the US withdrew), and other provisions. In addition, it updated some provisions that had become outdated and addressed the emergence of new issues (the commercial Internet did not exist at the time of signing NAFTA). These changes, while useful, did not require a new treaty. However, President Trump would not have been able to claim a complete success unless he got rid of NAFTA and introduced his own treaty.

China

President Trump campaigned on being a tough negotiator and ensuring that Chinese markets would be open to US companies on a fair and even level. Trade with China did not depend on the passage of a trade treaty and ratification by Congress: each country was able to impose rules and tariffs, subject to retaliation by the other country.

In 2017 the Trump administration began investigating China for unfair trade practices. While President Trump and President Xi Jinping had meetings, the tension around trade issues bubbled up, and in early 2018 Trump initiated tariffs on a variety of Chinese imports, including steel and aluminum, and filed a case at the World Trade Organization (WTO). In response, China imposed taxes on US products including fruits, nuts, pork, steel, aluminum, and bourbon (the majority of which comes from Republican Senate Majority Leader McConnell's home state of Kentucky). These tariffs led to a series of negotiations intended to reduce the tariff trade war, but the countries imposed more tariffs in the summer of 2018. Discussions extended for the next year and in summer 2019, the US increased tariffs again and China responded with increases of its own tariffs. Over the course of the next year, the governments increased some tariffs and exempted other products from them. In early 2020, they signed a trade deal intended to reduce tariffs somewhat. In addition, China agreed to increase, by hundreds of billions of dollars, its purchases of US goods as part of the negotiations. However, as of the end of 2020, China's imports from the US were about half of the amount it committed to in the agreements (Brown 2021). Not surprisingly to economists, the tariff wars have increased the prices of goods for American consumers (Oxford Economics 2021). At the same time the tariffs also may have protected some American manufacturing jobs such as at Whirlpool, which was protected by specific tariffs on washing machines, although its output has been constrained so its prices have increased and the job savings were very expensive for American consumers. Long (2019) cites research showing each job costs $800,000 to $900,000 per year in increased prices.

In addition to tariffs, the administration engaged in other trade-related policies around technology companies, including Tik Tok, WeChat, and Huawei. The Trump administration pressured these companies because of network security and the potential to extract confidential information from networks and consumers. The administration used provisions regarding the threat to national security to justify its actions and did not need congressional approval.

In sum, Trump challenged the Republican orthodoxy of free trade and his policies were costly to American consumers, saved some but not many jobs, and created tension in international trade relations.

COVID-19 SPENDING

In March 2020, Covid-19 began to ravage the economy. Over the course of two months, the unemployment rate tripled, from 3.5 percent in February to 4.4 percent in March and then leapt to 14.7 percent in April. Almost all non-essential retail stopped for a short period of time and resumed only gradually and in fits and starts. In a general recession, it is difficult for people to find jobs when there is low demand and a high rate of unemployment. With Covid, there was also a desire to keep people (both employed and unemployed) at home as much as possible to reduce the spread of the virus.

As a result, Congress stepped in with the Coronavirus Aid, Relief, and Economic Security (CARES) Act (2020) in an effort to stave off widespread economic depression. President Trump signed it into law on March 27, 2020. The speed of passage and the votes reflected more bipartisan agreement than almost any other economic issue during the Trump presidency. The CARES Act provided money to employed and unemployed citizens. All 2019 taxpayers with incomes below $75,000 received $1200 regardless of whether they were working or not. In addition, all workers receiving unemployment benefits received an additional $600 per week through July 31, 2020. The CARES Act and a subsequent stimulus bill also provided low-interest and forgivable loans to businesses and non-profits in an effort to have them retain employees.

The bipartisan consensus quickly shifted; from the initial CARES Act through the November election, Congress did not pass additional stimulus or relief bills. The Democrat-led House passed a $3 trillion follow-on bill in June (Health and Economic Recovery Omnibus Emergency Solutions [HEROES] Act 2020), but the Republican majority in the Senate did not take up consideration of it before the election. Discussions between Speaker Pelosi and Treasury Secretary Mnuchin did not lead to a compromise. President Trump did sign four executive orders on August 8, 2020, but those did not provide substantial relief: one slightly extended unemployment benefits, one recommended against evictions, one delayed (but did not reduce) payroll taxes in the hope that ultimately they would be eliminated, and one deferred (but did not eliminate) student loan payments.

After the elections, at the end of December 2020, Trump signed the Bipartisan-Bicameral Omnibus COVID Relief Deal for $900 billion (as part of a larger spending package) that provided an additional $600 check for the families that had received $1200 checks earlier in the year and reinstituted a $300 per week supplemental unemployment benefit through the end of March 2020.

In early March 2021, with the supplemental unemployment benefits running out, and a promise to add $1400 checks to the $600 December check, President Biden signed a $1.9 trillion bill (American Rescue Plan 2021) to provide myriad support mechanisms that was passed on party lines. The large spending and promised follow-on bills portend a need for more government revenue, larger deficits, or both.

NEXT STEPS

The longevity of the Trump Administration's economic policies depends on their success, how they were implemented, and what it will take to overturn them.

Environmental policy changes were early targets of the Biden administration. Since many of the Trump environmental regulation rollbacks were executive actions, it was somewhat easier to reverse them. There were few barriers to rejoining the Paris Climate accords and revisiting the social cost of carbon used in cost-benefit analyses by reinstating the Interagency Working Group and focusing on global damages.

Other regulatory changes take more time and effort to reverse, especially those overturned by the CRA that prevents enactment of similar rules without congressional approval. However, early signs were that the Biden administration would look to enact substantial environmental and consumer protection rules and to do so in a way that provided some longevity. President Biden hoped to entrench these rules by preventing their overturn by Republicans for several years, by which time they may show lower costs than expected, and with upfront costs already incurred, rollbacks will not pass a forward-looking cost-benefit test.

There are some Trump economic policies that Biden is unlikely to attempt to reverse. For example, labor-supported Democrats generally agree with the trade restrictions. While the Biden administration might not have entered the same agreements, it may be reluctant to overturn trade restrictions that labor favors despite the resulting higher consumer prices. In addition, there is a political benefit to being 'tough' on China regardless of party, so visibly enacting policies to facilitate China's exports may be less likely than letting other policies expire over time.

The federal budget deficit as a percentage of GDP is likely to remain higher than it has been historically, and to continue to increase. There will be more pressure from Republicans to worry about the deficit than there was during the Trump administration, but that pressure did not slow spending plans in the early months of Biden's term. Instead, the Biden team seemed wary of 'going too small' because of concern from many liberals that the Obama administration had not pushed for large enough economic support in the face of the Great Recession, resulting in sluggish recovery and ultimately Republican victories in Congress and the presidency. Biden's advisors responded to arguments that 'going too big' would lead to inflation by showing that conservatives expressed such fears in 2009 as well and that inflation never appeared. Also, the Biden team claimed that even if there were to be some inflation, it was less of an issue than having insufficient demand.

The Biden administration also declared its desire to double down (or more) on the oft-promised Trump infrastructure plan. Infrastructure is important for ensuring the economy can work smoothly, respond to crises, and provide access to the economy to all citizens through roads, bridges, airports, broadband, clean energy, and much more.

Biden's $1.9 trillion stimulus package, the American Rescue Plan (2021), was large and focused on relatively near-term needs, including $1400 checks for most people, increased child care tax credits, aid for state and local governments, and numerous other programs. While they are likely to be more expensive, the proposed infrastructure plans should provide longer-term benefits that can be paid for overtime. The Biden administration seemed to adopt the philosophy that increased government spending, and increased deficit spending, should be good for the long-term health of the economy and citizens.

The administration also seemed likely to propose tax increases, especially on high-income households. The Democrats' narrow majorities in Congress, though, made it look difficult, even using budget reconciliation, to increase revenues substantially as some Democrats object to tax increases given their more conservative constituency. For example, Democratic Senator Joe Manchin is from West Virginia, a state that voted nearly 70 percent Republican in the 2020 presidential election. As a result, even if the economy recovers substantially from Covid-19, the deficit (and debt) will likely remain high as a percentage of GDP.

Overall, the Trump administration's economic policy focused on easing restrictions on US businesses and lowering taxes. That philosophy set the stage for short-term business-led growth. The implications for the economy and the federal budget are less clear—large budget deficits, uneven economic growth and opportunity, and weakened environmental protections may lead to long-term harm.

References

Amadeo, K. 2021. Trump's NAFTA Changes. https://www.thebalance.com/donald-trump-nafta-4111368.

Autor, D. 2018. Trade and Labor Markets: Lessons from China's Rise. *IZA World of Labor* 431: 1–12.

Banerjee, A., and E. Duflo. 2019. *Good Economics for Hard Times*. New York, NY: Public Affairs.

Brown, C. 2021. US-China Phase One Tracker: China's Purchases of US Goods, February 1. https://www.piie.com/research/piie-charts/us-china-phase-one-tra cker-chinas-purchases-usgoods?utm_source=newsletter&utm_medium=email&utm_campaign=newsletteraxiosmarkets&stream=business.

Cogan, J. 2017. *The High Cost of Good Intentions: A History of U.S. Federal Entitlement Programs*. Stanford, CA: Stanford University Press.

Congressional Budget Office. 2020. The Federal Budget in 2019: An Infographic, April 15. https://www.cbo.gov/publication/56324.

Congressional Research Service. 2020. The Congressional Review Act (CRA): Frequently Asked Questions, Appendix A, January 14. https://fas.org/sgp/crs/misc/R43992.pdf.

Davis Noll, B.A. 2020. Tired of Winning, Judicial Review of Regulatory Policy in the Trump Era, forthcoming in *Administrative Law Review*, October 28. https://pol icyintegrity.org/documents/Davis_Noll_-_Tired_of_Winning_Oct_28.pdf.

DeLong, J.B. 2017. NAFTA and Other Trade Deals Have Not Gutted American Manufacturing—Period, January 24. https://www.vox.com/the-big-idea/2017/1/24/14363148/trade-deals-nafta-wto-china-job-loss-trump.

Executive Order 13771. 2017. January 30. https://www.federalregister.gov/docume nts/2017/02/03/2017-02451/reducing-regulation-and-controlling-regulatory-costs.

Gale, W. 2019. *Fiscal Therapy: Curing America's Debt Addiction and Investing in the Future*. New York, NY: Oxford University Press.

Interagency Working Group on Social Cost of Carbon. 2010. Technical Support Document: Social Cost of Carbon for Regulatory Impact Analysis Under Executive Order 12866, February. https://www.epa.gov/sites/production/files/2016-12/documents/scc_tsd_2010.pdf.

International Trade Administration. 2020. Mexico—Country Commercial Guide, August 17. https://www.trade.gov/knowledge-product/exporting-mexico-market-overview#:~:text=Mexico%20ranked%20number%20one%20among,supports%20mill ions%20of%20U.S.US%20jobs.

Krugman, P., M. Obstfeld, and M. Melitz. 2017. *International Economics: Theory and Policy*. New York, NY: Pearson.

Long, H. 2019. Trump's Steel Tariffs Cost U.S. Consumers $900,000 for Every Job Created, Experts Say, May 7. https://www.washingtonpost.com/business/2019/05/07/trumps-steel-tariffs-cost-us-consumers-every-job-created-experts-say/.

Niskanen, W. 2006. Limiting Government: The Failure of "Starve the Beast." *Cato Journal* 26 (3): 553–558.

Office of Information and Regulatory Affairs. 2020. Introduction to the Fall 2020 Regulatory Plan. https://www.reginfo.gov/public/jsp/eAgenda/StaticCon tent/202010/OIRAIntroduction.pdf.

Office of Management and Budget (OMB). 2003. Circular A-4, September 17. https://obamawhitehouse.archives.gov/omb/circulars_a004_a-4/.

———. 2019. OMB Memorandum M-19-4, 11 April. https://www.whitehouse.gov/wp-content/uploads/2019/04/M-19-14.pdf.

———. 2021. Historical Tables. https://www.whitehouse.gov/omb/historical-tab les/.

Oxford Economics. 2021. The US-China Economic Relationship: A Crucial Partnership at a Critical Juncture, January. https://www.uschina.org/sites/default/files/the_us-china_economic_relationship_-_a_crucial_partnership_at_a_critical_juncture.pdf.

Schultze, C. 1992. *Memos to the President*. Washington, DC: Brookings Institution.

Sunstein, C. 2018. *The Cost-Benefit Revolution*. Cambridge, MA: MIT Press.

Trump White House. 2017. Statement by President Trump on the Paris Climate Accord, June 1. https://trumpwhitehouse.archives.gov/briefings-statements/sta tement-president-trump-paris-climate-accord/.

———. 2020. Economic Report of the President, February. https://trumpwhiteho use.archives.gov/wp-content/uploads/2020/02/2020-Economic-Report-of-the-President-WHCEA.pdf.

United States Government Accountability Office (GAO). 2020. Social Cost of Carbon, June. https://www.gao.gov/assets/710/707871.pdf.

Villarreal, M.A., and I.F. Fergusson. 2017. The North American Free Trade Agreement (NAFTA). *Congressional Research Service Report*, May 2017. https://fas.org/sgp/crs/row/R42965.pdf.

Further Reading

Not surprisingly, the US federal budget and spending is the subject of an extensive literature. Schultze's *Memos to the President* (1992, Washington DC: Brookings Institution) provides a broad overview of federal fiscal policy in the form of short memos to the President. More recently, Cogan's *The High Cost of Good Intentions* (2017, Stanford: Stanford University Press) explores the history of federal entitlement programs and examines their costs. Gale's *Fiscal Therapy* (2019, New York: Oxford University Press), published just before the arrival of Covid-19, discusses the federal budget and proposes mechanisms to reduce costs and increase revenues in a way that he believes will lead to long-term economic growth with a sustainable federal budget deficit.

Sunstein's *The Cost-Benefit Revolution* (2018, Cambridge: MIT Press) provides a comprehensive overview of the myriad issues involved in federal regulation through a cost-benefit lens and shows how a technocratic approach can increase social welfare. Krugman et al.'s *International Economics* (2018, New York: Pearson) is a text that sets out the economic framework for trade policy and shows both the benefits and costs of free trade. Autor's 'Trade and Labor Markets' (2018, *IZA World of Labor* 431: 1–12) looks at how trade with China in particular has impacted jobs in the US. Banerjee and Duflo's *Good Economics for Hard Times* (2019, New York: Public Affairs) discuss the 'pains from trade' in addition to the traditional gains.

CHAPTER 15

Health Care Reform

Jonathan Oberlander

Health care reform has a long history of failure in the United States. During the twentieth century, presidents such as Harry Truman and Bill Clinton were unable to pass universal health insurance through Congress. In its absence, the United States developed an unsystematic patchwork of government programs and private insurance that covered most of the population but nonetheless left many Americans without robust protection against the costs of medical care. Consequently, the United States is an international outlier in health care policy. It is the only rich democracy in the world with a large uninsured population. The population that goes without health insurance is disproportionately low-income; and Hispanic and Black Americans are more likely to be uninsured than White and Asian Americans. While those without health coverage receive medical services from doctors, hospitals, and safety-net clinics (sometimes at no or reduced cost, though often at full price), they receive far fewer services and are more likely to delay or forego care than insured persons. Additionally, many Americans who do have coverage are underinsured as a result of insurance plans that leave patients responsible for paying a substantial portion of their medical care bills. The United States spends much more on medical care than any other nation, even as the quality of care remains highly uneven.

When the Obama administration took office in 2009, it sought to pass ambitious health reform that would address these problems. Overcoming fierce Republican opposition, in 2010 the administration and Democrats

J. Oberlander (✉)
Department of Health Policy and Management, University of North Carolina, Chapel Hill, NC, USA
e-mail: Jonathan_oberlander@med.unc.edu

G. Peele et al. (eds.), *Developments in American Politics 9*,
https://doi.org/10.1007/978-3-030-89740-6_15

in Congress succeeded in enacting a landmark law, the Patient Protection and Affordable Care Act (ACA). While the ACA, also commonly known as Obamacare, did not resolve all of America's health care challenges, it represented a major step forward. Advocates anticipated that the partisan division that accompanied the ACA's enactment would recede, and that they could build on and improve the ACA over time.

Yet the controversy surrounding the ACA intensified during its early years. The law barely survived legal challenges and many Republican-governed states refused to implement key provisions. When Republicans gained a majority in the House of Representatives in the 2010 elections, any chances of building on the ACA ended. And Donald Trump's victory in the 2016 presidential election, along with the election of Republican majorities in the House and Senate, threatened its existence. Trump came to office intent on making good on Republicans' promise to repeal and replace Obamacare. By the end of Trump's presidency, though, Republicans had failed to overturn the ACA through Congress and efforts to undermine it administratively were largely unsuccessful. Joe Biden's victory in the 2020 presidential election marked a new stage in the law's political life, with Democrats gaining their first opportunity in a decade to strengthen the ACA.

This chapter analyzes the ACA's turbulent political journey and the current state of health care reform in the U.S. That journey illustrates how contemporary political struggles over health policy are shaped by growing ideological and political divisions between Democrats and Republicans, and how partisan polarization has altered the normal political trajectory that follows the enactment of a major new social policy program like the ACA. I also explain how the adoption of piecemeal, incremental reforms during the twentieth century makes it difficult to enact more comprehensive solutions to the formidable problems in American health care.

The Politics of Health Care in the United States

Why is health care reform so difficult in the United States? Why is the United States the only rich democracy without universal health care? Why can the United States not contain the high costs of medical care spending? And why have so many legislative proposals to overhaul America's health care arrangements—including those with presidential support—failed to clear Congress?

There are myriad reasons why American health care politics are daunting. First, health policy takes place in an imbalanced political arena. The health care industry has an array of well-funded, politically active interests—associations of doctors, hospitals, insurers, pharmaceutical companies, and more—that have a powerful financial stake in maximizing the flow of revenue to their sector and minimizing any government regulation or intervention that threatens their income. Historically, that meant health system stakeholders strongly opposed national health insurance and, in the case of the American Medical Association (AMA), which represents physicians, fought against any role for the federal government in providing insurance (Starr 2011). In contrast, Americans who do not have any insurance at all are disproportionately low-income and lack organized representation, and during the twentieth century there were few influential interests which lobbied for universal insurance on their behalf. The politics of health care reform thus often tilt toward the health care industry. Consequently, the status quo, which provides enormous financial benefits to the industry, is resilient regardless of its inefficiencies, irrationality, expense, and inequities.

Secondly, the fragmented structure of American political institutions complicates the reformers' task (Steinmo and Watts 1995). The separation of presidential and congressional elections (in contrast to parliamentary systems) means that Congress can and often is governed by a different political party than that of the president. Even when such a divided government is avoided, presidents face major challenges to enacting their agenda. In 1993, Democrat Bill Clinton became president with large Democratic party majorities in the House and the Senate. Despite health care being a top campaign issue and Clinton making it an early legislative priority, his health plan came nowhere close to passing Congress. The Clinton administration's failure to enact reform underscored an axiom of American politics: a president who has majorities of their own party in Congress is not guaranteed success on any given piece of legislation. Members of Congress regularly defy presidents from the same party. The absence in the United States of mechanisms for a no-confidence vote in the government and early elections encourages legislators' independence. Even if the president loses a major vote as a result of defections from their own party, it cannot result in new elections being called whereby members of Congress would have to stand again for office ahead of schedule; they can thus vote against the president with less direct threat to their own political futures. If the United States had a United Kingdom-style parliamentary system of government that produced more party discipline, it might have enacted national health insurance in the late 1940s when it was proposed by President Harry Truman (Morone 1992).

The fragmented nature of American political institutions is also reflected in the organization of Congress. Health care legislation must pass through multiple committees in both the House and Senate. Traditionally, defeat in one key committee ended a bill's chances for enactment, meaning that opponents only had to trip reformers up once to block change. In more recent decades, the passage of legislation in the Senate has often required a supermajority of 60 out of 100 Senators to stop opponents from filibustering (and so preventing a vote on) legislation. Moreover, the influential role played by Congress in policymaking and its decentralized structure meant that the chairs of congressional committees often had their own reform plans that deviated from the president's or party leadership's preferred model. The result was that even when there was a potential majority in Congress for universal health insurance, as there was in the early 1970s, there was not a majority for any one proposal as support splintered among the different plans that lawmakers favored. No wonder, then, that political scientists declared Congress to be a 'graveyard' (Peterson 2005) where health reform went to die in the twentieth century.

Notably, health reform can be challenging in the United States even after legislation survives the congressional gauntlet, is signed by the president, and becomes law. Laws must survive potential challenges in the court system, including Supreme Court rulings that can overturn them. Additionally, in the American system of federalism, power is divided and shared between the national and state governments. A law that relies on states for its implementation may encounter varying degrees of compliance and opposition. As discussed later in this chapter, the Obama administration ran into both of these obstacles during the ACA's implementation.

A third factor in making health politics daunting is that skepticism and antipathy toward government is a prominent feature of American political ideology. Distrust of government, an impulse to limit federal intervention in the economy, and concern over threats to individual liberty are long-running themes in American politics. Proposals to create government insurance programs (and even to have government subsidize purchase of private insurance) have inspired charges of 'socialized medicine' for nearly a century. Solidarity and communitarianism, values which are integral to many health systems across the world, do not have the same resonance in an American political culture that comparatively places more emphasis on individualism and freedom from government (Oberlander 2003). Racism further undermines solidarity and community—proposed health programs are seen by some people as unfairly benefiting 'others' in 'undeserving' marginalized groups, especially Black Americans.

The United States has never reached the social and political consensus on universal health care that exists in other rich democracies. Health care debates are frequently ideological disputes about the boundaries between government and the market, and between social and individual responsibility. The fact that Americans have nonetheless enacted sizable government health care programs (some of which enjoy strong public support) demonstrates, though, that US political culture is more flexible than stereotypical views of the nation's commitment to rugged individualism and laissez faire capitalism might suggest.

Still, it is probably the case that universal health insurance has faced more ideological opposition in the United States than it has in many democratic countries. And even as the United States developed myriad public and private sources of health insurance during the twentieth century, they were piecemeal reforms that lacked the coherence and comprehensive protections provided by other nations' health care systems. During the 1940s, employer-sponsored private insurance, which was supported by government tax subsidies, took off and eventually came to cover most working Americans. In 1965, Congress enacted Medicare, a federal government insurance program for the elderly, and Medicaid, a joint federal-state program for specific categories of low-income persons such as pregnant women and children. These programs overcame the previously mentioned barriers to health care reform, but they were also shaped by them and the compromises required to secure enactment. For example, Medicare initially lacked robust controls on government payments to hospitals and doctors, reflecting a concession to the medical industry that opposed any such cost containment measures. Medicare and Medicaid did not cover all Americans but only groups seen as deserving of government assistance and public sympathy. And employer-sponsored insurance was a voluntary arrangement that not all firms offered, which left many workers and their families without access to affordable coverage. Thus the holes in America's patchwork insurance arrangements created a large uninsured population.

Nonetheless, over time the vast majority of Americans did come to receive health insurance from employer-sponsored insurance, Medicare, or Medicaid. The resulting patchwork created a fourth barrier to health reform: inertia. Most Americans with insurance are satisfied with their coverage and medical care. Reform plans can be portrayed as threatening to their existing benefits, especially for those with private coverage who are susceptible to opponents' charges that new government programs will lead to rationing of their medical care. The public and private foundations of health insurance developed constituencies dedicated to sustaining their operation—from elderly enrollees (in Medicare) to states (which administer Medicaid), businesses and insurance companies (which operate employer-sponsored coverage), and medical providers (which oppose cuts in payments from any insurer). Proposals to remake America's byzantine health care arrangements or unify the patchwork into a single national health insurance program trigger resistance from such constituencies who have grown accustomed to the prevailing (dis)order. The existence and institutionalization of these insurance programs generate a politics that is biased to maintaining the status quo (Oberlander 2019; Starr 2011).

BREAKTHROUGH POLITICS: THE AFFORDABLE CARE ACT

When Barack Obama took office in 2009, he was well aware of the treacherous terrain and mostly dismal history of health care politics in the United States. In particular, the health care misadventures of the last Democratic president, Bill Clinton—whose party lost majority control of Congress after the defeat of his reform plan—left a lasting impression on Democrats. President Obama and the Democratic Congressional leadership nonetheless decided in 2009 to again pursue ambitious health reform. They hoped to capitalize on the opportunities for change created by the Great Recession of 2008–2009, which once again laid bare the vulnerabilities of America's health financing arrangements as millions of people lost employer-sponsored insurance as the economy teetered. In addition, Obama's initial public popularity, his decisive victory (at least by the standards of contemporary American politics) in the 2008 presidential election, and Democrats' large majorities in Congress appeared to create auspicious conditions for reform. Crucially, Democrats won 59 Senate seats in the 2008 elections, and when Pennsylvania Republican Arlen Specter switched parties in April 2010, it gave them a filibuster-proof supermajority of 60 in the Senate, the first that either party had enjoyed since 1979.

The Obama administration and congressional Democrats still faced the daunting barriers that had previously stymied health reform, as well as questions about how to finance a large expansion of insurance coverage given soaring budget deficits and the vast sums being spent by the federal government to stabilize the economy. They also faced the prospect of intense Republican opposition.

Democrats, though, had learned the lessons of the Clinton administration's health care debacle and came to the 2009–2010 health care fight with a new set of strategies. Intent on avoiding a multi-front battle with stakeholder groups, they sought to build support for their plan among health industry groups (such as hospitals and pharmaceuticals) that stood to benefit from an increase in insurance coverage (avoiding both strict, centralized cost controls such as budgetary limits on national health spending and system-wide regulation of medical prices helped to win over those interests). Democrats also forged consensus on a health reform model, which emulated a 2006 law passed by the state of Massachusetts, that built on current government and private insurance arrangements, expanding coverage to the uninsured while minimizing disruption for the already insured and system stakeholders. That consensus enabled Democrats to mobilize an unusual level of coordination between various House and Senate committees involved in drafting health care legislation. Indeed, the Obama administration took the unusual step of deferring to Congress to craft the legislation and the compromises necessary to advance it (Brown 2011; Oberlander 2010).

Despite these strategies and Democrats' sizable Congressional majorities, health care reform had a tumultuous legislative journey through Congress. After Democrats lost their supermajority in the wake of Massachusetts Senator Ted Kennedy's death and a Republican victory in an ensuing special election, it appeared that health reform would once again fall short. This time, though, the commitment of Barack Obama, Speaker of the House Nancy Pelosi, and Senate Majority Leader Harry Reid to stay the course, the unity of Congressional Democrats who did not want to hand their president a major defeat, and the willingness of both the president and legislators to compromise, led to a landmark victory.

In March 2010, Congress enacted the Patient Protection and Affordable Care Act (ACA), the most important health care law in the United States in nearly half a century. However, in a sign of things to come, not a single Republican voted for the bill. Passage of the ACA was not the end of the health care debate in the United States but rather marked the beginning of a new, divisive chapter.

TRANSFORMATIVE INCREMENTALISM

The ACA built upon the status quo. Rather than eliminating America's patchwork insurance arrangements, the law contained a series of additional patches designed to make health coverage more affordable and accessible to the uninsured while disturbing the already insured as little as possible. In practice, that meant an incrementalist commitment to building both on government programs (extending Medicaid to more low-income persons) and private insurance (with new subsidies to help lower- and modest-income persons afford coverage and new regulations that prohibited companies from discriminating against those with pre-existing medical conditions). It also meant that the ACA embodied a series of compromises—including limits to the generosity of subsidies available to persons with modest incomes to buy private insurance—that ensured it would not achieve universal insurance, but rather take major steps in that direction.

The political rationale for such an approach—that it represented the only possible path to enacting ambitious reform—was compelling. But layering new policies, programs, and regulations on top of the messy architecture of US health care came at a cost. The ACA's implementation was rocky, with enormous problems surrounding the start of one of its main features, a new online health insurance purchasing pool where the uninsured could go to buy a private plan (Oberlander 2016). Moreover, the law affected different groups of people in different ways at different times, which contributed to confusion over the ACA's provisions and made it more difficult to build a political constituency around it. Public support for the ACA remained underwhelming. And the law's incrementalism did nothing to dampen opposition from Republican politicians who tried to undermine its implementation and fought to overturn the ACA in the courts, in Congress, and in the states.

Despite the ACA's limits as policy and the political opposition it faced, it has had a major impact on US health care. The uninsured population dropped from 46.5 million in 2010 to 26.7 million in 2016 after ACA's major coverage provisions took effect in 2014 (Tolbert et al. 2020). For many Americans, the ACA was transformative. It banned private insurers from refusing coverage or charging higher premiums to already sick persons and from setting annual and lifetime limits on coverage. It ended gender discrimination in insurance premiums (whereby women had been charged higher amounts). It required insurers to offer a standard minimum set of benefits that included coverage for hospitalization, physician visits, and other core services. And it extended eligibility for government programs and provided substantial financial assistance so low-income persons could obtain insurance. It also required most Americans to buy coverage or pay a penalty. In other rich democracies, such measures (and more) are taken for granted as policies necessary to ensure that all persons have access to health care (White 2013). In the US, however, these reforms represented a major change that enabled millions to access and afford insurance and produced health gains, including reduced mortality rates, among the newly insured. Moreover, this expansion of coverage was achieved while simultaneously moderating the growth in US health care spending, thanks in part to the ACA's cost containment provisions (even in the absence of centralized controls, the law contained measures such as new limits on federal Medicare payments to hospitals that generated savings).

To be sure, the law did not make coverage affordable for everyone. As noted earlier, resistance in some Republican-governed states to expanding Medicaid coverage for low-income persons created a major hole in the ACA provision. Moreover, under the ACA many people with modest incomes were eligible for only limited or no subsidies, leaving them to face private insurance plans with exorbitant premiums and high deductibles (the amount a patient must pay before their coverage begins). Democrats and reform advocates assumed that the law was a 'starter home' that could be improved and strengthened over time. They failed to anticipate Republicans' enduring resistance to the law.

Beyond Repeal: Obamacare and the Trump Administration

After the law's enactment, Republicans fought against Obamacare in Congress, in many states, and in the courts. Their campaign produced multiple legal challenges to the ACA that wound up in the Supreme Court, including *National Federation of Independent Business (NFIB) vs. Sebelius* (2012) and *King vs. Burwell* (2015) The court turned those challenges away, though just by a slim 5-4 majority, with Chief Justice John Roberts casting the deciding vote in the key *Sebelius* case (Jost and Keith 2020). The case challenged the constitutionality of the law's requirement that persons obtain insurance or pay a tax penalty (a decision against the so-called individual mandate could have resulted in the entire law being thrown out). In the same case, the court effectively made Medicaid expansion a state option, which set the stage for some Republican-governed states to refuse to implement that core reform even at the cost of turning away substantial federal financial assistance and leaving many lower-income persons in those states without access to affordable health insurance.

Thus, Republican resistance to the ACA found its greatest success at the state level. In Congress, though, Republicans achieved only modest victories during the Obama administration. They prevented passage of new legislation to address the ACA's problems, and in some cases succeeded in constraining the Obama administration's access to funds to implement the law. But as long as Barack Obama remained president, Republicans could not overturn the ACA because even when they had majorities in both the House and Senate during 2015–2016, they did not have the supermajority (a two-thirds vote in each chamber) necessary to override the president's veto of any legislation they passed.

When Donald Trump won the presidency in 2016, Republicans, having also had secured congressional majorities, finally appeared on the verge of repealing Obamacare and replacing it with a Republican health reform model.

Trump had campaigned on a pledge to overturn the ACA, promising to do so in his first 100 days as president. Repeal legislation was also a priority for GOP Speaker of the House Paul Ryan. Their 2017 repeal drive, though, ran into multiple problems (Hacker and Pierson 2018). Republicans had no viable replacement plan that could come anywhere close to insuring as many Americans as ACA did. Moreover, as part of repealing the ACA, Republicans also proposed major cuts in federal financial aid to states for the Medicaid program that serves tens of millions of low-income Americans. Despite Trump's assurances that Republicans had a 'great plan' that would provide 'insurance for everybody,' the actual GOP plan was full of holes. Nonpartisan estimates from the Congressional Budget Office (CBO) projected that Republican health care legislation would increase the number of Americans without health insurance by 23 million during the next decade. The CBO also concluded that the Republican's health care bill would weaken the ACA's regulations against discrimination by private insurers.

While public support for the ACA had been underwhelming, the repeal effort generated a backlash. The 2017 Republican health care bill became the least popular major legislation of the previous three decades (Nather and Gamio 2017). Many Americans worried about eliminating ACA's benefits and weakening its consumer protections. Most of the health care industry opposed the Republican plan, fearing that the cuts in Medicaid and the ACA would hurt their finances, erode insurance coverage, and destabilize the health care system. States, including some Republican governors, opposed the bill for similar reasons.

Despite its political and substantive problems, repeal legislation did pass the Republican-controlled House. However, it failed to clear the Senate. Republicans were using a special legislative procedure called budget reconciliation that only required a simple majority for passage, thereby averting a filibuster. Yet a narrow 52-48 Republican majority meant that Majority Leader Mitch McConnell could only afford two defections from his party. Senate Republicans, though, could not agree on what should replace the ACA, and without such a plan there was not a majority to overturn the law. Three GOP Senators (Susan Collins from Maine, Lisa Murkowski from Alaska, and John McCain from Arizona) ultimately joined with 46 Democrats and two independents voting against repeal. McCain, who was battling brain cancer and had only recently returned to Washington, cast the decisive vote to preserve the ACA, dramatically and unexpectedly giving a thumbs down on the Senate floor. After seven years of pledging to eliminate the ACA and only six months into the Trump presidency, Republican efforts to repeal and replace the signature achievement of the Obama administration had imploded.

The failure of the Trump administration and congressional Republicans to overturn the ACA reinforced familiar lessons about American politics: the limits of presidential legislative power, even when the president's party holds majority power in Congress; the challenges of maintaining intraparty unity in a political system that enables lawmakers' independence; the difficulties of coordinating action between the House and Senate; and of governing the Senate with a slim majority. Republicans had, in fact, run into many of the same institutional barriers that had often felled past Democrats' health reform proposals (Oberlander 2017).

The defeat of repeal and replace legislation in 2017 also demonstrated the extent to which the ACA had transformed health politics. The ACA had become part of the status quo in US health care that is so difficult to dislodge. As the years passed, a growing number of Americans experienced the law's benefits, giving it a political constituency. Public support for the ACA rose substantially in the face of Republican threats to its existence. And health system stakeholders adapted to the law and sought to protect it against repeal. Moreover, the ACA's core provisions—the regulation of private insurance, consumer protections against insurer discrimination, and financial assistance to help persons afford coverage—which in 2010 had represented a major change in U.S. health policy, became widely accepted and normalized as part of the new status quo. Even the Republican health care bill passed by the House retained, albeit in attenuated form, those key tenets. There was no going back to the status quo ante; the ACA had changed too much in US health care (Oberlander 2020). In the 2018 elections, Republicans lost 41 seats and majority control of the House of Representatives, a defeat which was widely attributed to their unpopular crusade against the ACA.

Still, the defeat of Republican repeal efforts in 2017 did not end the Party's attempts to undermine Obamacare. Since taking office, the Trump administration had sought to weaken the law through administrative actions such as shortening the period to sign up for the coverage in the ACA's insurance marketplaces and cutting federal advertising to promote enrollment in those insurance plans. Now, the administration took additional steps to destabilize the ACA, including canceling federal payments to private insurers that were required by the law to provide enhanced benefits to low-income enrollees. Having failed to roll back the entire ACA, Republicans in Congress turned to targeted repeal, passing a law that eliminated the penalty for not purchasing insurance (this individual mandate to obtain insurance had been viewed as essential to encouraging healthier persons to sign up for coverage). State Republican officials subsequently brought a legal case against the ACA, *California vs. Texas* (2021), that claimed the entire law should be struck down as unconstitutional because it rested on a penalty that no longer existed (a case eventually heard by the Supreme Court).

The Trump administration's efforts to undermine the ACA had consequences. During 2017–2019, America's uninsured population grew for the first time since the ACA's enactment, and attributable in part to Trump era policies that made it harder for persons to enroll in public insurance programs. Such barriers, including a new rule restricting the access of immigrants to government benefits, contributed to a substantial increase in the number of children without health coverage.

By the end of the Trump administration, though, the ACA remained mostly intact, demonstrating its political resilience (Levitt 2020). The steps taken by the administration and congressional Republicans to sabotage its operation did not unravel the law. There was not a precipitous decline in enrollment in the ACA's insurance marketplaces. Indeed, those marketplaces were more financially stable after being targeted by the Trump administration than before. The number of states that embraced Medicaid expansion increased during the Trump presidency, with voters approving ballot initiatives for expansion that bypassed the opposition of Republican governors and legislative majorities in Idaho, Maine, Missouri, Oklahoma, Nebraska, and Utah. It was one thing for Republicans to campaign against Obamacare, but actually overturning the ACA, taking away its substantial benefits, and reversing popular reforms to US health care proved to be a much more difficult task, one that the Trump administration could not complete.

The Pandemic

In January 2020, the United States had its first confirmed case of Covid-19. By March, much of the country was in lockdown as the novel coronavirus began to spread. During the following year, over 500,000 Americans lost their lives to the virus, with over 30 million confirmed cases. The pandemic's impact was unequal as it amplified preexisting socioeconomic, racial/ethnic, and health inequalities: it had a disproportionate impact on Hispanics, Blacks, and American Indians/Alaska Natives, who were more likely to die from Covid than Whites.

Beyond its staggering toll and unequal social impacts, Covid-19 again exposed the sizable gaps in Americans' health coverage. As the nation went into lockdown and the economy into recession, over 20 million people lost their jobs. Since insurance is tied to employment for most working-age Americans, many newly unemployed persons also lost their health coverage amidst a global pandemic that represented the greatest threat to public health in a century (Banthin and Holahan 2020). However, the combination of Medicaid and the ACA's insurance options appeared to have prevented a large increase in the uninsured population.

Still, there hardly could have been a greater indictment of the illogic of America's health insurance arrangements. Many nations, including those with universal health care, struggled to deal with Covid-19. Among rich democracies, though, only in the United States were people losing health insurance as the pandemic advanced; incredibly, access to medical care was threatened during a pandemic that required a community response to contain the spread of Covid-19. Because the United States lacks a comprehensive health care system, it had to adopt legislative and administrative measures to ensure that people, including those who lacked health insurance, had access to testing and vaccination at no cost. However, gaps in these policies meant that some Americans—such as those who sought care from medical providers that were not in their insurers' networks—still had to pay for Covid tests. Patients requiring hospitalization for Covid-19 faced high costs if their insurer did not cover the full bill (many though not all private insurers waived such costs). And a federal program to reimburse hospitals for Covid-19 treatment costs for the uninsured had limits. If a patient's primary diagnosis was not coded as Covid (Covid patients often present with multiple medical problems), hospitals could not receive government payments for their care (Schwartz et al. 2020). Some hospitals refused transfers of Covid-19 patients because they were uninsured or had Medicaid, which reimburses medical providers at lower prices than private insurance.

In other words, the piecemeal policymaking that has long defined US health policy and left sizable gaps in access to affordable medical care was again evident in America's response to Covid. Yet the ACA did provide a vital safety net during the pandemic. The increase in the uninsured population would have been much higher were it not for the insurance options that the law created for many workers who had lost employer-based coverage. The ACA's protections, though, were uneven. People who lost their insurance but lived in states that had not expanded Medicaid eligibility often did not have access to affordable coverage. The Trump administration also refused to reopen the ACA's insurance marketplaces during the pandemic (beyond their customary annual enrollment period), which further limited access to insurance for the uninsured. Even during a pandemic, then, the partisan politics of health care persisted.

RESTORATION: THE BIDEN ADMINISTRATION AND THE ACA REFORM

During 2010–2020, the politics of health care were a stalemate, with Republicans unable to repeal the ACA and Democrats unable to build on it. Despite the ACA's limitations and problems, including the continuing unaffordability of coverage for many middle-class persons, Congress did not pass any significant improvements to the law in the decade following its enactment. Republican opposition made such incremental improvements impossible and ensured that Obamacare remained stuck in an existential debate.

The 2020 elections broke that stalemate and transformed ACA's political environment. Barack Obama's vice president, Joe Biden, defeated Donald Trump in the presidential contest. Democrats' victories in ensuing runoff elections for two Senate seats in the state of Georgia gave them a de facto Senate majority by virtue of Vice President Kamala Harris's tiebreaking vote (Democrats had won a narrow majority in the House). In 2021, for the first time since 2010, a Democratic president had Democratic majorities in the House and Senate. The implications of unified Democratic control of government for US health policy were profound.

Biden wasted little time in reversing Trump administration policies that had been intended to weaken the ACA and restrict access to health insurance. As the Covid-19 pandemic continued, the administration opened the ACA's insurance marketplace in 2021 for a special enrollment period and reinstated federal advertising to encourage enrollment. Less than two months into the Biden administration, Democrats in Congress enacted measures, as part of a $1.9 trillion Covid relief bill, that would make private plans purchased via the ACA more affordable for lower-income persons, while also extending insurance subsidies to middle- and higher-income Americans. The American Rescue Plan Act of 2021 additionally subsidized private health insurance for workers who had lost their jobs during the pandemic, expanded Medicaid coverage for pregnant women, and established new financial incentives for states that newly adopted the ACA's Medicaid expansion.

Taken together, these provisions represented a return to a policy of expanding access to health insurance coverage. Their enactment also represented a significant legislative achievement for the Biden administration. Yet these provisions are time-limited; Congress must renew them or they will expire (most are set to end in 2023). Furthermore, the administration faces daunting obstacles to enacting additional health reforms. Democrats' slim congressional majorities mean that absent any Republican support, legislation cannot pass if even one Democratic Senator votes against it. As a presidential candidate, Biden outlined an ambitious agenda that included establishing a new government insurance program (known as a 'public option') that would be open to both uninsured persons and those with employer-sponsored coverage. The public option was part of Democrats' health plan during the Obama administration, but it failed to pass the Senate and thereby was left out of the ACA. Its reemergence signals both the persistent nature of problems and the policy remedies that are offered to fix them in US health care. It is, though, a controversial proposal fiercely opposed by much of the health care industry (which fears greater government control over payment) and conservatives (who oppose the expansion of federal intervention into private health care). Such a plan is unlikely to pass through the current Congress. Similarly, another proposal that Biden backed during the 2020 campaign— lowering the age of eligibility for Medicare from age 65 to 60—will be difficult to enact given Democrats' narrow majorities. Even as Covid-19 exposes the familiar inequities, irrationality, and failings of America's unsystematic insurance arrangements, the barriers to achieving universal health care remain strong.

In short, the Biden administration marks a new phase in US health policy. But its ability to enact major health reforms is severely constrained. If the administration is unable to pass additional major legislation, it could pursue executive actions to advance its health policy agenda, as the Trump administration did (albeit with a very different purpose). However, there are constraints on what can be done via executive orders and other presidential administrative actions. For example, it is not possible to achieve a major expansion of insurance coverage or adopt a new government insurance program through such mechanisms. And executive actions are impermanent, being easily overturned by a future president. While the Biden administration can reform the Affordable Care Act, it is not clear if Biden can move beyond that goal to realize more far-reaching changes.

Conclusion

Polarization between Democrats and Republicans is a defining feature of contemporary American politics. Democrats and Republicans in Congress are further apart ideologically than at any point in the past 150 years, a growing division driven mostly by the GOP's rightward shift (McCarty 2019). Moreover, American presidential and congressional elections have been closely contested over the past three decades, which gives the minority party in the House and Senate greater incentive to try to block the majority from any legislative successes in order to enhance their chances of winning the next election. And there is evidence of growing partisan polarization at the state level.

It is impossible to make sense of the long fight over the Affordable Care Act without this broader political context. Partisan polarization has impacted the ACA's implementation at the federal and state levels, fueled legal challenges to its existence, shaped divided public perceptions of the law, and ensured that the controversy surrounding the ACA's enactment did not abate. Given institutional fragmentation, interest group pressures, ideological ambivalence about government, and the inertia generated by existing arrangements, health care politics in the United States were already extraordinarily difficult. Polarization not only makes it harder to enact change, it also means that once enacted a program may continue to face partisan opposition that prevents it from building a bipartisan constituency and entrenching itself as an accepted fixture in US social policy. In that respect, the struggle over the ACA could be a harbinger of growing partisan conflict over US social policy.

What is the future of US health care policy? It is possible that the existential partisan war over ACA will finally fade during the Biden administration, as Republicans show scant appetite to pursue legislative repeal again and as their legal challenges to the law are exhausted. With each passing year, more Americans experience the ACA's benefits and, if the Biden administration succeeds in improving the ACA's performance, then overturning the law will become an even harder, and politically riskier, objective for Republicans. Moreover, the GOP still lacks a viable replacement plan, without which repeal remains a political fantasy rather than a realistic legislative possibility.

Even if the existential struggle over ACA recedes, there will be ongoing political conflict over how much to strengthen or weaken the law. The extraordinary partisan polarization of American politics means that the health care debate is far from over. In the short term, the prospects for reform always depend on how the results of the next congressional and presidential elections affect partisan control of government. In the long term, sustained progress in health policy is unlikely to come unless and until the United States can overcome the formidable political barriers to major policy change and move beyond the ACA and piecemeal measures to adopt more comprehensive reforms.

REFERENCES

Banthin, J., and J. Holahan. 2020. *Making Sense of Competing Estimates: The Covid-19 Recession's Effect on Health Coverage*. Available from: https://www.urban.org/sites/default/files/publication/102777/making-sense-of-competing-estimates_1.pdf.

Béland, D., P. Rocco, and A. Waddan. 2016. *Obamacare Wars: Federalism, State Politics, and the Affordable Care Act*. Lawrence: University Press of Kansas.

Brown, L.D. 2011. The Elements of Surprise: How Health Reform Happened. *Journal of Health Politics, Policy and Law* 36 (3): 419–427.

Hacker, J.S., and P. Pierson. 2018. The Dog That Almost Barked: What the ACA Repeal Fight Says About the Resilience of the American Welfare State. *Journal of Health Politics, Policy and Law* 43 (4): 551–577.

Jost, T.S., and K. Keith. 2020. ACA Litigation: Politics Pursued Through Other Means. *Journal of Health Politics, Policy and Law* 45 (4): 485–499.

Levitt, L. 2020. The Affordable Care Act's Enduring Resilience. *Journal of Health Politics, Policy and Law* 45 (4): 609–616.

McCarty, N. 2019. *Polarization: What Everyone Needs to Know*. New York: Oxford University Press.

Morone, J.A. 1992. Bias of American Politics: Rationing Health Care in a Weak State. *University of Pennsylvania Law Review* 140: 1923–1938.

Nather, D., and L. Gamio. 2017. The Most Unpopular Bill in Three Decades. Available from: https://www.axios.com/unpopular-health-care-bill-2454397857.html.

Oberlander, J. 2003. The Politics of Health Reform: Why Do Bad Things Happen to Good Health Plans? *Health Affairs* 22 (Suppl.), W3: 391–404.

———. 2010. Long Time Coming: Why Health Reform Finally Passed. *Health Affairs* 9 (6): 1112–1116.

———. 2016. Implementing the ACA: The Promise and Limits of Health Care Reform. *Journal of Health Politics, Policy and Law* 41 (4): 803–826.

———. 2017. Replace, Repeal, Repair, Retreat—Republicans' Health Care Quagmire. *New England Journal of Medicine* 377 (11): 1001–1003.

———. 2019. Lessons from the Long and Winding Road to Medicare for All. *American Journal of Public Health* 109 (11): 1497–1500.

———. 2020. The Ten Years' War: Politics, Partisanship, and the ACA. *Health Affairs* 39 (3): 471–478.

Peterson, M.A. 2005. The Congressional Graveyard for Health Care Reform. In *Healthy, Wealthy and Fair: Health Care for a Good Society*, ed. L.D. Brown, L.R. Jacobs, and J.A. Morone, 205–234. New York: Oxford University Press.

Schwartz, K., K. Pollitz, J. Tolbert, and M. Musumeci. 2020. *Gaps in Cost Sharing Protections for Covid-19 Testing and Treatment Could Spark Public Concerns about Covid-19 Vaccine Costs*. Available from: https://www.kff.org/health-costs/issue-brief/gaps-in-cost-sharing-protections-for-covid-19-testing-and-treatment-could-spark-public-concerns-about-covid-19-vaccine-costs/. Accessed 11 Apr 2021.

Starr, P. 2011. *Remedy and Reaction: The Peculiar American Struggle Over Health Care Reform*. New Haven: Yale University Press.

Steinmo, S., and J. Watts. 1995. It's the Institutions, Stupid! Why Comprehensive National Health Insurance Always Fails in America. *Journal of Health Politics, Policy and Law* 20 (2): 329–372.

Tolbert, J., K. Orgera, and A. Damico. 2020. *Key Facts About the Uninsured Population*. Available from: https://www.kff.org/uninsured/issue-brief/key-facts-about-the-uninsured-population/. Accessed 8 Apr 2021.

White, J. 2013. The 2010 U.S. Health Care Reform: Approaching and Avoiding How Other Countries Finance Health Care. *Health Economics, Policy and Law* 8 (3): 289–315.

Further Reading

The involvement of presidents from Franklin Delano Roosevelt to Barack Obama in health care reform is vividly explored in David Blumenthal and James Morone's (2009) *The Heart of Power* (Berkeley: University of California Press). Other excellent accounts of the history and politics of US health policy during the twentieth century include Paul Starr's (2nd edition, 2017) *The Social Transformation of American Medicine* (New York: Basic Books), Theodore Marmor's (2nd edition, 2000) *The Politics of Medicare* (London: Routledge), and Jacob Hacker's (1996) *The Road to Nowhere* (Princeton: Princeton University Press).

There is a large and growing literature on the politics of the Affordable Care Act (ACA). John McDonough's (2011) *Inside National Health Reform* (Berkeley: University of California Press) and Paul Starr's (2011) *Remedy and Reaction* (2011) (New Haven: Yale University Press) explore the remarkable constellation of political forces and choices that led to the law's enactment as well as the promise and limits of the ACA's design. The post-enactment conflicts over the ACA at the state level and in the context of federalism are skillfully analyzed by Daniel Béland, Philip Rocco, and Alex Waddan's (2016) *Obamacare Wars* and David Jones' (2017) *Exchange Politics* (New York: Oxford University Press). Jamila Michener's excellent (2018) *Fragmented Democracy* (Cambridge: Cambridge University Press) goes beyond the ACA to show how federalism reproduces inequalities in state Medicaid programs and how enrollment in such programs impact political participation by low-income beneficiaries.

Recent scholarship in American health politics has also examined the formidable barriers to controlling health care costs. Miriam Laugesen's (2016) *Fixing Medical Prices* (Cambridge: Harvard University Press) and Eric Patashnik, Alan Gerber, and Conor Dowling's (2017) *Unhealthy Politics* (Princeton: Princeton University Press) are exceptional accounts of the political forces that shape US health care spending. Beyond the scholarly literature, the Kaiser Family Foundation (https://www.kff.org/) and Commonwealth Fund (https://www.commonwealthfund.org/) are essential sources of news, data, and analysis of current issues in U.S. health care policy.

CHAPTER 16

Gun Policy and Politics

Robert J. Spitzer

On Valentine's Day in February 2018, a Biden high school student entered the Marjory Stoneman Douglas High School in Parkland, Florida with a semi-automatic assault weapon. In minutes, he had shot and killed 17 people, and injured 17 more. Within a week, President Donald Trump hosted an emotional White House meeting with the survivors and their families. Trump told them he would 'do something about this horrible situation' (Vitali 2018).

In a follow-up meeting with congressional leaders, Trump said he would 'take a look' when Senator Dianne Feinstein called his attention to a new proposal to ban assault weapons. According to Senator Amy Klobuchar, who also attended the meeting, Trump said he supported universal background checks for all gun purchases. The President also promoted the idea of raising the gun purchase age from 18 to 21. In perhaps his most surprising declaration, Trump said, 'I like taking guns away early. Take the guns first, go through due process second' (Jackson 2018).

Trump's comments squarely contradicted the tenets of the nation's leading gun rights organization, the National Rifle Association (NRA), which had enthusiastically endorsed him during his 2016 campaign for president. In fact, the NRA was among the first major interest groups to back Trump's candidacy.

R. J. Spitzer (✉)
Political Science Department, The State University of New York (SUNY), Cortland, NY, USA
e-mail: Robert.spitzer@cortland.edu

© The Author(s), under exclusive license to Springer Nature Switzerland AG 2022
G. Peele et al. (eds.), *Developments in American Politics 9*,
https://doi.org/10.1007/978-3-030-89740-6_16

Trump's seeming embrace of new gun laws did not last. Just four weeks after the Parkland shooting, Trump spoke with NRA leaders and proceeded to walk back on his promises. He appointed a commission, headed by Education Secretary Betsy DeVos, to examine school violence. Its report recommended no new gun laws.

Trump made no effort to advance new gun laws for the balance of his term. The only gun measure enacted during the Trump administration was an administrative regulation to ban 'bump stocks,' devices that can be attached to certain semi-automatic rifles (guns that fire one round as rapidly as a person can pull the trigger) that allows them to fire in the manner of a fully automatic firearm (fully automatic means that the gun issues forth a continual stream of bullets by simply holding the trigger down). Bump stocks were used by a mass shooter in Las Vegas in 2017. After the rule was announced, it was challenged, unsuccessfully, by gun rights forces in court—but not by the NRA (Savage 2018).

The NRA's monopoly of influence over the Trump White House would seem to typify the state of gun policy in America, where this powerful gun rights group appears to maintain a stranglehold on the course of national gun policy. Yet the contemporary political picture proves to be both more complicated and far more in flux.

Before examining the current political picture, some historical context provides an essential perspective, as the modern gun debate is sharply framed by the collision between gun myth and gun history. That collision is also reflected in legal and popular understanding of the U.S. Constitution's Second Amendment, the right to bear arms.

America's Gun History

A commonplace understanding of the history of guns in America generally supposes that the typical early American owned and was skilled in the use of guns; that few if any gun laws existed until the twentieth century; that many or most of these laws are suspect, because of the constitutional right to bear arms included in the Constitution's Bill of Rights in 1791; and that gun-carrying citizens were largely responsible for creating the country as we know it today. All of these suppositions are wrong, in part or in whole.

Gun possession is as old as America, but so are gun laws. From the colonial era through the nineteenth century, America's colonies and states enacted literally thousands of gun laws of every imaginable variety. In many respects, guns were more strictly regulated in the country's first 300 years than in the last 30. Moreover, gun laws and gun rights were perfectly compatible in most of US history (Spitzer 2015). Only in the last few decades, in this era of polarized politics, have gun laws and gun rights been viewed as 'zero sum': that is, a gain for one side is taken as a loss for the other.

Nothing illustrates this more clearly than America's so-called 'Wild West' of the nineteenth century. Contrary to popular notions of gun-toting Americans single-handedly settling western lands, westward expansion and settlement, though hazardous, was largely the result of agrarian and commercial expansion, with the role of guns and gunslinging wildly overstated. In fact, one of the first actions taken by local leaders during westward expansion was the enactment of strict gun regulations, including laws barring the carrying of concealed weapons, dueling, and the brandishing of firearms (displaying them in a threatening manner). State and local governments also enacted gun taxes, regulations concerning the sale and discharge of guns, registration requirements, and storage requirements. The kind of gunplay so often depicted in films, stories, and novels only occurred rarely (Spitzer 2021).

As for the Second Amendment, it played little actual role in establishing individual gun rights until recently. The amendment reads, 'A well regulated Militia, being necessary to the security of a free State, the right of the people to keep and bear Arms, shall not be infringed.' As the authors of the amendment explained in 1789, and as the courts interpreted the amendment for two centuries, the right it described pertained only to gun ownership in connection with citizen service in a government organized and regulated militia. The idea that it protected a personal, individual right to own guns unrelated to militia service was first established as law in the Supreme Court's 2008 ruling in *District of Columbia v. Heller*, when it ruled for the first time (and contrary to earlier rulings) that the amendment protected an individual right to own a handgun for personal defense in the home. Two years later, the court applied this interpretation to the states. Yet the court's decision also limited this individual right, essentially concluding that most existing gun laws would be considered constitutional. Of over 1400 court challenges brought against gun laws since 2008, the vast majority of those laws have been upheld (giffords.org 2021), although the current, more conservative Court is poised to change this.

THE MODERN GUN LAW REGIME

Two prevailing trends have long framed the modern American gun debate. The first is strong, durable, and consistent public support for stricter gun laws. Since the advent of modern public opinion polling in the late 1930s, consistent and usually large majorities of Americans have registered support for stronger gun laws. It is, in fact, one of the most consistent trends in all of public opinion (Spitzer 2021). The second trend is gun ownership. No precise tally of the number of guns in civilian hands is maintained, but the most likely estimates peg the number at about 300 million, for an average of nearly one gun per person in the country. About two thirds of those guns are long guns—rifles and shotguns—and the other third handguns. Yet that does not mean that most Americans own guns. In fact, only about 30 percent of homes report at least one gun, and about 25 percent of adults report personally owning at least one gun. Two other facts are also relevant: American gun ownership has been gradually declining across the last several decades while the average number of guns per owner has increased dramatically. In the 1960s, the average gun owner owned about 2½ guns. Today the average number is over eight (Cook and Goss 2020).

Beginning in the twentieth century, two types of events have spurred periodic calls for stronger gun laws: the spread and fear of gun-related crime, and political assassinations. Despite enduring popular support for tougher laws, new gun regulations at the federal level have been infrequent and limited in scope, owing in large measure to the intensity, single-issue focus, and political effectiveness of gun rights organizations. The vast majority of gun laws are, instead, state laws.

For example, gun-fueled gangsterism in the 1920s and 1930s prodded President Franklin D. Roosevelt (who was himself subject to an unsuccessful assassination attempt in 1933) to seek enactment of the first modern national gun law, the National Firearms Act of 1934, which strictly regulated gangster-type weapons, including sawed-off shotguns, machine guns (fully automatic weapons), and silencers. Similar moments of violence prompted new federal gun laws in 1968, 1993, and 1994.

These modest successes by supporters of stronger gun laws came to a halt with the 2000 elections. That year, the Democratic nominee for President, Vice President Al Gore, campaigned strongly in favor of stricter gun laws. His opponent, Republican Texas Governor George W. Bush, was endorsed by the NRA and embraced their agenda. Many Democrats attributed Gore's narrow loss to his position on gun control, and that prompted the party to largely abandon the issue.

The gun-friendly Bush presidency witnessed two major successes for the NRA and the gun community. First, in 2005, Congress enacted the NRA's top legislative priority, the Protection of Lawful Commerce in Arms Act, which barred civil suits against gun manufacturers and dealers. (Despite this major victory for the gun industry, it is neither very large, profitable, nor very powerful compared to most American corporations, although it has been a key source of funding for the NRA.) Second, a more conservative Supreme Court, which now included two Bush appointees, established new, personal gun rights under the Second Amendment in the *Heller* case.

Supporters of stronger gun measures were heartened by the election of Democratic Senator Barack Obama to the presidency in 2008, as Obama had a long history of support for gun safety measures. Yet he mostly avoided the issue in the campaign. During his first term as president, he proposed no new gun legislation to Congress, and even signed into law two minor provisions that loosened gun laws. In fact, the Brady Campaign, a pro-gun safety organization, gave him a failing grade on the issue after his first year in office (O'Brien 2010).

That all changed in December 2012, when a deranged man shot up the Sandy Hook Elementary School in Newtown, Connecticut, killing twenty children and six staff. The sheer horror of the event shocked the nation in a way not seen since a high school mass shooting in Littleton, Colorado in 1999.

These and similar mass shootings, while particularly heinous and attention-grabbing, often lead to the conclusion that they drive America's extremely high gun murder rate. But mass shootings account for only about one percent of all gun homicides per year. This does not, however, suggest that they cannot or should not receive the particular attention of lawmakers and the public.

Fresh off his 2012 re-election victory, and shocked by the Sandy Hook shooting, President Obama announced the appointment of a task force to make recommendations for new gun laws that were then sent to Congress in early 2013. Several measures, including the establishment of universal background checks for all gun purchases and re-imposition of the assault weapons ban (a limited federal ban, enacted in 1994, lapsed in 2004), were put to a vote in the US. Senate, but all were defeated. Congress's refusal to act put an end to any further legislative efforts, but Obama used the presidential 'bully pulpit' for the rest of his term to continue to decry gun violence and urge national action, which heartened and helped rally gun law supporters (Draper 2013).

The Sandy Hook shooting had another consequence: it spurred the creation of new gun safety organizations. In 2014, former New York City Mayor and billionaire Michael Bloomberg reorganized and expanded a gun safety group he had formed in 2006, Mayors Against Illegal Guns. The new entity, called Everytown for Gun Safety, combined and expanded Bloomberg's former group with another new group, Moms Demand Action for Gun Sense in America. The Moms group claimed over 200,000 members as of 2016. After combining with Everytown, it claimed a total membership of nearly 1.3 million, as of 2017. The Moms group had logged some successes by pressuring businesses through publicity and threat of boycott to not allow gun carrying in their places of business. These tactics proved effective in persuading businesses like Starbucks, Chipotle, Chili's, Sonic, Kroger, Panera, and Target to ban gun carrying. Bloomberg pledged to spend $50 million of his own money to advance his agenda, including the building of a grassroots organization and heavy spending in the 2014 and 2016 elections. In the 2020 election cycle, Bloomberg pledged $60 million to advance the gun cause, though the total amount spent proved to be less (Spitzer 2021).

The other significant gun control organization to emerge was formed by former congresswoman Gabrielle Giffords (D-Ariz.) and her husband Mark Kelly, a retired Navy captain and former astronaut. After Giffords survived a near-fatal shooting in 2011, the two formed Americans for Responsible Solutions in 2013. Their organization was also spurred, at least in part, by Sandy Hook. Both are gun owners and professed supporters of the Second Amendment who seek to reach out to gun owners, though their organization focuses on solutions to gun violence. In addition, they raised and spent $20 million for the 2014 elections—a significant accomplishment for the new organization. In the 2016 elections, they spent about $13 million; in 2018, they spent about $18 million. In 2016, the Giffords/Kelly group merged with the Law Center to Prevent Gun Violence, a gun safety research organization founded in 1993, and now goes by the umbrella name 'Giffords' (giffords.org 2021). Kelly entered politics directly in 2020 when he ran for and was elected to the U.S. Senate from Arizona as a Democrat.

Despite these organizations' differences, their common policy focus was on measures with wide and clear public support, including universal background checks for gun purchases, improved record keeping, more effective crackdowns on gun trafficking, ammunition magazine limits, extreme risk protection order laws (also called 'red flag' laws), and measures to keep guns from children and those at risk of suicide.

These groups sought to replicate the successes that marked the NRA's political activities in terms of group mobilization, electoral competition, money spent, and state policy change. To that end, they have pursued a three-part strategy similar to that of the NRA: the raising and spending of large sums of money comparable to that spent by the NRA; the establishment and cultivation of a motivated and committed grassroots base of supporters around the country; and playing the long game, meaning that they wanted to maintain and deepen their political influence over time, and not limit their efforts to a single election or to the immediate aftermath of shooting events that only temporarily rouse the attention of the nation.

Gun safety groups began to log political successes. The public lined up more strongly behind their agenda, and the NRA managed to shoot itself in the foot with some largely self-created financial, legal, and political problems.

NRA Woes and Shifting Gun Politics

As described at the start of this chapter, the NRA was an early and enthusiastic Trump supporter. Putting its money where its mouth was, it poured $31 million into his campaign, triple its spending for 2012 Republican presidential nominee Mitt Romney, and over $70 million in all into the 2016 elections (Stone 2017). The NRA's political gambit proved to be a big winner for them with Trump's improbable victory. Yet within two years the organization confronted a shocking series of cascading crises.

Media investigations reported disturbing and possibly illegal connections, perhaps including money laundering, between the NRA and Russian officials tied to the 2016 election. Revelations of significant mismanagement of organizational operating funds coincided with a series of severe cost-cutting measures, culminating in an angry and litigious split with the NRA's longtime public relations firm, Ackerman-McQueen, which had received decades of lavish annual fees—$40 million in 2017 alone. In 2019 the NRA pulled the plug on NRATV, an Ackerman-McQueen-designed online media outlet begun in 2016 that proved expensive and yielded little traffic (Spies 2019).

Validating the NRA's money woes, it was outspent in the 2018 midterm elections, for the first time ever, by gun safety groups, and a bevy of candidates around the country ran and won on a gun safety agenda. These reversals were spearheaded by a reinvigorated gun safety movement led by students from Parkland High School in Florida.

And then came the NRA's annual spring convention in 2019. Usually a picture of gun rights unity and pride, the 2019 event was a public relations debacle. The NRA's president, Oliver North, issued a letter to the NRA's board accusing NRA Executive Director Wayne LaPierre of profligate and improper personal spending at NRA expense, including $275,000 on clothing from a Beverly Hills boutique, multi-million-dollar travel to posh resorts, and a charge of sexual harassment. North insisted that LaPierre step down, calling the situation an 'existential crisis.' LaPierre (whose annual salary and perks topped $3 million yearly) fired back, accusing North of extortion and having an improper relationship with Ackerman-McQueen (which also represented North and paid him $1 million a year; ironically, LaPierre and his wife both had long ties to the ad firm). LaPierre prevailed, and North learned that he was out as president while the convention was still underway.

Yet bad news revelations did not stop there. Media reports disclosed that between 2010 and 2017, the NRA had drawn over $200 million in cash from its non-profit NRA Foundation to keep the doors open. The NRA Foundation is financially separate from the NRA itself; it has a privileged tax-exempt status under which the Foundation may only spend money on educational activities. It may not spend money on political activities; but in giving money to the NRA it could have been violating that rule. As of the end of 2017, NRA available assets were in the negative, to the tune of $31.8 million. In the previous ten years, while its revenues grew only 0.7 percent per year, its expenses grew on average 6.4 percent per year. Recent annual deficits ran to $40 million, and 2019 marked the fourth consecutive year the organization finished with a deficit, partly because membership revenue hit a seven year low in 2019. Some board members loudly condemned LaPierre's profligate ways, but the majority of board members continued to back him. Investigations also revealed that hundreds of millions of NRA dollars had been funneled to NRA executives, contractors, and favored vendors (Spies 2019).

On the legal front, a New York state agency ruled that the NRA's 'Carry Guard' insurance program, designed and marketed by Ackerman-McQueen to generate revenue by providing policies to cover self-defense shootings, violated state insurance rules. Critics dubbed it 'murder insurance' because it could provide coverage for a criminal act. The NRA sued but eventually paid a fine and ended the program in 2019. The state's Attorney General launched an investigation into the NRA's tax status (the NRA is chartered in New York), including whether it had violated the rules pertaining to its operation as a non-profit (tax-exempt) organization, as well as possible violations of campaign finance laws, improper payments made to board members, and tax compliance. NRA officials were served with subpoenas. Other entities conducted their own investigations. In 2020 the Attorney General issued a stinging 160-page summons and complaint detailing the NRA's misdeeds and calling for the dissolution of the organization. In 2021 the NRA filed for Chapter 11 bankruptcy and announced its intention to move to Texas.

From North's 2019 departure through the next twelve months, the NRA saw the firing or resignation of three executives (including LaPierre's heir apparent, Christopher Cox), eleven board members, three lawyers, and the layoff of over 100 staff. Several wealthy donors to the NRA announced that they would stop all contributions until LaPierre was dismissed (Van Sant 2020).

THE 2018 ELECTIONS

The Parkland High School shooting mentioned at the start of this chapter not only shocked the nation but emboldened some of its students to do something that had never occurred before. Within hours of the shooting, these students turned their private grief into public rage at government leaders who they accused of inaction on gun policy. Rejecting 'thoughts and prayers' from government leaders, they called for government action to strengthen the nation's gun laws. Beyond their initial outcry, the students became the driving wedge of a nationwide movement that had clear goals: to keep the gun issue at the forefront of the nation's consciousness; to mobilize young people to join the movement and register them to vote; to seek government policy change; and to bring the issue into the 2018 elections. Well-attended rallies that drew thousands were held throughout the country under the '#NeverAgain' banner. These efforts met with success, helped at least in part by the fact that in the past several years, national polls reported an upswing in already-strong support for stricter gun laws (Cullen 2019).

Efforts to enact new national gun safety laws failed, yet most gun laws in America exist at the state level, and state gun laws vary widely. In 2018, 27 states enacted over 60 new gun regulations, including traditionally gun-friendly states like Florida and Vermont. Some of these measures found bipartisan support. For example, fourteen states enacted 'red flag' laws after Parkland (as of 2020, a total of twenty states have such laws). These laws allow guns to be temporarily taken from persons considered to pose an imminent threat to themselves or others, subject to a subsequent hearing. Five of those laws were approved by Republican governors. In Congress, two keystone bills championed by the NRA, to enact concealed gun carry reciprocity (meaning that each state would be required to recognize the handgun carry laws of every other, which in effect would have lowered the national gun carry standard to that of the state with the least regulation) and to deregulate the purchase of gun silencers, stalled.

In the 2018 midterm elections, the NRA spent about $20 million; gun safety groups spent around $37 million. Voters reported that the gun issue was their third most important issue concern (with that support leaning overwhelmingly toward stronger gun regulation), a higher ranking for the issue than had been seen in decades. Among swing district congressional races, 38 of 59 candidates embraced gun regulation, compared to only four of 36 in 2016. A study of political ads nationwide found an increase by a factor of 22 in pro-regulation ads in 2018 compared with 2014 (Spitzer 2018). As if to punctuate the impact of this shifting tide, the Democratic-controlled House of Representatives passed two new gun measures early in 2019: one, to establish uniform gun purchase background checks (over a fifth of gun purchases occur without any checks) and another to extend and broaden gun purchase background checks. This marked the first time in twenty years that a house of Congress had passed a new gun bill. The Republican-controlled Senate took no action.

To be sure, gun rights forces logged some victories as well. Conservative states continued to loosen gun regulations. Up until the 1980s, any civilians who wanted to own and carry a handgun had to first obtain a permit from their state, although some states barred concealed carrying entirely. Some states had fairly strict requirements, some less so; but only one state (Vermont) did not require any permit for handgun ownership and carrying in society. Yet, beginning in the 1980s, the NRA launched a quiet campaign in the states to loosen or even repeal permitting requirements. The effort was highly successful, with most states reducing permitting requirements. Those states that had formerly barred concealed carrying all enacted carry laws. In fact, some states went further to eliminate state permitting entirely, meaning that citizens who could legally obtain a handgun (after passing a simple background check) could then carry their guns without the need to obtain a special permit for that carrying. In the years after Sandy Hook, several more states abolished permit systems for carrying a concealed firearm, bringing the total to twenty-one states as of 2021.

Finally, Second Amendment rights re-entered the political debate with the nomination of Amy Coney Barrett to the Supreme Court. During her confirmation hearings a month before the 2020 election, Judge Barrett was quizzed about her views on gun rights, along with many other subjects. Yet the most revealing piece of information came from a dissenting opinion she wrote as a federal judge in a 2017 court of appeals case upholding a law that barred felons from obtaining guns. The case involved a man whose felony conviction was non-violent. In her dissent, Barrett, a self-proclaimed constitutional originalist, said that the historical record of gun laws showed that guns could only be stripped from owners who had 'demonstrated a proclivity for violence.' The problem with her view is that the actual historical record of old gun laws demonstrates the opposite—that literally hundreds of gun laws in the colonies and states called for taking guns away from owners that had nothing to do with violent felony circumstances. Barrett's addition to the high court will undoubtedly provide a firm five-member majority for significantly expanding gun rights (Spitzer 2020).

THE 2020 ELECTIONS

The 2020 elections were dominated by three overriding issues that no one could have anticipated before the start of the year: the Covid-19 pandemic, the worst economic downturn since the Great Depression, and an explosive Black Lives Matter movement. One might have thought that these crises would have pushed the gun issue well down or even off the 2020 election agenda. In a certain respect that was true. Owing to the pandemic, 2020 was the first election year since 2012 that a statewide gun reform measure did not appear on any state ballot. The cause was no lack of enthusiasm on the part of gun safety advocates. Rather, the process of collecting petition signatures to place referenda on state ballots was short-circuited by health restrictions. Despite this, guns and gun controversies infused each of the dominant national issues. This was seen in right wing, sometimes armed, protests against restrictive pandemic policies designed to slow the spread of the disease; and it was seen in some-times armed counter-Black Lives Matter protests, in gun sales spikes, in gun interest group activity; and it was seen in the post-election insurrection in the nation's capital in early 2021.

Measures enacted to combat the spread of the virus provoked a sharp and sometimes armed response from right-wing groups. In the spring and summer of 2020, armed protestors showed up in over a half dozen state capi-tals to express opposition to pandemic lockdown policies they believed to be unnecessary and a violation of their rights.

But firearms-expressed anger extended beyond public protests, including, in one alarmingly extreme case, a foiled plot hatched by at least thirteen so-called militia group members in Michigan to kidnap that state's governor, Democrat Gretchen Whitmer, in reprisal for her administration's anti-virus measures. A similar plot was uncovered against Virginia's Democratic governor, Ralph Northam. Less dramatic, but arguably more significant, was the increase in shootings and homicides, especially in urban areas—an increase attributed, at least in part, to the interruption of programs devised to reduce gun violence because of the adverse economic effects of the pandemic, and possibly also to the surge of gun sales. That increase was all the more notable given that crime in virtually every other category continued to decline. Hovering over the entire fall election was the ominous specter of an armed presence during elec-tion time amidst the rallying of right-wing armed groups who spread fears that the elections would be somehow hijacked by opponents of President Trump.

All of this occurred in the context of mass demonstrations over racial injus-tice around the country. A series of legally dubious police shootings of Black people were the proximate motivation for widespread protests, coalescing under the Black Lives Matter movement banner. In a few instances these protests led to violence, including armed violence, most notably in Kenosha, Wisconsin, and Portland, Oregon. Yet despite news coverage suggesting that the nationwide protests were typically violent, the opposite was the case.

According to a study of the protests by the non-profit Armed Conflict Location and Event Data Project, of the 7750 protests held in all fifty states from May to August 2020, 93 percent of them were non-violent. Violent protests were defined as those that involved interpersonal clashes or property damage. Up to the end of August, virtually no gun violence occurred, although individuals did carry firearms in some instances. The one notable shooting instance occurred in Kenosha, when an armed 17-year-old counter-protestor shot three people, killing two of them. For his part, President Trump failed to condemn armed counter-protestors and expressed sympathy for the Kenosha shooter. He also sought to paint the demonstrations in dire terms, playing on fears of a breakdown of law and order. Biden denounced violence on all sides and urged calm.

The other notable trend spurred by the climate of uncertainty and concerns over violence was a record spike in gun sales. The spread of the pandemic in the spring of 2020 prompted an increase in gun sales, a seemingly puzzling response, given that firearms bear no relationship to viral infection. Yet this trend is not new; Americans with an affinity for guns increased purchases at past moments of national crisis as well.

Gun policy groups lined up with the candidates along expected lines. The National Rifle Association again swung support to Trump, but the organization's resources were severely strained by successive body blows. As of post-election day 2020, the NRA had spent $24.4 million on the campaign overall, roughly a third of that spent in 2016. Of that, $16.2 million went to the Trump campaign, half of what it spent on Trump in 2016. The gun safety groups Everytown for Gun Safety spent $26.9 million, and the Giffords group $2 million, in 2020 (Nass 2020). Despite polls showing that large majorities of Americans feared election-day violence, there was none - the election itself went off without any violence or disruption. A few scattered vote-counting protests emerged in the days after election day, including armed (but peaceful) pro-Trump right-wing protests in a half dozen swing states. Over a week after the election a pro-Trump rally was held in Washington D.C. and drew roughly 10,000 attendees, including members of right-wing so-called militia groups like the Oathkeepers and hate groups including the Proud Boys, Patriot Front, and American Guard (gun carrying is not allowed in D.C.; such groups are not militias under law, despite their appropriation of the term).

Trump supporters again convened in the nation's capital on January 6, 2021 where Trump spoke to the assembled thousands and exhorted them to march on the Capitol on the day Congress had convened to count the electoral ballots to formally declare the winner of the presidential contest. What ensued was a riot, labeled an insurrection by the US House of Representatives, where the mob forced their way past barricades and the outnumbered and out-staffed Capitol police to enter the home of the US Congress. The rioters vandalized the building; members of Congress narrowly avoided injury, death, or capture. The overwhelming majority of Americans were shocked, as was most of the world. Five died as a result of the melee, but only one from gunfire when an officer shot and killed a woman attempting to enter the area where members of Congress were located. A handful of rioters were later charged with illegal gun possession.

Conclusion: A Fork in the Road on Gun Control

Despite popular support for stronger gun laws, gun rights forces have often been successful because their strong feelings about gun ownership provide a degree of political motivation and intensity that supporters of stricter gun laws can rarely match (Lacombe 2021). Small but highly mobilized groups can often prevail in American politics against a larger but less motivated majority.

Yet the gun safety movement has found new vitality and organizational resources to log significant victories in the last few years, especially in the 2018 midterm elections, and the public continues to support stronger gun laws. On the other hand, the federal courts, populated with large numbers of very conservative Trump-era appointees, are poised to roll back many existing gun control laws that have formerly withstood legal challenge. The Supreme Court will undoubtedly lead that charge. This places the country in a position where legal doctrine on gun rights and laws may diverge sharply and dramatically from the public will, presaging two possible problems: a potential legitimacy crisis for the courts, and a reduced ability to fight gun-related crime.

References

Cook, Philip J., and Kristin A. Goss. 2020. *The Gun Debate*, 2nd ed. New York: Oxford University Press.

Cullen, Dave. 2019. *Parkland: Birth of a Movement*. New York: HarperCollins.

Draper, Robert. 2013. Inside the Power of the N.R.A. *New York Times Magazine*, December 13.

Giffords.org. 2021. https://giffords.org/lawcenter/gun-laws/second-amendment/protecting-gun-safety-laws-in-appellate-courts/.

Jackson, David. 2018. Trump Says Take Guns First and Worry About 'Due Process Second' in White House Gun Meeting. *USA Today*, February 28. https://www.usatoday.com/story/news/politics/2018/02/28/trump-says-take-guns-first-and-worry-due-process-second-white-house-gun-meeting/381145002/.

Lacombe, Matthew J. 2021. *Firepower: How the NRA Turned Gun Owners into a Political Force*. Princeton, NJ: Princeton University Press.

Nass, Daniel, 2020. How Much Is the NRA Spending to Reelect Donald Trump? *The Trace*, December 31. https://www.thetrace.org/features/nra-2020-election-spending-trump/.

O'Brien, Michael. 2010. Gun Control Group Gives Obama an 'F'. *The Hill*, January 19. https://thehill.com/homenews/administration/76717-gun-control-group-gives-obama-an-f.

Savage, Charlie. 2018. Trump Administration Imposes Ban on Bump Stocks. *New York Times*, December 18. https://www.nytimes.com/2018/12/18/us/politics/trump-bump-stocks-ban.html.

Spies, Mike. 2019. Secrecy, Self-Dealing, and Greed at the N.R.A. *The New Yorker*, April 17. https://www.newyorker.com/news/news-desk/secrecy-self-dealing-and-greed-at-the-nra.

Spitzer, Robert J. 2015. *Guns Across America: Reconciling Gun Rules and Rights*. New York: Oxford University Press.

———. 2018. The Gun-Safety Issue Is Actually Helping Democrats. *New York Times*, November 12. https://www.nytimes.com/2018/11/12/opinion/gun-control-con gress-mass-shooting.html.

———. 2020. Originalism, Shot Full of Holes: A Primer for Amy Coney Barrett. *New York Daily News*, October 14. https://www.nydailynews.com/opinion/ny-oped-conservatives-hold-your-fire-20201014-f3kmfsuirfgqxnw675gyeq3yxe-story.html.

———. 2021. *The Politics of Gun Control*, 8th ed. New York: Routledge.

Stone, Peter. 2017. NRA Spent More Than Reported During 2016 Election. *Miami Herald*, October 5. https://www.miamiherald.com/news/nation-world/national/article177313031.html.

Van Sant, Will. 2020. NRA Board Member Slams Group's Leadership for Secretive Layoffs. *The Trace*, April 8. https://www.thetrace.org/2020/04/nra-board-mem ber-slams-groups-leadership-for-secretive-layoffs/.

Vitali, Ali. 2018. Trump Hears Emotional Pleas from School Shooting Survivors, Familie. *NBCnews.com*, February 21. https://www.nbcnews.com/politics/white-house/trump-hears-emotional-pleas-school-shooting-survivors-families-n850011.

FURTHER READING

Criminologist Philip J. Cook and political scientist Kristin A. Goss co-author the scrupulous and comprehensive book, *The Gun Debate: What Everyone Needs to Know* (2nd ed., Oxford University Press, 2020). Historian Saul Cornell's book, *A Well-Regulated Militia* (Oxford University Press, 2006) is a widely respected treatment of the historical meaning of the right to bear arms. One-time NRA insider Richard Feldman's book *Ricochet: Confessions of a Gun Lobbyist* is a revealing insider look at the world of the NRA (John Wiley, 2008). The definitive analysis of the pro-gun control movement through the early 2000s is Kristin A. Goss's *Disarmed: The Missing Movement for Gun Control in America* (Princeton University Press, 2006). Pamela Haag's *The Gunning of America* is the most detailed account of the history of the gun industry (Basic Books, 2016). Political scientist Robert J. Spitzer is the author of *The Politics of Gun Control* (8th ed., Routledge, 2021) that examines the gun issue from legal, historical, criminological, political, and policy perspectives. His *Guns across America: Reconciling Gun Rules and Rights* (Oxford University Press, 2015) reframes gun law history and modern disputes including the assault weapons controversy and stand your ground laws. Legal expert Adam Winkler combines detailed gun history and law in *Gunfight: The Battle Over the Right to Bear Arms in America* (W. W. Norton, 2011). Among many available websites that cover gun issues, the Giffords Law Center (Giffords.org/lawcenter, a pro-gun safety group) chronicles court actions on gun cases. The Trace (thetrace.org) provides detailed news coverage of gun activities around the country.

CHAPTER 17

Social Policy and Poverty

Margaret Weir

As the pandemic upended life in America, it exposed the core weaknesses of American social policy: a complex set of work-oriented policies that offers only minimal assistance to those at the bottom of the labor market and still less for the unemployed. When jobs disappeared, workers lost their health insurance and state unemployment systems nearly collapsed under the weight of the demand for assistance. Without access to child care or sick leave, many families struggled to combine work and family life. Poor renters across the country faced eviction. Temporary emergency measures put a floor under Americans but the experience of the pandemic set the stage for a new debate about social policy. It highlighted the racial bias in the system because, even with extended benefits, Black and Latino families suffered the most with the least assistance. The 2020 election, which brought the presidency and both houses of Congress under Democratic control for the first time in a decade, ensured that many of the temporary measures adopted during the pandemic would become the focus of a national debate about updating American social policy. Yet, the longstanding partisan divisions surrounding the federal social role meant that any new initiatives would face strong political headwinds.

As president, Donald Trump departed from the traditional GOP social policy agenda in some ways, although in other respects he doubled down on Republican preferences for austerity, privatization, and benefit restrictions.

M. Weir (✉)
Department of Political Science, Brown University, Providence, RI, USA
e-mail: Margaret_weir@brown.edu

© The Author(s), under exclusive license to Springer Nature
Switzerland AG 2022
G. Peele et al. (eds.), *Developments in American Politics 9*,
https://doi.org/10.1007/978-3-030-89740-6_17

In contrast to Republican leaders, who for decades had warned of the need to overhaul Social Security and Medicare, Trump showed little interest in reforming entitlements, programs whose benefits are guaranteed to all who fit the program criteria. Recognizing how important these policies were to his older political base, Trump made it clear from the start that these programs were off-limits. He failed in his biggest retrenchment initiative: to eliminate the Affordable Care Act, President Obama's signature health reform program. Similarly, although Trump's annual budgets proposed major cuts to social programs that serve the poor, Congress declined to take up these initiatives. As a result, the Trump administration's social policy efforts aimed to use administrative tools to chip away at benefits that assist low-income Americans and disproportionately serve communities of color. These efforts included new regulations that sought to limit access to housing assistance, nutrition programs, and Medicaid, the program that provides health care to low-income people.

This chapter explores the political conflicts over America's work-oriented welfare state during the Trump years and considers how the pandemic set a new menu of policy possibilities for the early days of the Biden administration. It pays particular attention to the ways that Trump broke with the traditional Republican social policy agenda and where he embraced its long-standing agenda of limiting public social provision. The chapter examines the administration's budget proposals for slashing social programs for the poor and explores the efforts to use administrative means to introduce new restrictions on social benefits. It then shows how the pandemic broke the legislative deadlock that characterized Washington after Democrats took over Congress in 2018. Several bipartisan emergency measures greatly expanded the federal social role on a temporary basis. These acts allowed supporters of an expanded federal social role to write some of their priorities into law, albeit on a temporary basis. Many of the temporary measures provided a social policy agenda for the new Biden administration. Biden's first significant act, a major stimulus package that passed without Republican support, included some of these measures. But it went considerably further by providing new benefits designed to cut child poverty in half. The question for the future was which, if any, of these new initiatives would be made permanent. Before we turn to the Trump social policy agenda, we examine the emergence of the United States work-oriented welfare state and discuss what it has meant for workers in the low-wage labor market.

THE DEVELOPMENT OF WORK-ORIENTED SOCIAL POLICY

Welfare states across the developed world rely on keeping most of their workforce employed. As many European welfare states discovered in the 1980s, benefits become too costly and economies falter when a large swath of the workforce is unemployed. American social policy, too, rests on widespread labor market participation. But American social policy stands apart in the way that it links fundamental social benefits to jobs. Most working-age people receive medical care, sick leave, and supplemental pension benefits from their employer, not government. But over the past three decades, fewer employers have offered these benefits or required employees to pay more for them. American social policy also stands out for the lack of support it offers families: without a universal child benefit or funded family leave policies, Americans face daunting challenges in combining work and home lives. Although the federal government assists low-wage workers through the tax system, these workers face high levels of job instability. For those without work, benefits are scarce. America's system of unemployment assistance offers meager payments and excludes most low-wage workers. For the very poor, federal food assistance offers the most reliable source of support. Together, these features of American social policy make the United States an outlier among developed countries in the social risks that it expects individuals to manage on their own (Thelen and Wiedemann 2021).

The passage of the Social Security Act of 1935 jumpstarted the federal social role. Its provisions for old-age pensions (popularly known as Social Security), unemployment insurance, and Aid to Families with Dependent Children (AFDC) marked out new responsibilities for the federal government and the states. But its omissions—no provisions for health care or sick leave—laid the groundwork for a public–private welfare state that relied on private firms to provide these benefits (Klein 2010). Employers added pension benefits designed to supplement the basic public benefits offered through Social Security. The new system of workplace benefits resembled the model of firm-based welfare capitalism pioneered by some businesses in the 1920s. The federal government indirectly supported these programs through a system of tax expenditures that relieved businesses from paying federal taxes on the costs of the benefits they offered workers (Howard 1997).

This system of publicly supported private provision has atrophied over time, creating much bigger holes in the safety net. The loss of unionized jobs, the rising cost of benefits, and the pressure to produce profits have led employers to cut back on employee benefits since the 1980s. In 1998, 67 percent of working-age Americans were covered by employer-sponsored health insurance. By 2018, only 58 percent of workers received such benefits (Rae et al. 2020). Lower wage workers were much less likely to be covered by an employer plan. At the same time, benefits became more expensive and firms required workers to contribute significant sums to cover the cost of work-linked health insurance. Workplace pensions, too, have been eliminated or transformed over the past four decades. Thirty percent of workers have no employer-provided retirement plan (Bureau of Labor Statistics 2018). And in place of defined benefit plans, which guarantee a specified retirement income, most private firms have instituted voluntary defined contribution plans. But these plans have not ensured retirement security since many employees do not or cannot contribute to them. Families often dip into their retirement savings to tide them over during recessions or periods of unemployment. In 2019, half of all working-age families had no retirement savings at all. For those that had savings, only the top earners had sufficient funds for retirement (Morrissey 2019). These shifts in firm-based benefits have greatly increased inequality in access to social support, as high-earning college-educated workers reap the benefits and low-wage workers with less education experience mounting insecurity. Women and minority workers are disproportionately represented among those most exposed to insecurity.

As workplace protections have atrophied so too have social programs for those who are not in the workforce. The Social Security Act included two provisions to support people who are not working. Reflecting concerns that national programs could undermine work incentives, Congress designed them as federal-state programs, giving states considerable leeway in determining eligibility requirements. The first such program, unemployment insurance, is a state-financed and operated program. Designed for manufacturing workers periodically subjected to temporary unemployment, it is a poor fit for contemporary low-wage workers. These workers tend to experience unstable employment and frequent job turnover (Ananat et al. 2021). Because their work histories do not fit the rules governing unemployment insurance and because those rules have become more stringent in many states, low-wage workers are often unable to qualify for unemployment benefits. On average, unemployment insurance provides benefits to 28 percent of unemployed workers (Porter 2021). Those lucky enough to qualify for benefits cannot expect much: the average benefit is less than one-third of former wages. But there is great variation across the states: in Massachusetts the average benefit is $525 a week; in Mississippi it is $213 (Pavosevich 2020). The program provides 26 weeks of benefits, although some states lowered the limit to 20 weeks after the 2008 recession. Efforts to make unemployment insurance more generous routinely run into opposition from employers whose taxes fund the system. Many state governments, anxious to maintain a favorable business climate, resist improvements to the unemployment system because they do not want to raise taxes. During recessions, the federal government has stepped in to assist with temporary measures to extend the time period for which unemployment benefits can be claimed. But states have been reluctant to fund their share of extended benefits, thereby deeply undercutting the program's effectiveness (Porter 2021).

The second policy to support those not working has fared even worse. Once called Aid to Families with Dependent Children, now Temporary Assistance to Needy Families (TANF), the means-tested program was widely identified with African American women and disparaged for providing aid to undeserving recipients (Gilens 2000). Welfare, as the program was commonly known, became a decades-long political target for Republicans and many Democrats. Overhauled in 1996 and rebranded as TANF, the program requires that recipients work and it imposed a five-year lifetime limit on benefits. In 2020, TANF benefits in all states were 60 percent or more below the poverty line;

in some they were substantially lower (Center on Budget and Policy Priorities 2021). The reform left most low-income people without access to cash support, making food assistance through the Supplemental Nutrition Assistance Program (SNAP), the main lifeline for the very poor. After these changes to the welfare system, the numbers of Americans in deep poverty—one half of the poverty level—grew, the vast majority of whom were Black and Latino.

One consequence of deep poverty has been rising levels of homelessness and evictions. In 2016, 2.3 million households faced eviction and over half a million people were homeless (Eviction Lab 2018; HUD Exchange 2020). Centered on homeownership, American housing policy offers meager support for renters. The federal government helps to fund the construction of affordable rental housing through a complex public–private system that falls far short of what is needed. A federal program of vouchers also helps low-income renters secure housing in the private market. But, with limited funding, the program reaches only a quarter of those eligible. The local agencies that administer the program typically have long waiting lists that remain closed for many years at a time (Rosen 2020).

The growing gaps in American social policy have been the target of reforms initiated by Democratic administrations. In his 1992 campaign for president, Bill Clinton appealed for greater support for low-wage workers with the slogan "if you work, you shouldn't be poor." The reforms he proposed sought to update social welfare policies by addressing new insecurities caused by the growth of low-wage work, the shrinkage of firm-based benefits, and the rise of women in the labor force (Weir 1998). Clinton's plan to expand health insurance failed but he did usher through a significant expansion of the Earned Income Tax Credit (EITC), a program that provides cash to low-wage workers with children through the tax system. Clinton also enacted a Family and Medical Leave Program that allowed workers to take leave for medical reasons, childbirth, or to care for family members. The program represented a step toward recognizing the challenges of combining work and family, however the benefit has mainly assisted middle-class families—those in the median income range who do not qualify for means-tested programs—because it provided no funding for those taking leave. The Obama administration's Affordable Care Act (ACA) marked another effort to update the social policy system by making health care widely available regardless of employment status. With its provisions for expanding Medicaid and subsidies to help lower income people purchase private insurance on the new health insurance exchanges, the ACA succeeded in reducing the ranks of the uninsured by nearly 8 percentage points (Tolbert et al. 2020).

Even with these reforms, the United States remained an outlier compared to other high-income countries. In 2019, the OECD calculated that 17.8 percent of Americans were in poverty and 23.1 percent of American children were poor. These poverty rates were comparable to those in Latvia and Costa Rica and much higher than in other European countries. In Western Europe, Greece had the highest poverty rate at 12.1 percent, while the rate was 11.1

in the United Kingdom, and only 6.5 percent in Finland (OECD 2019). As a result of high poverty rates, Americans are more likely to be food insecure—meaning they lack access to sufficient affordable and nutritious food—than residents of other developed countries. Nearly 15 percent of Americans experience food insecurity, compared to 7.7 percent of Canadians, and 5.8 percent of the population in the older EU member countries (Gentilini 2013). Not surprisingly, Americans were also much more likely to rely on food banks than those in Western Europe.

On the eve of the Trump presidency, Democrats and Republicans viewed the social welfare system through very different lenses. Democrats pointed to poverty and rising need, arguing that social policies needed critical updates and expansions. Congressional Republicans, by contrast, had long opposed programs that could result in tax increases and were especially anxious to jettison the Affordable Care Act, which they feared could result in political credit to the Democrats.

Social Policies for the Elderly and Obamacare

The Trump administration's lack of concern with fiscal discipline departed from traditional Republican Party social policy orthodoxy. In contrast to congressional Republicans, Trump displayed little interest in entitlement reforms that threatened higher taxes and lower benefits for Social Security and Medicare recipients. On the other hand, Trump fully embraced the long Republican quest to eliminate Obama's Affordable Care Act and replace it with an unspecified alternative. As these diverse issue positions suggest, Trump's approach to social policy was intensely political and highly transactional. He protected policies that would redound to his credit and sought cuts in programs when it would not harm him politically and might even help.

As a candidate, Donald Trump vowed to keep Social Security and Medicare, the two core programs that serve the elderly, off the chopping block. "I will do everything within my power not to touch Social Security, to leave it the way it is," he announced on the campaign trail in 2016 (Eisenberg 2016). Republicans and Democrats had long struggled to agree on a strategy that would ensure the future fiscal viability of these programs. Both programs face funding shortfalls: Social Security is projected to be unable to pay full benefits by 2035, while Medicare's hospital insurance program faces a funding shortage as soon as 2026 (Social Security Administration 2020). Bipartisan entitlement reform commissions had made little headway since 1983 when the two parties had agreed on a major reform. But since then, neither side wanted to compromise. Republicans advocated benefit cuts and privatization, whereas most Democrats sought to avoid cuts and instead favored increasing the payroll taxes that fund these programs. Indeed, citing the changes to firm-based retirement plans, many Democrats had begun to argue in favor of expansions to Social Security.

In late 2017, House Speaker Paul Ryan declared his intention to push for a strongly partisan approach to entitlement reform, announcing that Republicans intended to pursue cuts in Social Security, Medicare, and Medicaid in order to get the national debt under control (Weixel 2017). A prominent champion of entitlement reform throughout his congressional career, Ryan saw his opportunity to act now that Republicans controlled both houses of Congress and the presidency. The major conservative Washington think tanks, including the Heritage Foundation and the American Enterprise Institute (AEI), had long promoted privatization as a way to reduce entitlement spending. But Speaker Ryan could not win Trump's support or the backing of Republican moderates. Senate Republican leader Mitch McConnell had little interest in pushing for entitlement reform that relied only on Republican support. Wary of unpopular cuts in advance of the 2018 elections, Republican moderates ensured that the conservative wing of the party made no progress on its proposed cuts. A frustrated Ryan retired from Congress in 2018 without having achieved entitlement reform but having enacted a major tax overhaul that greatly expanded the federal deficit. When Democrats regained control of the House after the 2018 elections, entitlement reform was effectively dead. The issue surfaced again briefly in early 2020, when President Trump expressed a willingness to "look at entitlement reform" in his next term. Faced with immediate pushback from Democrats, he quickly abandoned the idea (Haberman and Rappeport 2020).

When it came to the Affordable Care Act, Obama's signature health reform, President Trump was fully on board with the Republican effort to abolish the program. Since its passage in 2010, Republicans had introduced a number of bills to end the program. With President Trump behind them, congressional Republicans had high hopes that they would now succeed. Unusually for a major benefits program, the ACA had failed to win broad support in the years after its passage. A botched rollout and a concerted Republican campaign against it kept public approval ratings under fifty percent. Even though the program began to operate more smoothly and win additional support, most Republicans continued to oppose it. When the final showdown in Congress came in 2017, Republicans did not have the votes to overturn it. Three Republican Senators opposed the bill to replace the ACA with a slimmed down program that would have increased the number of uninsured. Senator John McCain (R. AZ), already suffering from the brain cancer that would soon kill him, cast the deciding vote, famously gesturing a thumbs down to express his opposition to the bill (Pear and Kaplan 2017).

The legislative battle over Obamacare repeal had ended but Republican opponents continued to pursue judicial and administrative strategies in their attempts to dismantle the law. The Trump administration issued new rules that made it harder to sign up for the insurance plans and allowed states to introduce less comprehensive plans. In 2019, a federal appeals court ruled that the requirement to purchase health insurance, known as the individual mandate and already undermined by congressional action in 2017 to eliminate fines, was unconstitutional. But concerns that these measures would lead to the ACA's unravelling proved unfounded. Although enrollments declined somewhat and the number of uninsured rose slightly, the shifts were not nearly as dramatic as the law's supporters feared (Keith 2020).

MEANS-TESTED BENEFITS FOR THE POOR AND MINORITIES

In contrast to his reluctance to tamper with programs that benefited the middle class and the elderly, Trump actively sought to pare back the means-tested programs that serve low-income people, including SNAP benefits, housing, and Medicaid. Enhancing work requirements was one of his central strategies. In 2018, the White House issued an Executive Order instructing cabinet departments to review every means-tested program to consider whether work requirements could be added, increased, or better enforced (Executive Office of the President 2018). In addition to promoting work requirements, the President's annual budget proposals called for deep cuts to programs that serve the poor.

Along with many congressional Republicans, Trump embraced the idea that recipients of means-tested benefits represented a drag on the economy. Echoing arguments long deployed by conservative Republicans, he questioned their deservingness and stoked resentment against them. In a 2017 speech announcing his support for cutting social assistance to the poor, Trump proclaimed that "the person who is not working at all and has no intention of working at all is making more money and doing better than the person that's working his [or her] ass off" (Stein 2017). Congressional Republicans also targeted these programs for budgetary reasons. With Social Security and Medicare off-limits, Republicans looked to achieve budget savings. Heading into 2018, having just enacted a major tax overhaul that would dramatically increase the budget deficit, programs that served the poor represented the best target for reducing spending.

SNAP benefits presented a priority target for adding work requirements. First created in 1964 under the name Food Stamps, the program was rebranded as SNAP in 2008 to emphasize its role in nutrition and to combat the stigma that surrounded the means-tested program. The number of house-holds receiving SNAP benefits shot up during the recession that started in 2008. As the only federal entitlement program available to low-income Americans, SNAP is the federal government's most extensive anti-poverty tool. Estimates show that SNAP lifted 3.4 million families out of poverty in 2017 and was particularly important for families in deep poverty, who accounted for half the benefits received (Sherman 2017).

Even before Trump's election, congressional Republicans had expressed concern that the number of SNAP recipients was too high. With more than 40 million beneficiaries in 2018, the caseload had not declined substantially even though the recession had officially ended years earlier. In 2017, congressional Republicans, including House Speaker Ryan, proposed ramping up work requirements for food stamps as a way to bring down the rolls (Stein

2017). Work requirements represented a potentially popular way to achieve cuts since most Americans support the idea of work. Major conservative think tanks, including the Heritage Foundation, backed work requirements as the key to self-sufficiency. When Congress failed to act, the Department of Agriculture, which administers SNAP, prepared a new rule that tightened existing work requirements for able-bodied recipients without children in the home. Scheduled to go into effect in April 2020, the new rule was projected to eliminate 700,000 from the SNAP rolls (Fadulu 2020).

Medicaid, the program that provides health care to low-income people, also imposed work requirements in some states for the first time. Because the program is jointly administered by the federal government and the states, states must get federal permission to experiment with major changes. Although some states governed by Republicans had earlier considered the idea of making work a requirement of access to Medicaid, the Obama administration had refused permission. The Trump administration granted waivers for ten states to impose work requirements on Medicaid recipients. Because these plans were immediately challenged with lawsuits, only one state, Arkansas, actually implemented work requirements. In the short time before a federal court halted the Arkansas program, an estimated 18,000 people had lost their health care (Goodnough 2020). The Department of Housing and Urban Development (HUD) also proposed new work requirements for federal housing programs but they were never finalized.

Curtailing immigration and deporting unauthorized immigrants occupied a central place in President Trump's domestic agenda. The administration pursued its immigration goals in the domain of social policy by introducing a new "public charge" rule in 2019. The new rule allowed immigration authorities to bar entry to immigrants who might use noncash social welfare programs, including medical care and nutrition programs such as SNAP benefits, from gaining permanent legal status. Public charge rules have been a feature of American immigration policy since the late nineteenth century's massive wave of European immigration; but those rules were mainly applied to those likely to need institutionalization or cash assistance, not noncash benefits. The new rule set off a wave of fear and misinformation in the immigrant community because many people live in mixed status families, where one or more parents is unauthorized but the children are American citizens. Although unauthorized immigrants qualify only for two social benefits—emergency medical care and public education—their American children qualify for a variety of noncash benefits such as SNAP and medical care. One study estimated that 260,000 children lost health insurance as anxious parents, fearing the impact on their applications for permanent residence, withdrew them from Medicaid coverage (Barofsky et al. 2020). The rule immediately met with legal challenges but was allowed to remain in effect while the challenges were being considered.

With Republicans focused on securing tax cuts and repealing the ACA in their first two years and the legislative stalemate after Democrats took back the House of Representatives in 2019, most of the deep cuts that Trump proposed failed to pass. And, with the exception of Medicaid work requirements actually implemented by only one state, the effort to reduce program participation by imposing additional work requirements remained on hold due to legal challenges.

POLICIES TO SUPPORT FAMILIES AND CHILDREN

Policies designed to support children and families have, on occasion, won bipartisan support. Since 1997, the Child Tax Credit (CTC) has offered a tax credit to families with children. Initially sponsored by Republicans aiming to support two-parent families with a nonworking spouse, the program offers families a tax credit for each child. Income limits were set high, making the program available to middle-class families. The program grew quickly and soon cost more than the Earned Income Tax Credit and TANF (Howard 2008). However, the bulk of the spending went to middle-class families, not families with children in poverty. Benefits to low-income families were limited by program criteria that disregarded the first $3000 of earnings, restricted the "refundable" portion (the amount greater than taxes paid) to $1000, and provided no benefits to families without earned income. The earnings requirements meant that low-income families did not qualify for the full $2000 benefit.

As part of the 2017 tax overhaul, Democrats and Republicans compromised on reforms that extended the benefits higher up the income ladder but also made the program more favorable to the poor by lowering the income threshold to $2500 and increasing the refundable portion of the tax from $1000 to $1400 (Matthews 2019). In 2020, the Child Tax Credit cost the federal government $117.6 billion compared to $68.3 billion for the Earned Income Tax Credit (U.S. Congress, Joint Committee on Taxation 2020). But because of the limits on assisting families with low-income or no income, the bulk of its benefits went to middle-income families: in 2020 about 40 percent of the benefit went to families making over $100,000 a year and only 15 percent to families making less than $15,000 a year. This pattern had racial correlates: in 2020 three quarters of White and Asian families received the full credit, whereas only half of Black and Latino families did (Wessel 2021).

The problem of child poverty had attracted considerable concern among congressional Democrats and research interest since the 1996 welfare reform. Much of that research culminated in a congressionally funded report on child poverty from the National Academies of Sciences, Engineering and Medicine in 2019. The 600-page report entitled *A Roadmap to Reducing Child Poverty* drew on a wealth of evidence-based research to recommend major changes in policies. Some recommendations called for expansions of existing work-oriented benefits, such as the Earned Income Tax Credit. Others departed from current policy by supporting payments to families with children regardless of work status. Democratic congressional members embraced the latter recommendation with the introduction of the American Family Act in 2019. The proposed legislation increased the annual benefit per child from $2000 to $3000 and it made the tax benefit fully refundable, meaning that even families with no income or very low income would receive the full benefit. Instead of paying benefits once a year, as did the child tax credit and the EITC, it called for monthly payments as a way to stabilize the budgets of poor households (Matthews 2019). The act drew broad support among House and Senate Democrats but, although there was some Republican interest in the Senate, it was not enough to forge a compromise.

COVID-19 AND EMERGENCY SOCIAL POLICY

The pandemic signaled an abrupt end to politics as usual. With the $2.2 trillion CARES Act (Coronavirus Aid, Relief and Economic Security Act), passed in March 2020, several smaller measures to support businesses and families, and another large spending package approved in December 2020, Congress pumped nearly $3.4 trillion into the economy to aid recovery and assist people thrown out of work by the pandemic. The legislation contained a wide variety of programs, many of them directed at remedying holes in the safety net that Democrats had long sought to address.

As the economy ground to a halt, Congress concentrated on getting cash into the hands of people who needed it. The centerpiece of the CARES Act was a $1200 check for individuals earning under $75,000 and $2400 for two-parent families making less than $150,000, as well as $500 per child. The legislation also provided substantial assistance to shore up unemployment insurance as official jobless rates rose from 3.8 percent just before the pandemic to a high of 14.4 percent. Due to the difficulties in counting the rapid shifts in employment, some estimates suggested that the true rate of unemployment might have been closer to 25 percent (Kochhar 2020). The CARES Act tackled the problem of low benefit levels by adding an additional $600 a month to unemployment insurance benefits. It also extended payments for an additional 13 weeks and expanded eligibility to include gig workers not normally eligible for the program. Even so, the deluge of applications for unemployment insurance made the weakness of the state-run systems glaringly apparent. Applicants waited for months as states struggled with administrative problems, including ancient IT systems unable to keep up with demand and new systems designed to err on the side of detecting fraud, not speeding up payments (Porter 2021).

In addition to these cash payments, Congress enacted measures that advocates for families and children had long supported. As the pandemic hit, Congress approved legislation that required employers with fewer than 500 employees to provide paid sick leave for workers who became ill, had to quarantine, or needed to care for children who were out of school due to the pandemic. It also provided additional funds to ensure that SNAP could meet new demand. Emergency waivers allowed states to expand monthly benefits for many SNAP recipients and work requirements were suspended. Congress also banned evictions in federally subsidized housing, protecting 28–45 percent of all rental households (Acosta et al. 2020).

This legislation represented a remarkable departure from the years of social policy inaction or retrenchment. Several studies showed that poverty did not increase in the early months of the pandemic and it may, in fact, have decreased (DeParle 2020). But the emergency measures were temporary, with the provisions set to expire after four months. Moreover, the Trump administration made several rulings that restricted benefits during the pandemic. It denied additional emergency SNAP benefits to those already receiving the maximum payment, meaning that 40 percent of recipients saw no increase in food assistance. Several states took the administration to court to challenge the restriction but did not succeed in boosting benefits for the poorest recipients (Larkin 2021). The federal government also refused to reopen the federal health insurance exchanges to allow people to sign up for insurance as they lost their job and their health insurance with it. As these measures suggest, the administration was wary of pandemic initiatives that could set the stage for expanded benefits in the future.

As the initial benefits began to expire, some parts of the administration and the Democratic House sought to renew them. When the initial eviction ban was about to lapse, the Centers for Disease Control (CDC) stepped in to impose a broad eviction moratorium. The Democratic House passed a $2.2 trillion package that extended many of the provisions in the original emergency legislation and introduced some more generous items. But the Republican Senate was unenthusiastic about another big package. Congress finally agreed on a second much smaller bill in the waning days of the Trump administration. The bipartisan legislation offered a cash payment of $600 to individuals, extended unemployment insurance benefits for an additional four months, and added $300 to the payments; it boosted food aid, and provided a one-month eviction moratorium.

Conclusion: Biden's Social Policy Agenda

Biden's 2020 election and the surprising victory of Democrats in both houses of Congress gave Democrats full control of the federal government for the first time in a decade. But with the Senate tied (with the vice president serving as tiebreaker) and a mere nine vote advantage in the House, Democrats did not have much room for intraparty disagreement. Democratic unity can never be assumed and divisions between progressives and moderates had intensified in the wake of the close election. Even so, there was plenty of room for the party to coalesce around an expanded public social role. Although Biden campaigned as a moderate, his agenda marked a major shift away from Republican preferences for reduced benefits, privatization, and stiffer work requirements. Congressional Democrats had a robust inventory of social policy priorities. Many wanted to make permanent some of the temporary provisions in the pandemic legislation, including paid family and medical leave, and they wanted more generous unemployment benefits. Democrats also hoped to overhaul the Child Tax Credit by expanding benefits to the poor and eliminating the requirement for earned income. How comprehensive social policy reform would be ultimately depended on where Democrats could forge agreement and how fast they could move in advance of the 2022 elections.

During Biden's first months in office, Democrats took initial steps toward realizing many of their social policy aspirations. With the president's executive orders and congressional approval of the $1.9 trillion American Rescue Plan in March 2021, not only did Democrats renew earlier emergency social support but they also reversed some of the Trump administration's restrictions on benefits. The online portals that allow people to sign up for health insurance under the Affordable Care Act were reopened and subsidies for purchasing insurance were increased significantly. The legislation also offered cash payments. All Americans with an income below $75,000 a year received one-time $1400 checks, and an additional $1400 for each child. And most generously, the Child Tax Credit increased benefits to $3000 each year per child and $3600 for each child under 6 years of age. The requirement that beneficiaries have earned income was suspended (U.S. Treasury 2021). Estimates showed that the key measures in the American Rescue Plan would cut poverty by 5 percentage points in 2021, dropping from a projected 13.7 percent to 8.7 percent. The benefits would be especially helpful to minorities: the poverty rate for Black Americans was projected to decrease by 42 percent, by 39 percent for Hispanics, and by 34 percent for non-Hispanic whites. At the same time, differences across the groups would decline (Wheaton et al. 2021). Even so, a projected 10.5 percent of Black Americans and 13.3 percent of Hispanics would remain poor compared to 6.4 percent of non-Hispanic whites.

Given his reputation as a moderate, President Biden surprised many with his decision to "go big" on the COVID relief package, even if it meant losing Republican support. As vice president during the Obama administration, Biden had witnessed the political cost of waiting to secure bipartisan agreement. In 2009, during the Great Recession, Democrats had greatly reduced the size of their economic rescue package in order to win Republican support. In retrospect, many Democrats felt that too small a package had dampened the economic recovery and set them up for electoral defeat in the 2010 elections. The Biden administration was determined not to make the same mistake. In another shift, in 2021, Democrats paid little heed to arguments that their policies would increase the federal deficit. This new approach marked a big change from earlier Democratic administrations, which, since Bill Clinton's presidency, had felt obliged to heed admonitions to keep deficits under control and reduce the national debt. Not only did Democrats believe that the emergency caused by the pandemic warranted expanding the deficit, they were also well aware that they had inherited large deficits caused by the

Republican 2017 tax cut. They seemed determined not to let new concerns about deficits or debt stand in their way.

The long-term impact of these measures remained in doubt because the expansive benefits in the American Rescue Plan were all set to expire in a year. Democrats hoped to make some of the key measures permanent, notably, the expanded Child Tax Credit. Unlike countries with comparable wealth, the United States had never enacted a child benefit program. Many countries have had such programs for decades and several have launched major anti-poverty initiatives in recent decades. Britain took steps that cut child poverty in half during the first decade of the 2000s; Canada enacted a very generous set of anti-poverty initiatives in 2019 (Waldfogel 2010; Employment and Social Development 2019). Even before the ink was dry on Biden's early executive orders, House Democrats introduced legislation to make the expanded credit, delivered in monthly payments, permanent. Many Democrats in the Senate expressed approval but whether all Democrats would support the measure remained uncertain. The prospects for winning Republican support seemed dim. Most opposed lifting the work requirement. As Marco Rubio, one of the main Republican champions of the pre-pandemic Child Tax Credit put it, "An essential part of being pro-family is being pro-work" (Faler 2021). Even so, once in place, changes in the tax code are hard to roll back. Because the credit benefits both middle class and poorer families, it was likely to garner broad public support and provoke a high-stakes political debate.

The Biden administration also proposed ambitious social programs soon after Congress enacted the American Rescue Plan. The American Jobs Act and the American Families Plan called for major new social spending, including measures to increase the pay of workers who provide long-term care as well as substantial increases to federal spending for child care, pre-kindergarten, and paid family leave. To pay for these plans, the administration proposed raising taxes on corporations and wealthy individuals. It remained uncertain if Congress would agree on even watered down versions of these bold proposals.

If none of the emergency measures was to be made permanent and if none of the new legislation was enacted, poverty was projected to grow substantially in 2022, as income and housing costs continued to pose challenges for many Americans. The United States entered the pandemic period with the paradox of low unemployment and high poverty compared to other rich countries. Even as the economy began to recover, studies suggested that many jobs would not return. The recovery that began after the first few months of the pandemic benefited higher income workers and left lower wage workers behind. Surveys showed that four in ten reported that someone in their household had lost their job or experienced reduced wages (Horowitz et al. 2021). Housing, too, caused concern for the future. One study showed that by January 2021, 9.4 million renter households owed an average of $5586 in back rent and that many had run up substantial credit card debt to pay the rent during the pandemic (Khouri 2021). Studies projected that it would take many households years to recover from the financial instability caused by the pandemic.

The social policy priorities of Republicans and Democrats have grown further apart over the past four decades. The two parties defend increasingly divergent views about the purposes of social policy and about the proper scope of social programs. Republicans have been centrally concerned to avoid dependency, promote privatization, and limit social spending. With the exception of making Social Security and Medicare off-limits, Trump shared these priorities and sought to advance them. His successes remained limited after the Democrats won the House in 2018 and the pandemic required massive government spending. Democrats, by contrast, view social policy as in need of updating. They prioritize improvements in the economic security of low-wage workers with precarious employment and no benefits. Democrats have also argued in favor of more generous policies to help lift families and children out of poverty. They are likely to make some strides toward their goals but how far they will succeed depends on their ability to remain united and to hold onto power after the 2022 elections.

REFERENCES

Acosta, S., A. Bailey, and P. Bailey. 2020. *Extend CARES Act Eviction Moratorium, Combine With Rental Assistance to Promote Housing Stability*. Center on Budget and Policy Priorities. July 27. Available at: www.cbpp.org/research/housing/ext end-cares-act-eviction-moratorium-combine-with-rental-assistance-to-promote.

Ananat, E., A. Gassman-Pines, and Y. Truskinofsky. 2021. Increasing Instability and Uncertainty Among Low Wage Workers. In *Who Gets What? The New Politics of Insecurity*, ed. F. Rosenbluth and M. Weir. Cambridge: Cambridge University Press.

Barofsky, J., A. Vargas, D. Rodriguez, and A. Barrows. 2020. Spreading Fear: The Announcement of the Public Charge Rule Reduced Enrollment in Child-Safety Net Programs. *Health Affairs* 39 (10): 1752–1761.

Bureau of Labor Statistics 2018. *National Compensation Survey: Employee Benefits in the United States*. Bulletin 2789, September. Available at: https://www.bls.gov/ ncs/ebs/benefits/2018/employee-benefits-in-the-united-states-march-2018.pdf.

Center on Budget and Policy Priorities. 2021. Chartbook: Temporary Assistance for Needy Families. February 2. Available at https://www.cbpp.org/research/family-income-support/temporary-assistance-for-needy-families-0.

DeParle, J. 2020. Vast Federal Aid Has Capped Rise in Poverty, Studies Find. *New York Times*, June 21.

Eisenberg, R. 2016. Social Security: Where Clinton And Trump Stand. *Forbes*, August 8.

Employment and Social Development Canada. 2019. Canada's Poverty Reduction Strategy, An Update 2019. Available at: www.canada.ca/en/employment-social-dev elopment/programs/results/poverty-reduction.html.

Eviction Lab. 2018. *National Estimates: Eviction in America*. Princeton University, May 11. Available at: https://evictionlab.org/national-estimates/.

Executive Office of the President. 2018. *Reducing Poverty in America by Promoting Opportunity and Economic Mobility*. Federal Register. 13 April. Available at: https://www.federalregister.gov/documents/2018/04/13/2018-07874/reducing-poverty-in-america-by-promoting-opportunity-and-economic-mobility.

Fadulu, Lola. 2020. Cities Prepare for the Worst as Trump's Food Stamp Cuts Near. *New York Times*, January 20.

Faler, B. 2021. Democrats' Plan To Lift Work Requirement Could Complicate Child Poverty Plan. *Politico*, February 8.

Gentilini, U. 2013. Banking on Food: The State of Food Banks in High-income Countries. IDS Working Paper 415, Institute of Development Studies. Available at: https://opendocs.ids.ac.uk/opendocs/bitstream/handle/20.500.12413/2323/Wp415.pdf?sequence=1&isAllowed=y.

Gilens, M. 2000. *Why Americans Hate Welfare: Race, Media and the Politics of Anti-Poverty Policy*. Chicago: University of Chicago Press.

Goodnough, A. 2020. Appeals Court Rejects Trump Medicaid Work Requirements in Arkansas. *New York Times*, February 14.

Haberman, M., and A. Rappeport. 2020. Trump Tries to Walk Back Entitlement Comments as Democrats Pounce. *New York Times*, January 23.

Horowitz, J., A. Brown, and R. Minkin. 2021. *A Year Into the Pandemic, Long-Term Financial Impact Weighs Heavily on Many Americans*. Pew Research Center. March 5. Available at: https://www.pewresearch.org/social-trends/2021/03/05/a-year-into-the-pandemic-long-term-financial-impact-weighs-heavily-on-many-americans/.

Howard, C. 1997. *The Hidden Welfare State: Tax Expenditures and Social Policy in the United States*. Princeton: Princeton University Press.

———. 2008. *The Welfare State Nobody Knows: Debunking Myths about US Social Policy*. Princeton: Princeton University Press.

HUD Exchange. 2020. 2019 AHAR: Part 1—PIT Estimates of Homelessness in the U.S. Available at: https://www.hudexchange.info/resource/5948/2019-ahar-part-1-pit-estimates-of-homelessness-in-the-us/.

Keith, K. 2020. Final Marketplace Enrollment Data for 2020. *Health Affairs*, April 2. Available at: www.healthaffairs.org/do/10.1377/hblog20200402.109653/full/.

Klein, J. 2010. *For All These Rights: Business, Labor, and the Shaping of America's Public-Private Welfare State*. Princeton: Princeton University Press.

Kochhar, R. 2020. *Unemployment Rose Higher in Three Months of COVID-19 Than it Did in Two Years of The Great Recession*. Pew Research Center, June 1. Available at: www.pewresearch.org/fact-tank/2020/06/11/unemployment-rose-higher-in-three-months-of-covid-19-than-it-did-in-two-years-of-the-great-recession/.

Khouri, A. 2021. Depleted Savings, Ruined Credit: What Happens When All The Rent Comes Due? *Los Angeles Times*, February 2.

Larkin, E. 2021. *Feds Defend Denial of Covid Benefits to Poorest of the Poor*. Courthouse News Service. January 5. Available at: www.courthousenews.com/feds-defend-denial-of-covid-benefits-to-poorest-of-the-poor/.

Matthews, D. 2019. Democrats Have United Around a Plan to Dramatically Cut Child Poverty. *Vox*, May 2. Available at: www.vox.com/future-perfect/2019/3/6/18249290/child-poverty-american-family-act-sherrod-brown-michael-bennet.

Morrissey, M. 2019. *The State of American Retirement Savings*. Economic Policy Institute, December 10. Available at: https://www.epi.org/publication/the-state-of-american-retirement-savings/.

OECD. 2019. Poverty Rate. Available at: https://data.oecd.org/inequality/poverty-rate.htm

Pavosevich, R. 2020. *Unemployment Insurance: Comparison of State Benefit Adequacy and Recipiency 2019*. National Academy of Social Insurance. April. Available at: https://www.nasi.org/sites/default/files/BAR2019_April162020.pdf.

Pear, R., and T. Kaplan 2017. Senate Rejects Slimmed-Down Obamacare Repeal as McCain Votes No. *New York Times*, July 27.

Porter. E. 2021. How the American Unemployment System Failed. *New York Times*, January 21.

Rae, M., D. McDermott, L. Levitt, and G. Claxton. 2020. *Long-Term Trends in Employer-Based Coverage*. Kaiser Family Foundation. Available at: https://www.healthsystemtracker.org/brief/long-term-trends-in-employer-based-coverage/.

Rosen, E. 2020. *The Voucher Promise: "Section 8"and the Fate of an American Neighborhood*. Princeton NJ: Princeton University Press.

Sherman, A. 2017. *Census: Programs Eyed for Cuts Keep Millions from Poverty*. Center on Budget and Policy Priorities. September 12. Available at: www.cbpp.org/blog/census-programs-eyed-for-cuts-keep-millions-from-poverty.

Social Security Administration. 2020. A Summary of the 2020 Annual Reports. Available at https://www.ssa.gov/oact/trsum/.

Stein, J. 2017. Republican Officials Say Targeting Welfare Programs Will Help Spur Economic Growth. *Washington Post*, December 6.

Thelen, K. and A. Wiedemann. 2021. The Anxiety of Precarity: The United States in Comparative Perspective. In *Who Gets What? The New Politics of Insecurity*, ed. F. Rosenbluth and M. Weir. Cambridge: Cambridge University Press.

Tolbert, J., K. Orgera, and A. Damico. 2020. Key Facts About the Uninsured Population. Kaiser Family Foundation. Available at: https://www.kff.org/uninsured/issue-brief/key-facts-about-the-uninsured-population/:~:text=However,%20beginning%20in%202017,%20the,2016%20to%2010.9%%20in%202019.

U.S. Congress Joint Committee on Taxation 2020. Estimates of Federal Tax Expenditures for Fiscal Years 2020–2024. November 5. Available at: www.jct.gov/publications/2020/jcx-23-20/.

U.S. Treasury. 2021. Fact Sheet: The American Rescue Plan Will Deliver Immediate Economic Relief to Families. March 18. Available at: http://home.treasury.gov/news/featured-stories/fact-sheet-the-american-rescue-plan-will-deliver-immediate-economic-relief-to-families.

Waldfogel, J. 2010. *Britain's War on Poverty*. New York: Russell Sage Foundation.

Weir, M., ed. 1998. *The Social Divide: Political Parties and the Future of Activist Government*. Washington, DC: Brookings Institution Press.

Weixel, N. 2017. Ryan Eyes Push for 'Entitlement Reform' in 2018. *The Hill*, December 6.

Wessel, D. 2021. *What Is the Child Tax Credit? And How Much of It Is Refundable?* The Hutchings Center on Fiscal and Monetary Policy, Brookings Institution. Available at: https://www.brookings.edu/blog/up-front/2021/01/22/what-is-the-child-tax-credit-and-how-much-of-it-is-refundable/.

Wheaton, L., S. Minton, L. Giannarelli, K. Dwyer. 2021. *Poverty Projections: Assessing Four American Rescue Plan Policies*. Urban Institute, March 11. Available at: www.urban.org/research/publication/2021-poverty-projections-assessing-four-american-rescue-plan-policies.

FURTHER READING

An excellent overview of the development and distinctive contours of American social policy is provided in *The Oxford Handbook of US Social Policy* edited by Daniel Béland, Christopher Howard, and Kimberley Morgan (New York: Oxford University Press 2015). For an insightful analysis showing how changes in jobs and work-related benefits have made American access to health care and retirement security more tenuous, see Jacob S. Hacker (2019), *The Great Risk Shift: The New Economic Insecurity and the Decline of the American Dream* (New York: Oxford University Press). The rise of deep poverty after the 1996 welfare reform legislation is examined in Katherine J. Edin and H. Luke Shaefer's (2015) *$2.00 a Day: Living on Almost Nothing in America* (New York: Houghton Mifflin Harcourt).

The intersection of race, poverty, and social policy has long drawn the attention of scholars. An excellent account of how African Americans were left out of New Deal social policy can be found in Robert Lieberman's (2001) *Shifting the Colorline: Race and The American Welfare State* (Cambridge: Harvard University Press). Public policy debates about social policy routinely raise questions about who is deserving of benefits. Martin Gilens (2000) provides an eye-opening study showing how race and deservingness are intertwined in American public opinion in *Why Americans Hate Welfare: Race, Media and the Politics of Anti-Poverty Policy* (Chicago: University of Chicago Press). Studies have also examined the distinctive ways that social policy benefits are delivered in the United States, with the middle class benefitting especially from tax expenditure policies and the poor receiving direct benefits. An incisive study examining the political repercussions of these arrangements can be found in Susanne Mettler's (2011) *The Submerged State: How Invisible Government Policies Undermine American Democracy* (Chicago: University of Chicago Press).

For timely analyses of a broad range of social policies The Center on Budget and Policy Priorities is the go-to source (https://www.cbpp.org). The National Academy of Social Insurance (https://www.nasi.org) offers excellent policy briefs analyzing social insurance policies, including Social Security, Medicare, Unemployment Insurance, and Disability policies. Both of these organizations tend to support more generous social policies. The Brookings Institution is a good source for in-depth analysis of economic developments and public policies. For conservative perspectives that call for more work-oriented policies and a smaller government role see The Heritage Foundation (https://www.heritage.org) and the American Enterprise Institute (https://www.aei.org).

CHAPTER 18

Foreign and Security Policy

Trevor McCrisken

Two decades after the September 11, 2001 terrorist attacks, and three decades after the end of the Cold War, the US may have reached another crossroads in its foreign and security policy. In 1989–1991, the fall of the Berlin Wall and the collapse of the Soviet Union signaled the end of the central organizing principles that had guided US foreign policy for almost half a century. The debate over what direction the US should then take appeared to be answered finally by the violence of '9/11' and the subsequent 'war on terror.' The 'new' security threat posed by non-state terrorist organizations such as al Qaeda was elevated to the center of Washington's narratives of existential threat. Gradually, over the last 20 years, that threat appears to have diminished.

Presidents Obama, Trump, and now Biden have attempted, with varying levels of success, to extract the US from the 'forever wars' that were started in response to '9/11' and to expand the focus of US foreign policy. The pendulum swings of partisan domestic politics have had a significant impact on the differing approaches to foreign policy, between the more multilateralist and progressive leadership of Democratic administrations to the more unilateral and traditional strategies of Republicans. Great power rivalries have returned to the core of US concerns as the perceived threats from China and Russia grow. Yet the events of 2020–2021 made clear to policymakers in both US political parties that they ignore or downplay at their peril the

T. McCrisken (✉)
Department of Politics and International Studies, University of Warwick, Coventry, UK
e-mail: trevor.mccrisken@warwick.ac.uk

© The Author(s), under exclusive license to Springer Nature Switzerland AG 2022
G. Peele et al. (eds.), *Developments in American Politics 9*,
https://doi.org/10.1007/978-3-030-89740-6_18

significance of transnational threats such as pandemics and climate change, as well as internal threats to security and stability such as racial injustice and domestic violent extremism. Policymakers will be wary of dropping their guard against the traditional security threats they perceive in the strategic ambitions of Moscow and Beijing, as well as Pyongyang and Tehran. Yet the challenges of the first quarter of the twenty-first century, both to global peace and stability and to the more specific interests of the US, suggest the need for transformative thinking in foreign and security policy if it is to develop and adapt effectively.

This chapter will give a brief overview of the approaches to foreign policy adopted by successive US administrations since the end of the Cold War. In particular, it will consider whether President Trump's unorthodox personal approach undermined his limited foreign policy achievements and whether his freedom to maneuvre in the international sphere was diminished by his domestic political vulnerabilities, including his handling of Covid-19. It will also address the question of whether Trump's attempts to radically shake-up US foreign policy largely failed, or whether his legacy will long be imprinted on policymaking in ways that will be difficult for President Biden to unpick. Specific analysis will be offered of the 'forever wars' and the use of military force, relations with Iran, China, and Russia, and the growing challenges from 'non-traditional' security threats such as climate change, pandemics, and domestic racial injustice. The chapter will consider whether US foreign and security policy can be taken in new, transformative directions.

From Cold War to Trump, Via the War on Terror

The end of the Cold War raised fundamental questions for US foreign policymakers. For decades, the USSR had been perceived as an existential enemy and the core US objective was preventing the global spread of communism. The sudden demise of this threat was celebrated by some scholars as the triumph of liberal democratic capitalism (Fukuyama 1992) and others as establishing the 'unipolar moment' with the US as the world's hegemon (Krauthammer 1990). However, fears of uncertainty and new emergent threats haunted the thinking of other analysts and policymakers unsure of what the emphasis should now be in US policy, and how Washington should respond to the fledgling post-Cold War world (Hoffmann 1998). Far from celebrating in the afterglow of victory, these security conscious Americans fretted over questions of who is our enemy and what is our purpose?

The '9/11' attacks appeared to answer these questions, at least for President George W. Bush. In the aftermath of the destruction in New York and Washington, Bush and his closest advisers constructed the narrative of the 'war on terror' that characterized all forms of international terrorism as an existential threat to US security that must be met with the full force of the national security state. Bush established the new guiding principles of US foreign policy, institutionalizing the assumptions and discourse of the 'war on terror' so deeply within the national security structures and political culture of the US that it has since been the fundamental focus of security policy (Jackson 2005; Croft 2006). Bush pursued the 'war on terror' relentlessly and often to excess, including the commitment to long term, intractable conflicts in Afghanistan and Iraq, as well as utilizing extreme interrogation tactics and extraordinary rendition to intern suspected terrorists at CIA black sites and Guantanamo Bay. In doing so, Bush was accused of undermining the very values and principles that he argued the 'war on terror' was designed to uphold and protect.

President Obama was expected by his supporters to be something of an antidote to Bush. Yet while he rejected much of his predecessor's foreign policy approach, particularly with regard to the tactics of the 'war on terror,' Obama was nonetheless a 'true believer' in the threat posed to the US by al Qaeda and other associated groups (McCrisken 2011). The nature and tactics of US counterterrorism shifted from full-scale interventions to targeted killing using drones and 'leading from behind' in multilateral interventions such as Libya. Obama attempted to reassert other priorities to the foreground of US policy. He rejected Bush's simple Manichean constructions of global politics as good versus evil, emphasized complexity and nuance in international affairs, and acknowledged that stability, prosperity, and security required more than a robust defense against international terrorism and performative demonstrations of US military might. Nonetheless, his administration perpetuated involvement in the main conflicts of Bush's 'war on terror', struggling to extract the US from Iraq and especially Afghanistan (Bentley and Holland 2014).

President Trump was a vociferous critic of Obama's largely multilateralist approach to foreign policy. He vowed to put 'America First.' Trump was certainly a stark contrast to his predecessor in his highly personalized foreign policy approach. Trump was brazen and often aggressive in his language and attitude. His highly individualized, self-confident, nationalistic approach upset not only Democratic political opponents, but also critics within his own Republican party who warned he would prove to be a 'dangerous President' who would put US national security 'at risk' (*New York Times* 2016). Despite his often combative relationship with other Republicans, his administration nonetheless shared much of the approach and assumptions that had long underpinned his party's foreign policy. Trump and his advisors claimed their policy was driven by the basic principle of 'peace through strength,' an approach associated most closely with Ronald Reagan's presidency in the 1980s.

Trump rejected Obama's 'globalism' and asserted notions of what he called 'principled realism' whereby the US would promote its own interests above all others unapologetically. The pursuit of these interests would be achieved through a determined application of 'peace through strength.' Trump did not believe US objectives could be achieved by offering compromise and cooperation through multilateral engagement, as had been the preference in the previous Democratic administrations of Carter, Clinton and Obama.

Instead, adopting the 'peace through strength' approach required the US to use assertive rhetoric and act resolutely, overtly threatening and using force when necessary, in order to project an unambiguous perception of strength to allies, potential adversaries, and purported enemies alike. Only once this credible resolve was established should Washington move to conduct diplomacy and negotiate disputes, utilizing this perceived position of strength to deliver outcomes beneficial to the US.

The 'peace through strength' approach is extremely risky, however, and can cause more problems than it solves. Allies may be offended by their aggressive treatment at the hands of Washington and withdraw much needed cooperation; adversaries can be antagonized so they are more resolved to oppose US objectives; and conflictual situations with perceived enemies can be exacerbated and escalate into crisis and damaging confrontation. To be effective, such a strategy requires a degree of consistency and finesse that the Trump presidency lacked. Although 'peace through strength' was used as a framing device by Trump and advisers such as his second Secretary of State Mike Pompeo, the president's unpredictable character, lack of attention to policy detail and the frequent personnel changes in his foreign policy team made a sustained approach to any element of policy difficult to maintain effectively.

By the time Trump left office, the administration had shown little indication of moving to the conciliation phase that the 'peace through strength' approach implies. Their emphasis remained heavily on the 'strength' side of the equation in the trade war with China, the 'maximum pressure' campaign against Iran, and the burden-sharing war of words with NATO allies. Despite campaign pledges to 'bring our soldiers home,' the administration continued to engage militarily in Afghanistan, Syria, Yemen, and Somalia. Only in relations with North Korea did the approach appear to follow the transition from establishing a position of strength to negotiating for peace. In 2017, Trump had threatened to 'totally destroy' the country should North Korea use its nuclear weapons against the US; but by 2018 he was meeting Supreme Leader Kim Jong Un face-to-face and declaring an end to the North Korean nuclear threat. In 2019, the pair symbolically crossed back and forth over the Demilitarized Zone (DMZ) between North and South Korea. By 2020, however, talks had stalled. Trump left office having made no concrete progress in establishing a more cooperative relationship with Pyongyang let alone ensuring the promised denuclearization of the Korean peninsula.

Trump's strong-arm tactics and lack of diplomatic finesse caused damage to his presidency. Trump's first impeachment in early 2020 stemmed from pressure he placed on Ukrainian President, Volodymyr Zelensky, to investigate Joe Biden and his son Hunter's activities in Ukraine. Although he was acquitted by the Republican-led Senate, the impeachment raised questions among allies and adversaries alike about the stability and reliability of the Trump administration. Within days of surviving impeachment, Trump was confronted with rapidly rising infection and death rates in the US due to the Covid-19 pandemic. Trump initially downplayed the pandemic's serious-ness and struggled to provide effective leadership in confronting the virus as it spread. His brash, even dismissive attitude and rejection of expert advice threatened to compound the damaging political and economic effects of the crisis. A month before the November election, Trump tested positive and was hospitalized with Covid-19. His relatively rapid recovery, however, appeared to reinforce his view that the pandemic could be survived by the US without significant government intervention and that the major restrictions being recommended by his scientific and medical advisors were unnecessary.

Trump's foreign policy agenda was at risk of being overwhelmed first by the Ukraine scandal and then by the dire impacts of coronavirus. The increasing domestic political and civil unrest pivoting around the Black Lives Matter campaign further projected to the world an image of the US in crisis under Trump's leadership. Trump's freedom to maneuvre in the international sphere in 2020 was seriously diminished by these domestic political vulnerabilities. Trump had entered his fourth year looking for a 'big win' abroad that would help him secure a second term, but his lack of foreign affairs experience, his penchant for rejecting diplomatic niceties and speaking his mind, and an increasingly demanding and complex domestic situation, frustrated most of his ambitions for securing significant achievements in foreign policy. When Biden won the 2020 presidential election, he vowed to restore American global leadership, to reinvigorate US diplomacy, and return Washington to a more engaged, cooperative, and multilateral approach to foreign and security policy.

'FOREVER WARS'

One of the most fundamental questions facing presidents is when, where, and how the US should threaten or use its vast military power. Obama was expected to reverse the Bush administration's deployment of large-scale force to combat the threat of terrorism and to draw to a close the Afghanistan and Iraq wars. Although he was determined to make US counterterrorism more adaptive, nimble, and effective, Obama nevertheless regarded the threat posed by al Qaeda and associated groups as both very real and serious. Even while he changed the language and practice employed, replacing mass interventions with drone-launched targeted killings, the underlying assumptions of the 'war on terror' were maintained.

Obama had opposed the Iraq war and promised to end direct US mili-tary involvement. He ordered the last contingent of US combat troops to leave Iraq in August 2010 and all remaining forces to withdraw in December 2011. Obama regarded Afghanistan as the real frontline in the war against terrorism and after an extensive policy review, he initially intensified the mili-tary campaign there. By May 2014, however, he announced an intention to end US combat operations that December. Some 9800 US troops remained on a NATO mission, however, to provide training and other support for the

Afghan military and security forces. The US and its allies continued to partici-pate in ground offensives and conducted extensive air strikes against a Taliban insurgency and Islamic State targets, particularly with drone attacks. With the situation on the ground worsening, Obama announced in July 2016 that approximately 8400 US troops would remain in Afghanistan until the end of his presidency. Despite Obama's earlier hopes and promises, he was unable to bring to an end direct US military involvement in Afghanistan.

Obama's main Middle East policy objective was to defuse conflict, build trust, and establish stability and security. By late 2015, however, it appeared that his most lasting legacy in the region might well be one of renewed intervention and conflict rather than the peaceful end to a decade of war. His administration was rather reluctantly drawn into the Syrian civil war and used air power to stem the military successes of Islamic State there and across the border in northern Iraq. Rather than bringing the US into a new era of peace, Obama embarked on another long-term military engagement that would outlast his presidency. Trump made the defeat of Islamic State a central objective that was largely achieved by working closely with coalition partners—Syrian militia, Iraqi government forces, Kurdish forces and coordinating to some extent with Russia and Turkey. While Trump's administration succeeded in pushing back Islamic State and recapturing territory, they failed to develop a comprehensive plan for confronting the issues inherent in the Syrian civil war.

Trump's frustration at what he called the 'endless wars' in Syria and Afghanistan led to his controversial announcement in December 2018 that he would withdraw all US troops from these countries regardless of the situation on the ground or the consequences of a precipitous extraction. Secretary of Defense James Mattis resigned amid widespread criticism that Trump's decision would give advantage to adversaries in the region such as Iran and Russia. Trump relented, but in mid-October 2019 he gave a more specific order to pull back US special forces from the Turkey–Syria border in a disputed area held by Kurdish forces. Trump brushed off criticism he had abandoned Kurdish allies and soon declared a major victory when he revealed US forces had raided the compound of IS founder Abu Bakr al-Baghdadi who committed suicide to avoid capture. For Trump this was the fulfillment of the 'top national security priority of my administration' and the strongest possible response to critics who claimed his policies were weakening the US. When Trump left office, however, the Syrian civil war continued unresolved and US rivals Russia and Iran retained opportunities to exploit the situation to their advantage rather than Washington's.

In Afghanistan, under threat of a congressional resolution to force the maintenance of troop commitments, Trump made his desired withdrawals contingent on the success of US-Taliban peace talks. In February 2020, the 'Agreement for Bringing Peace to Afghanistan' was signed, including provision for a complete withdrawal of US forces by May 2021. The Taliban pledged not to offer support or haven to al Qaeda and a timeline was established for peace talks between the Taliban and the Afghan government. Critics feared a premature withdrawal of US troops could trigger renewed levels of violence and instability in Afghanistan and the wider region contrary to US interests. Trump nonetheless pushed to reduce the remaining US troop commitment to a negligible level before he left office.

President Biden shares Obama's preference for a relatively small, nimble, and adaptive US military presence in the Middle East coupled with diplomatic engagement rather than large-scale deployments and aggressive confrontation. Biden's early decision to withdraw US support for offensive operations in Yemen while reinvigorating diplomacy was an indication of his wider approach to regional conflict. On becoming president, Biden ordered his Secretary of Defense Lloyd Austin to undertake a Global Posture Review to determine appropriate levels for deployments across US commitments and priorities, including Afghanistan, Iraq, and Syria. Although the emphasis would be on reducing the levels of US military commitments where possible, analysts expected Austin to recommend a long-term residual deployment of US special forces in Iraq and Syria to continue counterterrorism operations, combat the Islamic State threat, and temper the regional objectives of Iran, Russia and Turkey.

Biden initially viewed the 2020 US-Taliban agreement as hastily negotiated and doubted the May 1, 2021 withdrawal date was realistic. Biden was determined, however, to conclude involvement in 'wars that have dragged on for far too long.' Biden's emphasis on bringing those wars to a 'responsible end' led him to announce that the final US withdrawal from Afghanistan would *begin* on May 1, 2021 and be completed by the symbolically important 20th anniversary of the September 11, 2001 attacks. Finally ending the almost 20 year war was a significant achievement for the fourth US president to preside over the Afghanistan conflict, although the chaotic final evacuation of US forces and allied Afghans in August 2021 led to international criticism of Biden's handling of the withdrawal.

A significant factor in Biden's calculations in ending the 'forever wars' is his extensive personal experience with the conflicts. Biden supported the 2003 invasion of Iraq, a decision for which Obama believed he still 'felt burned' during his time as Vice President, informing his cautious approach to further deployments in both Iraq and Afghanistan (Obama 2020). Biden admits his attitude toward the use of the US military 'is personal for me' since his son Beau was deployed to Iraq for a year. Biden's sense of personal responsibility for these wars means he is determined to bring US involvement to an end. He also recognized the importance, however, of leaving Afghanistan and Iraq in a situation stable and secure enough to warrant all the sacrifice and commitment of the last two decades. Critics remain doubtful that a sustainable peace will follow the US departure, but Biden was determined that America's longest war should now finally end.

One of the biggest problems for successive presidents is that US military force is proving to have limited utility. While the US certainly has the largest

and best-equipped military in the world, Washington has failed to achieve its
political or strategic objectives in several military interventions since World
War II. The Vietnam war is the most obvious example, but there are others,
such as the 1992–1993 Somalia intervention and the Afghanistan and Iraq
wars. In these and other conflicts, the US's brute military power has proven
ineffective at overcoming the challenges of asymmetric warfare and struggled to fully secure its goals or to extricate itself from intractable conflicts.
Heavy emphasis on air power, including drones, has rarely been sufficient to
weaken enemy resolve or capabilities to the point where Washington could
claim victory. The complexities of politics in civil conflicts, and the diversity of
ethnic and religious groups often involved, make it very difficult for the US
to resolve situations comprehensively when they intervene militarily. Critics
argue that US policies over the past 20 years have fueled the fires of civil war
and exacerbated regional conflicts, particularly in the Middle East, by creating
'longer-lasting, more violent wars that create terrorist safe havens and cause
mass refugee flows.' Goldenberg and Thomas (2020) argue the answer is to
de-escalate situations by pursuing 'pragmatic diplomacy' instead of advocating
regime change and military solutions. Only then will the 'forever wars' be fully
resolved.

Engagement or Confrontation: The Case of Iran

Obama's approach to Iran may offer a model for the benefits of choosing
engagement over confrontation and conflict. His administration refused to
discount the possibility of using force to prevent Iran from acquiring nuclear
weapons, but made serious efforts to resolve the issue peacefully through
engagement and negotiation. The JCPOA (Joint Comprehensive Plan of
Action), better known as the Iran nuclear deal, was signed in July 2015.
While other elements of his nuclear non-proliferation and disarmament agenda
stalled, Obama succeeded in finalizing a solution to one of the thorniest and
potentially most dangerous of all confrontations involving nuclear proliferation. It seemed Obama had secured a significant victory through constructive
engagement with an adversarial state that would be central to his legacy.

President Trump was unimpressed, however, calling the JCPOA 'the worst
deal ever' and vowing to terminate it. He demanded unsuccessfully that the
deal be renegotiated, then withdrew the US from the agreement in May 2018.
The administration ramped up its rhetoric and pushed for the imposition of
more stringent sanctions against Iran in an approach similar to that taken
with North Korea in 2017. Describing Iran as a 'rogue state' led by a 'fanat-
ical dictatorship,' Trump accused Tehran of sponsoring terrorism, aggressively
fomenting violence in other Middle Eastern states, and brutally oppressing
its own people. Trump's advisers were somewhat divided over the issue, with
some warning that the Obama-era nuclear deal, whatever its perceived short-
comings, was better than no deal at all. The changes to Trump's foreign policy

team in 2018, however, brought a more consistent hardline on Iran through National Security Advisor John Bolton and Secretary of State Mike Pompeo.

Trump's willingness to turn aggressive rhetoric into action was tested in June 2019 when Iran's Islamic Revolutionary Guard Corps (IRGC) shot down a US drone flying near to the strategically important Strait of Hormuz. Trump's initial reaction was to order a retaliatory missile strike, but he aborted the attack at the last minute to avoid deaths he believed would 'not be proportionate to shooting down an unmanned drone.' Provocations continued throughout mid-2019, but after the hawkish Bolton resigned, tensions seemed to ease. Pompeo indicated that Trump had no interest in initiating another long-term military engagement in the Middle East. Drawing direct comparisons with the administration's recourse to 'peace through strength' with North Korea, Pompeo highlighted Trump's 'willingness to talk to even the United States' staunchest adversaries,' suggesting that the aim of the 'maximum pressure' policy was to bring Iranian leaders to the negotiating table (Pompeo 2018).

Any such prospects diminished greatly in January 2020, however, with the targeted killing of Major General Soleimani of the IRGC. Trump claimed Soleimani was 'the number one terrorist anywhere in the world' who he alleged had 'targeted, injured and murdered hundreds of American civilians and servicemen' and was 'plotting imminent and sinister attacks on American diplomats and military personnel.' Iran condemned the assassination as an act of 'state terrorism' and launched retaliatory missile attacks against bases in Iraq. Fears of a full-scale war soon dissipated when Tehran admitted they had accidentally shot down a Ukrainian airliner, killing all aboard, during the retaliatory strike. With further military action averted, the US continued to increase sanctions pressure on Iran, and Tehran symbolically issued a warrant for the arrest of Trump and other US officials accused of responsibility for Soleimani's death. Something of a diplomatic stalemate ensued, not least as both countries struggled to contain Covid-19.

Through all this posturing, the other signatories to the JCPOA (China, France, Germany, Russia, UK, and EU) continued to hope for its revival. Biden entered office determined to recommit to Obama's approach of engagement with Iran. Early indications are that Biden will work to rebuild trust by reducing sanctions and move to return the US to the JCPOA, provided Iran complies with the original terms of the agreement. Any US return to the JCPOA or a successor agreement, however, will remain vulnerable to being negated again by a future Republican administration or by political change within Iran, demonstrating again the significance of domestic politics to foreign policy developments.

RUSSIA

Another development in recent years has been the revival of Great Power rivalries between the US, Russia, and China. Under Vladimir Putin's leadership, Russia has become increasingly assertive in its foreign policy, whether annexing Crimea during the Ukrainian crisis or intervening in the Syrian civil war in close proximity to US forces. Russia was also accused of making wide-ranging attempts to influence the outcome of the 2016 US presidential election in favor of Trump. US intelligence services concluded that Russia had conducted extensive cyber espionage against Hillary Clinton's campaign and there were also accusations of direct collusion between the Trump campaign and the Russian government. Trump denied all involvement, but suspicions of obstruction plagued the FBI's investigations. In May 2017, Special Counsel Robert Mueller was appointed to formally examine the allegations, resulting in the conviction of several former Trump campaign members and associates and indictments against Russian individuals and companies over the election meddling. The 2019 Mueller Report stated rather ambiguously that 'while this report does not conclude that the President committed a crime, it also does not exonerate him.' Even so, Trump confidently proclaimed the report proved there was 'no collusion.' This lack of a clear resolution did not end the desire among some opponents to seek his impeachment for attempting to obstruct justice, a campaign that would soon shift to the President's conduct with Ukraine.

The evidence of Russian interference and allegations against Trump's presidential campaign complicated US–Russian relations. Trump toed a fine line between denying collusion over election interference while proclaiming a strong personal connection with Putin. Other administration officials, including second National Security Advisor H. R. McMaster and Secretary of Defense Mattis, made clear publicly their concerns about a resurgent Russia. Their views were reflected in a series of policy documents including the 2017 National Security Strategy (NSS), the National Defense Strategy and the Nuclear Posture Review. Along with China, Russia was characterized as being in direct and deliberate competition with the US and seeking to 'shape a world antithetical to US values and interests.' The NSS declared that Washington must 'counter Russian subversion and aggression' (National Security Strategy 2017).

In March 2018, the alleged Russian-sanctioned poisoning of former Soviet double agent Sergei Skripal and his daughter in the UK added weight to arguments for taking a harder line against Russia. Trump supported sanctions and a co-ordinated expulsion of 153 Russian diplomats by the UK, the US, and 27 other countries, to which Moscow responded in kind. Nonetheless, Trump maintained his positive attitude toward Putin. At the July 2018 Helsinki summit, Trump refused to criticize Russia's policies and stated clearly that he believed Putin's denials of election interference, implying he trusted the

Russian President more than his own intelligence services. Although he subsequently claimed to have misspoken, his comments drew strong condemnation not only from opponents but also from a number of influential Republicans and gave further impetus to the Mueller investigation.

In the latter half of 2018, Bolton, Pompeo and Mattis began to push for a more critical stance on Russia. In late October, Trump announced the US would unilaterally withdraw from the 1987 INF (Intermediate Nuclear Forces) Treaty, claiming Russia had been in violation of the agreement for many years. Critics argued that ending the treaty would trigger a destabilizing nuclear arms race between the US and Russia, as well as potentially undermining efforts to denuclearize North Korea and to prevent Iranian proliferation. Trump completed the INF withdrawal in August 2019, leaving the 2010 New Strategic Arms Reduction Treaty (New START) as the only limit on US and Russian nuclear arsenals, although that treaty was due to expire in February 2021. Mattis and Bolton both resigned amid concerns that Trump's determination to reduce the US military presence in Syria would play to Russia's advantage. For the remainder of his presidency, the relationship with Russia remained ambiguous, not least due to the inconsistencies between Trump's positioning and that of his more hardline advisers.

The Biden administration indicated early on that it regarded Russia as a state 'determined to enhance its global influence and play a disruptive role on the world stage.' They vowed to stand against any Russian provocations but made clear that they did not wish to enter into 'costly arms races.' Biden moved quickly to extend New START and expressed an interest in pursuing new nuclear and emerging technology arms control agreements with Moscow (Biden 2021). The risk of deliberate US-Russia military confrontation has remained relatively low despite the heightened tensions of recent years. These initial overtures suggest the potential for a more stable, or at least clearer, policy toward Russia to emerge under Biden.

CHINA

An important aspect of Obama's attempts to broaden foreign policy beyond counterterrorism was the so-called Asia 'pivot.' This policy shift was designed chiefly to reinvigorate significant diplomatic, economic, and strategic relationships in Asia, especially with Japan and South Korea. The context was the increasing nuclear threat from North Korea but most significantly the growing ascendency of China.

Obama sought to maintain the fundamental approach of competitive engagement with China that had characterized US relations since the 1970s rapprochement with Beijing. This approach is predicated on the idea that the best route to minimize China's threat potential and encourage democratic progress is to facilitate economic liberalization through engagement. However, fears over the 'rise' of China gained traction across the political divide in recent years. China is viewed unfavorably in US public opinion, especially as an economic threat to US interests. Consumers have raised significant concerns about the quality and safety of Chinese-made products ranging from children's toys to dog food. Congressional support has been high for forcing a revaluation of China's currency and reversing the trade deficit with the US. China's assertive moves over disputed territories in the East and South China Seas intensified during the Obama years, as did tensions over Hong Kong, Taiwan and the Chinese treatment of minorities. China's economic expansion and hegemonic ambitions in Africa and Latin America caused increasing consternation in Washington. China was also accused of sanctioning or carrying out major cyberattacks against US government and business targets. All these factors contributed to relatively strong anti-Chinese sentiment among Republicans and Democrats. Donald Trump tapped relentlessly into this 'China fear' in his 2016 presidential campaign, blaming Beijing's trade and finance practices for many of America's economic woes, and carried these campaign narratives into his presidency.

While declaring a positive relationship with Chinese President Xi Jinping, Trump's China policy was distinctly adversarial. The 2017 NSS listed China alongside Russia as the most hostile competitors of the US. Both were accused of challenging US power, influence, and interests while 'attempting to erode American security and prosperity.' The NSS promised the Trump administration would 'contest China's unfair trade and economic practices and restrict its acquisition of sensitive technologies' (National Security Strategy 2017). In March 2018, Trump ordered the first in a series of tariffs on Chinese imports, to which Beijing responded with its own tariffs against US imports, thereby launching a trade war which escalated throughout 2018–2019. Trump argued that the tariffs placed the US 'in a very strong bargaining position' in negotiations for a comprehensive trade deal, again following the 'peace through strength' maxim. Despite the short-term domestic political gain for Trump, critics argued the effects of the tariffs on US and global economic prosperity and stability would be highly damaging.

Tensions eased sufficiently for a Phase One trade deal to be agreed and signed in January 2020. Although comprehensive trade deal talks continued, with the US presidential election drawing near, Trump and his advisers increased their critical rhetoric toward China. They condemned cyber activities and alleged election interference by Beijing. Communications company Huawei was blacklisted over alleged national security risks and Chinese-owned cell phone applications were blocked. Human rights abuses of the mainly Muslim Uyghurs in Xinjiang province and the imposition of new security measures in Hong Kong led to sanctions on Chinese officials. Despite initially cooperative overtures, the Trump administration accused China of failing to deal effectively with Covid-19 and blamed Beijing for the spread of the pandemic globally. Trump labeled Covid-19 the 'Chinese virus' and the 'plague from China', attempting to reignite the anti-China sentiments that had proven so beneficial in his 2016 election campaign.

Trump had overturned the long-preferred US policy of competitive engagement with China by opening an escalatory trade war designed to force China to adopt economic and trade practices more palatable and beneficial to the US. Trump was determined to shake-up the Asia–Pacific region and confront the perceived threats from China head on. President Biden might well prefer a return to a less acrimonious relationship with China, steeped as he is in the diplomatic traditions of the last 50 years including arguments in favor of engagement over confrontation. He faces pressures from within his own party to maintain a strong stand, however, especially on human rights abuses and cybersecurity and increasingly on trade. The initial meeting between his foreign policy team and a Chinese delegation to Anchorage, Alaska in January 2021 suggests that the tensions of the Trump years will not subside easily. Secretary of State Anthony Blinken and National Security Advisor Jake Sullivan made clear the administration's 'deep concerns' over China's human rights record, cyberattacks on the US and economic coercion against US allies, all of which Blinken argued 'threaten the rules-based order that maintains global stability.' The Chinese response was to lambast the US for its hypocrisy, particularly on human rights and the use of force, with senior foreign policy official Yang Jiechi condemning the 'slaughter of the black people' in the US and the use of force abroad to 'topple other regimes' or 'massacre the people of other countries' (US Department of State 2021; Zhou 2021). Although both sides insisted they do not seek conflict with each other, this public trading of barbs suggests the tension within the relationship will remain for some time to come.

Black Lives Matter, White Supremacists, Climate Change, and Global Pandemics

It is not only the Chinese leadership which finds hypocrisy in the treatment of Black Americans. The history of racial injustice in the US has long been a weakness at the core of its claims of a principled and values-based foreign policy. US domestic social and political developments contributed significantly to disquiet over the Trump administration's policies abroad. Trump's reaction to the Charlottesville, Virginia demonstrations against a right-wing rally in August 2017 fuelled claims that he condoned racism and white supremacism. Trump compounded these views with his use of deeply offensive scatological language, describing some African and Central American nations as 'shithole countries' in a meeting with US senators on immigration in January 2018. Attracting widespread rebuke and claims of blatant racism, Trump projected a much more complimentary attitude at the UN General Assembly, insisting that he and his wife Melania 'both love Africa. Africa is so beautiful, the most beautiful part of the world, in many ways.'

The killing in police custody of African American man George Floyd in May 2020 reinvigorated the Black Lives Matter movement in the US and brought strong reactions across the globe, resonating particularly across African states.

Chair of the African Union, Moussa Faki Mahamat, denounced 'the continuing discriminatory practices against Black citizens of the United States of America.' Protest marches in solidarity with African Americans were held in Kenya, South Africa, Ghana, Uganda, Nigeria, Liberia, Senegal, and other states, with a broad focus on issues of police brutality, racism, colorism, and the legacies of colonialism, as well as the relationship between US domestic issues of racism and its policies toward African states.

Racialized attitudes could also be discerned in Trump's immigration policies. He characterized Mexican immigrants as drug dealers, criminals, and rapists and pledged to build a wall along the US-Mexico border. He used executive orders to impose a so-called 'travel ban' on citizens from seven Muslim-majority countries, mostly in the Middle East, from which his administration suspected potential terrorists might come. Subsequent legal actions against the travel ban caused delays and revisions, and the southern border wall was only partially built, but Trump had succeeded in further securitizing the issue of immigration.

Trump's unwillingness to condemn white supremacist groups and his often less than tacit support and encouragement came to a violent climax with the events of January 6, 2021 on Capitol Hill in Washington, DC. In its October 2020 Homeland Threat Assessment, the Department of Homeland Security had already identified white supremacist extremists as the 'most persistent and lethal threat' to the security of the US homeland (Department of Homeland Security 2020). Researchers at the Center for Strategic & International Studies (CSIS) found that violent far-right groups and individuals were responsible for ten times as many plots and attacks than Salafi-Jihadists, whether foreign or homegrown, during the first eight months of 2020 (CSIS 2020). The Department of Homeland Security issued a National Terrorism Advisory Bulletin in late January 2021 that warned of a 'heightened threat environment' across the US for weeks to come, due to 'ideologically-motivated violent extremists' who were emboldened by the attack on Capitol Hill and held grievances against 'the exercise of governmental authority and the presidential transition, as well as other perceived grievances fueled by false narratives.' The expectation was that they 'could continue to mobilize to incite or commit violence' (Department of Homeland Security 2021). Almost twenty years after the 9/11 attacks, the source of greatest risk to the security of the US homeland was no longer international terrorism but domestic white supremacist groups and individuals. This stark reality suggests the need for a reorientation of security thinking on how to best protect the US public in their homeland environment, who poses a threat to national security, who is most threatened, and what are the root causes of those threats.

It is not only domestic terrorism and racial injustice that are challenging traditional conceptions of US security. The final twelve months of the Trump presidency also exposed the full vulnerability of the US to two existential transnational threats—climate change and global pandemics. In 2020, the US National Oceanic and Atmospheric Administration (NOAA) reported that there were 22 weather and climate disasters in the US where the overall damages and costs exceeded $1 billion, including deadly wildfires in Western states and seven hurricanes in the South and East coast. The number of such events per year has increased significantly since recording began in 1980, with a third taking place in the last five years. Since 2016, the total cost has been $606.9 billion and 3696 people have lost their lives (NOAA 2021). The death toll in the US over the last decade due to weather and climate disasters far exceeds losses due to terrorist attacks, whether foreign or domestic, and the economic impacts are far greater. This evidence is significant since the Trump administration was highly resistant to the linkages between climate change and security.

Trump repeatedly challenged the scientific evidence on climate change, variously referring to it as 'alarmist' or blaming 'hoaxters,' 'prophets of doom' or even 'the Chinese' for creating the 'myth' of global warming. Most consequentially, he withdrew the US from the 2015 Paris Agreement on Climate Change, claiming it unfairly punished US companies. Trump's position was in striking contrast to Barack Obama's, as it was on so many issues. Obama had claimed in 2009 that 'climate change poses a grave and growing danger to our people.' He had asserted that 'Unchecked, climate change will pose unacceptable risks to our security, our economies, and our planet' (Obama 2009). President Biden shares these sentiments and has made 'restoring our leadership and working alongside others to combat the acute danger' of climate change one of the central pillars of his interim national security strategy. He re-joined the Paris Agreement within hours of taking office and has appointed former Secretary of State John Kerry as his Presidential Special Envoy for Climate (Biden 2021). Environmental degradation and extreme weather are not only direct threats to the security of the US but also act as threat multipliers, exacerbating other aspects of security policy globally.

The Covid-19 pandemic has been described as the 'most invasive global crisis of the postwar era' that poses a fundamental threat to US hegemony 'in terms of both US capabilities and US leadership' (Norloff 2020). By the end of March 2021, more than 30,485,200 people in the US had been infected with the novel coronavirus and 551,638 people had died (*New York Times* 2021). While President Trump took a largely dismissive attitude toward the virus, it nonetheless had a disproportionate impact on the US. Although the US has just four percent of the world's population it suffered a quarter of all Covid-19 infections and deaths by March 2021. As Ed Yong wrote in *The Atlantic* in August 2020: 'A virus a thousand times smaller than a dust mote has humbled and humiliated the planet's most powerful nation' (Yong 2020). The pandemic has demonstrated that the US is 'woefully unprepared' for the types of disruptive crises and threats to its national security that it is likely to face in the coming decades: climate shocks, cyberattacks on vital systems, and indeed more pandemics (Sitaraman 2020).

US policymakers are at a crossroads in foreign and security policy thinking. They can fall back into traditional approaches that were designed for a wholly different era of international relations. Or they can adapt and develop new and transformative ideas about security and how to best protect the US and its people, while also promoting greater peace and stability globally. The US track record, particularly over the last four years of divisive rhetoric, dangerously polarized domestic politics, and a return to power politics internationally, suggest this will be a difficult transition to achieve. Yet early indications of the foreign policy positions and approach being taken by the Biden administration suggest there could be reason for some optimism. They appear to both recognize the complex nature of contemporary challenges and that new, transformative notions of security may be required in order to face them effectively. As Biden and his national security team write in their Interim National Security Strategic Guidance (March 2021):

> Recent events show all too clearly that many of the biggest threats we face respect no border or walls, and must be met with collective action. Pandemics and other biological risks, the escalating climate crisis, cyber and digital threats, international economic disruptions, protracted humanitarian crises, violent extremism and terrorism, and the proliferation of nuclear weapons and other weapons of mass destruction all pose profound and, in some cases, existential dangers. None can be effectively addressed by one nation acting alone. And none can be effectively addressed with the United States on the sidelines. ...the need for American engagement and international cooperation is greater than ever.

REFERENCES

Bentley, M., and J. Holland (eds.). 2014. *Obama's Foreign Policy: Ending the War on Terror*. London: Routledge.

Biden, J.R. 2021. Interim National Security Strategic Guidance, March, at: https://www.whitehouse.gov/wp-content/uploads/2021/03/NSC-1v2.pdf.

Center for Strategic & International Studies. 2020. The War Comes Home: The Evolution of Domestic Terrorism in the United States, 22 October.

Croft, S. 2006. *Culture, Crisis and America's War on Terror*. Cambridge: Cambridge University Press.

Department of Homeland Security. 2020. Homeland Threat Assessment, October. https://www.dhs.gov/sites/default/files/publications/2020_10_06_homeland-threat-assessment.pdf.

———. 2021. National Terrorism Advisory System Bulletin, 27 January. https://www.dhs.gov/sites/default/files/ntas/alerts/21_0127_ntas-bulletin.pdf.

Fukuyama, F. 1992. *The End of History and the Last Man*. New York: Free Press.

Goldenberg, I., and K. Thomas. 2020. 'Demilitarizing US Policy in the Middle East', Center For A New American Security, 20 July.

Hoffmann, S. 1998. *World Disorders*. Lanham, MD: Rowman & Littlefield.

Jackson, R. 2005. *Writing the War on Terrorism*. Manchester: Manchester University Press.

Krauthammer, C. 1990. The Unipolar Moment. *Foreign Affairs* 70 (1): 23–33.

McCrisken, T. 2011. Ten Years On: Obama's War on Terrorism in Rhetoric and Practice. *International Affairs* 87 (4): 781–801.

National Oceanic and Atmospheric Administration. 2021. Billion Dollar Weather and Climate Disasters. https://www.ncdc.noaa.gov/billions/.

New York Times. 2016. A Letter from G.O.P. National Security Officials Opposing Donald Trump, 6 August.

———. 2021. Coronavirus in the US: Latest Map and Case Count, Updated, 1 April. https://www.nytimes.com/interactive/2020/us/coronavirus-us-cases.html.

Norloff, C. 2020. Is COVID-19 the End of US Hegemony? *International Affairs* 96 (5): 1281–1303.

NSS. 2017. *National Security Strategy of the United States of America*, December.

Obama, B. 2009. Remarks by the President at the Morning Plenary Session of the United Nations Climate Change Conference, White House Office of the Press Secretary, Press Release, 18 December.

———. 2020. *A Promised Land*. New York: Viking.

Pompeo, M.R. 2018. Confronting Iran: The Trump Administration's Strategy. *Foreign Affairs* 97 (6): 60–70.

Sitaraman, G. 2020. A Grand Strategy of Resilience. *Foreign Affairs* 91 (5): 165–174.

US Department of State. 2021. Secretary Antony J. Blinken, National Security Advisor Jake Sullivan, Director Yang and State Councilor Wang at the Top of Their Meeting, March 18, 2021, Office of the Spokesperson, Press Release.

Yong, E. 2020. How the Pandemic Defeated America. *The Atlantic*, September. https://www.theatlantic.com/magazine/archive/2020/09/coronavirus-american-failure/614191/.

Zhou, V. 2021. What the American Interpreter Got Wrong. *Vice*, 22 March. https://www.vice.com/en/article/epdy4p/us-china-interpreter-mistranslation.

FURTHER READING

A detailed overview and engagement with the historical context of US foreign and security policy, the domestic political sources of policymaking, and their consequences for a range of foreign policy problems and issues can be found in Greg Hastedt (12th edition, 2020) *American Foreign Policy: Past, Present and Future* (Lanham, MD: Rowman & Littlefield). For a lively analysis of US foreign policy from the end of World War II to the 'war on terror' see Seyom Brown (3rd edition, 2015) *Faces of Power: Constancy and Change in United States Foreign Policy from Truman to Obama* (New York: Columbia University Press). For a critical view, see Noam Chomsky (2004) *Hegemony or Survival: America's Quest for Global Dominance* (London: Penguin).

An engaging exploration of how the increasingly polarised US political environment plays out in foreign policy battles between Republicans and Democrats can be found in Peter Hays Gries (2014) *The Politics of American Foreign Policy* (Stanford, CA: Stanford University Press). For a series of challenging essays on how the US moved from the internationalism of Barack Obama to the 'America First' stance of Donald Trump's foreign policy see Hal Brands (2018) *American Grand Strategy in the Age of Trump* (Washington,

DC: Brookings Institution Press). The deep antecedents of conservative thinking in US foreign policy are explored in Colin Dueck (2019) *Age of Iron: On Conservative Nationalism* (Oxford: Oxford University Press). Whether the much vaunted American-led liberal international order can survive the Trump presidency is explored in a number of recent books and articles, with several perspectives drawn together in the edited volume by Robert Jervis, Francis J. Gavin, Joshua Rovner, and Diane N. Labrosse (2018) *Chaos in the Liberal Order* (New York: Columbia University Press).

A number of books are challenging conventional thinking on US foreign policy and have enjoined the call for transformative thinking in security policy. For a diverse and challenging set of essays on the possibilities see Edwin Daniel Jacobs, ed. (2017) *Rethinking Security in the Twenty-First Century* (New York: Palgrave Macmillan). Specific themes are explored in greater depth in Charles L. Chavis, Jr. and Sixte Vigny Nimuraba, eds. (2020) *For the Sake of Peace: Africana Perspectives on Racism, Justice and Peace in America* (Lanham, MD: Rowman & Littlefield); Arie Perliger (2020) *American Zealots: Inside Right-Wing Domestic Terrorism* (New York: Columbia University Press); Peter Hough (2nd edition, 2021) *Environmental Security* (Abingdon: Routledge); and Colin Kahl and Thomas Wright (2021) *Aftershocks: Pandemic Politics and the End of the Old International Order* (New York: St Martin's Press). These contemporary debates over US foreign policy and its possible future directions can be traced by regularly consulting the journal *Foreign Affairs* (www.foreignaffairs.com) for the competing views of academics, policy makers, think tank analysts and even US presidents.

CHAPTER 19

Assessing Trump's Legacies

Gillian Peele

Rarely, if ever, in recent American history has the end of a presidency prompted such introspection and trauma as occurred in the closing weeks of Trump's. Of course, sudden death and assassination have generated national grief and a sense of dislocation as occurred in 1945 with the death of FDR and in 1963 with the shooting of JFK. However, the period between election day on November 3, 2020 and the inauguration of Joe Biden to succeed Donald Trump on January 20, 2021 witnessed a series of unprecedented events, culminating in the invasion of the Capitol building by a mob which had rallied to protest the legality of the presidential election results and to prevent the certification of Joe Biden's victory. Although the disruption did not in fact prevent the certification of Biden's election, the violence renewed intense criticism of Trump himself and his handling of the office. It also placed question marks over a number of features of the American political system and the ability of its Madisonian constitutional arrangements to work effectively. Equally, it highlighted deep fissures in the wider society; some of them—like race and the contrasting mindsets in relation to science and religion—were ones with a long history; others such as divisions over political correctness and cancel culture were of more recent vintage. These divisions had increasingly become the basis of a pervasive identity politics which seemed likely to outlast the Trump presidency (Fukuyama 2018) and they threatened to polarize further a political system already deeply marked by fault lines and tensions (Klein 2020). Finally,

G. Peele (✉)
Lady Margaret Hall, University of Oxford, Oxford, UK

© The Author(s), under exclusive license to Springer Nature
Switzerland AG 2022
G. Peele et al. (eds.), *Developments in American Politics 9*,
https://doi.org/10.1007/978-3-030-89740-6_19

although a defeated president does not usually command such attention, the reaction to Biden's victory threw into sharp relief the changed character of the Republican Party and the extent to which it had been captured by Trump and his highly personal and combative style of politics.

In this chapter I explore the legacies of Trump's controversial presidency and its impact on the course of American political development. It is important to remember that contentious though Trump's personality, rhetoric, and actions were before, during, and after his tenure of the White House, his presidency must be seen in part at least as a response to a complex knot of social, economic, political and cultural changes which had created new identities, loyalties and antagonisms in the United States as well as profound disillusion with established elites and institutions. His appeal and his style reflected acute tensions between different sections of the American population as well as profound disagreements about the meaning and strength of American democracy.

The chapter proceeds as follows. It first discusses briefly Trump's political style and its legacy and the way that his appeal tapped into themes familiar to scholars of populism. It then moves to examine his escalation of identity politics including race and religion but it also examines the issues associated with political correctness on such matters as ethnicity, gender and, in the context of the Covid-19 pandemic, mask-wearing. The next section explores Trump's policy legacy and then his impact on the Republican Party. It looks at his effect on the GOP especially after the 2020 election loss and at the divisions within the Party as to what its strategy should be in the future in order to ensure its survival. The chapter concludes by asking long-term questions about the strength of American constitutional democracy and whether the Trump presidency should be seen as an aberration or as an indicator of a new pattern of politics which is likely to endure.

TRUMP'S STYLE

It was clear from the moment that Trump entered the race to secure the 2016 Republican presidential nomination that his would be a highly unusual candidacy. Trump had no previous political or governmental experience and indeed he had not always been a registered Republican. His rhetoric was crude and abrasive and he projected an aggressive personality which seemed likely to alienate large sections of the public. As Renshon has written, Trump's was a highly personal style that would have been difficult to maintain in any traditional organizational setting where there were norms, expectations, routines, and paths to advancement. As Renshon points out, Trump's experience as the sole decision-maker in the Trump organization encouraged a style which included 'flamboyance, combativeness, risk taking, rhetorical sleight of hand ("truthful hyperbole"), impulsiveness and flexibility that enabled him to pursue personal and business indulgences with a cool calculation, enormous levels of hard work, creativity, and resilience in a peripatetic and wide-ranging business career' (Renshon 2020: 12).

Doubtless the different elements of Trump's personality and psychology will continue to intrigue observers for many years to come. Here it is worth noting just three points. The first is that Trump's candidacy and presidency had the impact it did precisely because he was not constrained by the norms and expectations of the political system. His message was a call to make a new beginning and to break from the established pattern of doing politics. His policies were a radical departure not just from the progressive policies which had been espoused by the Democrats but also from the Republican orthodoxy in domestic and foreign policy. He wanted in short to be a disruptor. The second point is that many aspects of Trump's appeal—his campaigning tactics and indeed the conduct of his presidency—may be analyzed as an expression of a populist wave which has challenged many liberal democracies recently and which has a long pedigree in American political life (Kazin 1995). In Trump's case, as in earlier populist eruptions, his candidacy was a reaction to the perceived gridlock and frustrations associated with a complex constitutional system and an apparent lack of responsiveness to popular grievances and disillusion with orthodox politics. That populism was made more powerful by its yoking to a mastery of new social media.

Trump's presentation of himself as an outsider who could make a clean break with a corrupt establishment and a compromised set of political elites marked him out from the crowd of Republican contenders. He claimed he would move beyond the policies and politics which he argued were destroying America and make it possible for America to reassert its primacy and be a winner once more. His ability to project himself as the savior of a nostalgic vision of the United States—to make America great again—and to identify and defeat its enemies depended apparently on a supreme self-confidence and ego, although some have noted that Trump also displayed a good deal of insecurity. The techniques of modern communications fitted Trump's style of campaigning very well, allowing him to connect with his supporters via Facebook and Twitter, although they of course proved deeply unsettling to the policy process once he was in office.

Trump's appeal would not have been successful without the underlying public dissatisfaction with the direction in which the United States was headed and a disenchantment with politics as usual. Polls taken in 2016 showed that six in ten Americans thought the country was on the wrong track, reflecting concern about partisan polarization and gridlock in government (Jordan 2016). Trump was better able to present himself as an agent of change than Hillary Clinton who was a consummate Washington insider.

What Trump offered was a narrative—direct and simple—of what had undermined American greatness and how it could be retrieved. It was designed particularly to appeal to groups who felt their own economic and cultural values and positions were threatened by demographic and social changes. His appeal was to those who wanted to preserve their way of life from global influences and entanglements, the undermining of employment from international competition, and alien elements inside the United States—immigrants, radicals, socialists, humanists, and secularists. Trump's appeal in 2016 also drew on a changing pattern of white working-class voting which had been occurring for some time (Carnes and Lupu 2021). It drew on a rising tide of distrust in government, which had found expression in the Tea Party movement's reactionary insurgency and transformation of the Republican Party (Blum 2020; Skocpol and Williamson 2012). It also tapped into a reservoir of racial resentments and cultural fears which few other politicians had dared to highlight as explicitly or as directly. One aspect of this exploitation of cultural and racial fears was the strengthened appeal to white Christian nationalism. As Samuel Perry noted the 'greatest ethnic dog-whistle the right had ever come up with was the label "Christian" because it meant "people like us"' (quoted in Griswold 2021). From the beginning of Trump's 2016 campaign his tactics and derogatory rhetoric toward immigrants, toward Mexicans, and toward Islam were designed to distinguish various minority groups from 'people like us' and those tactics reframed the debate and often made it hard for his critics to retaliate. Trump had learned the art of maximizing publicity for himself and he was not squeamish about expressing his policies in ways which would inevitably gain attention. His narrow victory in the 2016 election not merely surprised many pundits but also shocked many Republican insiders who had earlier dismissed his presidential aspirations (Boehner 2021).

Identity Politics, Division, and Polarization

Polarized identities had been key to Trump's campaign for the presidency in 2016, and were to his bid to retain it in 2020. Clarifying those identities became a major tactic of Trump's presidency and pushed what Sides et al. (2019) called 'identity-inflected issues' like immigration up the political agenda. Stoking awareness of those identities also involved giving the key elements of his coalition what they wanted. For example conservative religious groups wanted and received judicial appointments sympathetic to their agenda on strengthening the role of religion in public life and exemptions from what they saw as intrusions on the free exercise of religion. Not surprisingly Trump's defeat in 2020 further inflamed the antagonisms which had come to mark American political life and the heightened awareness of which groups would be the losers and which the winners with a change of administration. The assertion that the election had been fraudulent and stolen from Trump was not merely calculated to undermine Biden's legitimacy but fuelled further the anger of Trump's supporters.

The refusal to accept the fairness of the election results also reflected two features of American political life which had become marked during the Trump presidency: the abandonment of the notion of objective truth for alternative versions of the facts and the spread of conspiracy theories. As a *Washington Post* study of Trump's fragile relationship with truth noted, every president lies at some point (Washington Post Fact Checker Staff 2021). But as the same publication highlighted, Trump stood out as 'the most mendacious' president in US history, one known not for one big lie but for a 'constant stream of exaggerated, invented, boastful, purposely outrageous, spiteful, inconsistent, dubious and false claims' (*Washington Post*: x). The well-documented assault on truth eats into the fabric of public trust and, as the *Washington Post* study argued, has a 'mind-numbing effect' on Americans, making them tune out the torrent of presidential misstatements. Interestingly, it also seems to have reduced the significance that Republican identifiers attributed to the importance of politicians being truthful. Thus, while polls found similarly overwhelming numbers of Democrats and independents in 2007 and 2018 saying it was extremely important for presidential candidates to be honest, there had been a marked shift in the number of Republicans who thought that honesty was important—down to 49 percent in 2018 from 71 percent in 2007.

The allure of conspiracy theories is a familiar phenomenon in American history. But conspiracy theories have recently taken on new forms and become more widely accessible as a result of the proliferation of new social media platforms and the popularity of Facebook, Twitter, Reddit and YouTube and websites such as Breitbart, Daily Caller and Infowars. There were a number of conspiracy theories circulating during the Obama presidency and under Trump social media provided an outlet and rallying point for many others. One such conspiracy theory is QAnon which had an extensive number of followers on Facebook and other outlets, although the major companies have tried to ban it. QAnon, which seems to have emerged in 2017, alleges that Democratic politicians (including the Clintons) and a range of other prominent figures are involved in a Satanic pedophile ring. In this theory Trump was seen as the savior who would destroy the evil-doers in a great confrontation. It is not clear precisely how far this seemingly absurd sort of conspiracy theory has spread in the United States but it is clear that there is an enthusiastic audience for it. A report by AEI in 2021 showed that white evangelical protestants were more likely than other groups to believe the QAnon theory and that white evangelicals also were likely to believe other conspiracy theories (Cox 2021). It is also clear that on the right there has been a rising skepticism about scientific expertise. The advent of the Covid-19 virus witnessed a major division on partisan lines as, encouraged by Trump, many Republicans rejected the necessity of mask-wearing and social distancing and refused to be vaccinated against the virus.

Many of the raw political, racial, religious, and cultural divisions that had come to mark American life and new developments in its political conflicts could be seen in the demonstrations that occurred just prior to and on the day the presidential election results were due to be certified. The crowd that gathered to protest the validity of the election was largely white and among the emblems carried during the protests was the confederate flag, an increasingly unacceptable symbol of white supremacy. QAnon supporters were visibly present in the invasion of the Capitol showing that it had gained a foothold in the conservative base. Religious motifs were evident in the banners and placards carried at the demonstrations. As Robert Jones wrote, there was a juxtaposition of white supremacist symbols and Christian ones among the protesters including 'Jesus saves' and 'Jesus 2020 flags' which mimicked the Trump flags (Jones 2021). The Christian flag was carried into the Capitol and there was even a Jericho march around the Capitol using shofars to draw the comparison between the pro-Trump protests and the biblical siege of Jericho by the Israelites. What was apparent from the participants' diverse collection of symbols is the intermingling of themes and motifs and of their mutual reinforcement.

Importantly, there was also a visible element of violence both in the presence of organized militia groups such as the Proud Boys and the Oath Keepers, the use of threatening props such as a noose and gallows, and in the rhetoric and sentiments expressed by the crowd. The prospect of domestic violence around political issues had grown substantially over the years of the Trump presidency. The protests of the Black Lives Matter (BLM) movement had frequently been met by organized resistance and the summer of 2020 saw riots across US cities. Although the BLM protests had largely been peaceful at least initially, the Trump administration and right-wing groups claimed it had been infiltrated by militant anti-fascist groups. The demonstrations by BLM supporters offered an opportunity for an array of right-wing groups to engage in violence. Although the threat posed by right-wing militia groups to national security had been apparent for some time, there was a general sense that it had been downplayed in the Department of Homeland Security by the Trump administration. The Biden administration by contrast has identified the threat of domestic terrorism from armed right-wing groups as a major priority.

Race

The Republican Party has long been overwhelmingly dependent on white voters for its support. Since the 1960s when the civil rights revolution precipitated a realignment of the South (taking the white South into the Republican camp and making the Republican Party more southern) the GOP has become increasingly white. But there have been subtle and not so subtle changes in the role of race in the US political equation. First, demographic changes have created a sense of urgency and fear as white Americans are projected to become a minority by 2055, overtaken numerically by a combination of the fast growing Hispanic and Asian communities and Black Americans. For many white Americans this transformation threatens their culture and their values and this sense of threat has strengthened an explicit appeal to white identity and a changing pattern of white political behaviors (Jardina 2020). Second, the relative decline of the white American proportion of the population has also been an important factor prompting Republican-majority states to change their voting laws to tighten access to the polls. Finally, racially charged issues have become more prominent in public debate, intersecting both with issues which had established racial connotations (such as law and order, immigration, and welfare) and with the newer issues associated with the pandemic. Not surprisingly the focus on ethnic and racial minorities in political discourse and Trump's often inflammatory rhetoric seems likely to have caused minority groups to be fearful of attack. The incidence of hate crimes in the United States rose dramatically over the period of Trump's presidency with a marked increase in its later period. Asian-Americans in particular experienced a surge of attacks which some attributed to Trump's assertions that China had deliberately allowed the spread of Covid-19, dubbed by the president as the Wuhan flu or, playing even more on racial stereotypes, Kung Flu.

Trump himself came to the presidency with a long history of racism, despite him proclaiming his own freedom from it. His father's real estate business was charged with racial discrimination by the Department of Justice in the early 1970s; he had called for the death penalty for five black youths who were wrongly accused of a brutal assault and rape in New York; and he had become extremely hostile to Native Americans when they appeared to challenge his casino business. In 2011 he took up the claim that Barack Obama had not been born in the United States and was therefore ineligible for the presidency. The charge gained Trump extensive publicity and indeed by later that year about half of Republican voters thought that Obama was a Muslim. This 'birther' campaign served two purposes. First it cast doubts on Obama's legitimacy; but it also spread the image of Obama as somehow a threat to American cultural and religious values, even a terrorist threat (Serwer 2020).

Trump's 2016 campaign explicitly appealed to public hostility to immigrants and fears of terrorism. The language used deliberately defied normal conventions about the terms in which racial issues would be discussed. In office, presidential initiatives were designed to stoke fears among his support groups, including the travel ban against people from predominantly Muslim countries on security grounds and building a wall to protect the United States from an 'invasion' of Latin American would-be immigrants. His speeches were laced with hostility to black Americans and to black politicians and sought to portray them as not properly American or not grateful for the chance the United States had given them. In 2019 members of the Squad, a group of young non-white progressive female Democrats, were attacked by Trump who asked why they did not go back to help fix the 'totally broken and crime-infested places' from which they came. The remark prompted the House of Representatives to pass a motion deploring the racist comment, although it passed on a vote in which all but a small number of Republicans voted against the reprimand. Trump also savaged Elijah Cummings, a black Congressman who was Chair of the House Oversight Committee and a key figure in the first impeachment of Trump. The president called Cummings's district, which included much of Baltimore, a 'disgusting, rat and rodent-infested mess.' Such personal attacks were designed to gain publicity and mobilize his base.

Two episodes in Trump's presidency underlined how Trump sought to exploit the sharpening of racial antagonisms in building his base. The first was his response to violence which erupted at a Unite the Right rally in Charlottesville. The second was the reinvigoration of the Black Lives Matter campaign which occurred in the wake of the death in police custody of George Floyd. Charlottesville became a significant indicator of Trump's attitude toward the growing militancy of the so-called alt-right, a loose confederation of right-wing nationalist and neo-Nazi groups including the Ku Klux Klan and David Duke who had gathered in Charlottesville to protest about the decision to remove a statue of Robert E. Lee from Emancipation Park (which had formerly been called Lee Park). The removal of statues and the renaming of public monuments especially those deemed to be associated with slavery, segregation, and discrimination had become an increasingly important cause of contention in American political debate. Trump and many Republicans had increasingly tried to reverse the pressure for change, arguing that it was an ideologically inspired move which denied the reality of American history. At Charlottesville the right-wing groups (many of them uniformed and armed) clashed with peaceful protesters. In the disturbances which followed one of the protesters against the rally was killed and nineteen injured when James Alex Fields drove his car into the crowd. Trump apparently refused to condemn the actions of the right-wing groups saying that there were some 'very fine' people on both sides and defending the right of groups to resist the removal of the statue. What Charlottesville did was to signal Trump's sympathy for groups anxious to defend, if need be with force, a particular view of American culture and history, one which was based on white nationalism rather than multiculturalism.

The escalation of organized opposition to police brutality toward black Americans provoked through the BLM movement saw the Trump administration emphasizing the choice between the anarchy and disorder which came in the wake of protests and the protection of law and order and property. Trump saw the electoral advantage to be gained from highlighting the dangers associated with BLM inspired protests and took every opportunity to highlight the need to defend the values which BLM was allegedly threatening. The most extreme example of Trump projecting his administration's identification with the wider defense of American civilization occurred in the context of a BLM demonstration in Washington DC at the beginning of June 2020. Trump had earlier made a speech warning state governors that they should use the National Guard to re-establish order and regain control of the streets. If the governors would not take action, Trump stated that he would deploy military force to protect law and order in the United States. Following a speech, an area in front of the White House was cleared of protesters and Trump marched to St. John's Episcopal Church to be photographed holding up a bible. The message of a choice between Trump's defense of law and order and religion on the one hand and Democratic lawlessness on the other could not have been clearer. The use of the bible and the church as a backdrop angered many including the clergy; but it projected Trump's deliberately polarising message of Republican values standing in marked contrast to those of their liberal opponents.

Religion

Although many members of the clergy were critical of Trump's attempts to co-opt religion onto his side, religious adherence and religious issues had become increasingly salient in America's identity politics and an important factor in Republicans' campaign strategy.

Since the late 1970s the Republican Party has counted white religious Americans, especially evangelicals but also Roman Catholics, as an essential element of its coalition. Trump's appeal to evangelicals when he first became a candidate seemed limited both because of his personal morality and his own very limited commitment to any religious beliefs. But he appreciated the significance of the religious vote and the role of churches and conservative religious groups in mobilizing voters and moved to cement its role in his coalition. In power Trump moved quickly to give the conservative religious groups what they wanted—in the form of judicial appointments, limitations on abortion and contraception, restrictions on the use of fetal tissue in scientific research and limitations on the rights of gay and transgender people. The Trump administration promoted a Religious Freedom initiative; and it appointed a number of committed conservative Christians to key positions including Mike Pence who became his vice-president, Ben Carson and Mike Pompeo.

It is worth emphasizing the radical nature of some of the goals of the religious groups on the right. White evangelicals had been integrated into the conservative movement and the Republican Party from the late 1970s in opposition to a perceived attack on conservative moral values and the traditional family. But the early twenty-first century had seen a growth in the ambitions of a number of groups and individual pastors dedicated to restoring the idea of the United States as a Christian commonwealth and eradicating the influences of such perceived enemies as Islam and secularism (Posner 2020). They lent support to a number of attempted legislative initiatives especially at the state level such as the banning of sharia law and the restoration of mandatory school prayer and bible readings. Increasingly some elements of conservative Christianity in America seemed to blend with nativism and to advocate a reconstruction of the United States as a theocracy rather than a pluralist multicultural democracy.

There were some critics of the increasing association of the Republican Party with Christianity. Within the evangelical movement figures such as Russell Moore and Jim Wallis had been strong opponents of the Trump candidacy and there were signs of some crumbling of evangelical support at the elite level toward the end of Trump's presidency when *Christianity Today* blasted Trump's unfitness for the presidency (Galli 2019). Beth Moore, a very prominent evangelical with a special outreach to women through her Living Proof ministries, announced in early 2021 that she was leaving the Southern Baptist

Convention in large part because it had become too closely associated with Trump and right-wing causes. There were a set of not unfamiliar scandals affecting the reputation of celebrated televangelists including Jerry Falwell Jr. Some Roman Catholics openly criticized Trump's policies and indeed some of the issues which gained attention—such as the separation of children from parents seeking asylum—caused discomfort among religious believers especially in the liberal churches. There was also an increasing and painful exploration of the relationship between Christianity and white supremacy in the United States (Jones 2016, 2020; Butler 2021). Some of this exploration revisited the extent to which much of the history of religion in the United States, especially in the south and in the evangelical community, was intrinsically entwined with assumptions about black inferiority and indeed violence toward blacks.

There were also important works highlighting the shades of opinion about the proper relationship between church and state within the United States and highlighting the importance not so much of religious belief and observance per se but of what could be called Christian nationalism (Whitehead and Perry 2020). What this work suggested was that there was a divide between those whose commitment was to the defense of a cultural vision of the United States as a distinctively Christian society and those whose commitment was to the doctrinal and religious elements of their faith and who might increasingly see contradictions between it and the historical legacy of Christianity in America and the Republican Party's efforts to co-opt it for a political cause.

It was also increasingly apparent that, although emphasizing the cultural primacy of Christianity in the United States might prove attractive in the short term, its longer term value to the GOP might be limited as increasing numbers of Americans do not identify with a religious group. This group—dubbed 'nones' by commentators—constituted about 23 percent of the US population by the end of Trump's presidency. Its members were more evident in younger age groups and increasingly self-confident about their lack of religious belief (Campbell et al. 2021).

Culture Wars and Political Correctness

The concept of Christian nationalism highlights the set of values which Trump often championed very successfully. Whatever his earlier policy positions, Trump sought to make the Republican Party the defender of both patriotic sentiments and a version of American history not encumbered by guilt or embarrassment about slavery and racial segregation. Trump took advantage of a host of symbolic opportunities to identify his position on cultural issues and to paint opponents as unpatriotic and anti-American. Players who followed Colin Kaepernick's initiative of 'taking the knee' at football games during the national anthem were lambasted by Trump. Trump in 2020 highlighted what he saw as a disgraceful tendency to make pupils hate their country by focussing on slavery and racism rather than its contribution to freedom and democracy.

Efforts to reform the school curriculum to reflect the experience of slavery as exemplified by the *New York Times* 1619 Commission were treated with scorn, and a version of materials to promote a patriotic history through a 1776 Commission was initiated (Balingit and Meekler 2020). (Biden immediately ordered the project terminated on taking office.) Any attempt to introduce critical race theory, which focuses on deeply embedded structural and institutional inequalities, into the curriculum met intense official disapproval and Trump threatened to defund any institutions which sought to use it. While his own approach to family life and sexual morality might be suspect, he saw no problem in upholding traditional patterns of family values and excluding efforts to recognize equality claims on behalf of those with alternative sexual identities. Although he claimed to be supportive of promoting women in politics, his attitudes toward women were markedly contemptuous and in his 2016 campaign he openly flouted convention and civility by personal attacks on critics. Female candidates were attacked for their looks and a disabled reporter was publicly mocked.

In striking these attitudes Trump was not merely displaying his pugnacious determination to defend the values of his supporters but was attempting to push back against a campaign for political correctness which to many seemed to threaten free speech in its desire not to offend individuals or groups. This debate is not of course one confined to the United States but it has become a highly significant one there. The debate takes many forms and sometimes deeply divides opinion as in the case of a number of Dr. Seuss children's books which came under fire for their alleged depiction of racial stereotypes. Sometimes it has involved sensitivity about the use of pronouns and prefixes. Sometimes it has become a symbol of the tribalism which has become such a feature of American life. Thus in the Covid pandemic, mask-wearing or not became an indicator of broadly liberal or conservative attitudes to government. Regardless of the public health issues, those who refused to wear a mask were seen by conservatives as asserting their rights; those who wore them were often attacked for following government injunctions. In a remarkable broadcast in 2021 Tucker Carlson, the Fox TV celebrity, encouraged viewers to call the police if anyone saw a child wearing a mask, which in Carlson's view constituted assault.

THE POLICY AND GOVERNANCE LEGACY

Although Trump came to the presidency with an ambitious and radical agenda his capacity to promote long-lasting policy change was limited. Certainly he was able to launch a number of symbolic initiatives by executive order but, as Biden showed on taking office in 2021, the executive orders of one president can be quickly reversed by his successor. Trump's change of emphasis on trade policy may last longer but his legislative achievement has actually been quite slight, not least because of the capture of the House of Representatives by the Democratic Party in the 2018 midterm elections. Trump's failure to deploy the resources of the executive branch adequately also explains why in some issue areas he achieved far less than his ambitious agenda predicted. As Andrew Wroe has shown in an earlier chapter, on immigration he was unable to deliver the radical policy changes he wanted and even on his key pledge to build a wall there was failure. Similarly as Bert Rockman has shown, many of his most radical policies came to nothing because of procedural irregularities which proper preparation and attention to detail might have avoided.

However, in addition to increased polarization and the dysfunctional effect of Trump's style on policy, the Trump presidency left a number of legacies for the political system. As Bauer and Goldsmith argue Trump's years in the White House exposed a number of gaps in the law and norms governing the office and broader weaknesses in presidential accountability (Bauer and Goldsmith 2020). Apart from the key point that partisan loyalty saved the president from conviction in two impeachments even when it was clear that Trump had encouraged an insurrection, his willingness to defy convention and expectations about ethical behavior in office highlight important gaps in the governmental framework. Bauer and Goldsmith point to Trump's refusal to submit tax returns and his merging of the office of the presidency with his personal interests. And they point also to the extent to which Trump was able to attack and undermine a range of institutions such as the press, the judiciary, Congress, state and local governments and many elements of his own executive branch, especially the Department of Justice and intelligence agencies. Although Bauer and Goldsmith are as they put it mindful of the uncertain prospects for reform, they are adamant that many of the constitutional problems revealed by the Trump presidency need to be addressed.

Trump's Legacy for the Republican Party

In many ways perhaps the most perplexing legacy of the Trump presidency relates to its impact on the Republican Party. How did Trump come to achieve such domination over the party and how will the loss of the 2020 election shape its strategy for the future? Is it possible that the Republican Party is, in the words of Thomas E. Patterson, "destroying itself" (Patterson 2020)?

The Drift to the Right

Patterson highlighted five traps which faced the Republican Party in the contemporary era—the drift to the right, demographics, tax policy, the media and disregard for democratic norms. Each of those traps is important in its own right and underlines ways in which the Republican Party appears to have locked itself into politically constraining positions. Perhaps the most significant of these traps is the drift of the GOP to the right. The movement of the Republican Party toward the right of the political spectrum was a slow process which had its origins in Goldwater's 1964 campaign and the series of ideological, organizational, and issue shifts which occurred thereafter. There emerged a new and powerful conservative movement. The Reagan two-term presidency was both built on that movement and indeed consolidated its influence on the Republican Party. New stages of the rightward move occurred in reaction to subsequent Democratic presidencies—those of Bill Clinton and Barack Obama. Obama's capture of the presidency in 2008 had a dramatic impact on the polarization of American political life, prompting the formation of the Tea Party movement as a grass roots eruption of anti-government sentiment and transforming aspects of American conservatism (Skocpol and Williamson 2012). The Congress elected in 2010, itself reflecting a Republican victory driven by Tea Party strategies, was the first with no ideological overlap between members of the opposing parties, a dramatic change from the 1960s. As Patterson notes, established Republican leaders in Congress found themselves marginalised: 'the Tea Party movement exposed a shift in power within the GOP. Republican lawmakers were no longer in charge of the party's agenda. They had become captives of the party's base' (Patterson: 25). Patterson is correct to note the disappearance of moderate Republicans and the change in the orientation of the Republican Party.

Crucial to the equation also however is the element of organizational development which has occurred since the Reagan years. The early period of building a new conservative infrastructure of think tanks and policy institutes as well as fundraising and electoral initiatives has been well documented. In the twenty-first century the character of the American right has changed subtly. The emphasis on the intellectual influence of think tanks and policy institutes appears muted; but there has emerged a series of organizational networks especially at the state level which enable wealthy donors to influence Republican policy direction. The Koch brothers and their organization Americans for Prosperity (AFP) which was founded in 2004 provide a key example of this financial leverage supporting right of center campaigns, causes, and candidates. Republicans at the state level were also able to tap into the pre-existing networks of right of center groups such as the American Legislative Exchange Council, the police unions, and the churches (Hertel-Fernandez 2019). These cross-state linkages, while they did not always agree about policy strategy and tactics, had sufficiently much in common to maintain a common front against Democrats. There have been efforts to resist the rightward drift of the GOP but moderate Republicans have felt themselves increasingly marginalized. Part of that sense of marginalization was the increased power of the Republican base and the sidelining, more obviously marked after Trump's ascendancy, of previously influential Republican elites in such areas as foreign policy and law (Saldin and Teles 2020).

Yet once he had gained the nomination and the presidency, the Party gradually became evermore subservient to Trump. Initially there was opposition to some of Trump's policies as for example occurred when the Party was unable to find a replacement policy for the Affordable Care Act. Also, as has been noted earlier, while there was a policy legacy from the Trump administration, the legislative accomplishment was limited. As Trump became increasingly dominant inside the Republican Party and projected his personal popularity with the Republican base there was little independent action by the GOP. As the Republican Party prepared to enter the 2020 elections there was much discussion of the Party as having been hollowed out. There was no separate GOP platform but the Party prepared to fight the elections on Trump's agenda. The two impeachment efforts occasioned by his presidency saw only a limited defection to vote against him. For those Congressmen and Senators who did try to take an independent line there was swift reaction both from Trump himself who denounced his Republican critics as RINOs (Republicans in Name Only) and from the threat of well-funded primary challenges. This threat became ever more apparent within GOP ranks as Trump lost the election but continued to deny that he had lost it properly.

Efforts to remove members of Congress who voted against Trump in the impeachment process served both to keep potentially errant members in line and to remove moderates either by defeat at the polls or by forcing them into retirement. Liz Cheney, the third most powerful Republican in the House of Representatives, lost her leadership role as she struggled to defend the view that the 2020 election results were not fraudulent. Although the attack on her position was initially rebuffed with support from Kevin McCarthy, the Republican House leadership subsequently failed to defend her and championed her ousting in the name of party unity. After the election it was clear that many of the party's established leaders were in an uncomfortable situation especially if they harbored future presidential aspirations. There was in short little incentive for Republicans to come out against Trump or challenge the view that the 2020 elections had been rigged, especially as successive polls showed that 70 percent of Republicans believed that the elections had indeed been stolen from Trump. The fantasy which Trump had persuaded so many to believe in a sense meant that the GOP was increasingly living in a different universe from their opponents and reality.

The growth of right-wing media has been an essential element of the story of the rise of the right since the 1970s. But now the population is divided in its bubbles and subject to very few countervailing viewpoints. Although Fox News is a key player in shaping political consciousness on the right, there is competition for its audience from other right-wing platforms such as Newsmax and the One America News Network. All of these sources promote a distinctive view of the world shaped by extreme right-wing ideas and attitudes, including conspiracy theories. It is also relatively easy to set up new media platforms to avoid regulation and newer platforms (such as Twitch) can host a range of groups, some of them violent. There is little media accountability and some media platforms can operate both as fundraising and information mechanisms.

The Republican Party in the 117th Congress elected in 2020 has struggled to adapt to the loss of the presidency and is torn between concentrating on its opposition to the Biden agenda and restoring party unity. Some of the extreme factions of the GOP in Congress threaten to embarrass the Party and constrain any attempt to broaden the GOP appeal. Thus the most pro-Trump and hard right members of the House of Representatives (including Marjorie Taylor Greene, Matt Gaetz, and Louie Gohmert) attempted to start an America First Caucus to promote the view that the United States is 'a nation with a border and a culture, strengthened by a common respect for uniquely Anglo-Saxon political traditions.' The self-evident white supremacist implications of the caucus caused Republican leaders to distance themselves from it and Marjorie Taylor Greene to backtrack. However there is an America First Policy Institute and, although Greene was forced to deny her association with the potential caucus, there is a group of far right members of the House and Senate who have the capacity to place an imprint on the Republican brand pushing it further from the center.

At the state level a series of Republican-controlled states—including Florida, Texas, and Georgia—moved to impose restrictive new voting laws which would make it harder for some groups to vote. In Georgia the new law exerted revenge on Brad Raffensberger who had resisted Trump's attempt to manipulate the 2020 outcome there. Georgia's new voting law removes the Secretary of State from decision-making on Georgia's electoral board.

Trump himself has thus far remained relatively quiet about his future intention. Although spending most of his time at Mar-a-Lago, his Florida house, he did appear at a Conservative Political Action Committee Conference in Florida in February 2021 to demonstrate his enduring popularity with the base by winning a presidential straw poll. Yet it seemed that even in this most pro-Trump venue, a clear majority, 68 percent of delegates, did not think he should run again and seemed to want to take forward Trump's agenda without Trump as the candidate. How this tension will be resolved remains to be seen but Trump at present is keeping his options open. Certainly, he has taken care to protect his own donor base and brand. He established in early 2021 a Save America PAC to encourage donations to him rather than the GOP and lawyers representing Trump took legal steps to stop the Republican National Committee and other Republican groups using Trump's name.

When political parties lose an election they normally hold a post-mortem to see if there are lessons to be learned for the future. The loss of the presidency in 2012 saw precisely that with the Party urging a widening of its big tent and urging outreach to voters in minority groups. The divisions which emerged in the GOP after the 2020 defeat were of a different order. Internal hostilities and debate about Trump's future role in the GOP threaten to preclude the Republican Party from moving on.

CONCLUSION: TRUMP'S LEGACIES

Although he served only one term, Trump's period in the presidency was by any standards an extraordinarily controversial one. As argued here and in many of the other chapters, his rhetoric and style and his deliberate exacerbation of political divisions seemed calculated to produce heightened social tension.

Whether that tension with its potential implications for a rise in hate crimes and violence can be reduced by the policies of his successor remains to be seen. Rebuilding the social fabric is not impossible but it will certainly take time. In the short term, the antagonisms and angry negativity of the Trump era seem likely to endure. Trump's policy legacy is less easy to assess. Certainly in a number of policy areas such as health care reform and immigration his achievement fell below his own ambition. In other areas such as trade and tax policy his approach may be longer lasting, although both will be subject to correction and rebalancing by the Biden administration. One of the most disturbing features of the Trump presidency was the willingness to attack key institutions of American democracy. By denying his defeat at the polls, Trump encouraged his supporters to reject the validity of the electoral process. Trump's legacy for the American constitutional order is thus one which, in addition to intensified politicization in areas such as the courts and the bureaucracy where it threatens their effective operation, is also a dangerous loss of public confidence in the whole American democratic system.

Trump's major legacy may however be to the character of the Republican Party. The future of the Party is of importance beyond the ranks of its supporters. Its character is of major significance for the efficiency and integrity of governance in the United States and the operation of constitutional democracy. We have seen that the GOP has steadily moved right over the period since Reagan, responding to a new coalition of voters built around moral and cultural issues and becoming increasingly negative in its attitude toward its opponents' values. The ideological sorting and the shift away from the center ground had profound implications for the ability to work the complex institutions of Madisonian democracy which require a degree of compromise and conciliation. That point has been well made in a number of studies, notably the insightful analysis by Thomas Mann and Norman Ornstein (2012). With the Republican Party becoming so evidently the Party of Trump a further twist has been added to the saga because Trump's whole message was calculated to show how only a strong individual appeal, such as that offered by himself, can cut through the problems facing America. It saw the constitutional framework, although revered in theory, in practice as part of the problem, something to be overcome. Fear of alternative perspectives and of groups deemed outside the Trumpian definition of the American people creates a deeply dysfunctional politics in a country which is objectively highly diverse on every demographical dimension. Added to this Manichean view of political conflict is the fact that extremist elements with a commitment to defend their view of American democracy, if necessary by force, were given legitimacy by Trump's rhetoric and his conduct in the presidency. Even if Trump himself decides not to run in 2024, he will retain an influence not least because of his popularity with the base of Republican voters, his fundraising ability and the absence of any obvious leadership figures who can frame an alternative approach. The temptation will be for the Party to try to recapture the Trump appeal through the choice of a standard bearer who is willing to use Trump's techniques. If the

GOP is going to move from Trump himself, it will be tempted to look for someone with his kind of popular appeal and therefore likely to try to push the same polarizing messages as he pursued, despite the need to win back swing voters alienated by Trump—educated women, suburbanites, younger voters, and secular Americans. Would-be candidates for the 2024 nomination are likely to want Trump's endorsement and indeed there is already a trail of politicians to Mar-a-Lago to cultivate his support. It is of course possible that with time and the working out of longer term trends in the electorate the incentives for Republicans to pursue the strategies it has adopted recently will weaken. In the short term, however, the Party seems likely to continue with strategies which will render it less and less able to unite the country.

References

Balingit, M., and L. Meekler. 2020. Trump Alleges 'Left Wing Indoctrination' in Schools, Says He Will Create National Commission to Push More Pro-American History. *Washington Post*, September 17.

Bauer, B., and J. Goldsmith. 2020. *After Trump: Reconstructing the Presidency*. Washington, DC: Lawfare Press.

Blum, R. 2020. *How the Tea Party Captured the GOP: Insurgent Factions in American Politics*. Chicago: University of Chicago Press.

Boehner, J. 2021. *On the House: A Washington Memoir*. New York: St. Martin's Press.

Butler, A. 2021. *White Evangelical Racism: The Politics of Morality in America*. Chapel Hill: University of North Carolina Press.

Campbell, D., G. Layman, and J. Green. 2021. *Secular Surge: A New Fault Line in American Politics*. Cambridge: Cambridge University Press.

Carnes, N., and N. Lupu. 2021. The White Working Class and the 2016 Election. *Perspectives on Politics* 19 (March): 155–172.

Cox, D. 2021. Social Isolation and Community Disconnection Are Not Spurring Conspiracy Theories. Survey Center on American Life. https://www.americansurv eycenter.org/research/social-isolation-and-community-disconnection-are-not-spu rring-conspiracy-theories/.

Fukuyama, F. 2018. *Identity: The Demand for Dignity and the Politics of Resentment*. New York: Farrar, Straus and Giroux.

Galli, M. 2019. Trump Should Be Removed from Office. *Christianity Today*, December 19.

Griswold, E. 2021. A Pennsylvania Lawmaker and the Insurgence of Christian Nationalism. *The New Yorker*, May 9.

Hertel-Fernandes, A. 2019. *State Capture: How Conservative Activists, Big Business and Wealthy Donors Reshaped the State and the Nation*. Oxford: Oxford University Press.

Jardina, A. 2020. *White Identity Politics*. Cambridge: Cambridge University Press.

Jones, R. 2016. *The End of White Christian America*. New York: Simon and Schuster.

———. 2020. *White Too Long: The Legacy of White Supremacy in American Christianity*. New York: Simon and Schuster.

———. 2021. Taking the White Christian Nationalist Symbols at the Capitol Riot Seriously. *New York Times*, January 7.

Jordan, W. 2016. Does "Right Direction/Wrong Track" Matter? You Gov Polls, August 12. https://today.yougov.com/topics/politics/articles-reports/2016/08/12/americans-are-unhappy-other-side.

Kazin, M. 1995. *The Populist Persuasion: An American History*. New York: Basic Books.

Klein, E. 2020. *Why We're Polarized*. London: Profile Books.

Mann, T., and N. Ornstein. 2012. *It's Even Worse Than It Looks: How the American Constitutional System Collided with the New Politics of Extremism*. New York: Basic Books.

Patterson, T. 2020. *Is the Republican Party Destroying Itself? And Why It Needs to Reclaim Its Conservative Ideals*. Seattle, WA: KDP Publishing.

Posner, S. 2020. *Unholy: Why White Evangelicals Worship at the Altar of Donald Trump*. New York: Random House.

Renshon, S. 2020. *The Real Psychology of the Trump Presidency*. New York: Palgrave.

Saldin, R., and S. Teles. 2020. *Never Trump: The Revolt of the Conservative Elites*. Oxford: Oxford University Press.

Serwer, A. 2020. Birtherism of a Nation. *The Atlantic*, May 13.

Sides, J., M. Tesler, and L. Vavreck. 2019. *Identity Crisis: The 2016 Presidential Campaign and the Battle for the Meaning of America*. Princeton: Princeton University Press.

Skocpol, T., and V. Williamson. 2012. *The Tea Party and the Remaking of Republican Conservatism*. Oxford: Oxford University Press.

Washington Post Fact Checker Staff. 2021. *Donald Trump and His Assault on Truth*. New York: Simon and Schuster.

Whitehead, A., and S. Perry. 2020 *Taking America Back for God: Christian Nationalism in the United States*. Oxford: Oxford University Press.

Further Reading

There are already many studies by academics and participants of Trump's character, style, and the conduct of his presidency. A thoughtful analysis grounded in both political science and psychology is Stanley Renshon, *The Real Psychology of the Trump Presidency* (2020, New York: Palgrave). Although there are as yet no definitive studies of the 2020 presidential election, the 2016 presidential election is well covered in John Sides, Michael Tesler, and Lynn Vavreck in *Identity Crisis: the 2016 Presidential Campaign and the Battle for the Meaning of America* (2019, Princeton: Princeton University Press). Efforts to explain the alienation of American voters can be found in a number of works including Russell Hochschild, *Strangers in Their Own Land: Anger and Mourning on the American Right* (2018, New York: The New Press).

The role of religion and attitudes toward its role in the American political system are well explored in Andrew Whitehead and Samuel Perry, *Taking America Back for God* (2020, Oxford: Oxford University Press), which uses extensive survey data to analyse the strength of Christian nationalism. Sarah Posner *Unholy: Why White Evangelicals Worship at the Altar of Donald Trump* (2020, New York: Random House) offers a well-informed journalistic perspective on the ambitions of the contemporary religious right.

The Republican Party's evolution and contemporary problems are well covered in Theda Skocpol and Vanessa Williamson, *The Tea Party and the Remaking of Republican Conservatism* (2012, Oxford: Oxford University Press) and Theda Skocpol and Caroline Tervo, *Upending American Politics: Polarizing Parties, Ideological Elites and Citizen Activists from the Tea Party to the Anti-Trump Resistance* (2020, Oxford: Oxford University Press).

Index

Milton Keynes UK
Ingram Content Group UK Ltd.
UKHW021855240124
436644UK00002B/30

9 783030 897390